ENGLISH
LANGUAGE
AND
LITERATURE

FIVE GREAT MEN OF LETTERS
SHAKESPEARE, CHAUCER, JOHNSON, SHAW AND DICKENS

ENGLISH LANGUAGE

AND

LITERATURE

A COMPREHENSIVE GUIDE TO THE STUDY OF
ENGLISH LITERATURE, LANGUAGE AND SELF-
EXPRESSION, TOGETHER WITH CHAPTERS ON THE
TECHNIQUE OF POETRY, DRAMA, THE NOVEL, THE
SHORT STORY, FILM-WRITING AND BROADCASTING

CONTRIBUTORS

Michael Balcon *J. W. Marriott*
W. J. Blyton *Dr. Bruce Pattison*
Richard Church *L. A. G. Strong*
St. John Ervine *Frank Swinnerton*
Lord Gorell *Gwynneth Thurburn*
John Lehmann *Professor Ernest Weekley*

ODHAMS PRESS LTD · LONG ACRE · LONDON

CONTENTS

MEDIEVAL PRINTING SCENE

The effect of the invention of printing in Europe, which took place about 1440, was to hasten the revival of learning and the growth of new ideas—ideas which revolutionized the old orders of man's relationship to the State and the Church. Indeed, although many large libraries were founded by princes and churchmen, attempts were made to repress the industry because the spread of the printed word encouraged too much independence of thought. Without printing, it is safe to say, the urge for reformation, which was the outcome of the Renaissance, could not have had the overwhelming result of plunging Europe into physical and intellectual strife, for it was the rapidity with which new ideas circulated that caused the incurable schism. In England a printing press was first set up in 1476 at Westminster by William Caxton, who had learned his trade at Bruges. Unlike other European printers, who printed their books in Latin, Caxton used only his own language; a man of considerable gifts, he made many of his own translations, and printed about eighty separate books. The early print reproduced above shows Continental printers at work.

CHAPTER 1

INFLUENCES ON THE ENGLISH LANGUAGE

THE influences that can affect the growth and structure of a language are of two kinds, which can be called internal and external, the former resulting from the character and pursuits of the race that speaks it, the latter from the historical contacts and the political or religious movements and literary fashions that have come from outside.

The English people is impatient of useless detail and of strict logic and has an innate gift for improvisation and "muddling through." It is to these characteristics that we owe the almost complete disappearance from English of all the inflexional machinery which still encumbers the other European languages, the replacement of grammatical gender by natural gender, the freedom and looseness of our syntax, and our obstinate retention of an artificial spelling which sometimes fails completely to represent the sound of the spoken word. A great Danish scholar has written: "The English language would not have been what it is, if the English had not been for centuries great respecters of the liberties of each individual and if everybody had not been free to strike out new paths for himself" (Jespersen, *Growth and Structure of the English Language*).

From outside have come the successive waves of invaders whose languages, gradually amalgamating, produced by the time of Chaucer, who died in 1400, a composite language to which there is no parallel in linguistic history, a language in which the various elements had become so completely fused that no joins were visible. The fifteenth and sixteenth centuries witnessed the two great movements of the Renaissance of Learning and the Protestant Reformation, the first enriching English with numbers of words taken from Latin and Greek, the second familiarizing the people with the language used by the great Bible translators of the Tudor age, a language which has

never been equalled, except by Shakespeare, in beauty and nobility. This period has been called the age of Caxton, who transferred his printing press from Flanders to England in 1476 and was thus the chief agent in making education, hitherto almost the monopoly of the Church, gradually accessible to the nation at large.

Then came the golden age of English literature, the age of Shakespeare, and the gradual development of English into a form which, for all literary purposes, reached its perfection with Milton (1608-1674). This was also the age of seafaring, of the great geographical discoveries, of widely extended trade and of the beginnings of the British Empire.

With the Restoration of Charles II (1660) begins a new phase, chiefly characterized by the imitation of French models and a gradual reaction in the direction of that clarity and sententiousness which culminated in the epigrammatic neatness of Pope and the stately, latinized prose of Dr. Johnson, whose famous *Dictionary*, published in 1755, was erroneously thought by his contemporaries to have stabilized the language, an enterprise as hopeless as an attempt to halt the rising tide.

The Romantic movement of the later eighteenth and early nineteenth centuries (represented by Gray, Coleridge, Scott, Shelley, Keats and finally Tennyson), with its enthusiasm for the historical or legendary past and for natural beauty, did much to reverse the work of Johnson, giving back to the language a poetic vocabulary and a poetic ideal which had been absent from it for a century. The early nineteenth century had also an intense preoccupation with political, social and economic questions and at the same time the Industrial Revolution was transforming English life and bringing in the age of steam.

Since then the rapid progress of all forms of science and the constant succession of new inventions have naturally affected the language. The gradual decay of classical studies has almost destroyed what little grammar English still had, and the American invasion of recent years has further dislocated its structure, while giving to colloquial speech qualities of "pep" that add greatly to its power of expression.

Starting, roughly speaking, from the period of the Renaissance and of the great geographical discoveries, we have borrowed words from almost every language in the world, with the result that such a national work as the great *Oxford English Dictionary* contains a larger number of words than are registered in any other European language. The twenty thousand or so which we inherited from Anglo-Saxon have increased to nearly half a million, though few people ever need to use more than a twentieth part of this vast vocabulary. Here it may be well to kill a ridiculous fiction, due to Max Müller and still often repeated by people who ought to know better, to the effect that the agricultural labourer's vocabulary numbers only a few hundred words. The vocabulary of the agricultural labourer is as great as the vocabulary used by Shakespeare in the whole of his plays and three times that of Milton in the whole of his poems.

Coming of the Anglo-Saxons

The history of English begins with the landing in A.D. 449 on the coast of Kent of two Jutish pirates, Hengest and Horsa, in quest of plunder and land. This date is given by the Venerable Bede, writing nearly three centuries later, but as already in the third century the Romans had appointed a Count of the Saxon Shore to protect the east and south coasts against such marauders, it is probable that there were earlier attacks and possibly infiltrations. Other adventurers followed and in the course of a century the whole island, except for some remote corners, was subdued, for the civilized Ancient Britons, accustomed so long to live in safety under the stern, but just, Roman rule, were helpless against these fierce invaders. It is a mistake to suppose that they were exterminated or driven into the wilds of Cornwall, Wales and the

Scottish Highlands and islands—"The Britons were not exterminated, but absorbed by their Saxon conquerors. Their civilization and language vanished, but the race remained" (Jespersen). They lived on as a subject race, the Anglo-Saxon word *wealh*, foreigner, Welshman, taking also the sense of slave. Most of our place-names in *Wal-*, such as Walcott, Walton, Walford, etc., were named from the Ancient Britons who inhabited them. But, except where protected by remoteness, their language gradually disappeared, persisting only in geographical names, especially those of rivers. Our Avon, Esk, Usk, Exe are Ancient British names for water.

Ancient British Survivals

Usually a conquering race takes much of its vocabulary from the conquered, or even adopts its language altogether, as the Franks did in Gaul, which thus became France, or the Northmen in Neustria, renamed Normandy. But the Anglo-Saxons did not adopt more than half a dozen British words. Theirs was not a mere conquest, it was a mass migration.

The Ancient British languages still survive, most vigorously of all in Wales. In some villages on the Welsh coast only Welsh is spoken, except to visitors from England, while up in the hills there are plenty of people who neither speak nor understand English. A few Ancient British words have drifted into English from time to time, but it was not until the Scottish Highlands began to attract visitors and Scottish writers made known the romance of their country, that picturesque words like glen, corrie, loch, clan, claymore, coronach, pibroch, began to appear in our literary vocabulary. In 1749 William Collins wrote his *Ode on the Popular Superstitions of the Highlands*, in 1771 Thomas Pennant published his *Tour in Scotland*, and in 1775 Dr. Johnson his *Journey to the Western Islands of Scotland*. Before this period the Highlands were regarded as "frightful," "horrid" and "most of all disagreeable when the heath is in bloom" (Trevelyan, *English Social History*).

The Angles and Saxons came from various regions of North-west Germany

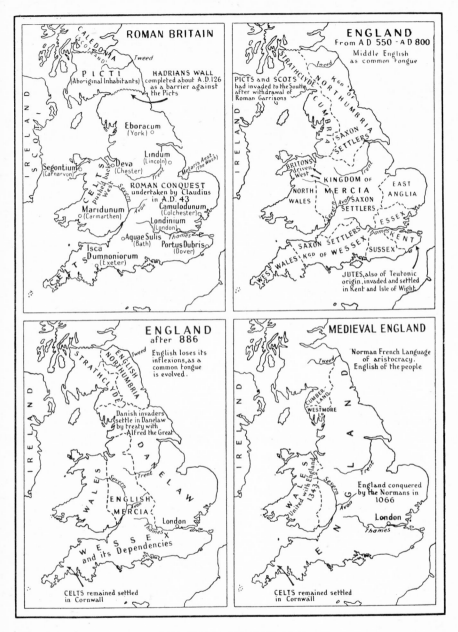

The four maps show the settlement in England of waves of invaders—from Rome, from North Germany (the Saxons), from Scandinavia (the Danes or Vikings), and finally from Normandy (the Norman-French). Each succeeding group of invaders left its mark on the Anglo-Saxon language and by the fourteenth century English was a fusion of Anglo-Saxon, French and Latin elements. Out of this language has been evolved our modern English.

and spoke various dialects of what is called Low German or *Plattdeutsch*, closely allied to Dutch and still the language of the peasantry in many parts of North Germany. These dialects differed considerably in vocabulary, inflexions and pronunciation, and tended to diverge even more widely during the six centuries before the Norman Conquest, but eventually the prestige of Alfred the Great, King of Wessex, whose capital was Winchester, caused West Saxon to be regarded as the dominant tongue and it is on this principle that our Anglo-Saxon dictionaries are compiled.

Shedding Useless Grammar

Anglo-Saxon, which some scholars prefer to call Old English, was a very complicated language, and the general tendency in its conversion *via* Middle English (*circa* 1150-1450) into Modern English has been in the direction of simplification, the race holding, with Bernard Shaw, that "useless grammar is a devastating plague." All European languages show the same tendency, but none to such an extent as ours. German, especially, so near akin to English, has preserved a tremendous number of inflexions, e.g. corresponding to our definite article *the*, it has forms for three genders (*der, die, das*) with four cases and separate plural forms.

Ever since the coming of the "Danes," English has been steadily shedding its grammar, partly from that linguistic laziness which is so marked a national quality, partly as a result of contact with Old Norse and Old French. Particularly characteristic is the gradual substitution of natural gender for grammatical gender, a piece of practical common-sense in which English stands alone among European languages. In Anglo-Saxon, *muth*, mouth, was masculine; *nosu*, nose, feminine; and *eage*, eye, neuter; genders which the corresponding German words still keep.

Anglo-Saxon was the speech of the common people, until, by about 1150, it had completed the transition into what is called Middle English, which in its turn began to develop into early Modern English after the introduction of printing and the circulation in the early part of the sixteenth century of the Bible in the English tongue.

Anglo-Saxon nouns were divided into a number of declensions with case-endings often characterized by the full vowel sounds of *a, o* and *u*. These dropped off in Middle English or were replaced by a vague *e* sound which later became silent, though it is still syllabic in Chaucer, e.g. the seventh line of the *Prologue*—"The tendre croppes and the yonge sonne"—contains ten syllables, the -*e* at the end of the line not being counted. Of the case inflexions of Anglo-Saxon only the genitive (possessive) in -*s*, has survived. Feminine nouns had no such ending in Anglo-Saxon, but gradually adopted it in Middle English. We still say Lord's-day, but Lady-day, Thurs-day from the god Thor, but Fri-day from the goddess Freya. There were various plural endings, but, towards the end of the Anglo-Saxon period, two of them, in -*as* and -*an*, prevailed over the others, becoming Middle English -*es* or -*s* and -*en*. The final triumph of the former was no doubt helped by the French plural -*s*. Of the -*en* plurals only oxen survives, for brethren and children are not quite simple cases.

The pronouns, from syntactical necessity, kept some of their cases (he, his, him), though these were reduced in number, e.g the nominative ye was gradually replaced by the objective you, though the distinction is still observed in the Bible, e.g. "Blessed are ye, when men shall revile you and persecute you" (Matt. v, 11).

Verbs were divided into weak and strong, the former represented by such modern verbs as bless, blessed, build, built, the latter showing change of vowel in the past tense and a past participle in -*en*, e.g. shake, shook, shaken, drive, drove, driven. This -*en* has generally dropped off, as in sing, sang, sung, and there has been a general tendency to assimilate the vowel of the past tense to that of the past participle, e.g. broke, for the Biblical brake, because of broken, and got for the Biblical gat, because of gotten, which survives in the compounds begotten, forgotten and in the old phrase "ill-gotten gains." Gotten is still usual in America, and in the Authorized Version and the Prayer Book forms in -*en* are still common, e.g. "graven image," "bounden duty," etc. Here again much simplification has taken place. The rustic who, in spite of elementary education, says "He's been took ill," or "Who done it?" is merely continuing the work of our ancestors, who adopted the labour-saving device of one form instead of two for the past tense and past participle. Strong verbs have been constantly transferred to the weak conjugation. Examples are climb, help, melt, but Coleridge wrote, with conscious archaism, "Till clomb above the Eastern bar the horned moon . . ."; *holpen* is used in the Prayer Book and one can still speak of "molten lead." A consequence of this reshuffling of the verbs is one more of those inconsistencies in which our language delights, e.g. we can have a "swelled head," but a "swollen face," we speak of a "cleft chin," but a "cloven hoof," and can be thunderstruck, but poverty-stricken.

Of the personal inflexions of the Anglo-Saxon verb we have kept only the -*st* of the second person singular, now confined to Biblical language and poetry, and the -*s* of the third person. The latter struggled for a long time against the -*th* form, which alone is used in the Authorized Version. Milton has always -*s* except for hath and doth.

Alliteration in Anglo-Saxon Verse

It was during the Middle English period that we developed those progressive tenses (I was writing, shall be writing, would have been writing, etc.) which hardly exist in other European languages, but which give precision to a statement, and also the use of *do* in the negative and interrogative. Here again the Bible, poetry and the dignified style prefer the older and simple constructions, e.g. from the Authorized Version —"While he yet talked to the people, behold his mother and his brethren stood without" (Matt. xii, 46), "Whence comest thou, Gehazi?" (2 Kings v, 25), "Swear not at all" (Matt. v, 34). "The increased precision of modern English, though it be a great gain for matter-of-fact statement, is sometimes the reverse of an advantage for the language of emotion and contemplation. Hence we find that our poetry and our higher literature often return to the less developed grammar of the Elizabethan

age" (Bradley, *The Making of English*).

One feature of Anglo-Saxon is of special literary interest, namely, its love of alliteration. Its poetical effects were produced by the recurrence of consonant sounds within each line, and, though French and Church-Latin influence replaced alliteration by rhyme in the Middle English period, our greatest Middle English poetical work except that of Chaucer, the *Piers Plowman* of his contemporary, William Langland, was written in alliterative verse. "On a May morning on Malvern Hills" is its opening line. Not only Anglo-Saxon poetry, but also rhetorical prose, adopted the same device, which is still used effectively in modern poetry and prose. Here are two examples from one of our greatest poets, Coleridge:

> Five miles meandering with a mazy motion.
> > (*Kubla Khan*)

> The fair breeze blew, the white foam flew,
> The furrow followed free.
> > (*Rime of the Ancient Mariner*)

A recent example of its use in prose is Mr. Winston Churchill's "Let it roar and let it rage. We shall not fail or falter," and alliteration is responsible for many of our most expressive collocations of words, such as "might and main," "kith and kin," "hale and hearty," " without fear or favour," as also for the choice of the noun in such comparisons as "as bold as brass," "as cool as a cucumber," "as dead as a doornail," "as proud as a peacock," etc. Some of these collocations preserve words which are otherwise obsolete, e.g. kith (acquaintance), main (strength), while few of those who use "spick and span" know that spick meant a bright new nail and span a clean new chip of wood.

Viking Influence

In 597 Augustine landed in Kent with his forty missionary monks and became the first Archbishop of Canterbury. In the course of a century the Anglo-Saxons were converted to Christianity. They did not, however, at once beat their swords into plough-shares, for there were long and bloody conflicts between the various kingdoms; but, at any rate, they ceased to make piratical attacks on neighbouring countries. It was a kindred race whom we call collectively, the "Danes," though they came from all three of the Scandinavian countries, who began to repeat the performances of Hengest and Horsa. The conflict between the English and these invaders, for whom the better name is "Vikings," was to some extent religious, for the Danes were still pagans. The great English hero of the struggle, which lasted two centuries, was Alfred the Great and it was he who concluded with the Danish chieftain, Guthram, in 878 the Peace of Wedmore, by which the Danes were given the country north of Watling Street, known in history as the Danelaw and comprising Northumbria, East Anglia and part of the midland kingdom of Mercia. Our place-names ending in -by, -thorp, -dale, -thwaite, always indicate a Danish settlement. When, in 1014, the Witan, the national Council of England, accepted the Danish Knut (Canute), the Christian son of a pagan father, as King of England, the country was unified, the two races became one and a composite language had being.

The Old Norse spoken by the Vikings, from various forms of which modern Danish, Norwegian, Swedish and Icelandic are descended, was closely allied to Anglo-Saxon in vocabulary. The two races had little difficulty in understanding each other, but, where they came in contact, they tended to drop the inflexions which differed in the two languages. Consequently, it was in the Danelaw that the process of simplification was most rapid.

The completeness of the fusion of the two languages is shown by the homely and everyday character of the Old Norse contribution. To it belong such familiar nouns as anger, egg, fellow, husband, leg, plough, root, skill, skin, sky, trust, window, wing, and even such an intimate word as sister, such adjectives as ill, loose, low, meek, odd, rotten, scant, ugly, wrong, and such verbs as call, cast, drown, put, take, thrive. As a rule words borrowed from another language belong to these three classes (nouns, adjec-tives, verbs), but from Old Norse came also the pronouns, they and them, and the prepositions, till and fro, the latter surviving only as an adverb in "to and fro." There are also a few doublets, i.e. pairs of words of identical origin, but of different form and meaning. Corresponding to the Anglo-Saxon church, raise, shirt, whole, yard, we have from Old Norse, kirk, rear, skirt, hale, garth. The Vikings also introduced a number of administrative words, such as law, but these were mostly replaced after the Conquest by French terms.

To sum up, by the end of the Anglo-Saxon period, c. 1150, the spoken language of the Englishman was a blend of two closely related Teutonic tongues, the original vocabulary had been greatly enriched and the complicated inflexional system of Anglo-Saxon had been simplified to an extent without a parallel in the other Teutonic languages.

The process of simplification went on during the Middle Ages, with the result that the language of the Wycliffite Bible (c. 1380) presents little difficulty to a modern reader, whereas the Anglo-Saxon version is quite unintelligible except to a student of the science of language. Thus, in the verse, "The queen of the south shal ryse in dome with this generation and shall condempne it; for she came fro the endis of the erthe for to here the wisdom of Salomon, and loo! here is more than Salomon" (Matt. xii, 42), the only archaisms, apart from the spelling, are the use of doom for judgment and of more for greater, as still in "more's the pity" and "more fool you."

Fusion of Tongues

With the Norman Conquest begins one of the most curious and interesting phenomena in linguistic history, the complete fusion of two languages, one purely Teutonic, the other of Latin origin. Just as before 1066 and up to c. 1150, when Middle English may be said to begin, our speech was a mixture of the original Anglo-Saxon and Old Norse, so, from the Conquest onward, it became gradually blended with Old French. It should be understood that such words are not, as a rule, identical in form with those of Old and Modern

French, but have been considerably altered in form and sound.

The saturation of Middle English with French words was not the immediate result of the Norman Conquest. The invaders were not numerous, and, unless reinforced, would gradually have adopted the language of the conquered, just as their Viking ancestors had adopted French when they converted Neustria into Normandy. For centuries after the Conquest England and France were in ceaseless contact. William and his sons were still Dukes of Normandy, the Plantagenet kings ruled vast provinces in France and much of the country was subject to the English crown during the Hundred Years War, which began in 1337.

These centuries were a rather barren period in English literature, while the thirteenth century was the golden age of Old French literature, which was admired, imitated and translated all over Europe.

Some of the most important literary works produced in England between the Conquest and the revival of English literature in the fourteenth century were written in Norman-French or the later Anglo-French by subjects of the English king, such as Wace, the Jerseyman, author (*c.* 1150) of the famous *Roman de Rou*, with its account of the Battle of Hastings, and Marie de France, who wrote her delightful lays at the court of Henry III.

Language of Polite Society

French was not only, until 1362, the language of the law and of administration, but also that of polite society. The town crier's *Oyez!* Old French for "Hear," is an interesting survival, and, when the Countess of Salisbury dropped her garter, King Edward III's remark was "Hon(n)i soit qui mal y pense!" As late as the fourteenth century schoolboys construed their Latin into French, all who aspired to

FROM A PAGE IN THE ANGLO-SAXON CHRONICLE
The Anglo-Saxon Chronicle was probably inspired by King Alfred and is the first attempt in English at a national historical record and describes the Danish wars. The extract above refers to the defeat of the Danes in the Vale of the White Horse in 871.

social elegance interlarded their remarks with French words and phrases, and educated products of the schools were generally trilingual. Chaucer's friend, "Moral Gower," the poet and philosopher, who died in 1408, wrote one book in English, one in French, and one in Latin.

Words from France

It was natural that the first French words introduced should be those of a ruling race. The native king and queen survived, but borrowed their throne, crown and sceptre from Old French. Our titles of nobility, with the curious exception of earl, which adopted a French feminine, are of Old French origin, as are also the titles of the chief officers of the crown, chancellor, marshal and constable. The same applies to most words connected with the administration of justice, e.g. judge, jury, assize, prison, gaol, and the formal names of crimes such as felony, arson, larceny. These terms belong to Law French, a barbarous form of Anglo-French which was not formally abolished till 1731. From the same source come most of our words connected with property, e.g. lease, tenant, heir. Peace and war and most of the words connected with the latter are also French, e.g. host, later replaced by army, armour, banner, battle, fortress, siege, tower. Sir and madam, master, mistress and servant are evidently from the vocabulary of a dominant class and one might moralize on the peremptory sense which the French *demander*, to ask, acquired in English. Ecclesiastical words which point to the influence of the Norman churchmen are abbey, altar, clergy, cloister, parish, saint, sermon and the verbs pray and preach.

It was a seventeenth-century grammarian who first pointed out that, while the names of the domestic animals are English, the meat they provide has French names, such as beef, mutton, pork and veal. The inference drawn by Wamba, in the first chapter of Scott's *Ivanhoe*, as to Norman luxury and English privation, is probably erroneous, as the reason may well have been the superiority which French cooking still has over English. It may be remarked that the chief meal of the day, dinner, has a French

name and that epicures like to employ a *chef* as the ruler of their *cuisine*. Aristocratic sport gave us chase, park, leash, quarry, scent, falconry, etc., and from knightly exercises we have tourney, joust, lists. The superiority of the foreign architects is seen in aisle, arch, column, nave, dungeon, palace, pillar, porch, vault, etc. Our names of relationship outside the family circle, uncle, aunt, cousin, nephew, niece, are all French, while in grandfather, grandmother we have a half translation. The humbler trades remained English, as, for example, baker, miller, smith, weaver, while the luxury trades took French names—draper, spicer, tailor.

It was probably during the early period, when the two languages existed side by side, but had not yet become one, that it became the practice to add an explanatory French word to an English word. Familiar examples are "goods and chattels," "law and order," "ways and means," "lord and master." Later this became merely a literary mannerism, as in the "acknowledge and confess" of the Prayer Book or the "shield and buckler" of the 91st Psalm.

Chaucer's English

By Chaucer's time the fusion was complete. The nation and the language were both unified, and the noble of Norman descent, whose ancestors had despised the conquered English, now gloried in the name of Englishman. "In Chaucer's time the English people first clearly appear as a racial and cultural unit. The component races and languages have been melted into one. The upper class is no longer French, nor the peasant class Anglo-Saxon: all are English. England has ceased to be mainly a recipient of influences from without. Henceforward she gives forth her own" (Trevelyan, *English Social History*).

The French invasion did not greatly affect English grammar. In Anglo-Saxon the adjectives sometimes followed the noun, as still occasionally in poetry, e.g. Milton's "old man eloquent," Wordsworth's "vision splendid" or Dickens's "Ivy green that groweth on ruins old," but in such administrative terms as heir apparent, body politic, proof positive, princess royal,

FIRST TRANSLATOR OF THE BIBLE

John Wycliffe (c. 1320-1384), a forerunner of the Reformation, stood for the right of every man to read the Bible for himself, and to make this possible undertook its translation into English. His doctrines were condemned, but he escaped the fate of the heretic.

treasure trove, court martial, malice afore-thought, the last of which is a half trans-lation of the Anglo-French *malice prepense* as knight errant is of *chevalier errant*, the position of the adjective is due to French influence.

Anglo-Saxon used the possessive or geni-tive case much more freely than we do, e.g. in the passage from Wycliffe quoted on p. 12 the Anglo-Saxon version, if modern-ized, would read "Southland's queen came from earth's ends to hear Solomon's wis-dom." This genitive was replaced under French influence by the use of "of" so that now we only use it with names of persons, in a few poetic or stereotyped phrases such as "journey's end," "heart's desire," "the river's brink," "out of harm's way," or in expressions connected with time such as "this week's *Punch*," "the year's harvest," "a night's rest," etc. The use of the plural you for the singular thou is also partly due to the influence of the French conqueror.

So complete was the fusion of the two languages that we are not conscious of using an English and a foreign word in such familiar collocations as "wholesale and retail," "touch and go," "a happy release," "a blessing in disguise," in alliterative phrases like "without fear or favour," "slow and sure," "rack (originally *wrack*) and ruin," or in compounds such as absent-minded, poverty-stricken. We can add an English suffix to a French word as in dukedom, artless, or a French suffix to an English word as in riddance, eatable. Many compound nouns, e.g. arm-chair, time-table, gentleman, grandfather, commonwealth, are hybrid formations.

The borrowing of French words has gone on steadily through the centuries. During the long reign of Louis XIV (1643-1715) France was the dominant power in Europe and French manners, literature and fashions were everywhere imitated. From approximately this period dates the greater part of our military vocabulary, words such as colonel, lieutenant, brigade, reconnoitre, sortie, etc., some of which are ultimately Italian, for it was in Italy that the military organization of the gunpowder age originated. Since the Peace of Nymwegen (1678) French has been recognized as the diplomatic language of Europe, hence such words and expressions as *ballon d'essai*, *chargé d'affaires*, *démarche*, *démenti*, *entente*, etc., and in recent times a great number of French words and phrases have become current English, justifiably so when they express an idea for which our language

LUTTRELL PSALTER

A fine example of the medieval illuminated manuscript which preceded the printed book, the Luttrell Psalter was completed about 1340. It is a collection of psalms made for the household of Sir Geoffrey Luttrell. Note the wealth of detail in the painted work.

PAGE FROM BEDE'S ECCLESIASTICAL HISTORY

This is an extract from the illuminated manuscript of Bede's history of the English Church, written in Latin in 731. Because Church and lay government were closely connected the history becomes in fact a general record of the country's affairs.

has no exact equivalent. Such are *agent provocateur, camouflage, canard, cliché, coup d'état, flair, laissez-faire, nonchalant, sabotage, succès d'estime.* *Pince-nez* is a French singular which our best-sellers insist on treating as a plural, while they usually reverse the correct genders in *bête noire* and *crime passionnel.*

What We Took from Latin

The other great foreign element in our language is Latin. The most potent influence on the civilization of Western Europe was that of the Romans. From Latin come Italian, French, Spanish and other Romance languages with only trifling contributions from other sources. The Teutonic races took from Latin only those words which might naturally be useful where the two races came in contact. The earliest are, apart from the religious element, mostly short words of a purely material character, descriptive of the improved standard of life due to the superiority of the Romans in the useful arts. Our names

of fruits, except the native apple and berry, come either immediately from Latin or indirectly through French and the same applies to vegetables, among which only the homely bean is English. From Latin come also wine, cook, kitchen, dish, butter and cheese, and the superiority of Roman building is reflected in the words tile and wall Commerce and administration have given us mile, inch, mint, pound.

The early Church words are mostly Greco-Latin and some of them, such as angel, devil, minster, church, were known to the Anglo-Saxons before they arrived in this country, for, though they had never worshipped in Christian churches, they had often sacked or burnt them; but the great mass of Church words came in with St. Augustine and his successors. The Anglo-Saxons took over the chief ecclesiastical titles, such as bishop (*episcopus*), abbot (*abbas*), monk (*monachus*), etc., but they generally translated other Church words. The Greco-Latin *evangelium*, good tidings, became *god-spel,* now gospel, and *sanctus*

DUKE OF BEDFORD'S MISSAL

A masterpiece of fifteenth-century penmanship and illumination this missal (a document containing the office of mass) was probably a gift from the Duke of Bedford to his duchess, Anne, on the occasion of their marriage in 1423.

was rendered by *helga*, holy one, as still in All Hallows; but in the Wycliffite Bible most of this vocabulary was replaced by words of Latin origin, e.g. Trinity instead of the Anglo-Saxon *thrines* and resurrection instead of *ærist*.

Language of Scholarship

Latin was in Anglo-Saxon and medieval times practically the only subject of instruction in schools, and serious literature, from the time of the Venerable Bede (675-735) down to that of Francis Bacon (1561-1626), was generally written in that language. The

great prestige of French literature during the Middle Ages familiarized people with a vocabulary of Latin origin and the Wycliffite translation of the Bible, made from Latin texts, brought further reinforcements. The consequence is that English, alone of the Teutonic languages, is saturated with Latin, and a census of our vocabulary would show that the Latin element is the largest of all. As it was for a long time the regular vehicle of scholarly writing, it was natural that pedants should latinize to a fantastic extent, so that the schoolmaster became a stock figure of fun. An example is

Holofernes, in *Love's Labour Lost*, with his "posteriors of this day, which the rude multitude call the afternoon."

So greatly did the Latin influence grow during the seventeenth and eighteenth centuries, that English, in the hands of such great writers as Sir Thomas Browne or Dr. Johnson, almost ceased to be a Teutonic language. Thomas Blount, who published in 1656 a *Dictionary of Hard Words*, says that he has "in a great measure shun'd the old Saxon words, as finding them growing every day more obsolete." It was the Romantics and Wordsworth who gave back its rights to the English tongue.

Opinions differ as to the value or otherwise of this great importation of Latin into English. Scientific writers, from T. H. Huxley to H. G. Wells, have usually been very hostile to classical studies. The latter tells us that "the universities imposed a proud, defensive pedantry upon the whole scholastic scheme. The quintessence of learning was the boring grammatical study of these dead and eviscerated languages"; but in the book (*Phœnix*) from which this is taken, he makes use himself of such Latin tags as *homo sapiens, a priori, quid pro quo, ad hoc, sine qua non*, reminiscent of the medieval theologians and philosophers for whom Latin was a kind of native tongue.

Few people realize what an immense number of Latin words and phrases we use in an unaltered form, e.g. such nouns as genius, index, omen, tribunal, or such phrases, many of them from Law Latin, as *prima facie*, bona-fide, post-mortem. We have made nouns from the adverbs alibi, interim, item, tandem (at length!), from the verb forms memento, fiat, propaganda and innuendo. We have a dative plural in omnibus, a genitive plural in quorum. The adverb quondam has supplied us with an adjective. We are hardly conscious of using Latin words when we say junior and senior, maximum and minimum. Often we indulge our love of abbreviation, as in *postscript-(um)*, *infra dig(nitatem)*, *pro tem(pore)*, *nem(ine) con(tradicente)*, or indulge in ellipses as in *in statu quo (ante)*. These examples, taken at random, might be multiplied many times over to illustrate a

kind of lazy acquisitiveness which has no parallel in the other European languages.

One result of our wholesale adoption of Latin words, to save the trouble of building up from native material, is that the adjective connected with a noun is often remote from it in origin. Thus, corresponding to the nouns mouth, nose, eye, we have the adjectives oral, nasal, ocular, the ox is bovine, the dog is canine, the cat is feline, etc., whereas in a kindred language like German the adjective is constructed from the noun. Some consider this a defect in the English language.

One result of the great Latin invasion of the language was that many words were reconstructed in accordance with their derivation. The *parfit* which Chaucer had taken from Old French became perfect, with a changed pronunciation, but victuals for the earlier *vittles* (French *vitailles*) is still sounded as it was by our ancestors. We also have many pairs of words, often with different meanings, e.g. frail, poison, fealty, caitiff, from Old French, are now accompanied by fragile, potion, fidelity, captive, from Latin.

In spite of the fact that our language is now a complete fusion of Old English (i.e. Anglo-Saxon and Old Norse), French and Latin, it is still, by its essential vocabulary, its grammatical structure and what may be called its machinery, a Teutonic tongue. For many ideas we now have three words, native, French and Latin, e.g. kingly, royal, regal, each with its own special appropriateness, but it will generally be found that the native word is the richest in emotional and picturesque content—"The peculiar depth of meaning of our native English words is largely due to the existence of the less vigorous synonyms of Latin origin, which enables us to reserve the nobler words for nobler uses" (Bradley).

What We Took from Greek

The Greek element in English was, until recent times, rather insignificant. The earliest words from this source, such as apostle and bishop, reached us in a latinized form through the Roman missionaries. Few men knew Greek in the Middle Ages, but some essential words, such as arithmetic, astronomy, mathematics, comedy and tragedy, physic, are recorded. These usually came through Old French with a phonetic spelling, e.g. *fisicien*, now restored to physician. So also French *fantaisie* gave our fantasy, soon reduced to fancy and later accompanied by the learned form phantasy. At the Renaissance Greek words began to be adopted freely, often in an unaltered form, e.g. analysis and synthesis, climax, hypothesis, nemesis, pathos, all recorded in the sixteenth and seventeenth centuries. Since that time any one who has had a new idea, made a discovery or an invention, is apt to give it a Greek name It was thus that Napier of Merchiston invented logarithm, i.e. word-number, and

the coinages of later scientists are innumerable. The compounds of such prefixes as *meta-, para-, hyper-, hypo-* run into hundreds and the same applies to words beginning with *auto-, hetero-, hydro-, phono-*, etc., or ending in *-ology* and *-ism*! This vocabulary is rather algebraic than linguistic, but is of great value for international currency. Greek is peculiarly fitted for scientific language because of its richness in affixes and its adaptability to new formations. Being almost unused material, it has a clarity free from the ambiguity which might result from the associations of more familiar words. *Suppositio* is the exact Latin translation of the Greek *hypothesis*, but nobody would deny that for scientific purposes *hypothesis* is the better word.

Many Dialects

It will have been realized that, when Caxton started printing in England, he had to deal with a language compounded of three elements, native, French and Latin. It was also a language divided into various dialects, often showing great differences of vocabulary and pronunciation. It was the East Midland dialect, spoken in Cambridge and London and, to some extent, in Oxford, which eventually became standard English. Caxton himself was a native of the Weald of Kent, where, says he, a very "rough" English was spoken. He tells an amusing story of a north-countryman, who, landing on the coast of Kent, went to a farmhouse to buy eggs and was told by the good wife that she did not understand French. Egg is a Scandinavian word which has quite supplanted the native word *ey*.

The dialects are now dying out, the result of universal education and the B.B.C., but well into the nineteenth

FIRST ENGLISH PRINTED BOOK

A page from "The Recuyell of the Historyes of Troye" (Collection of Stories about Troy) which Caxton translated and printed in Bruges about 1475. The printed matter looks like the old written manuscripts.

century, not only the peasantry, but also the more well-to-do class still spoke more or less like their forefathers. In the past many expressive words have passed from the dialects into standard English and it is interesting to know that in Shakespeare's "mobled queen" (*Hamlet*), "blood-boltered Banquo" (*Macbeth*) and "nook-shotten isle" (*Henry V*) we have three adjectives belonging to his native Warwickshire. To the popularity of Scott's novels we owe glamour, gruesome, raid and uncanny and Carlyle familiarized us with the Scottish feckless. The disappearance of the dialects may be practically desirable, but it is a matter of regret to the student of the science of language and lover of the past—"Time was in the House of Commons," said Lord Baldwin, "when you could tell a member from Worcestershire from a member from Yorkshire by his talk. You cannot do it now and I think more's the pity."

Founding of Schools

The fifteenth century marks a turning-point in the history of English. It begins what might be called the book age or perhaps the school age. Hitherto learning had been almost monopolized by the Church and generally confined to the monasteries. There were schools, but they were few and scattered. In the fifteenth century grammar schools were being founded all over the country, sometimes by great ecclesiastics, but perhaps more often by the new middle class which had grown up at the end of the Wars of the Roses (1455-1485). The great extension of commerce, due in large measure to the geographical discoveries, had called into existence a class of enterprising merchants. Nor were they actuated by the profit motive alone. Religion was a very real thing to these ancestors of ours and good works were regarded by them as obligatory on a Christian. A very large proportion of our ancient schools and famous hospitals owe their existence to successful merchants and enriched yeomen of the Tudor age.

It must not be supposed that education at once became general. Little provision was made for the real poor before the so-called charity schools of the eighteenth century. In the grammar schools the sons of the aristocracy and of the comparatively poor studied side by side and were flogged impartially. The foundation deeds of the oldest of the great schools, Winchester, built and endowed by William of Wykeham at the end of the fourteenth century, expressly state that a certain proportion of the scholars should be the sons of men of position.

Bible Influence on Speech

Education continued to be based almost entirely on Latin and the diffusion of books in English was slow and scanty. The scholarly still regarded Latin as the proper vehicle of literature. More's *Utopia* was published in Latin in 1516 and not put into English till 1551. In 1620, four years after Shakespeare's death, Bacon had so little confidence in the English language that he wrote his *Novum Organum* in Latin and the great Sir Isaac Newton still followed his example towards the end of the century.

An exception was the circulation of the Bible in English. There were various translations before the publication, in 1611, of the Authorized Version, but the two great names connected with the English Bible are William Tyndale and Miles Coverdale, both of whom worked in exile in Germany. Tyndale translated from Greek and Hebrew texts, Coverdale from Latin and from Luther's German version. Tyndale excelled in accuracy and vigour, while Coverdale is more graceful and musical. The Authorized Version is almost entirely based on Tyndale, while to Coverdale's translation we owe the Prayer Book version of the Psalms. The Bible was for centuries the chief reading and moral stand-by of all classes and was studied in this country as nowhere else, with the result that English acquired a special vigour and dignity— "Very many people of all classes at the time of Waterloo knew the Bible with a real familiarity which raised their imaginations above the level of that insipid vulgarity of mind which the modern multiplicity of printed matter tends rather to increase than to diminish" (Trevelyan, *English Social History*).

The consequence is that English, both

spoken and written, teems with scriptural quotations and allusions, e.g. from the Old Testament, "the fat of the land," "olive branch," "Egyptian darkness," "mess of pottage," "a broken reed," "a howling wilderness," "the skin of the teeth," "the writing on the wall," "the fly in the ointment," "bread upon the waters," or, from the New Testament, "pearls before swine," "a whited sepulchre," "the fatted calf," "the widow's mite," "to wash one's hands of," "old wives' fables," etc. To these may be added allusions to persons and places, such as a Nimrod, a Jehu, a painted Jezebel, a Job's comforter, a good Samaritan, a Prodigal Son, etc. Even a professed agnostic is apt to demand "chapter and verse" for a statement. It is true that, with the contemporary neglect of Bible reading, this picturesque element now tends to disappear along with such once familiar classical allusions as "a Greek gift," and "crossing the Rubicon."

Word-makers at Work

With the diffusion of the Bible in the vernacular we can begin to trace the progress of word-making in English. There must have been a certain amount of word-making in the Middle Ages, but it remains anonymous, while, beginning with the period of the Renaissance and the Reformation, we can watch the word-makers at work, from Coverdale and Tyndale onward. To Coverdale we owe such expressive compounds as bloodguiltiness, kindhearted, lovingkindness, tender mercy. Tyndale gave us long-suffering, broken-hearted, stumbling-block, filthy lucre, mercy-seat and even such a necessary word as beautiful, while his scapegoat, though possibly a mistranslation, is now indispensable. The other great contributor to our vocabulary and phraseology is Shakespeare, whose influence on English has no parallel in language history.

Between the English Bible and Shakespeare comes Spenser, "the poets' poet." His language is a rather artificial medley. He was an enthusiastic admirer of Chaucer, "well of English undefiled," but was also much influenced by the great Italian and French poets of the Renaissance. From these various elements he constructed a picturesque vocabulary to which the poets of the Romantic period often turned for inspiration. He invented the words blatant and braggadocio, possibly also elfin, and was the first to imitate the Greeks by calling the dawn rosy-fingered.

Shakespeare's Mint

With Shakespeare the Renaissance, which earlier had made itself felt only in a small circle, had to some extent reached the people or, at any rate, the new great prosperous middle class, and there was now a real reading public. An immense number of words are, as far as we know at present, first recorded in Shakespeare's works. Examples are aerial, bump, countless, dwindle, eventful, fitful, gnarled, hurry, lonely, monumental, etc. He is even our earliest authority for blood-stained. Among his creations are such wonderful epithets as fancy-free, ill-starred, proud-pied (used in describing April), cloud-capp'd (towers), heaven-kissing (hill), lacklustre (eye), while Shakespearian phrases now form an integral part of our everyday vocabulary, e.g. "the mind's eye," "caviare to the general," "a pound of flesh," "the bubble reputation," "a tower of strength," "the sere, the yellow leaf," "yeoman's service," "to the manner born," "not wisely but too well," "by flood and field," "to wear one's heart upon one's sleeve." From *Hamlet* alone it would be possible to enumerate some fifty such expressions, and many a man who has never read a line of Shakespeare quotes him unconsciously every day.

In the age of Shakespeare the rules of English grammar had not been formulated. In fact, men of learning did not regard their own language as worthy of serious attention. Consequently Shakespeare is often very ungrammatical. He indulges freely in false concords, double negatives, double comparatives and even superlatives —"the most unkindest cut of all." By Milton's time English grammars had been written and the irregularity of the Elizabethan age had been reduced to order. For all poetic and literary purposes English reached perfection with Milton. His own contribution to word-making is represented

TITLE PAGE OF COVERDALE'S BIBLE PUBLISHED IN 1535

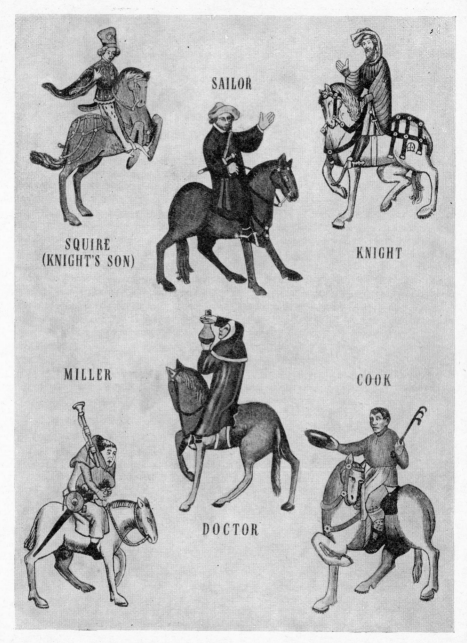

SAILOR

SQUIRE
(KNIGHT'S SON)

KNIGHT

MILLER

COOK

DOCTOR

MEDIEVAL PILGRIMS IN HOLIDAY SPIRIT

From these early fourteenth century drawings of some of Chaucer's characters we know how different social types looked and dressed in the Middle Ages. They were among Chaucer's companions on the journey to the shrine of St. Thomas à Becket. The illustrations are taken from the illuminated Ellesmere manuscript.

by pandemonium, and the present meaning of gloom, darkness, is due to him. Familiar phrases from his poems are "darkness visible," "human face divine," "dim religious light," and the frequently misquoted "fresh woods and pastures new."

Between Milton and the Romantic movement there was little word-making and phrase-making by the poets. Pope is often quoted, but usually in sententious couplets. Scott is the only real word-maker among the later poets. To him we owe free-lance, red-handed, Norseman, "passage of arms," "Caledonia stern and wild," "to beard the lion in his den," "foemen worthy of their steel." He also revived many Shakespearian words and phrases such as fitful, "coign of vantage," "towering passion," "yeoman's service."

The Romantic poets themselves were, apart from Scott, not great word-makers, but they revived a number of archaic words, largely from Spenser, which had long ceased to be in familiar use. The consequence is that it is impossible to read a page or two of a Romantic poet without encountering words that we should never use in speech and rarely in writing. Examples are the knell and lea of the first verse of Gray's *Elegy*, the hail and blithe of the first line of Shelley's *Ode To A Skylark*.

Science and Invention

In the period between Shakespeare and the Romantics word-making was mostly left to the prose-writers. The age of Pope especially was rationalistic and matter-of-fact, with little use for the imaginative. The invented words due to the prose-writers often supplied a felt want, e.g. Sir Thomas Browne's precarious, hallucination and antediluvian, or the fortuitous and central of his contemporary, Henry More. The later eighteenth century was much preoccupied with political and social questions. Hence Burke's colonial, electioneer and municipality, Bentham's international and utilitarian. In the nineteenth century Macaulay gave us constituency and influential. More recent coinages are Huxley's agnostic, Galton's eugenics and Shaw's superman. Scientific invention and discovery have necessitated much word-making, usually from Greek materials. Such words as photograph, dynamite, cinematograph, neolithic, etc., explain themselves immediately to any one who has a smattering of Greek.

Words from the World at Large

In addition to the three main sources dealt with we have borrowed words from all over the world, beginning with the Hebrew contribution from the Bible, e.g. cherub, sabbath, shibboleth, and the scientific terms which we owe to the Arabs, who were the great preservers of science during the Middle Ages, e.g. alchemy, algebra, zenith, zero. From about the period of the Renaissance European travel became the fashion and the chief country visited in making the "grand tour" was Italy from which we took a host of words dealing with music, art and architecture. The Spanish element in English gives a clue to our struggle with Spain and the conflict for the wealth of the New World, while from Holland we have taken, as might be expected, seafaring words and part of our art vocabulary. From the Scandinavian languages we have borrowed little since the time of the Vikings and from modern German chiefly a few words dealing with mineralogy; but Coleridge translated homesickness from German, as Carlyle did "a bolt from the blue," while Matthew Arnold and Carlyle between them naturalized Philistine in its modern figurative sense. Some European borrowings have made long journeys to reach us, e.g. boss (governor) has crossed the Atlantic twice on its way from Holland to England and the Portuguese cobra and padre were picked up in India. Accident may give sudden popularity to a word, e.g. bosh, the only Turkish word in common use, occurs frequently in an Oriental story, *The Adventures of Hajji Baba of Ispahan* by Morier (1834), mascot dates from Andrane's operetta, *La Mascotte* (1880) and the Czech robot from Karel Capek's play, *R.U.R.* (*Rossum's Universal Robots*), produced in London in 1923.

With the exploration of the world we have acquired an immense number of words, mostly the names of strange animals and products, and, unlike the South African Dutch, who made up their own names for animals and flowers (whence such words as springbok), we have taken them ready-made from the natives. The consequence is that our dictionaries contain a very much larger number of exotic words than those of other countries. Our collection of Indian words, especially, is very large and contains many terms so familiar that we hardly think of them as foreign, e.g. bungalow, cot, loot, pyjamas, toddy. It is only occasionally that this element in our language is other than purely materialistic. The Red Indian totem and the South Sea Island tabu have supplied useful terms to anthropologists, the Australian boomerang has given us an effective metaphor, from Chinese we have translated the expression "to save one's face," and nirvana, from India, expresses what cannot be expressed otherwise.

By far the most important recent contribution to colloquial English has come from America. There is something very expressive about such monosyllables as boom and slump, crank and crook, hunch, pep and stunt, though they do not belong to literature, and the same is true of such concise descriptions as brain-wave, dope-fiend, highbrow, sob-stuff, tightwad, wisecrack, live wire, raw deal, etc.

Curious Revival

But the American language has, within the recent years, had a remarkable influence on our grammatical construction in the revived use of the subjunctive. Except for stereotyped expressions of wish, such as "hallowed be Thy name," "Thy kingdom come," from the Lord's Prayer, "God save the King!" "Heaven forbid!" or concessive sentences, such as "Be that as it may," the subjunctive had become almost limited to the use of were after if, whether, as though, or after the verb to wish, e.g. "I wish he were here." In 1904 Henry Bradley wrote: "Perhaps in another generation the subjunctive forms will have ceased to exist except in the single instance of were." This shows the unwisdom of prophesying in matters of language, for the subjunctive is now more alive than at any period since

the time of the Authorized Version. This revival began in America under German influence. Here is an example from the letters of Walter Hines Page, who was U.S. Ambassador in London during the first World War—"I am going down to Garden City till the President send for me; or, if he do not send for me, I am going to his house and sit on his front steps till he come out." Contemporary American novels are full of such sentences as "She insisted that he knock before entering and she demanded that he admire her hats," and the same construction is now accepted English and can be read every day in our newspapers. The word, should, tends to disappear completely from such a sentence as "He suggested (requested, proposed, insisted, etc.) that we arrive not later than noon."

English Love of Abridgement

The present state of the English vocabulary is largely the result of our slack pronunciation. An Englishman can talk quite comfortably with a pipe in his mouth, whereas a foreigner must first remove anything that obstructs his vocal efforts. In such a word as pardonable only the first syllable is uttered distinctly, the others petering out in a vague murmur. Our pronunciation tends always to contract a long word, e.g. to make halfpennyworth into haporth and God be with you into good-bye, or to clip off unstressed syllables, as in sport for the older disport or raiment for the older arrayment. We often deliberately use only the first or last syllable of a word, e.g. van, which stands for both vanguard and caravan, the quite modern mike for microphone and tote for totalizator. Where a long word does not easily contract, we often substitute a shorter one, e.g. most people call a telegram a wire, and hunch tends to supplant premonition or intuition. We even leave our sentences unfinished, feeling that we have supplied an intelligent listener with enough, when we have said "for the duration," "that depends," "not an earthly," "Well! I never!" or "loitering with intent." The consequence of this love of abridgement is that English is now the most monosyllabic of European languages and that, whereas in such a language as Italian practically every word ends with a vowel, the abrupt consonantic finish is characteristic of English. This may be exemplified by the lines in which Coleridge so wonderfully describes the sudden nightfall of the tropics:

> The sun's rim dips; the stars rush out:
> At one stride comes the dark.

What the language has thereby lost in musical quality it has undoubtedly gained in manly vigour. Words of learned length and thundering sound may impress the ignorant, but it is the monosyllable that is really effective. As *The Times* said of Mr. Winston Churchill: "His monosyllables strike home like conscience or like fate— 'We will have no truce or parley with you or the grisly gang that work your wicked will. You do your worst and we will do our best. Perhaps it may be our turn soon; perhaps it may be our turn now.' "

One of the most curious features of English is the way in which it can interchange the parts of speech. Partly as a result of our loss of inflexions, partly from that linguistic laziness so often mentioned in this chapter, nouns and the corresponding verbs early became identical in form. This may be illustrated by an example. The German for comb is *kamm*, the verb is *kämmen*, with change of vowel. Similarly from Anglo-Saxon *camb* was formed the verb *cemban*, of which the past participle survives in unkempt; but already in Middle English this verb began to be replaced by comb; for why have two words, when one will do? Now we can not only use concrete nouns as verbs, as when we floor a room or an opponent, beach a boat, ditch a car, book a seat, pocket a tip, etc., but we can use abstract nouns in the same way, e.g. we can countenance proceedings or recondition a house, whereas in other languages a new formation or an explanatory phrase

MEDIEVAL FARMING
Our knowledge of life in the Middle Ages is based on contemporary writings, such as the Paston Letters, and contemporary drawings, such as this one from the Luttrell Psalter. (See also photographs on pages 16, 28 and 33). The farmer and his wife use primitive wooden mallets to break up the stony ground.

would be necessary. Other parts of speech can be similarly used colloquially as verbs, e.g. we can black our shoes, down tools, out an opponent and even pooh-pooh a suggestion.

Most of our nouns can be used as adjectives, as in gold watch, stone wall, field sports, recreation ground. Almost peculiar to English are such compound epithets as a matter-of-fact man, an up-to-date idea, a never-to-be-forgotten kindness.

Lack-logic English

As for syntax, so long as the meaning is conveyed, we trouble little about logical construction. Such sentences as "I was given this watch by my grandfather" or "The troops have been issued with winter clothing," defy grammatical analysis, but nobody complains. English alone omits the relative, as in "The book I am reading" and the conjunction, as in "He said he felt ill." It is interesting to note that the more scholarly writers do not indulge in this freedom. Dr. Johnson described the omission of the relative as a "colloquial barbarism," and it is said to occur only seven or eight times in Milton and only twice in Macaulay's *History of England*.

To conclude, English, apart from comparatively recent and often unnecessary accretions, is a perfect fusion of three elements—Old English (i.e. Anglo-Saxon and Old Norse), Old French and Latin. It is this wealth of vocabulary, combined with the practical use made of it by the national temperament, that makes English the richest, most expressive and most flexible of European languages. The extent to which this or that particular ingredient prevails depends upon the instinct of the writer or the fashion of the day. It is possible to write simple prose or verse in which every word is from Old English, just as it is possible, in a more ornate style, for all the essential words to be ultimately of Latin origin. The following paragraph by Dr. Johnson translates into "Latin" the proverb "Take care of the pence and the pounds will take care of themselves": "The proverbial oracles of our parsimonious ancestors have informed us that the fatal waste of our fortune is by small expenses, by the profusion of sums too little singly to alarm our caution and which we never suffer ourselves to consider together." Here English has practically ceased, except for the connecting machinery, to be a Teutonic language. On the other hand, Bunyan's wonderful opening to *The Pilgrim's Progress*, "As I walked through the wilderness of the world . . ." is almost pure

SERVING AT TABLE

Another illustration from the Luttrell Psalter gives a vivid impression of a feudal dining-hall.
It will be noticed that the food is eaten from platters; knives, but no forks are used.

Anglo-Saxon. It is interesting to take any famous passage and analyse its vocabulary, e.g. from Wordsworth's great Ode:

> There was a time, when meadow, grove
> and stream,
> The earth and every common sight
> To me did seem
> Apparelled in celestial light.

Here a series of simple native words (except for common) seem to lead us naturally to the gorgeous foreign epithets of the fourth line. As a rule it would seem that the most intimate feelings are best expressed by an Old English vocabulary, as in the immortal line which ends the Ode—"Thoughts that do often lie too deep for tears." Compare the monosyllabic homely music of the Victorian Poet Laureate, Alfred Tennyson, in:

> Break, break, break,
> On thy cold grey stones, O Sea!
> And I would that my tongue could
> utter
> The thoughts that arise in me,

in which every word is Anglo-Saxon, with the stately Latin vocabulary of Prospero's great speech. (The words or parts of words which are of Latin origin are italicized):

> And, like the *base*less *fabric* of this
> *vision*,
> The cloud capp'd *towers*, the *gorgeous*
> *palaces,*
> The *solemn temples*, the great *globe*
> itself,
> Yea, all which it *inherit*, shall *dissolve*
> And, like this *insubstantial pageant*
> *faded*,
> Leave not a rack behind.

Test Yourself

1. The Angles and Saxons, coming from various regions of North-west Germany, spoke several dialects. Which of these became the dominant tongue and the principal source of Anglo-Saxon (or Old English)?

2. Name six verbs deriving from Anglo-Saxon and six nouns deriving from Old Norse.

3. At the end of the Anglo-Saxon period (about 1150) the original language had been greatly enriched and the complicated inflexional system of Anglo-Saxon had been greatly simplified. How did this come about?

4. What was the influence of Norman-French upon the language? Write a short essay of 500 words upon the main effects, using the following headings for guidance:

   (*a*) Introduction of French as a literary language (cf. *Roman de Rou*).

   (*b*) French words introduced for court, military and legal functions (cf. throne, army, judge).

   (*c*) English used as the language of the common people (cf. brewer, baker, smith).

   (*d*) Gradual fusion of the two languages.

5. Give six words illustrating the influence of Latin on the language.

6. Can you list six examples of words in common use which appeared for the first time in Shakespeare's works?

Answers will be found at the end of the book.

GEOFFREY CHAUCER

Soldier, traveller, diplomat and prolific poet, Geoffrey Chaucer (1340-1400) was the author of "The Canterbury Tales," "Troilus and Criseyde" and the "Legende of Good Women."

CHAPTER II

THE BEGINNING

A SOUND taste in literature is a guarantee against boredom, and the key to a fuller mental life. We may say to begin with that the appreciation of books and the ability to discriminate between good and bad workmanship is one aspect of general judgment and good taste, and as such can be improved and perfected by use and practice. The man or woman who can talk intelligently about books bears the hallmark of a cultured mind, and therefore, apart from any consideration of personal enjoyment, a knowledge of literature is a great social asset.

This work covers, among other things, the main periods of English literature, and is carefully designed to familiarize readers with the books best worth knowing, to show their relative importance, and to illustrate the close connexion which great literature has with the pattern of history and the growth of ideas.

Dainties Bred in a Book

With a bold, simple and comprehensive plan, readers can go ahead with confidence, whether they read at the fireside or in a library. Some of the best minds have been formed by reading; William Shakespeare, for instance, says: "He that hath never fed of the dainties that are bred in a book, he hath not eaten paper, as it were, he hath not drunk ink; his intellect is not replenished; he is only an animal, only sensible in the duller parts." Charles Dickens, Robert Burns, and John Keats were self-educated on books at home, as were many others. "I would rather be a poor man in a garret with books than a king who did not love reading," said the famous historian-statesman, Lord Macaulay; and many, speaking from experience, have praised it as an insurance against an empty old age and as a delightful topic of thought and talk free from bitterness. William Wordsworth found, in the "strong book-mindedness" of the Cumberland dalesmen's homes, that "books are a substantial world wherein

solid happiness can grow." He was right.

But rules and methods are needed. Moods are all very well, but sometimes we should control them just as we do if we are learning music or a language. A backbone of dates and facts is a positive help to intelligent appreciation.

Our appraisal will begin with Geoffrey Chaucer and the fourteenth century. It must be realized, however, that there is no definite line of demarcation at which English literature appears in our history. There were, in fact, six hundred years of Anglo-Saxon poetry and tale-telling before Chaucer, and today much of this may be followed in translation.

Two decisive events happened in English history before the Norman Conquest in 1066. The Angles and our other Scandinavian ancestors invaded and settled in Britain, and then, in A.D. 597, St. Augustine and his fellow monks began the Christianizing of those heathen bands, whose minstrels had sung of the exploits of the heroes of Germanic Europe and of the struggle against the Danes. With the coming of Christianity the celebration of heathen deeds necessarily declined, but the clergy themselves possessed the art of writing and records no longer depended upon the handing down of verbal traditions and rhymes from father to son.

Beowulf: Epic from the Past

The Angles came in the sixth century with a folk-tale called *Beowulf*, which lived by the *skalds* (poets) repeating it; but about A.D. 1000 it was written down. For hundreds of years, it is supposed, the manuscript was in the Cotton collection, now in the British Museum, but in 1732 it was slightly damaged by a fire. Fragments of a companion Anglo-Saxon saga, *Waldere*, were found in 1860 in the Royal Library at Copenhagen.

Beowulf is not about England nor even about the Angles; it is sheer Scandinavian mythology, of monsters and rescues—in long, alliterative lines and stark imagery. It is somewhat tempered, in its manuscript version, by the Christianity which was beginning to take hold. Still, its main tone is of northern melancholy, fatalism, and heroic defiance. It is the largest and most characteristic of all the salvaged epics of the period.

Christian missionaries could not destroy these pagan myths, but they influenced them, and a blend can be seen in *Andreas* (St. Andrew) in which Andrew rescues St. Matthew. The new religion gradually gained the ascendant, and this was expressed by Caedmon (*d.* 680), a Whitby monk drawn from the people. He was cowherd of the monastery, the dunce of the brethren, yet it is by him largely that the ruined monastery on the Yorkshire cliff is remembered.

Bede and Caedmon

The Venerable Bede (673-735), the learned monk who put the Gospel of St. John into Old English and who justly earned the title of "Father of English history," tells us that the harp was pushed around the hall at supper, and each had to sing, like the gleemen, his own story. Caedmon was dumb, and slipped out into the night. Once, while he was dreaming in the stable, a stranger asked him to sing something, and when Caedmon told of his plight the apparition said: "Sing the Creation." When he awoke Caedmon felt he had the gift, and he began his paraphrase of the Genesis story—in wild short lines, full of fire and imagery.

Those who will be at the pains of comparing a modernized version of Caedmon's graphic lines with John Milton's more elaborate *Paradise Lost* (fully dealt with in Chapter V), written almost exactly one thousand years later, will discover with an agreeable shock the length of our literary history, and the tenacity of certain traditions.

The development of the vernacular tongue was checked by the influx of the Normans, who for a time imposed French as the educated language, but this influence was not to last, and by the reign of Edward II (1307-1327) we find English metrical romances, like *Guy of Warwick* and *Bevis of Hampton*, which were the staple literary entertainment of the people.

By this time the Crusades, which opened a channel for the importation into Europe of knowledge as well as goods from the Mediterranean countries, had stimulated a zest for study (philosophy, natural and divine—what we call physical science and theology). This resulted in the form of philosophy known as Scholastic, the exponents of which were known as Schoolmen.

Medieval Inquirers

Much of the discussion which occupied the time of the Schoolmen strikes the modern reader as being outdated. They believed that man's earthly life was of less importance than his life after death, and because of this their writings contrast sharply with the humanitarian, economic, and sociological theories which later philosophers evolved. It must be realized that the great Schoolmen had many lesser imitators whose writings and discussions often degenerated into obscurity and playing with words. But at its best the Scholastic approach contributed nobly to the evolution of ideas and, more important, to the crystallization of the Christian attitude towards life.

The principal Schoolmen were known as Doctors, the title being prefixed by an adjective denoting their character. Thus the fine, ringing name of the Admirable Doctor was accorded to the English monk, Roger Bacon (1214-1294), a member of the Catholic Order of St. Francis (whose members included many of the most learned churchmen). The life of Roger Bacon shows that Britain counted for a good deal in the world of thought; after his death his successors gave him the title of *doctor mirabilis*. He was a far more *practical* scientist and investigator than the Francis Bacon (1561-1626) whom we reach with the other Elizabethans shortly; and is never to be confused with him. Roger's inquiries were into theology, grammar, ancient languages, geometry, astronomy, chronology, geography, music, optics, mechanics and chemistry. He mastered what was then known of these subjects, even if that was

SOWING IN MEDIEVAL DAYS

From the Luttrell Psalter comes this picture of country life in the fourteenth century. The farmer is seen sowing his wheat, while his dog drives off a thieving crow.

far less than we possess now. Although he did give credit to the changing of base metals into precious ones (alchemy) and the foretelling of the future by astrology, he had one of those universal minds that colonize fresh bits of country for other writers later to explore fully.

We are tracing rapidly the growth of this tree of letters from the days of parchment, vellum, and then folios up to William Caxton's slow hand-press at Westminster, which he set up in 1476. Caxton's press was taken over and improved by his pupil, Wynkyn de Worde. The latter put out a few copies each of four hundred and eight works. Then Richard Pynson, who set up for himself, became the first King's Printer, and published two hundred and twelve works (translations and oddments included). All this called new authors into being, and there was a larger sprinkling of those who could read out to the illiterate. It is astounding how precarious, before printing, was the life of literature—yet it lived, thanks to hand copyists in monasteries and schools.

Nationalism in the period we are surveying was nothing like so conscious or exclu-

HARVESTING

Again from the Luttrell Psalter: medieval thrashers use wooden flails to separate the grain.

E.L.L.—B

sive as we have known it in modern days. There was a lively coming and going of envoys, teachers and missioners about Western and Southern Europe, including Britain. It was not uncommon for a man to speak English and French equally fluently; while the use of Latin in writing provided an international means of communication between the learned.

For long, kings of England were kings of a goodly part of France. They and their courtiers, bishops and soldiers were constantly crossing and recrossing the Channel. Manuscripts were moved about, too.

Now let us stand back from these sources of the stream of English literature and look at the broadening river ahead, and plan our personal journey along it.

Stream of Literature

Periods in history and literature fade into one another as night into day. After glancing, as we have done, at some of the principals of our origins (before works were written which can be read with ease today) it is wise to remember, not periods, but a few peak names which stand for summits of ability. They are: Chaucer, Shakespeare, Ben Jonson, Spenser, Sir Francis Bacon, Milton, Dryden, Pope, Swift, Defoe, Addison, Samuel Johnson, Gibbon, Fielding, Blake, Burns, Scott, Coleridge, Wordsworth, Byron, Shelley, Keats, Tennyson, Browning, Dickens, Trollope, Thackeray, Macaulay, Hazlitt, Lamb, Carlyle, Ruskin, and Swinburne.

And then those nearer today: Hardy, Meredith, G. B. Shaw, Conrad, Wells, Bennett, Galsworthy, Yeats, Chesterton, Kipling, D. H. Lawrence, Somerset Maugham, Masefield, and Aldous Huxley, whose work—or much of it—will continue to live for many a year. These names trace our course as we proceed.

Admittedly the list gives but a scanty idea of the luxurious garden or forest of the adventuring mind—as scanty as it would be to tell a foreigner that the amazing opulence of beauty, skill, and human interest in the British Isles consists of a dozen peaks and cities, with Westminster, St. Paul's, York Minster, Lincoln Cathedral, and Windsor Castle—omitting all the crowded if less conspicuous treasures.

Here is a moment for some plain rules on this tour. Several methods will be laid down here as alternatives. The student therefore should not mix them nor flounder from one to the other. The multitude and the tempting quality of books are astounding. Their numbers today even destroy the reputation of many rather good ones. A big over-variegated crowd of subjects and styles is as paralysing to the literary instinct as a swollen evening party is to the social, friendly instinct.

Another prescription: in every recommended case, know something of the author's actual *text*. A knowledge of what critics have said about the big man is a poor substitute for a knowledge of what he has said himself; and second-hand, hearsay knowledge, however glibly repeated later in talk or writing, is seen to be quoted and derived by shrewd people acquainted with the sources. It is not the real thing, and it will not yield the intense pleasure and profit of the real thing.

Attend to the *manner* often, as well as to the matter. In many noble works the style is quite as much as—or more than—the mere information conveyed. It is this tasting of the words, sentences, and shading which discriminates a true connoisseur of literature from a hurried reader eager for plot, stories or facts. To bolt one's mental food is as harmful as to eat fast and greedily.

Poetry should be read slowly and carefully; pay the author the compliment of crediting him with ideas as important as any in a work of science. When the meaning is mastered, the poem should be read over again—perhaps aloud—to catch the magic of the diction and movement. Even in prose, too, never allow oneself to be lulled by sound. Reading is an intellectual, not an hypnotic exercise.

Do not hesitate to pencil notes and impressions on a loose paper or card, to be kept in the book. Subsequent reference to these will indicate how far you have advanced in discernment.

Do not surrender to any cliques, coteries or sects which exist to trumpet some particular man or school. They are invariably

LINDISFARNE GOSPEL

This page from the Lindisfarne Gospel, a manuscript written in Latin at the end of the seventh century by Eadfrith, Bishop of Lindisfarne, shows the Anglo-Saxon glosses added between the lines about 950 by Alfred, Bishop of Durham. The glosses represent the earliest form in which the gospels are extant in English.

unjust to other and greater men who are not of that exclusive circle; and they soon become dated, parochial, and slightly ridiculous. Listen to what the centuries say against the years, and the years against the passing hour. The moment's "genius" or the topical "masterpiece" may have sunk into oblivion by the year after next. Meanwhile, the mental conscience of cultured mankind has more or less justly graded the outstanding men and settled what their special powers are.

The writers of greater stature, who tower above their fellows, will of themselves afford any one a noble and adequate culture and a lifetime of intellectual pleasure. But knowledge of their works opens up other fascinating avenues of exploration—into history, philosophy, sociology, biography, and the literature of other countries.

Make full use of your civic rights at your local public library, and submit to the librarians any suggestions for new books. Periodically examine the displays at the second-hand booksellers, and keep up a gentle flow of discriminating recruitment to your bookcase, which, in a sense, is the noblest part of any home.

Remember, too, that there are fine interpreters of literature, among them Sir Arthur Quiller-Couch, Edmund Gosse, George Saintsbury, John Bailey, Walter Raleigh and Desmond McCarthy; and never scorn good books about literature.

More advice—strong and definite. Never drop a fine book because here and there it expresses something that is not *your* opinion. This is to mistake the whole purpose of literature; that purpose is to lift us out of our stagnant self-approval. Ask only of a book: "What did the creator of this work set out to do, and did he do it?" It is impertinent to ask:

"Is this done as *I* would have done it?"

Independence and stability of judgment are as rare in literary matters as in politics or anything else. One would suppose that, having felt a writer's force and beauty, individuals would not be forgetful or ungrateful. But, in fact, estimates become dulled, they are even reversed, and fluctuate like Stock Exchange quotations. The long-sighted critic, or the experienced reader, both rightly resent this. Broad popular preferences (for Shakespeare or Dickens, for instance) are more reliable because they represent a fairly constant point of view. But the way in which a great man's stock slumps, especially after his death, is a humiliating substitute for judgment. It then takes some influential creator or critic to rescue the disparaged name. Whereupon there is a stampede of the victims of fashion back to board the train they had left.

These pages deal in values and reputations which vary but slightly:

> For sense survives, when merry jests
> are past ;
> And rising merit will buoy up at last.

As Pope also said:

> A perfect judge will read each work of
> wit
> With the same spirit that its author
> writ :
> Survey the whole, nor seek slight faults
> to find
> Where nature moves, and rapture
> warms the mind.

Never neglect a good author because of a prejudice in fashion at the moment. Judge a writer by his best, or his average, or his total, never by his few blots.

Test Yourself

1. What was the name of the folk-tale brought by the Angles?
2. Who is called "the Father of English History"?
3. Who were the Schoolmen? Name one of the most famous English Schoolmen, who inquired into many subjects, including chemistry.
4. What was the date when printing was introduced to England? Who was the man who introduced it?

Answers will be found at the end of the book.

GEORGE INN, SOUTHWARK

The George Inn in Southwark, or "The Borough," as this part of London is known, is the only surviving London tavern to retain its galleries. It was from a Southwark inn that Chaucer's pilgrims set forth for Canterbury, and later, in the yards of inns such as this, early Elizabethan plays were presented by strolling players.

And when I sangne · it wolde be no bette
I obeyed · vnto his byddynge
And as the lawe · me bounde in alle thynge
As I koude · with a ful pale chere
Ay tale I ganne · anone as ye shal here
Explicit prologus

Prima pars
Here begynneth the Segge of Thebes ful
lamentably tolde · by John lidgate Monke of
Bury annexynge it to ye tallys of Caunbury
Sirs quod I · fich of yowre Curtesye
I entrede am · in to youre Companye
And admytted · a tale for to tele ·
By hym that hath power to compele
I mene oure hoste governere and gyde
Of youre erbeone · rydenge here by side

PAGE FROM THE "CANTERBURY TALES"

A page from a fifteenth-century manuscript version of Chaucer's "Canterbury Tales"
shows some of the pilgrims making their way to the shrine of St. Thomas à Becket,
"the holie, blisful martyr," murdered in Canterbury Cathedral in 1170.

CHAPTER III

THE DAWN OF ENGLISH AND CHAUCER

IN the year 1356 a writer, styling himself "Sir John Mandeville," dedicated to King Edward III a narrative of "Travels" through China, Turkey, Persia, Armenia, India, and Ethiopia. There is some evidence that the writer was a Frenchman, a physician of Liége. He claimed to have worked his passage through great dangers by knowing something of medicine, and returned with some tall stories of wonder. The point is that it was worth while to turn them out of Latin into French *and English*. The book proved immensely popular in England.

In the year 1362, Parliament was first opened by a speech in English. John Gower, a moral and lengthy rhymer, was writing in English, and more parts of the Bible were being translated by John Wycliffe and others. These facts indicate the pro-English set of the lingual tide. The time was ready for a genius to give lustre to the now popular language. Geoffrey Chaucer was the fortunate answer.

His century, the fourteenth, was the most important up to then in the life of Europe. It was the slackwater between the decay of chivalry and feudalism in England, and the young flood of the Renaissance, or Revival of Letters, or the New Learning as it is variously called.

Of all men Chaucer is most representative of that age which was the sunset of the (not always) "good old times": the age of chivalry, merry pilgrimages, carols, and wandering entertainers was about to perish for ever.

The comfort-loving Chaucer, master of quiet laughter, sly character-drawing and fresh observation, did not write of the problems of his age. He took his fables and plots from the past. He does not hint at the religious controversies of the period, the revolt of the Lollards against established religious usage, or the worldliness in the Church which angered the earnest soul of William Langland in his *Piers Plowman*. He knew more about life, Court, travel and the military pride caused by English victories in France.

It is this new gladness of a young and growing people which utters itself in the verse of Chaucer. He was born in Thames Street, London. As a young man he fought against the French in 1359, and was taken prisoner. Soon after he was released he found at home a patron in John of Gaunt (father of King Henry IV), and thrice went to Italy on diplomatic errands. There he may have met the Italian writers Boccaccio and Petrarch, whose tales and sonnets he loved and, with Dante's name, remembered in his own verse. In Government employ, he was busy with building at Westminster, Windsor and the Tower. For years he seemed to have the knack of making himself cheerful in every kind of circumstance, as he cheered his readers—or listeners—with his debonair ways and fun.

" The Canterbury Tales "

He had gifts and pensions from Court, including a daily gallon of wine; he also knew disfavour after a London riot raised by one of his influential chiefs, and had to flee to the Continent for eighteen months until he exhausted his supply of money by helping other English refugees. Returning, he was flung into the Tower, and while imprisoned there he had to sell his two pensions to save his family from starving. However, the sun shone on him again; but he chose a country backwater—probably Woodstock—in 1391, and there he settled to write *The Canterbury Tales* by which he is known to students in Britain and in all other nations besides. King Henry IV doubled his pension. On a visit to town, lodging in Westminster, he fell ill, and found an honoured grave in the Abbey— the first of a long line of great men whose

SIR THOMAS MORE

This English statesman, born in 1478, was both lawyer and scholar. He came under the influence of Sir John Colet, promoter of Renaissance learning in England, and of Erasmus, the Dutch humanist. More's "Utopia," a satire on government and society, was published in 1516; in 1529 he was created Lord Chancellor in succession to Cardinal Wolsey. More was beheaded for opposing King Henry VIII's claim to be head of the Church.

illustrious dust reposes there. *The Canterbury Tales* are his masterpiece. If Chaucer is read in the right mood, by those who are not put off by the archaic spelling, his poetry is among the greenest and freshest in our language. He has inspired a number of critics (Samuel Taylor Coleridge, William Hazlitt, James Russell Lowell and George Saintsbury among them) to lively appraisals, and at least two poets (Dryden and Wordsworth) to write modern versions of part of his *Canterbury Tales*; but, though the latter are good as poems, something sweet and youthful is forfeited in the adaptation. In the original, Chaucer seems to suggest to us that what we call antiquity was really the youth of the world. He seems, besides, to be not an artist apart from his subject, but one more voice of nature added to the others, and one among his own party of pilgrims from the Tabard Inn, Southwark, travelling through Kent to Canterbury Cathedral and the shrine of the "holie blisful martyr," St. Thomas.

Realism Comes to Literature

It is a merry, broad-jesting, frank and English party, untouched by puritanism and pretence. The Wife of Bath is uproarious fun, and is (with Shakespeare's Falstaff) one of the greatest comic creations in literature. But the stories told on that long, jolly open-air ride through the orchards and hopfields cover the whole field of medieval poetry.

The thirty pilgrims are distinct characters. Sharply defined in the clear air we watch them start on a May morning; courtly knight, curly-headed squire, poor parish priest, high-born nun, the host of the Tabard Inn, the miller, the shipman, the pardoner (or seller of pardons from the Pope) and all the rest of the motley cavalcade. Notice their free and easy democracy —before the word was coined. Learned men are there, in the portly person of the doctor of physic, rich with the profits of the pestilence; the busy serjeant-of-law, "that ever seemed busier than he was"; the hollow-cheeked clerk of Oxford with his love of books and his pathetic and charming story of Grisilde; the haberdasher, carpenter, tapestry-maker, each in

the livery of his craft—not forgetting the honest ploughman who would dyke and delve for the poor without pay. It is the first time in English literature that we are brought face to face with thirty living and breathing people, all very definitely drawn, with sly humour and keen relish.

Beginning of a Tradition

It is the first of what later became known as picaresque stories (i.e. of wanderings), a class to which belong some of the most vivacious things in fiction—the novels of Fielding, Smollett, Sterne, Scott, Borrow, Dickens, and, in our time, J. B. Priestley's *The Good Companions*. For we all love journeys, tours, pilgrimages, holidays, new acquaintances, "fresh faces, other minds," and a continually changing scene. This great story-teller derived his skill and sharpness of eye from actual life and experience, not from theory and books. He had known war, exile, courts, business, travel, and the pell-mell of London and foreign cities. His wide tolerance, humour, large heart and affectionate satire enabled him to reflect, as none but Shakespeare has done for us, the pageant of the times. The nearest to him, in keeping a story briskly on the move, are Sir Walter Scott, Charles Dickens and Robert Browning.

There is fun as well as song in him, prose as well as rhyme. If he had not given us the very feel of moist meadows and summer skies, and love, and colourful ceremonials, he might have been a shrewd master of irony and comedy like Jonathan Swift and the French essayist, Michel de Montaigne. Yet he does far more than this. The ripple of laughter is never far away, and there is no cruelty in him. Like Shakespeare, he borrowed stories from abroad; anything that seemed specially addressed to Geoffrey Chaucer would serve, and what he did was to recreate it in his own original way. Edmund Spenser, generations afterwards, called him:

> That renowned poet,
> Dan Chaucer, well of English undefiled,
> On Fame's eternal beadroll worthy to be filed;

and Dryden describes him as "a fountain of good sense," adding: "Here is God's plenty." It is interesting to remember that for one hundred and fifty years Englishmen were as proud of Chaucer as a purifier and settler of our tongue, as the Italians were of Dante.

However, thirteenth and fourteenth century life was not all sunshine and skittles for the people. There were dark spots of ignorance, oppression, and disease. In six years the Black Death killed six million people, and in such an atmosphere the promise of life eternal might well seem more attractive than life on earth. Corruption extended into the Church itself; and, among the preachers who called for reforms, there was a poet, William Langland, whose *Vision of William concerning Piers the Plowman* is a sombre foil to Chaucer's work. Langland was a west-countryman well acquainted with Severnside, Shropshire and the Wrekin. His tall, thin, protesting figure

was long a tradition there and in London; this reformer-poet-churchman illustrated the seamier side of life. The Plowman, as he calls himself, picked out the abuses and sufferings of the age and the common people, and denounced the political causes in short, sharp, accusing verse, popular and alliterative. His poem, which was frequently re-copied up to A.D. 1400, is a series of visions dissolving into one another, which needs a running marginal commentary if we, of today, are to understand it. Langland wrote under a sense of danger, for his outspoken social criticism offended high persons in Church and State.

The gay pilgrims of Chaucer's story seem a pleasant dream, far from the world of wrong and ungodliness revealed by this gaunt rebel of a class-conscious poor. Some took the moody clerk for a madman, obsessed by the inequalities of human lot and the social chasm. To him the time was out of joint, and he had no faith in his

SPENSER'S HANDWRITING

Above is part of a letter, signed by Edmund Spenser, "the poets' poet." He is the author of the "Shepherd's Calendar" and the "Faerie Queene," which is by far the longest epic in English and was written in honour of Queen Elizabeth.

power to put it right with all his moral preaching and his angry outbursts of coarse, moralizing humour which is akin to that found later in the engravings of Hogarth.

Piers the Plowman is, in parts, a striking allegory. Like other fine work which will be mentioned as we proceed, it is best left till the student has a grip on more wonderful and less difficult parts of our literature. It affords a lively picture of some aspects of manners and conditions in the fourteenth century, and of the spirit of criticism and revolt which even then began to stir. Yet the full storm did not break for nearly two hundred years.

New Scholarship

It is astonishing, but true, that, after Chaucer, there was well over a century's dearth of anything great in literature. What was happening? History, like Nature, contains no vacuums and great events were on their way. Renaissance (or rebirth) is the name given to the immense expansion of knowledge which now took place. Highly cultured, fugitive scholars from Constantinople and the Byzantine empire, which the Turks had captured in 1453, were pouring into the West with their knowledge of the great Greek philosophers and poets, such as Plato and Euripides, and texts of the best Latin masterpieces, which had been neglected by the eager, one-track Schoolmen, and by their students who had dwindled sadly in numbers for lack of new stimulating subjects for research. Education acquired a new meaning. From about A.D. 1420 onward, men of means, often church dignitaries, built colleges. In the fifteenth century nearly forty new universities were founded in Europe: at Oxford, Lincoln College by a Bishop of Lincoln, All Souls by Archbishop Chicheley, Magdalen by the Bishop of Winchester and Lord Chancellor; at Cambridge, King's College (1441) by Henry VI—with Eton as its "preparatory"; Queens' by Queen Margaret of Anjou. At St. Andrews and Glasgow a similar work was started, Glasgow University being founded in 1450 by Bishop Turnbull under a bull of Pope Nicholas V.

The New Learning seemed to strike native original genius dumb, because men found it difficult to cope with the forceful tide of incoming ideas. The higher ranks, lay and clerical, supported the general movement; many monks and obscure clerks, on the contrary, believed Greek to be the language of the evil one, and science a sort of black art. Indeed, in May, 1456, Parliament (at Henry VI's request) confirmed protections to three alchemist favourites of his because of "a certain most precious medicine, the mother and queen of medicine, called by some the inestimable glory; by others the philosopher's stone; by others the elixir of life or quintessence, is a most sovereign antidote against all poisons and is capable of preserving to us and our kingdom other great advantage, such as the transmutation of other metals into real and fine gold and silver."

Man of the Renaissance

An important development in the next hundred years was the birth (about 1467) of Desiderius Erasmus in Holland. This sage, wit and courageous critic lived in London, Oxford and Cambridge, and was befriended by so many of our great men, that we seem to consider him an Englishman. He taught himself the new golden-key language, Greek, and studied the early New Testament text.

His parents, whose story is fascinatingly told in *The Cloister and the Hearth* by Charles Reade, and who were well-to-do, had been prevented from marrying by interfering relatives. The father died in a monastery; the mother was left with her child, and soon afterwards she, too, died. Little Erasmus was heir to a moderate fortune, and his guardians, with an eye on this, put the boy into a harsh school to be prepared for a monastic life where the orphan's resistance was about as effectual as Oliver Twist's. The Archbishop of Cambrai heard of him later, and sent him to the University of Paris, where he dispensed with monk's frock and acquired as much knowledge as he could.

Two English noblemen brought him over to England when he was twenty-eight to the Court of King Henry VII. He was given a church living in Kent, and as a bigger bait Henry VIII later offered him a pension and palatial house to induce him to remain there. But he wanted freedom, not a livery. He had in him those shining *Essays and Dialogues* and his *Praise of Folly* which translate so well. He afterwards lived at Louvain, where he corresponded—very candidly—with Popes, cardinals, kings and statesmen on the need for quiet, timely reforms in the Church; advice which, had it been taken, would have saved centuries of disaster and trouble. Still, it is highly curious to see the extreme freedom with which they allowed him to propose to them his plans for true reform. But inertia won the day. Those in power were tragically out of touch with the world-awakening.

More's "Utopia"

Among his friends were Bishop Fisher and Sir Thomas More, and the latter, in his beautiful, daring, free-spirited *Utopia* (a title made of two Greek words and meaning "Nowhere") written about 1516, showed how disturbed he was by the prevailing opinions concerning Church and State. *Utopia*, which is a description of an ideal state, can be read in excellent translations. When More opposed Henry VIII's claim to be regarded as head of the Church, and was beheaded in consequence in 1535, the news of his death stunned Europe. It hastened the death of Erasmus. Splits within the Church were increasing, his advice was spurned, his translation of the New Testament (a landmark in the history of intellectual development) was seized and condemned though he was a true member of the pre-Reformation Church, and his bosom friends, More and Fisher, were executed. Erasmus lost the desire to live and passed out of a world whose follies and errors he had so often satirized. He had pleaded for the *real* gospel—"love is the whole fulfilling of the law"—but his message was not heard.

Ironically enough, knowledge, through the Greek and Latin literatures, was encouraged by men whose cause, though they did not realize it, was to suffer from the popularization of the new ideas. Pope Nicholas V added five thousand Greek manuscripts to the Vatican; and English bishops and nobles were equally keen.

Criticism grew bold. Even More, in his *Dialogue concerning Heresies* (1528), says: "Some priest, to bring pilgrims to his parish, may devise some false fellow feigning himself to come seeking a saint in his church, and there suddenly say he has gotten his sight. Then shall ye have the bells rung for a miracle."

A lesser but interesting figure of the period was the rhymester, John Skelton (1460-1529), said to have been a native of Diss, in Norfolk, whose hard-hitting coarseness became popular in his attacks on Cardinal Wolsey, favourite and counsellor of Henry VIII:

Our barons be so bold
Into a mouse-hole they wold
Run away and creep
Like a flock of sheep
For all their noble blood
He plucks them by the hood
And shakes them by the ear.

But the new learning was also producing a great religious division and a wholesale reorganization of the Church.

Tyndale and Coverdale

William Tyndale (1490-1536) is in many ways the hero of the struggle to make the Bible available in the English tongue. The influence of the Bible upon English literature cannot be over-estimated: its influence extends right down to the work of John Ruskin, Algernon Swinburne and Rudyard Kipling. It has been the well-spring of much of the best in our legacy of prose and poetry.

Tyndale found that England was not a safe place for such a daring innovation and went to Germany. In spite of efforts made to impede the publication of his New Testament, he succeeded in issuing it in octavo form in 1526. He then turned his attention to the Old Testament. In 1530 appeared his English translation of the Pentateuch and that of Jonah in 531. In 1535 he was tried for heresy and condemned. In 1536 he was seized, strangled and his body burnt at the stake.

DESIDERIUS ERASMUS

The great Dutch humanist, born in 1476, enjoyed the friendship of many English scholars, including Sir Thomas More and John Colet. Erasmus pleaded for reform within the Church, and among his many works the most important is his edition of the Greek New Testament.

Tyndale's version is racy and colloquial and, to many Christians, offensive. An example of his style may be given: "And the Lord was with Joseph and he was a lucky fellow."

Meanwhile Miles Coverdale had published the first complete English Bible, probably from Zurich, in 1535. It must be realized that the background of this struggle was the more important issue known as the Reformation, which resulted in most of Northern Europe adopting the doctrine of the Reformed Church as opposed to that of the Church of Rome.

The final cleavage between the Pope and the English Church resulted in a Bible that was a composite of Tyndale and Coverdale, published "with the King's most graycous lycence" in 1537. The Authorized Version, for the production of which a committee of divines was responsible, was published in 1611, in the reign of James I, and this remained virtually the only Bible used in the Church of England until the Revised Version was published in the nineteenth century.

Impact of the Bible

As an accompaniment to general reading for pleasure and study, the student should certainly make a resolve to read the outstanding Books of the Bible—Genesis, Kings, the Psalms, some of the Proverbs, Job (certainly), Isaiah, and the New Testament. It is wise to read a whole gospel through at an hour's sitting, with a fresh mind, as far as possible freed from associations of previous piecemeal hearings. Great literary critics—and creators—know greatness when they encounter it here. There is probably no more beautiful mode of narrative extant than the first chapters of St. Luke's gospel. The Acts may be compared to a simple, vivid war despatch, travel log, or pioneer's diary. Epistles like St. Paul's letters to the Corinthians, the Ephesians and Colossians are an example of forceful yet persuasive exhortation lucidly and beautifully expressed.

Something like literary justice can in this way be done to all these books in a study of the Bible in one month of evenings, if taken consecutively. But take this interesting side-adventure one evening a week, apportioning the rest to (a) poetry, and (b) recognized prose.

At first the impact of the Bible on the unprepared crowd who thronged St. Paul's Churchyard and other places to hear it read out (because literates were few) was but one more excitement in the general bubbling cauldron of new knowledge, tales of returned travellers, and religious unrest. Shakespeare expressed the new pride of man and the Renaissance in his *Hamlet*:

> What a piece of work is a man! how noble in reason! How infinite in faculty! in form and moving, how express and admirable! In action, how like an angel! In apprehension, how like a god! The beauty of the world! The paragon of animals!

And then, the sudden reaction:

> And yet, to me, what is this quintessence of dust? Man delights not me: no, nor woman neither. . . . I have of late lost all my mirth, foregone all custom of exercises; and indeed it goes so heavily with my disposition, that this goodly frame the earth, seems to me a sterile promontory; this most excellent canopy, the air, look you, this brave o'erhanging firmament, this majestical roof fretted with golden fire, why, it appears no other thing to me than a foul and pestilential congregation of vapours.

That, by the way, is perhaps the first modern prose: all the grit and crabbedness washed from it; fluid, vivid, and lucid. Shakespeare's prose is as notable as anything else in him. The point to seize, however, is the sensitive way in which it expresses so many emotions. The minds of men in Shakespeare's time can hardly cope with a world so altered by discovery in literature, science and geography. Hamlet's mercurial changes, his caprice, his feigned madness, his uncanny thrusts of wit and wisdom, his excited and morbidly speculative mentality and his moody disgust—all this is typical of the Renaissance period:

> O God! I could be bounded in a nutshell, and count myself a king of infinite space, were it not that I have had bad dreams.

How different from the settled, cheerful tone of naïve faith in Chaucer and the earnest morality of *Piers Plowman* generations earlier. How different from the more ordered ethical minds of John Milton and Andrew Marvell a few years later, when even the fanciful speculations of Sir Thomas Browne (1605-1682) in his *Religio Medici* keep within hail of orthodoxy and normality.

Yet both outlooks result in stirring, stimulating literature. Genuine belief can inspire great books; but so can sincere unsettlement and speculation. Anything may be grist to the mill of poet, dramatist, or the teller of tales. Anything which deeply moves the emotions of men will loosen their tongues and wing their pens. Many men of that time lived intensely and dangerously. A result was writing which will live. Science itself was a dangerous adventure, far more so than in the nineteenth century when men were already prepared for the progress to be made in scientific discovery.

Discovering the World

Travel and exploration, described nobly by plain sailormen in books by the English geographer, Richard Hakluyt, gave our island people this window into the wide unchartered world and the mystery beyond the horizons.

To the original Anglo-Saxons the sea had been something desolate, and their tone about it was plaintive, as of a place of dubious wandering and unmarked graves. They were emphatically a home-staying island folk, whose coastal settlements looked *inland* with backs to the ocean; they tilled their fields, tended cattle, and bartered wool, and even Chaucer's shipman, almost the sole representative of the sea in our medieval literature, plied only a coastwise trade.

In a fifteenth-century map in Hereford Cathedral, Jerusalem is placed at the junction of what Shakespeare in after days called "The three corners of the world"—Europe the region of light, Africa of darkness and Asia of mystery. Round the whole mass rolled the vague, void Ocean; the medieval mind did not find it possible to think of an outer circumference to Ocean, any more than we find it easy to think of an outer circumference to Space.

To them, the British Isles appeared as the last foothold of habitable land in the European corner of the world. "Nothing," says a naval historian, "could be more natural than that the inhabitants of Britain should turn towards the Continent and away from the Atlantic; away from storms and mists and angry breakers towards the vineyards of France, the orange groves of Spain, and all the shimmering loveliness of Italy."

The real reason was that most ships were then unseaworthy for long voyages. In Plantagenet and early Tudor days men felt a passion of curiosity about Asia, and a superb indifference to Africa (of which only the northern shore was known). This, too, is easily understood. Out of the east had come the evangel of Christianity; out of the east had come the menace of Islam; and beyond the battlefields of Cross and Crescent lay markets packed with strange merchandise, and trade routes whence came stories of fabulous wealth and wonder-working kings. So men were for years content to "mark the embarked traders on the flood."

Brazil, when discovered, was believed to be the mythical lost continent of Atlantis; while the intrepid sea captains, Columbus, Amerigo Vespucci and Cabot brought back accounts which fired the popular imagination. The dramatists and poets, for the greater part of a century and until the time of Milton, held the mirror up to the voyagers, and hardly a tale or poem but breathed of "the unplumbed, salt, estranging sea." In his sea-glimpses in *Paradise Lost* Milton shows us "the night-foundered skiff" and the huge Leviathan, "largest of those that swim the ocean stream," and the "cany wagons light" of the Chinese and far Cathay and "Araby the blest." And his less partisan friend, Andrew Marvell,

PTOLEMY'S MAP OF THE WORLD

Ptolemy, the Greek geographer, drew up his world map in the second century, but its authority was unchallenged until after America was discovered.

sings of "where the remote Bermudas ride on the ocean's bosom unespied."

It is necessary to give the reader this outlook upon the great world, because the revolution in the thoughts of men—now familiar to us, but staggering to them—affected all future literature. England, whose white cliffs had for ages been the last human foothold in the barren west; England, whose sullen skies and windy sea-wall had been accepted as the natural threshold of chaos ("the Ginnunga-Gap" of our Scandinavian forefathers), was now no longer on the rim of the world, but excellently placed for those who would voyage to the Orient and its marvels. They gazed on the sea with new curiosity. Could it be that far beyond the horizon lay continents which they might one day populate? Hence they dreamed, lived recklessly, coveted knowledge, glory and wealth. And literature, which is the echo and mirror of all human thought, hummed with the new disturbance.

Has not something similar been seen among us in late years? Tales, poems, plays, letters have always had a two-fold relation to life as it is lived: as both a mirror of it and an escape from it. In our own short memory, there have been the "grim" novels of world war; there have been scores of books about Polar and Antarctic journeys, about farming adventures far from town, adventures in Tibet and Central Africa, exploits in the air; scientific fantasias, Sir James Jeans's thought-provoking work, *The Mysterious Universe*, where we played among the stars; Rudyard Kipling disclosed India to us, and Joseph Conrad the East Indies and the South Seas. So much for escape.

By contrast we have the "realist" or photographic chronicle of some fictional family, shadowing each character so closely that the result reads like an affidavit or a verbatim report.

Now we are coming to Spenser, Marlowe and Shakespeare in that order of date. Picture the frugal home surroundings of our imaginative, inquisitive forefathers about 1500. Most people still had to sleep on hay or straw, had rushes strewn for carpets, rushlights or candles for illumination, logs and peat for fuel, salted beef through the winter and no fresh milk or cheese till spring grass revived the milch cows and ewes; no tobacco or potatoes.

no coffee, tea or cocoa, and, as yet, no glass windows. Without these accessories of modern civilization they had home life, the human heart, open-air toil or pastimes, song, religion, pageant and tales.

The vast mass of our people could not be egged on by warring theologians to take definite or violent sides in the quarrel between old and new, Catholic and Protestant. Monarchs changed sides for political reasons, and gradually the people acquiesced in these changes—and changed back when a new regime was proclaimed. They kept to their older traditions and occupations, especially in the countryside. It took nearly a century for the Bible to saturate the folk or our literature. As we have seen, the Authorized (King James's) Bible was only published in 1611—the same year in which Shakespeare, it is believed, finished

CHAINED BIBLE

The chained Bible seen here is that in Canterbury Cathedral. After the Bible had been translated into English during the Reformation it was made accessible to the common people by lying open in the churches in this way for all to read.

writing, and retired to Stratford. Spenser's career was over by then; no wonder, therefore, that neither of them shows its verbal or other influence, as later men do. As for Christopher Marlowe and other wild dramatists, they were not the sort to study the sacred literature closely, even if it had been available.

After the death of Chaucer in 1400, the stream of English song vanished until the beginning of Elizabethan times. Sir Philip Sidney strove with half-successes and some failures after a nobler poetry and prose; Sidney, who, born in 1554, lived only thirty-two years, has a symbolical relation to his time. Queen Elizabeth called him one of the jewels of her crown, and at the age of twenty-three—so fast did genius ripen in that summer time of the Renaissance—William the Silent (who sought to deliver the Netherlands from Spanish oppression) called him "One of the ripest statesmen of the age." The author of *Arcadia* and the *Apology for Poetry* travelled, knew many languages, and dreamed of adventure in America and on the high seas. His death, while fighting in the Netherlands, intensified the halo of romance that gathered round his name. "Look in thy heart and write," was one of his fine phrases; and another concerned poems so enticing that they "hold children from their play and old men from the chimney corner."

For Sidney, writing was an occasional pursuit; but for his friend, Edmund Spenser (1553-1599) one of the great figures in our annals, it was his first love. This Spenser realized after a stay in the North of England, when he wrote his *Shepherd's Calendar*, which was hailed with delight. Following disappointments at Court, he was sent to Munster as ruler and colonist among hostile people; and there he was guilty of political severities which, however, must not detain us nor warp our purely *literary* judgment. His castle was burnt down, and his child perished in the flames.

" The Faerie Queene "

After the *Shepherd's Calendar*, he began his long allegory, *The Faerie Queene*, a large volume in itself. It is certainly no poem to read through, without breaks into other reading. Poets then were not afraid of big tasks. Up to the time of Milton and, later, of Dryden, they were ambitious to write long epics. There was less in the world to read, and readers' appetites were more robust. Yet every one should be cordially advised to dip from time to time into this work, which is chequered with lovely stanzas that resemble subtly coloured tapestry swaying in the breeze. Then it will be seen why he has been called "the poets' poet," why such men as Milton, Cowley, Dryden and Keats proclaimed their debt to him, why Byron fell in love with his stanza-form and reproduced it, and why his fluid diction and idealistic outlook has nursed the young genius of others.

"Never mind the allegory of it, ' said Hazlitt; "it will not bite you." Indeed, it will escape most readers, and even the story is elusive, since the long fantasy never had its last book in which all that went before was to have been explained. It has been this noble dreamer's ill-luck to be excluded from most anthologies and golden treasuries precisely because of his leisurely length. Never does he compress; his genius consists in dilation. Colour as of the sunrise in the tropics pours over every page—or over many pages. He is "gaudy" in the older English sense of the term—joyous, tinted, prismatic with the shifting lights of an opal. In the prologue to his *Masque at Court* he has unwittingly described his spiritual home, a land wherein it is always afternoon:

> Wherein no wild, no rude, no antic sport,
> But tender passions, motions soft and grave,
> The still spectator must expect to have.

That sounds like a very passive programme for the reader, and so it is. But who has not such a receptive mood at times? One has known lovers of the *Faerie Queene* who, after a score of pages, are lulled to sleep. But what of that? It is pleasant, romantic sleep, better than some awakenings: only it is not for any time or mood. Here are three individual lines which convey the typical feeling he gives us:

> The woods shall to me answer and my echo ring.
> A gentle knight was pricking on the plain.
> Fierce wars and faithful loves shall moralize my song.

Test Yourself

1. When was Parliament first opened by a speech in English?
2. What is the name of Chaucer's greatest work, and what was its theme?
3. Who has been called "the poets' poet"?
4. How did the ordinary people live during the early sixteenth century?
5. Write a short account of the background which affected the literature of the early sixteenth century.

Answers will be found at the end of the book.

WILLIAM SHAKESPEARE

William Shakespeare, born in the country town of Stratford on Avon, an actor in a London playhouse, became the world's greatest playwright and the inspiration of writers throughout the world. None has equalled him in breadth of outlook, depth of feeling, or diversity of characterization. His monument in Westminster Abbey provides this picture.

CHAPTER IV

THE ELIZABETHAN CHORUS

IT is with some excitement that we approach the Elizabethan drama. In its beginnings, drama in England was religious —the playing of some part of the story of Christ's life suited to a church feast. These plays originally were no doubt over-shadowed by a choral element. Gradually the very human aptitude for mimicry and drama gained the upper hand and the drama passed from the church porch to the street.

This change occurred in the twelfth century. Elaborate cycles or recurring series of plays were founded which were performed at Whitsuntide, beginning at sunrise and lasting all through the day till dusk. Each town had its own cycle, and of these the cycles of York, Wakefield, Chester and Coventry still remain. As far as possible each company or guild of craftsmen took some Bible story fitted to its trade. The tone of these plays was often broadly humorous. Shakespeare and his fellow playwrights quite probably saw the Coventry or other cycles in youth.

A set called the "University Wits"— Christopher Marlowe, Thomas Kyd, Robert Greene, Thomas Nash and George Peele—went to London determined to fashion plays for the crowd. They haunted the taverns and theatres and gave full rein to their Bohemianism.

Christopher Marlowe stands out from the rest. Born at Canterbury in 1564, he was the head of a new movement which carried spoken and acted English at a bound nearer to the language we now know. He is, in order of time, the first maker of verse in which we have not to make much allowance for obsolete words and spellings. More than any other (except Lord Byron much later) he typifies the wild, vehement young man hungering after power and knowledge, combat and sensation. In him it has been called "a hunger and thirst after unrighteousness," but it was rather a yearning for the vast untried and the extreme of passion. He changed blank verse into something rich and ringing and rapid; "Marlowe's mighty line" became a label for him. Much of Marlowe is "young man's rant," but an actor today can still declaim it effectively. At that vigorous but child-like period, people enjoyed this musical magniloquence, but today a critical conscience is awake, and we tend to understatement and the avoidance of excessive emotion in our writing.

Marlowe's Mighty Line

Marlowe's imagination is unhallowed by anything but its own energy. He died at thirty in a dagger fight in a tavern. Though younger than he, Shakespeare enjoyed Marlowe's violent rhetoric; even echoing him in places, and parodying him in others. And the poet, Michael Drayton (1563-1631) said that Marlowe had in him:

> Those brave translunary things
> That the first poets had; his raptures
>   were
> All air and fire, which made his verses
>   clear;
> For that fine madness still he did retain
> Which rightly should possess a poet's
>   brain.

For those who like sounding theatrical speeches Marlowe is the man. As a dramatist, he was indifferent to plot, character or subtlety. He is saved by lofty style alone, for he had little thought, no message, and no humour. His *Jew of Malta* is a precursor and model of Shakespeare's *Merchant of Venice*; his *Tamburlaine* is a celebration of the power of conquest; his *Edward II* is a forerunner of those plays about English history with which Shakespeare was to delight the later Elizabethan playgoers; it exhibits the emotional antics of a shilly-shallying king whose murder at the climax of the play was praised by Charles Lamb as being the most tragic scene in drama. But his *Tragicall History of Dr. Faustus*, in which he first touched that legend of

evil curiosity, gives his measure and reflects
the restless era. Ambition mad, Faustus
exclaims:

> Divinity, Adieu!
> These metaphysics of magicians
> And necromantic books are heavenly.
> Oh what a world of profit and delight,
> Of power, of honour, of omnipotence,
> Is promised to the studious artisan!
> All things that move between the quiet
> poles
> Shall be at my command. . . .

A good angel begs him to lay the damned
book aside. An evil one urges him on to
doom. "Be thou on earth as Jove is in the
sky—lord and commander of the elements."
Faustus resolves to surpass the Delphian
oracle and the wonder-workers; and so
keeps tryst with the Furies. He calls up
spirits from the deep—and cannot exorcise
or lay them. The fatal signal is to be the
stroke of midnight: then the Devil will
come to claim his own. We can imagine
the theatre audience tensely waiting for this
horror. The agony of fear mounts, till
Faustus cries to himself:

> Ah, Faustus,
> Now hast thou but one bare hour to
> live,
> And then thou must be damned per-
> petually!
> Stand still, you ever moving spheres
> of heaven,
> That time may cease and midnight
> never come—
> That Faustus may repent and save his
> soul!
> O lente, lente, currite noctis equi!
> The stars move still, time runs, the
> clock will strike,
> The devil will come, and Faustus must
> be damned!
> . . Who pulls me down?
> See, see, where Christ's Blood streams
> in the firmament!
> One drop will save my soul: ah, my
> Christ!—
> Ah, rend not my heart for naming of
> my Christ!
> Yet I will call on him: Oh spare me,
> Lucifer. . . .

Sonority and splendour are in such speeches,
and the London theatre mobs highly
favoured such bursts of eloquence. Horror
was presented at least in glorious words.

To be obliged to put a quarter of the
truth about Shakespeare into a few pages
would make the most hardened summarizer
quail. We can picture the soil from which
this miraculous plant sprang — the surroundings of the tiny town of Stratford,
his father's gradual decline in fortune after
dabbling in agriculture and land values, so
that after being local bailiff or mayor in
1568 (four years after William's birth),
eleven years later his poverty exempted him
from a levy for a public calamity.

Shakespeare's Early Life

Thus, the poet-to-be was at the latter
date fifteen or sixteen, and by all accounts
was not himself an aspirant for any good-
conduct prize at the local grammar school,
where he had the right of free tuition.
There he would get scraps of the Latin poet
Virgil, a chapter from Caesar's *Commentaries*, possibly classical fables and some of
the Greek historian Plutarch's *Parallel
Lives* like the other boys; only he was to
make startling use of these things. There
is a tradition that the teacher used him as
a "monitor" for the juniors, what we should
call an unpaid pupil teacher. Some critics
believe that they have demolished the
legend of his poachings in Sir Thomas
Lucy's park near Stratford. What is certain
is, that he left his native town in 1586, at
the age of twenty-two, when his parents'
means were particularly cramped, and
when he had been married four years to
Anne, daughter of a smallholder at Shottery,
two miles away. Anne was seven and a half
years older than he. It may be added, in
the modern "realistic" way, that her relatives expedited the wedding. In the next
year a girl child was born, and in the next
twins (one of whom, a boy, died at twelve).

These personal details are of more use to
us than the folk-lore with which Shakespeare has been embroidered and disguised
by sentimentalists. Moralists have frowned
because he did not take his wife and
children up to London with him. They do
not explain what he should do with them

ELIZABETHAN PLAYHOUSE

The artist has reconstructed an Elizabethan theatre, such as the Globe, where Shakespeare's plays were performed. Unroofed, it was built with an "apron" stage on which the player could soliloquize among the audience standing in the "pit." Seats in surrounding galleries were more expensive. Sometimes nobles or wealthy people had seats on the stage.

in the noisy and, in some ways, dangerous capital. He left them with his parents at Stratford in a cheaply run household, to which he was soon the main contributor for the twenty-five years of his absence, earning his own and their keep.

As for the will, in which he left his wife the second-best bed with furniture, censorious critics overlook the fact that as Shakespeare's property was chiefly freehold, his wife was legally entitled to benefit without any formal mention in her husband's will. A minor puzzle to us is this: how did he maintain himself from eighteen, when he got married, to twenty-two, when he went to London to try his luck? Many aspects of Shakespeare's life will forever afford material for speculation.

He went to London not merely to get out of a groove and to avoid the helpless spectacle of poverty with no prospects, but to *see life*—of which he was to be the world's master.

Globe Theatre

The new profession of acting was clamouring for new recruits: so where was the need for such an exceptionally intelligent youth as Shakespeare to hold horses' heads at theatre doors for a coin, as tradition has it? The story is nonsense, for there were no horses' heads to hold at doors which opened on the narrow Bankside site of the Globe Theatre, to which people went on foot or in boats. Besides, he was at this time writing those earliest short poems having in them genius which would be recognized by any theatre-haunting Elizabethan. Within three years of arriving in town (in 1589, that is) he was one of the sixteen shareholders of the Globe, who divided the profits among them. He also added the duties of arranger of pieces, and actor. He made other men's shapeless plays readable, and then began as original author, turning out thirty-seven dramas in twenty-five years—three every two years. No wonder he did well, financially. From what he earned, he saved and invested shrewdly. Obviously he did well to leave his family in their comfortable native spot while he concentrated on things that were "not for an age but for all time"; on things

which, nevertheless, kept them in comfort.

Soon his name is fifth among only eight shareholders, and later it is second. He was doing so well that a spiteful pamphlet came out about him; it was withdrawn with apologies. The Globe evaded the censorships and prosecutions which dogged the other theatres; but when Shakespeare retired, it got into trouble with the licensers like the rest. At the age of thirty-three (after eleven years in London) he had enough money to buy New Place in Stratford, and reconstructed it—this fact alone indicating that he must have paid visits to his home and family.

When aged thirty-eight he purchased one hundred and seven acres of land and most probably (like his father before) speculated a little in farming or produce-dealing, along with his brother Gilbert. At one time, it is computed, he made £1,500 a year—perhaps £30,000 or £40,000 in our present currency, although such comparisons in values cannot be drawn too closely. His daughter, when he was forty-three, married a Dr. Hall and prospered. With them he went to live at the age of forty-eight, but enjoyed this serenity for only four years, dying on the anniversary of his own birthday, April 23, in 1616.

Shakespeare's Vision

These facts make waste paper of numerous fanciful stories about our chief of poets. They show his normality, and his strong practical sense of this world and the main chance. His genius was not of that sort which *seizes* a man and uses him as a mouthpiece. He spoke of "the poet's eye in a fine frenzy, rolling from earth to heaven," but this was no self-portrait. He had width and depth of imagination, but not tumult. His was the poetry of thought and human motive and nature. The most characteristic Shakespearian mood was one of understanding all sorts of human beings, now with humour, now with pity. Some of his best endings are on a note of tolerance and forgiveness. "Men must endure their going hence, even as their coming hither: ripeness is all." He was a great pardoner, with something of a generous sadness in his outlook on human kind.

ANNE HATHAWAY'S COTTAGE

Shakespeare's wife, Anne Hathaway, came from the small village of Shottery. Above is the farmhouse, owned by her father and believed to be her birthplace.

We of today have come to see Shakespeare as though he towered above his companions, but at the time others saw him as "Will Shaxpere" or "Master William Shakespear" (even spelling was fluid), pleasant to work with, amusing at the Mermaid Tavern, fond of quips and word-play (even to the detriment of some plays), gentle (that is, well-bred), honest (that is, honourable and open), quick-witted and (as a rival said) "jack-of-all-trades." Milton, in his first printed poem, spoke of Shakespeare's "Delphic lines" (i.e. deep and oracular) which "makes us marble with too much conceiving"—that is, transfixes us with pondering thought:

Thou in our wonder and astonishment
Hast built thyself a life-long monument.

The playwright Ben Jonson, too, in his "To the memory of my beloved master William Shakespeare, and what he hath left us," says:

Soul of the age!
The applause! delight! and wonder of our stage!
My Shakespeare, rise! I will not lodge thee by
Chaucer, or Spenser, or bid Beaumont lie
A little further, to make thee a room.
Thou art a monument without a tomb.

This is how the Elizabethans appraised in verse. Their verse thinks, their thought is musical as well as intellectual. Jonson, roughly candid, tells his friend's shade, "though thou hadst small Latin and less Greek," nevertheless he would call forth thundering Aeschylus, Euripides and Sophocles to live again and hear Shakespeare "shake a stage" for the comparison of all that insolent Greece or haughty Rome sent forth. This is terrific tribute from such an intense classicist as Ben. "Triumph my Britain," he adds, "thou hast one to show, to whom all scenes of Europe homage owe. He was not for an age, but for all time."

We have this unbribable critic's word for it that Shakespeare knew how to revise: "for a good poet's made, as well as born: and such wert thou!" We are told here by one who knew Shakespeare's very voice, gesture and smiles that "his mind and manner brightly shines in well-turned lines —in each of which he seems to shake a lance as brandished at the eyes of Ignorance." The next great writer to praise Shakespeare was the congenial Dryden; then Pope and Dr. Johnson. Coleridge, too, spoke of the many moods of the poet. Keats, however, hit upon an essential secret: Shakespeare's *experiencing* nature, his watching eye and listening ear.

Shakespeare's work shows detailed knowledge of many modes of livelihood—of farming and the sights of the country, of inns and ostlers, of characters on the roads, folk-lore, current legal terms, and, of course, the life of players. We do not know how he won his knowledge of practical affairs. He cannot have had first-hand experience of all the things and trades he writes about.

His Verbal Dexterity

He arrived at the right time. The English language was young and flexible, its edges unworn by repeated use or misuse. It was not formalized or "literary," and even rough sailors wrote their adventures in a fresh heroic diction. Part of the wonder, then, is in the fortunate state of our mixed tongue. The rest of the miracle was of his own making.

Clearly, his consummate mastery of all sorts of verbal expression was matured by continually being amid lively *talk*, action, movement and speculation. When he read, he read for hints, facts and stimulus; to borrow and improve upon and transfigure; he "brought to his reading a mind equal or superior." His art followed life closely, and he thought more about man than about theories. Great writers are never slaves of a formula or a system. It is only those of the second class who are merely aestheticists or moralists or theorists.

His Sympathetic Imagination

And Shakespeare, in an extreme degree, was all imaginative sympathy. It was his *nature* to enter into others' minds and realize their lot and view-point—from scallywags haunting taverns to kings and cardinals, from his girl heroines to common soldiers, from hired murderers to nobler humanity.

If he had a creed and a morality, it was to understand and experience nature and human nature in all their created varieties. Existence was to him a spectacle, not a subject for argument. And this all-including tolerance and appreciation may be a more moral attitude than the incurable moralist's. It widens and deepens us, moves and teaches us more than the rigorous and narrow method can. Shakespeare is the wholesome opposite of the types who start with a prejudice or theorem before they know life, and who bend everything to their preconceptions. He was himself aloof from the dynastic, social or religious quarrels of the time: he saw and felt through them, round them and over them. And these look crude and childish now: it is he who looks wiser, greater, more adult and attractive.

He, first in our literature, had that gift of indicating character, of opening up whole unending vistas of thought by a single phrase. It looks so easy as to seem luck. The words smack of the real thing, as in no other writer; they do not seem to have been contrived or meditated, but to be a windfall. If he speaks of earth, the words have the tang of earth. Or a line or phrase leaps out and, as the American essayist, Ralph Waldo Emerson, said, "sweetly

A
Midſommer nights
dreame.

As it hath beene ſundry times pub-
likely acted, *by the Right Honoura-*
ble, the Lord Chamberlaine his
ſeruants.

VVritten by VVilliam Shakeſpeare.

Printed by Iames Robèrts, 1600.

"A MIDSUMMER NIGHT'S DREAM"

*Although this play was probably written during the year 1595-96, it was first published in
"quarto" form in 1600, and above is seen the title page of this edition. A complete edition
of Shakespeare's plays was not published until 1623. Rowe's edition, produced in 1709,
was the first to divide the plays into acts and scenes.*

torments us with invitations to its own inaccessible home. His magic spoils for us the illusions of the green room. Read the old documents from which he took his material—and now read one of those skyey sentences—aerolites—which seem to have fallen out of heaven."

Very soon he had far surpassed his predecessors and models; his production was incessant and continually bettering. After three or four plays, he was a long way beyond the drum-and-trumpet tone of Marlowe, a longer way beyond Peele, Greene and John Lyly (who originated the affected style of writing known as euphuism). His meaning is more complex, farther-ranging than theirs, and so are his form and versification. The real Shakespeare cannot help showing himself, if only by a flash here and there, quite early; and then we are in the presence of something new and free and masterly, eclipsing any faults of haste.

Shakespeare's Range of Characters

Then in his maturity, when he gave us the gorgeous comic creation Falstaff, the half-brute Caliban, the tragic Othello and Desdemona, Macbeth and his lady, Lear and the daughters and the Fool, Perdita, Imogen, Shylock and Portia, Romeo and Juliet, Henry and the others, all the sweetness and the terrors of the human lot lay in his mind.

A good reader can, as it were, get *inside* the mind of the Greek philosopher, Plato, or Bacon, or Milton, and think from there; but not into Shakespeare's. For he is too many-sided and myriad-minded for that; he is everywhere, and out-of-doors—the farthest reach of subtlety and versatility compatible with an individual self. The astonishing thing is that, with this wisdom of life and knowledge of all sorts of minds, there are imaginative and lyric power, and wizardry with words, which are as exceptional as his penetration of nature.

It is a mistake to assume that his character-drawing required a large canvas. The whole of the Falstaff scenes in the first part of *Henry IV* do not contain above fourteen thousand words. In about twenty thousand words Shakespeare has elaborated the characters of all that wonderful gallery of humours: Falstaff, Bardolph, Nym, Pistol, Dame Quickly, Justice Shallow, Prince Hal and Poins. And how effective in so few pages are Dogberry and Verges, and the gravediggers in *Hamlet*.

Open the last of his plays, *The Tempest*, the ripe fruit of his feeling for life and its mystery and beauty. Previously every order of mind from king to beggar has spoken; he has uttered the lore of fairyland in *A Midsummer Night's Dream*, fate and law in the universe in *King Lear*, the drama of conscience in *Macbeth*; now it pleases him to create Caliban, neither man nor fairy, a something between brute and human nature who speaks with these words:

> . . . wouldst give me
> Water with berries in't; and teach me how
> To name the bigger light, and how the less,
> That burn by day and night: and then I loved thee,
> And show'd thee all the qualities o' the isle,
> The fresh springs, brine-pits, barren places and fertile.
> . . . Let me bring thee where crabs grow;
> And I with my long nails will dig thee pig-nuts;
> Show thee a jay's nest, and instruct thee how
> To snare the nimble marmoset; I'll bring thee
> To clust'ring filberts; and sometimes I'll get thee
> Young scamels from the rock.

These words are transparent, and seem to be the very things spoken of. Then there is the crystal-clear evocation of landscape near the shore, by Iris:

> . . . thy pole-clipt vineyard;
> And thy sea-marge, sterile and rocky-hard,
> Where thou thyself dost air:

and Prospero's farewell to "elves of hills, brooks, standing lakes, and groves." *The Tempest* contains the most noble meditative passage in the plays, on the dissolving of

FIRST FOLIO EDITION
Published in 1623, this edition of Shakespeare's plays, known as the First Folio, bears this authenticated portrait of Shakespeare engraved by Martin Droeshout on the title page.

SHAKESPEARE MEMORIAL THEATRE

*The memorial to William Shakespeare, including a library, picture gallery and theatre,
was erected at Stratford on Avon in 1877, but the theatre seen above was built after 1926
when the original was destroyed by fire. Each year a company of actors and actresses
presents a repertory of Shakespeare's plays and those of his great contemporaries.*

this fabric of a vision, the world itself.

Unlike the fluid grace and streaming colours of Edmund Spenser, Shakespeare's verse ripples swiftly by, glittering with reflected suns to match the wealth of metaphor. Words carry a more than logical or factual meaning; they are sounds and symbols suggesting a meaning beyond the reach of words.

Wonder though he is, even Shakespeare was indebted to his time and its atmosphere, to Chaucer, Spenser, the voyagers, chroniclers such as Holinshed, translations and Plutarch's *Parallel Lives*. They were the capital he started with—and vastly in-

creased; for the ready coining of such a phrase (one of a thousand) as

> Shake the yoke of inauspicious stars
> From this world-wearied flesh,

is beyond the reach of his forerunners.

Any one who intends to journey in Shakespeare ought to start by way of *A Midsummer Night's Dream, Romeo and Juliet, The Tempest, Julius Caesar, The Merchant of Venice*; the historical *Henry* plays; *Macbeth, Hamlet, King Lear* and *Antony and Cleopatra*, with *The Merry Wives of Windsor* for a finer kind of farce.

"Divinely rich, varied, strong and attractive," Matthew Arnold calls him. "With royal ease," said Robert Browning, "he walks up the steps and takes his seat on the throne while we poor fellows have to struggle hard to get up a step or two." "He is a second *nature*," says Leigh Hunt; "how near does he come to us with his thousand touches." So does he wind his way into the human heart and brain; for he is not so much a prophet or bard singing down to the people, as a portrayer and interpreter of many human beings as from within them.

There is no room to enlarge upon his view of men's ultimate destiny, save to say that he saw it with the solemn sympathy of men who reflect with their heart and soul, and never with the unreal definiteness of the intellectualist and doctrinaire, His love of common men and women in the dignity of their humanity was tempered by distrust of mobs, parties, or powerful groups.

His English comes straight from the spring, bright as its source: there is nothing stilted or second-hand about it. Therefore many masters since have found that to read him is to *clear* as well as to enrich their own vocabulary and rhythm.

Shakespeare as an Education

Therefore, too, it should go without saying that any or every course of English literature should bring the best of Shakespeare in early, and that whoever else is read or not read, *he* must be. Learning to discount, as we must, Shakespeare's flaws of taste and haste—especially in his earlier work when he was courting a very miscellaneous public, mixing others' coarser journey-work with his own—it is a first duty, in the culture of any English-speaking person, to form wide and intelligent ideas of his mind and poetry and style.

If English literature can be a liberal education, a university in itself, even making us independent of the Greek and Latin classics in the original, then indubitably Shakespeare is a large proportion of that education.

A very different being was his burly boon-companion and rival, Ben Jonson, ten years Shakespeare's junior, oracle and chairman

at the Mermaid Inn, the Falcon in Southwark, and of the Old Devil at Temple Bar. His construction of plot and drama shows the strength of an oak; his lyrics have the delicacy of flowers. A romantic, passionate and adventurous man, he was a theorist laying down the law about play-making and versification; a classicist with a "system" and a blow of the ferrule for transgressors.

From Bricklayer to Playwright

His early life, full of hardship, tells us much. His father came from Scotland, became a poor parson in Westminster, and died before Ben's birth. After being schooled awhile at Westminster School Ben was apprenticed to the bricklaying trade, from which he enlisted as a soldier. Soon he was fighting in the Low Countries, and is said to have killed one of the enemy in single combat in "no man's land": this and other exploits he did not hesitate to tell to his admiring cronies when, at Shakespeare's death, he inherited the sovereignty of the English stage. At twenty he was back in London, married, and an actor at a minor theatre at Clerkenwell. There he quarrelled with another busker, and killed his rival in a duel, coming, as he says, "very nigh the gallows."

In 1598, when he was twenty-five, he wrote his play, *Every Man in his Humour*, in which Shakespeare, then aged thirty-four, performed a part. Several years later Ben violently assailed John Marston and Thomas Dekker, rival playwrights, in *The Poetaster*; he was feeling his strength and had the Queen's occasional favouring notice. Then followed a queer two-years' silence, when, a diary of the time says, he "lived upon one Townesend and scorned the world."

James I (and VI of Scotland) now came to the throne, and as ill-luck would have it, the comedy, *Eastward Ho*, by Ben, his former foe Marston, and George Chapman (the translator of Homer from the Greek) reflected on the Scottish nation. A courtier, Sir James Murray, brought this to the King's attention, and "Jamie" threw the authors into prison and threatened them with the loss of their ears and noses.

Finally, they were not tried but set at liberty. The only trace we have of the satire now is an allusion to Scots: "There are no greater friends to Englishman and England, *when they are out on't.* I would a hundred thousand of them were in Virginia." The King's resentment was soon soothed by Jonson's masques (with Inigo Jones, who designed the Palace of Whitehall, as producer), in which Jonson showed his mastery of compliments which are never fulsome.

He took a genial enough view of Scotland when, in 1619, on his appointment as first Poet Laureate, he walked to that country; visiting, among others, the poet William Drummond of Hawthornden, who left an ill-tempered but possibly true thumbnail character-sketch of the positive, boastful, but generous Ben ("Given rather to lose a friend than a jest, jealous of every word and action of those about him, especially after drink . . .").

In the crowd of dramatic talents—Elizabethan and Jacobean—he was surpassed in tragedy by John Webster and John Ford, in grace by Philip Massinger, and in invention by the collaborators Francis Beaumont and John Fletcher: but in other ways he was surpassed by Shakespeare alone. His gifts waned with age, but he was buried with honours—upright—in Westminster Abbey, with the inscription "O Rare Ben Jonson!"

He wrote sinewy prose, too, which was echoed in later men. For instance:

> What a deal of cold business doth a man misspend the better part of life in! in scattering compliments, tendering visits, gathering and venting news, following feasts and plays, making a little winter-love in a dark corner.

Those last nine words and their cadence belong to him and his time. Despite his

INTERIOR, ANNE HATHAWAY'S COTTAGE

Preserved as a national monument to Shakespeare since 1892, Anne Hathaway's cottage at Shottery, not far from Stratford on Avon, is visited by admirers from all parts of the world, and has remained largely unaltered throughout three centuries.

BEN JONSON

When Shakespeare retired from playwriting, his rival, Ben Jonson, who began life as a bricklayer and killed a man in a duel, became England's leading dramatist. His plays include "Volpone," "The Alchemist" and "Bartholomew Fair," while he was also associated with Inigo Jones, designer of sets and costumes, in the presentation of court masques.

immense reputation and the homage of Robert Herrick, the poet, and others, he fell out of fashion, and has never been caught up in an eddy of taste or been lifted, as some other old writers, on a great wave of sudden understanding and appreciation.

Some of his plays have been revived in the last few years. Leonard Woolf, Aldous Huxley, Gregory Smith and T. S. Eliot have paid tribute to the author of many exquisite lyrics and epigrams, of *Drink to me only with thine eyes*, as well as the plays *Every Man out of his Humour, Catiline, Volpone, The Alchemist* and the masques. Jonson,

with his burly figure, his stormy good nature and his dogmatism was a "character." In *Bartholomew Fair* he gave us a hard, realistic picture of London types, Dickensian, but without Dickens's sentiment or exuberance.

To the reader for pleasure, whose time is limited, Jonson may well come at a later stage in his experience. This is just as true of Kyd, Webster, Dekker, Ford, Massinger and the whole bevy of tragedians and comedians who wrote for the Elizabethan and Jacobean stage. Shakespeare apart, there are works soon to be mentioned, no less enduring and easier for the student.

SAMPLE OF BEN JONSON'S WRITING

Twice imprisoned, a swashbuckling, witty talker with a quick temper, a haunter of London taverns, Jonson was yet patronized by two kings of England, James I and his son, Charles I. Here he is writing to a member of the royal family, signing himself an admirer of "your Highness's virtues." Jonson was buried in Westminster Abbey.

JOHN FLETCHER

Collaborator with Francis Beaumont in many plays, including "The Maid's Tragedy," Fletcher is believed to have worked with Shakespeare on "The Two Noble Kinsmen."

If any descriptions of the period can breed appreciation of them, William Hazlitt's zestful talks on the Elizabethan poets and Charles Lamb's *Specimens of English Dramatic Poets* will do it. The former, though a rich and quotable book, is even too loaded with praise: Hazlitt wanted to praise them all as near equals of Shakespeare, a contention with which critics now will have nothing to do. Let the inquiring reader first taste them embedded in Hazlitt's animated prose.

"That Other Harmony of Prose"

Francis Bacon is an exalted name in prose literature as well as in scientific and philosophical speculation. All that need detain most readers at first are his shrewd, condensed *Essays* which resemble what Ben Jonson said of his speech, that if a listener turned his head aside or missed a sentence

he lost something weighty and perhaps lost the thread.

"Reading maketh a full man, conference a ready man, and writing an exact man," says Bacon; and it may be added that reading Bacon as he deserves makes a careful, concentrated man. His chequered career of intellectual glory and political and social disgrace (from 1561 to 1626) is narrated with ringing emphasis in Lord Macaulay's essay, and more fully and justly by Dean Church.

Here a remark on the Bacon-Shakespeare controversy may be pardoned. Bacon was far too busy a man, in his State duties and in literature, and too distressed by public anxieties, ever to have had time to write the mass of Shakespeare's plays; and Shakespeare was too full and unmethodical a genius ever to have consented to the right Latin forms of Bacon's legal, matter-of-fact prose. Bacon distrusted English and preferred Latin. Shakespeare had little Latin. Moreover, Jonson, who knew both men, has left us brief character sketches of them which prove that they were two distinct persons, very remarkable for incompatible qualities. The modern attempt to make one man of two prodigies could issue only in failure.

All this time "that other harmony of prose" was becoming more the flexible servant of thought. Bacon's was too crowded with meaning; the English clergyman, Richard Hooker's (on the Church), was stately and latinized; it is Sir Thomas Browne (1605-1682), physician of Norwich, who, especially in the little gem, *Religio Medici* (written near Halifax, in Yorkshire), made a new music for ear and mind. He is no thinker with anything much to tell us; but he is a word-artist of the first flight. There are still men of taste to be met in this year of grace who often make this book of solemn fantasy, queer and inexact learning and wandering speculation their pocket companion; though others are impatient because he "gets us nowhere." (But do dreams, elegies, sonatas or requiems take us anywhere definite?) At least he is easily read and, as Lytton Strachey says: "It is pleasant to start out for a long walk with such a splendid phrase upon one's

FRANCIS BACON

Born in London in 1561, Francis Bacon was statesman, essayist, philosopher and even some-thing of a scientist. He surveyed the progress of knowledge in "The Advancement of Learning" and did much to popularize the idea of basing knowledge on experience and on inference drawn from experience and experiment.

BACON'S HANDWRITING

For his service to the Crown under the reigns of both Elizabeth and James I, Bacon was created Baron Verulam and Viscount St. Albans, and was given the posts of Attorney-General and Lord Chancellor. His fall from power was due to a charge of bribery in connexion with the hearing of chancery suits, a charge which Bacon admitted.

lips as: 'According to the ordainer of order and mystical mathematics of the City of Heaven,' to go for miles with the marvellous syllables still rich upon the inward ear, and to return home with them in triumph."

Sir Thomas Browne and John Donne

Browne's is a dreamy, echoing prose, with a grave Latin element, touched with quaint erudition, more to our taste, perhaps, than Sir Richard Burton's queer and interesting *Anatomy of Melancholy* because more contemplative and harmonious. Men of that time—John Donne, especially, in his poems and sermons, which have had a remarkable latter-day revival—were fond of whatever is curious, strange and hallucinatory. Browne interrupts a midnight meditation under the stars thus: "To keep our eyes open longer, were to act our antipodes! The huntsmen are up in America; and they have already passed their first sleep in Persia." And here, too, is noble, suggestive prose, such as Coleridge, Lamb and others rejoiced to listen to:

Let true knowledge and virtue tell the lower world thou art part of the higher. Let thy thoughts be of things which have not entered into the hearts of beasts: think of things long past, and to come. acquaint thyself with the choragium of the stars, and consider the vast expansion beyond them. Have a glimpse of incomprehensibles; and thoughts of things, which thoughts but tenderly touch. Lodge immaterials in thy head; ascend unto invisibles; fill thy spirit with spirituals and the mysteries of faith, the magnalities of religion, and thy life with the honour of God.

Do not these cadences recall the English of the Authorized Version of *The Wisdom of Solomon* and *Ecclesiastes*?

It is a good thing, almost a necessary thing, to know the style of some periods quite other than our own. Hence the deeply enriching effect upon any mind of knowing the Bible, the Church liturgies, and the roomy prose of the seventeenth century with its deep-chested music, which began with Ben Jonson and ended with

Dryden, who suddenly modernized it. Once more, here is Browne:

I thank God for my happy dreams. And surely, it is not a melancholy conceit to think we are all asleep in this world, and that the conceits of this life are as mere dreams, to those of the next, as the phantasms of the night to the conceits of the day.

Music is a sensible fit of that harmony which intellectually sounds in the ear of God.

The earth is a point, not only in respect of the heavens above us, but of that heavenly and celestial part within us. There is surely a piece of divinity in us, something that was before the elements, and owes no homage unto the sun.

These imaginative undertones and overtones were to be heard long afterwards in the prose of Charles Lamb, Thomas De Quincey, Cardinal Newman and John Ruskin.

That odd Dean of St. Paul's, John Donne (1572-1631) above referred to, is divided against himself—passion-ridden, yet analysing his passions: and so is in our day strangely attractive.

Mystic with a Zest for Life

John Donne began his career as a young gallant, and ended as a mystic with tortured sceptical moments. He essays to put a quart of meaning into a pint vessel of form, and sees things or analyses emotions so swiftly and subtly that he baffles the slower comprehensions of his readers. Disconcertingly fresh in his points of view, his restlessness and self-discontent, his colloquial bluntness (he begins one poem "For God's sake hold your tongue and let me live"), his intense individuality was eager to find a north-west passage of his own. Donne reminds one in style of Robert Browning generations ahead, and he showed a mixture of misgiving, sense of mortality, vehement faith; peering into every corner of love and death and life and religion with sleepless curiosity. He is not recommended except to readers of experienced taste of very adventurous inclination.

Equally devotional and mystic, but more easily appreciated, are his contemporaries, George Herbert, Vaughan, Crashaw and Traherne, sometimes called the fantastics, or the metaphysical school, or Platonists. There are beautiful passages in them. More delightful in some ways is the parson. Robert Herrick (1591-1674), one of Jonson's Mermaid "boys" who was exiled as parson of Dean Prior in Devon. His *Hesperides* is a delicious and quaint collection of nearly one thousand glees, catches and roundelays. In verse, often as bright and complete as dewdrops, he can sing thrillingly of harvest homes, and country sounds and sights, but he can move us in epitaphs and little hymns:

Here a solemn fast we keep
While all beauty lies asleep.

His simple grace of utterance is deceptive: here is a wonderful artist in miniatures, as good as Jonson, who sometimes nearly equals Shakespeare's songs.

The Jacobeans and Carolines demand, some day, to be read as they deserve. For instance, no lines are more fiery, sincere and passionate than Crashaw's glowing lines to St. Teresa. Richard Crashaw (c. 1616-1649) underwent long neglect, until recent days when (it is interesting to recall) Arnold Bennett, quoting his "seraphic" poem in the story of *Hilda Lessways*, made it known to a wide public.

How odd are the fluctuations of judgment! Sometimes for a whole century an old writer remains unappreciated. The mental climate is unfavourable; the acoustics unsuited to his kind of music; the general mind obtuse to his thought. Thus, many literary surveys of sixty and eighty years ago dismiss Crashaw as hectic or exotic. More modern criticism will have none of this summary treatment. In the lifetime of persons still with us, we have retrieved the reputations of Jonson, Crashaw, Donne, Marvell, Dryden, Blake, Smart and Clare, all of whom were long the victims of neglect.

Who brings about these reversals of taste? None other than he who can form a judgment and express it—the man or woman who can feel an enthusiasm and make others share it.

Finally, the coming easier idiomatic prose was forecast in Izaak Walton's *Compleat Angler* and *Lives*, and in Thomas Fuller's *Worthies*, attaining greatest simplicity in the work of Bunyan, the tinker.

Test Yourself

1. What were the origins of the drama in England?

2. Who were the "University Wits"?

3. Write an outline of the career of William Shakespeare from the following headings. his boyhood, education and family history; his career as actor-manager and playwright; his greatest plays; what constitutes his greatness?

4. Compare the career of Ben Jonson with that of Shakespeare. In what respect did Jonson fall short of his great contemporary?

5. Read or re-read *Hamlet, Othello, Macbeth* or *King Lear*. Write a note on the main character, discussing his good qualities and indicating the weakness that led, step by step, to his downfall.

Answers will be found at the end of the book

A BLAKE ILLUSTRATION

The imaginative grandeur of Milton's epic poem, "Paradise Lost," is reflected in William Blake's conception of Satan exhorting the rebel angels to continue the struggle. Blake's appreciation of the solidity and power of this great work and of the nobility of the "Prince of Darkness" is to be seen in the strength of his pictorial impression.

CHAPTER V

MASTER OF THE GRAND STYLE

WE come to one who towers above his age in majesty of style and grandeur of subject. This is John Milton: and the proof of the words just used of him are in the "divine" epic, *Paradise Lost*, and its successor, *Paradise Regained*, in *Comus*, *Samson Agonistes*, and in the wonderfully pictorial early poems.

A liking for Milton's verbal harmonies can be an abiding pleasure for the reader who will take the steps to acquire it. His praises are sung by all scholars, poets and critics whose voices carry any weight; and their mere names would (as in the case of our next greatest poet, Wordsworth) fill a page. To him, the Anglo-Saxon race may point confidently as their one sure triumph in the grand style, fit to be named with the Greek Homer, the Roman Virgil, and the Italian Dante. John Dryden, a younger contemporary, was the first boldly to proclaim his supremacy and sublimity; Joseph Addison further championed his chief work through the *Spectator*; Dr. Johnson reluctantly, yet generously, added his tribute; and with the poets Thomas Gray and William Cowper, the eighteenth century was cordially pro-Milton.

From boyhood Milton dedicated himself to the ideal of being a poet in the greater mould, and to "build the lofty rhyme." Patiently, through youth and early manhood, he absorbed the best Hebrew, Greek and Latin and Italian literature. His father had faith in John's poetic ambition, and the means to back it. He was a scrivener—a lender, financier, agent and adviser, discharging some of the functions of the lawyer. Though he prospered, he continued to live over his shop in Bread Street, Cheapside. It bore the sign of the spread eagle, the family crest.

Here John Milton was born in 1608, and went to St. Paul's School, which was then close at hand. His home had something of that "liberal cultivation which, if not imbibed in the home, *neither school nor college ever confers*." (These words came from his biographer, the Rector of Lincoln College, Oxford, Mark Pattison.) At sixteen, he went to Christ's College, Cambridge, where a Fellow, by name Chappell, who was a narrow ecclesiastic, drove him into an opposition which probably influenced his opinions in later life.

Here was a boy of eighteen who, in the lines beginning "Hail, Native Language," showed a vision and a power of expression far above his teachers. He looks forward to the time when he can sing:

> . . . Such where the deep transported
> mind may soar
> Above the wheeling poles, and at
> heaven's door
> Look in, and see each blissful deity
> How he before the thunderous throne
> doth lie,
> Listening to what unshorn Apollo
> sings
> To the touch of golden wires. while
> Hebe brings
> Immortal nectar to her kingly sire:
> Then, passing through the spheres of
> watchful fire,
> And misty regions of wide air next
> under,
> And hills of snow, and lofts of pilèd
> thunder,
> May tell at length . . .

The astonishing maturity of this owed nothing to such tutors as existed in 1625, and his protest against the slavish traditions of learning was justified. He was "sent down" from Cambridge for a short time. His mind could not constrict itself to the then current theological-ecclesiastical tests; it was never a submissive mind, but made its opinions as it went along.

That he enjoyed life—music, society, landscape and study—in his serious way, is proved by the two lovely poems written about 1632, when he was twenty-four and left college to live with his mother at Horton, Buckinghamshire, studying there for five happy years. These two light masterpieces were *L'Allegro* and *Il Penseroso*, but they could not relieve the inner anxiety he expressed in the sonnet:

> My hasting days fly on with full career,
> But my late spring no bud or blossom
> shew'th

This "late spring" produced the poetic masque, *Comus*, and that touchstone of taste, *Lycidas*. He thought of chambers at one of the Inns of Court, of "towered cities" with plays and masques, of the busy hum of men, and visits to some shrine:

> Where let the pealing organ blow
> To the full-voiced choir below
> In service high and anthems clear . . .

lines which prove his love of beauty of worship was as pronounced as his dislike of one sort of ecclesiastic. His generous father agreed that John should travel through Italy, where he stayed for fifteen months amid musical, painting and poetical circles in Rome, Florence and Venice, visiting Galileo, the astro-physicist. Italian poetry always had a special charm for Milton; and his stay produced some short poems of rich vintage.

Cheerful Man and Pensive Man

We shall never exhaust nor dull the freshness of the country air and domestic charm of that simple school piece, *L'Allegro* (the cheerful man); that is, if we like

> To hear the lark begin his flight,
> And singing startle the dull night
> From his watch-tower in the skies,
> Till the dappled dawn doth rise. . . .
> While the cock, with lively din,
> Scatters the rear of darkness thin,
> And to the stack, or the barn door,
> Stoutly struts his dames before,

or to watch the sun colour the clouds, while the ploughman whistles in the furrows; and beyond, on russet lawns or fallows, the flocks nibble, and a cottage chimney smokes between two aged trees; and the upland hamlets invite—and so through the long daytime till dusk, with nut-brown ale and stories. In *Il Penseroso* other exquisite landscapes pass across the mind's eye:

> To behold the wandering moon
> Riding near her highest noon,
> Like one that had been led astray
> Through the heaven's wide pathless
> way,
> And oft, as if her head she bow'd,
> Stooping through a fleecy cloud;

or we hear the distant wind in woods or sea, from a snug ingle-nook by the light of glowing embers and to the sound of crickets on the hearth. "All rural sights and sounds and smells are here blended," says Mark Pattison, in his biography, "in that ineffable combination which once or twice perhaps in our lives saluted our young senses before their perceptions were blunted by alcohol, by lust, or ambition, or diluted by the social distractions of great cities." Milton had far less first-hand knowledge of soil, crop or worker than Shakespeare, Tennyson, or a dozen more; but he has gathered a choice bouquet of experiences in these early poems.

They are cited because we shall hear echoes in later verse—the *home* motif which is so English. We are nearly all ex-villagers at three or four removes, and domestic in instinct. Shakespeare had, in *Pericles*, a marvellous song about the house at night, when only the cat is awake staring at the mouse-hole and the logs die down into ashes. The note was to be heard again in Oliver Goldsmith's *Deserted Village* and in the work of many later poets.

Milton's cultivated dreaming in Italy was interrupted by the beginnings of the civil war which was to overthrow monarchy for a time and bring about the Parliamentary wars. On his arrival in London (in 1640) all he could do was to open a small school. This life did not suit him. He was a man of furious political feeling: all his tastes and culture were Cavalier, his protests and convictions were Cromwellian. For years he was to be obsessed by political disputation, consuming time and energy in a succession of violent pamphlets, which show the breadth and depth of his social conscience. His prose is not very good as prose—nothing like so enjoyable as Bishop Jeremy Taylor's or Sir Thomas Browne's at that time, and its value now chiefly consists in its autobiographical hints and in a few fine rhetorical passages.

His public-spiritedness made him write tracts for the times, in which he gave as good as he got.

Those who think that Milton should have stuck to poetry are asking for a different man and a different poet. The author of *Paradise Lost* had his politics and religion in him.

Puritan and Republican

The importance of John Milton's political career can easily be overlooked; but to a great extent the Puritanism which forced him into active political life in the Puritan State is also expressed in his later works, *Paradise Lost, Paradise Regained* and *Samson Agonistes.* Had he ceased to write before his entry into politics in his thirty-second year he would be remembered as an exquisite minor poet, but it was apparently the years spent in fierce political advocacy that enlarged his literary instrument from the sweet flute of *L'Allegro, Comus* and *Lycidas*, to the reverberating cathedral organ heard in his epics.

As Latin secretary to Oliver Cromwell, to which position he was appointed at the age of forty, he had the duty of translating into Latin letters sent to, and received from, foreign states. He continued in this office until and beyond Cromwell's death, in 1658, despite failing eyesight. Towards the end he had Andrew Marvell as his assistant.

Milton stood for fierce and uncompromising republicanism, the disestablishment of the Church of England—a step from which Cromwell recoiled—and for the strengthening of the power possessed by Parliament. His hopes were disappointed. After Cromwell's death the general feeling was for a restoration of the monarchy in the person of Charles II; Cromwell cautiously refused to disestablish the Church; and the authoritarian regime of the Commonwealth sapped Parliament of its capacity for decisive and independent action. This last it took time to recover.

Milton's republicanism included emphasis upon individual freedom. His *Areopagitica, A Speech of Mr. John Milton for the Liberty of Unlicensed Printing, to the Parliament of England,* published in 1644, towards the end of the struggle between Charles I and Cromwell, was a powerful blow for Press freedom. So unanswerable was his forceful logic that the whole system of licensing and censorship received its death blow, though it did not wholly pass away for many years.

His personal courage was beyond doubt, for when the Restoration was completely settled, and many of his friends were trimming their sails to the new wind, Milton continued to protest against the recall of the Stuarts. How he escaped with his life is one of history's minor mysteries. It is certain that he was protected by powerful friends with influence at Court, among them probably Andrew Marvell.

Milton and Women

At thirty-five (in 1643) Milton married Mary Powell, aged twenty, daughter of a reduced Oxfordshire Royalist squire. She found life under Milton's city roof too austere, and went back by a stratagem to her parents. Milton was angered more than most husbands, for he had enormous self-esteem and a strict view of women's subordination. He was about to marry again (he made his own divorce laws), when Mary returned suddenly and on her knees asked pardon. Milton could not resist her plea, and he took her back. The reader will see traces of these emotional events when perusing the Eve passages in *Paradise Lost.* Four years after her death he married again, but the second wife died within a year: she is the subject of a lovely sonnet recollecting a dream of her appearance. In 1663, when blind, he married his third wife, who survived him by fifty-three years.

Dr. Johnson quaintly says of *Paradise Lost*: "no one ever wished it longer"; but that is true of many of the world's popular books. Homer's *Iliad*, Virgil's *Aeneid*, Cervantes' *Don Quixote*, Defoe's *Robinson Crusoe*, and Bunyan's *Pilgrim's Progress*; yes, and Byron's *Don Juan*, Tennyson's *Idylls of the King*, some of Scott and

Dickens—not to mention many a modern trilogy of novels! It is also "unequal": what human work is not? As for human interest (as distinct from incessant battle), it is full of it; Eve is a genuine heroine. The interviews with the angels, fallen and unfallen, are noble in execution. Only when argument intrudes itself does the swell of the sonorous music weaken.

it is meant to be used. So long as you think the corkscrew was meant for opening tins, or the cathedral for entertaining tourists, you can say nothing to the purpose about them."

Therefore, expect a grand composition, not subtle and crowded and worldly like Shakespeare's canvases; not dreaming and pictorial like Spenser; nor rapturously

JOHN MILTON

John Milton, the great English poet and political writer, was the author of our noblest epics, "Paradise Lost" and "Paradise Regained," in which he set out in sonorous blank verse to give the Protestants' justification of "the ways of God to man."

Spots on the sun are an interesting study, but it is a poor heart that never forgets the spots in order to revel in the lord of day. In his *Preface to Paradise Lost*, C. S. Lewis says: "The first qualification for judging any piece of workmanship, from a corkscrew to a cathedral, is to know *what* it is—what it was intended to do and how

lyrical like Shelley. His theme is the Fall of Man, the revolt of Lucifer and his angels, the Creation, the temptation of Adam and Eve—adding much of his own to the data in Genesis. We must allow him this convention, as we allow (without a tremor) the fiction writer today *his* convention.

Whole books have been written about

Milton's artistic management of rhyme and blank verse, and his vivid phraseology, exceeded in expressiveness by Shakespeare alone. *Paradise Lost*, especially, is full of geographical and historical allusions, for it is a panorama of all seas and lands, of many ages, and of "Night powdered with stars." The poet, blind with much study and pamphleteering, dictated it each day after nightly composition. The *Morning Hymn in Paradise* is one of the best examples of Milton's command of sound and imagery:

> Fairest of stars, last in the train of Night,
> If better thou belong not to the Dawn,
> Sure pledge of day, that crowns't the smiling morn
> With thy bright circlet, praise Him in thy sphere,
> While day arises, that sweet hour of prime . . .
> And ye five other wandering Fires, that move
> In mystic dance, not without song, resound
> His praise who out of Darkness raised up Light.

The ancients could have done no better. He is famous also for his spacious, elaborate similes:

> . . . As when by night the glass
> Of Galileo, less assured observes
> Imagined lands and regions in the moon:
> Or pilot, from amidst the Cyclades,
> Delos or Samos first appearing, kens
> A cloudy spot.

> . . . Not that fair field
> Of Enna, where Proserpine gathering flowers,
> Herself a fairer flower, by gloomy Dis
> Was gathered, which cost Ceres all that pain
> To seek her through the world; nor that sweet grove
> Of Daphne by Orontes, and the inspired
> Castalian spring, might with this paradise
> Of Eden strive.

No fragment can convey an impression of the *imaginative* power and unity of any Miltonic section—hardly even the rhythm of the invocation:

> Hail, Holy light, offspring of Heaven first-born!

or Satan's address to the sun, or the march of the angel armies to celestial battle, or the mounting of the heavenly guard in Eden. Listen to his description of Satan starting to address his host of rebellious immortals. "—Angel Forms, who lay entranced, Thick as autumnal leaves that strew the brooks in Vallombrosa":

> . . . He, above the rest
> In shape and gesture proudly eminent,
> Stood like a tower. His form had yet not lost
> All her original brightness, nor appeared
> Less than Archangel ruined, and the excess
> Of glory obscured: as when the sun new-risen
> Looks through the horizontal misty air
> Shorn of his beams . . . Darkened so, yet shone
> Above them all the Archangel: but his face
> Deep scars of thunder had intrenched, and care
> Sat on his faded cheek, but under brows
> Of dauntless courage, and considerate pride
> Waiting revenge. Cruel his eye but cast
> Signs of remorse and passion, to behold
> The fellows of his crime . . . Attention held them mute
> Thrice he assayed, and thrice, in spite of scorn
> Tears, such as Angels weep, burst forth . . .

The starry endlessness of existence was present to his view: this world was not enough to detain him. It is this which caused Keats to call him "scholar of the spheres" and Lamb to fancy that the ideal

ANDREW MARVELL

Andrew Marvell, poet and Member of Parliament for Hull, is remembered for two things —the charm of his verses such as those "To His Coy Mistress" and "Thoughts in a Garden," and his friendship with John Milton. Milton was foreign secretary during the Commonwealth under Cromwell, and when his eyesight began to fail him Marvell was appointed as his assistant. As a parliamentarian Marvell was conscientious and hardworking, as may be observed from the letters he sent to his constituents from London. His political and satiric verses are not well known, but they exercised a considerable influence on Jonathan Swift, to the greater profit of English literature.

preparation—or accompaniment—to Milton's noble numbers was a voluntary cn the organ. Indeed, if Shakespeare was a manifold interacting orchestra, Milton was a cathedral organ—with, however, a concert organ's range of stops.

Even in his boldest flights, he is calm and master of himself, not carried away like Shelley, nor haunted by questionings like Wordsworth, nor myriad-minded in sympathy like Shakespeare. He fuses seventeenth-century theology and enormous classical and scriptural learning, a whole which defied imitation or parody.

Many men in the eighteenth century tried hard to recapture Milton's style—among them James Thomson in *The Seasons* and John Dyer in *The Fleece*, and not one of them could bend the bow of Ulysses.

Marvell's Friendship with Milton

Andrew Marvell's is a small name by comparison: but Marvell (1621 1678) is at last receiving justice. Son of a Hull grammar schoolmaster, he became Member of Parliament for the city after being a diplomat in Constantinople, giving instruction in the family of Fairfax, and later assisting Milton in the Latin-Secretaryship.

His political uprightness, his satires and controversies—which did, however, influence Jonathan Swift—are forgotten now in two facts: his friendship with Milton, and some five intensely felt yet fanciful poems. Before glancing at the best known let us notice some that are often missed. Take his lament as he sees Cromwell lying in state:

> When up the armed mountains of Dunbar
> He marched, and through deep Severn, ending war . . .

> I see him dead: a leaden slumber lies,
> And mortal sleep, over those wakeful eyes . . .
> O Human glory, vain! O Death! O wings!
> O worthless world! O transitory things!

And in his lines to Milton, which appear in old editions of *Paradise Lost*, are several of sound descriptive criticism:

> Thou singest with so much gravity and ease,
> And above human sight dost soar aloft,
> With plume so strong, so equal, and so soft . .

Every one should know his verses *To His Coy Mistress*, in which he rises from the badinage of courtesy and compliment to passion and solemnity:

> But at my back I always hear
> Time's wingèd chariot hurrying near,
> And yonder all before us lie
> Deserts of vast eternity.
> Thy beauty shall no more be found,
> Nor, in thy marble vault, shall sound
> My echoing song. then worms shall try
> That long-preserved virginity,
> And your quaint honour turn to dust,
> And into ashes all my lust:
> The grave's a fine and private place
> But none, I think, do there embrace.

Then the gathering wave of passion falls in these urgent, stirring lines:

> Let us roll all our strength and all
> Our sweetness up into one ball,
> And tear our pleasures with rough strife
> Through the iron gates of life:
> Thus, though we cannot make our sun
> Stand still, yet we will make him run.

Possibly his best-known lines (from *Thoughts in a Garden*) are those describing the mind withdrawing into its happiness, creating,

> . . . Transcending these,
> Far other worlds and other seas,
> Annihilating all that's made
> To a green thought in a green shade.

Another, a compliment to Charles I at his execution, is:

> He nothing common did, nor mean,
> Upon that memorable scene.

George Wither (born 1588) lived to be nearly eighty. He began in the Civil War as a church and king man, and when over fifty was captain of cavalry against the Scots Covenanters. He was possessed all his life by the notion that he had a genius for public affairs, and when he was ignored he turned Roundhead and wrote some brisk satires with biting titles, *Abuse Stript and Whipt* and *Almonds for Parrots*. He ended in the Marshalsea prison—where he wrote some delicious praise of poetry and of the comforts it had brought. His, too, are the lines:

Shall I, wasting in despair,
Die because a woman's fair?
. . . If she be not so to me,
What care I how fair she be?

William Davenant, reputed by some to be a natural son of Shakespeare—he himself would not seem to have denied the suggestion—left one delightful lyric, *The lark now leaves his watery nest*; William Browne's *Pastorals*, smooth and tuneful, are worth reading. Robert Herrick's *Hesperides* are gem-like songs of love and wine and rural joys. Richard Lovelace with his famous lines:

I could not love thee, dear, so much,
Loved I not honour more;

Sir John Suckling, Thomas Carew, and others are in the anthologies

"Pilgrim's Progress"

John Bunyan, the strangely gifted tinker of Bedford (1628-1688), is a more typical Puritan than the many-sided richly cultured Milton. The Bible and his own lively imagination made him. *The Pilgrim's Progress* is a book of genius for the people, and scholars have long come to see its unique quality as prose, as narrative, and as allegory. The journey of Christian from the City of Destruction to the Celestial City is simply a record of such a life as Bunyan's, seen through an imaginative haze of spiritual idealism in which its commonest incidents are heightened and glorified. He tells his tale with such

naturalness that the Slough of Despond and Doubting Castle are as real as places we daily see. We know Mr. Facing-Both-Ways, Mr. Talkative, Mr. Worldly-Wise-Man, Mr. By-Ends and Mr. Legality as if we had met them in the street. It is in this amazing reality of personification that his dramatic genius displays itself. In its bold character drawing, humour, suspense and acute human interest, in its sunny kindliness and easy suggestion of landscape, it is among the noblest of English poems, for poem it is, though it is all in prose simple enough for a child to understand.

Persecuted Preacher

He has told us all about himself in one work or another, especially in *Grace Abounding*; of the lonely, despairing mental struggle which theology often inflicted on a sensitive, imaginative soul. He exaggerates his youthful "vices," which apparently went no further than the statutory games and a drink of ale at the inn. At twenty-seven he joined the local Baptist meeting, and soon disclosed singular preaching power. Persecution began at the Restoration of Charles II to the throne, and Bunyan was gaoled for over twelve years at Bedford. In prison, whose routine was gradually relaxed for him, he saw friends, met other prisoners, wrote a little, and made tagged laces. His family and blind daughter visited him, and in the eleventh year he was often out on leave.

It is strange that the astonishing literary excellence of the *Life and Death of Mr. Badman* should have escaped equal notice for many years after *Pilgrim's Progress* was household property. In dialogue it gives the realistic biography of a prosperous scamp, from which Daniel Defoe learnt some craftsmanship, as did later writers too. One of its episodes is that story of "old Tod," told perfectly in twenty lines. Bunyan's *Holy War* is well written, but great in passages rather than as a whole.

Two of his contemporaries, Thomas Hobbes (1588-1679) and Samuel Butler (1612-1680) are in remarkable contrast. The former, who is thought to have been Francis Bacon's secretary, was the author of *The Leviathan*, a theory of society which

JOHN BUNYAN

Author of "The Pilgrim's Progress," a book as simple in style as it is rich in Puritan faith, this nonconformist spent twelve years of his life in Bedford gaol. Among the works which make him the greatest allegorist in English literature are "Grace Abounding to the Chief of Sinners" and "The Life and Death of Mr. Badman."

anticipated modern totalitarianism written in a cold, acrid, but logical style; and the latter, a Cavalier satirist who wrote in short, witty measure of the cant and humbug of the time. Butler's *Hudibras*, refreshing and quotable, ought to be known to every bookman.

Even the non-expert reader of good literature will notice, at this stage, a change coming over its tone. Poetry and glamour are receding; prose, medium of wit and cool sense is coming in. Eloquence and feeling held out longest in the pulpit; this was in fact "the golden age of preaching."

The English then put most of their philosophy into this moral and religious form, and some books on theology have seams of true gold. Still, the new atmosphere was that of inquiry, science, and criticism, typified in the Royal Society founded under Charles II. Its members gave it a European reputation. The Essays on *Human Understanding*, on *Toleration, Education, and Government* of John Locke (1632-1704) show common sense without much depth, a clear head and pedestrian style without idealism.

Sir Isaac Newton (1642-1727) was the intellectual Titan of this time. His physical discoveries made as much stir as those of Darwin and Einstein later. Though he does not strictly come within our scope, his *Principia Mathematica* (1687) is a masterpiece of clarity: he is the boast of Trinity College, Cambridge.

Our road has already climbed to a height from which is seen a panorama which few literatures can show—four supreme masters, Chaucer, Spenser, Shakespeare, Milton and a host of remarkable writers, yet the year is only about 1600: another three hundred and fifty years of high performance are still to come; and printing was, at this date, only a two-hundred-year-old device!

The methodical reader—or anyone with serious purpose behind his entertainment—is strongly enjoined, at this stage, to take up with an open, impressionable mind:

Shakespeare's *A Midsummer Night's Dream*, or *Twelfth Night*, or *The Tempest*; and especially the wonderful short songs scattered through the plays. Also *Hamlet*, or *Macbeth*, or *Othello*, or *King Lear*.

Milton's *L'Allegro* and *Il Penseroso*, for their colour and picture-evoking power; everyone should have these and his *Lycidas* by heart, or at least in the heart.

The Faerie Queene—an hour or two with this epic will introduce you to the wonderland of Spenser, in which the human and the enchanted meet and merge.

Chaucer's *Prologue* to the *Canterbury Tales* or the boisterous, sly, comic tale told by the Wife of Bath.

Spend an hour, too, with the eloquent Book of Job, in the Bible; and the Wisdom of Solomon in the Apocrypha; and the first four chapters of St. Luke. Each of these, in its kind, is supreme; and is pure criterion of merit elsewhere.

Test Yourself

1. Write a two-hundred-word account of the life and works of John Milton, mentioning salient points in his personal life and as many of his works as you remember.

2. Name the great scientific writer who lived between 1642 and 1727 and who discovered the force of gravity.

3. Write a two-hundred-word summary of the career of John Bunyan, mentioning four of his books.

4. Name the poet, a contemporary of Milton, who wrote *Thoughts in a Garden*.

Answers will be found at the end of the book.

SAMUEL PEPYS

Samuel Pepys (1633-1703) is famed in literature for his diaries covering the years 1660-1669. These journals, which give a lively and informative picture of Restoration life and an excellent self-portrait of the author, were written in cipher which was not translated until the nineteenth century. In his own day Pepys was known as a hard-working civil servant, and was appointed Secretary of the Admiralty in 1672 and for a further period in 1684.

JOHN DRYDEN
Acknowledged as the leading poet and satirist in the years following the Restoration,
John Dryden turned his hand to literary criticism and playwriting; his lucid style influenced
many writers. His satire was merciless to opponents and rivals.

CHAPTER VI

THE YEARS OF PROSE AND GOOD SENSE

FROM the heights of imagination and poetry outlined in our previous chapter we now come with a marked change in style to a level table-land. The late seventeenth and eighteenth centuries were marked by the rule of taste. Correctness and elegance were qualities sought rather than freedom. In this respect the age of Louis XIV (1638-1715) of France set a fashion for all Europe and certainly influenced the writers of the Restoration Period in England. Because patronage flourished much work was done directly or indirectly in praise of the regime. Thus, the age of Queen Anne is called Augustan, its writers contributing to the glory of the State as Virgil and Horace had contributed to the glory of Rome under the Emperor Augustus. Virgil, indeed, was a model consciously adopted; translated and emulated, for example, by John Dryden.

The rule of taste continued through the eighteenth century and is seen in operation in the critical judgments of Dr. Johnson in his *Lives of the Poets*. There grew out of it a tendency to make reason, rather than undisciplined instinct, the touchstone of literature; for, as London grew and the trading middle class prospered, courtly elegance changed into or merged with a sturdy good sense; wild nature was regarded with distrust and the town was considered the only place for the writer to live and also the main source of his inspiration. The fops, the merchants and the writers alike congregated in the social centre of the Coffee House. The proper study of mankind was man. In saying that "the man who was tired of London was tired of life," Dr. Johnson was very typical of his age.

"Glorious John Dryden" (1631-1700) was the first great writer of this age of good sense. Dryden came of country landed stock, being a grandson of Sir Erasmus Dryden, Sheriff of Northamptonshire, who was one of the original baronets created by James I in 1611. He went to Westminster School and studied for seven years at Cambridge, where the records say he showed "disobedience to the Vice-Master, and contumacy in taking punishment." In this he resembled Milton (his forerunner at Cambridge) whom Dryden used to visit when the great poet was old and blind.

It is typical of the change of times that Dryden, although not inactive in politics, never attained Milton's fierce incorruptibility and passionate belief in religious and political dogma. Dryden was left a small income by his father and thus saved from the heart-breaking literary drudgery which was the common lot of many of his contemporaries. His first work showed his genius. This was the *Heroic Stanzas* (1658) to the memory of Oliver Cromwell, a fine tribute to the Lord Protector which showed both the author's command of stately compliment and his close study of Latin poetry. Nevertheless, when Charles II assumed the throne, Dryden felt no difficulty in forgetting the memory of Cromwell and lauding the new regime in two panegyrics—*Astraea Redux* (1660) and *Panegyric on the Restoration* (1661). Dryden planned his life according to the dictum that "he who lives to please, must please to live," and thus his writings reflect very closely the tendencies in public taste.

Within a year of two of the Restoration he set his hand to playwriting—at a time when the bawdy comedy and flamboyant drama in imitation of the French were the typical products of the English stage; and when women actresses trod the boards for the first time, female parts having previously been played by boys. Snobbery and social caste became a factor in playwriting, for the Restoration had resulted in a large, impoverished class of aristocrats whose lack of security, dislike of the new, powerful merchant class, and debauched manner of life were depicted in the theatres. Dryden

SAMUEL BUTLER

Samuel Butler (1612-1680) was a satirist in an original vein. His poem "Hudibras" caricatures a Puritan knight.

possessed an easy, colloquial prose style, without subtlety, but with a directness that is unequalled. In his plays, however, he was lacking in the self-discipline that is essential to a playwright, and he falls below the excellence of his three great contemporaries — William Wycherley, William Congreve and Sir George Etherege. He had a large output, engaging at one time to write three plays a year for the Theatre Royal. Perhaps his best comedy is his *Marriage-à-la-Mode* (1672), which should be read both as an example of Dryden's writing for the theatre and for its social commentary on the period. In addition to comedy he wrote historical tragedy, preferring the Shakespearian tradition to the conventional rigidity of the French dramatists. His *All for Love*, a conscious imitation of Shakespeare's *Antony and Cleopatra*, is the best example. In addition, he was responsible for "revising" Shakespeare for public presentation, a fashion that was to continue until it became realized in the nineteenth century that the original text was better than any "revision."

Meanwhile, Dryden turned his great power of public address and capacity for satire to public affairs. Towards the close of 1681, when the problem of the accession to the English throne was the question of the day, he took the field on the side of the Court party in his satirical poem, *Absalom and Achitophel*, which ran into nine editions and caused a tremendous stir. Other works further illustrate his talent for invective— *The Medall* and *MacFlecknoe*—and show his gifts and also his weaknesses. We can hear the hearty, although not vindictive laugh, as he exposes some crooked public figure or some would-be literary rival in a dozen resonant couplets. He preserved for ever in the amber of his words a vain busybody who, eager for fame, jostles into public life and

> . . . not to miss
> Of being known (his last and utmost bliss)
> He rather would be *known for what he is.*

These deadly summings-up crowd his pages and cause a smile even when the unfortunate victim has long been forgotten along with his folly.

Dryden is something more than the wielder of a pretty gift for sarcasm and invective. While his successor in this field, Alexander Pope, was the artful versifier of polished society, Dryden's freer feet still walked in the English countryside, and we can tell from his translation of Virgil from the Latin, and his *Fables, Ancient and Modern*, that he had his roots in green England. In *Religio Laici* (writing as an Anglican) and *The Hind and the Panther* (writing as a Catholic) there are passages of manly piety; while he could, like Ben Jonson before him, forget for a while his classicism in a few lovely lyrics. He never quite stormed the highest peaks of composition, but he gave literature a form and a directness that paved the way for the writers who followed him. His prose—"The style

DEFOE IN THE PILLORY

Daniel Defoe, journalist and Jack-of-all-trades, fathered the novel by starting to write faked autobiographies purporting to be about real people. He was a prolific pamphleteer, and his "Shortest Way with Dissenters" landed him in the pillory.

we would all use if we could" in Matthew Arnold's opinion—is all couched in clear, flowing, rather loosely jointed English, carefully avoiding rhetoric and eloquence to attain the mellow ease of cultured talk, rather than the tighter, closely knit style of literary prose. For that reason, literary men envy the manner of the Prefaces to this day. Edward Fitzgerald ("Omar" Fitzgerald), Gerard Manley Hopkins, whose poems have influenced many moderns, the American essayist, James Russell Lowell, and many other critics have pardoned Dryden's occasional coarseness and want of finish for the sake of his very

exceptional qualities no less in prose than in poetry.

So far we have not come to any mention of the term "novel," and this is due to the fact that the novel, as we know it, took longer than any other literary form to emerge. It is true that *Euphues* by John Lyly, a tedious work on manners and etiquette which enjoyed immense popularity in 1579, is in its form an early work in the direction of a novel, and that early in the seventeenth century Sir Thomas Overbury and John Earle pointed the way by writing character studies concerning milkmaids and other stock characters. John

Bunyan's *Pilgrim's Progress*, although intended as a moral story by its author, escapes from the confinement of a religious thesis and becomes an intensely dramatic and finely told experiment in what we today call the novel. But although these trends seem clear enough to us today they were not recognizable at the time, and the evolution of the novelist's art became almost a matter of accident.

Birth of the Novel

It was Dryden's contemporary, Daniel Defoe (born about 1659), who attempted the first conscious step in what was to become the most popular literary form; he had the plainness and popular appeal of a great journalist. Though now best known by *Robinson Crusoe*, written when he was sixty, his earlier works—reputed to be nearly two hundred—have great interest,

ROBINSON CRUSOE
Robinson Crusoe is Defoe's most famous creation. Defoe had never been to sea; much less had he lived on a desert island.

and got him into hot water with the authorities. After trying three trades, hosier, tile-maker and wool merchant, and learning every trick of the trade of writing, from 1704 to 1713 he conducted, and wrote entirely by himself, his famous *Review*, a prototype of the later periodicals. He was ill advised to put forth the notorious pamphlet, *Shortest Way with the Dissenters*, whose irony was not understood by the Government. Irony is a most dangerous weapon, which even in Jonathan Swift's hands caused his career to be frustrated; Defoe was prosecuted, fined, pilloried and imprisoned; and promptly wrote a *Hymn to the Pillory*. Many indeed of the best-known English writers have been stormy petrels, involved in trouble and adventure; they have been distinctly "characters."

Defoe's greatness lies in his mastery of lucid and plausible narrative. Like Shakespeare he had an amazingly exact knowledge of many trades; for a landsman he exhibits a remarkable grasp of all matters pertaining to seamanship, and his studies of criminal types, although deplored by the Victorian critics, such as Sir Walter Scott (*Lives of the Novelists*), are drawn with that stark realism which has found favour in the modern novel. His work is badly constructed and rambling, for he wrote at top speed without troubling to revise or plan. So graphic is his style that the first readers of *Robinson Crusoe* firmly believe that they were learning of an actual happening (in part the book is based upon the adventures of one Alexander Selkirk). *Moll Flanders*, a study of a harlot and a shoplifter, ranks as one of the greatest English novels of all time, and his *Journal of the Plague Year* illustrates his capacity for reconstructing past events so that they read like an eye-witness account. An amusing sidelight to his activities is his *True Relation of the Apparition of one Mrs. Veal*. A bookseller acquaintance of Defoe had a large and unsaleable stock of a dull book which instructed its readers how to prepare for death! Defoe stimulated demand for this white elephant by publishing an ingenious and circumstantial account of a Mrs. Veal, who returned to a friend after death and, among other things, advocated a perusal of the book. The pamphlet's interest lies in the subtlety of the suggestion. The injunction to obtain the publicized volume is not overstressed, but cunningly introduced among a mass of convincing domestic detail. In this Defoe showed a knowledge of psychology unsurpassed by later publicists.

Swift the Satirist

Jonathan Swift (1667-1745) possessed an outstandingly plain style, but one which differed from that employed by Defoe (who was self-taught) in that it sprang from careful revision and a calculated use of words. Swift is the greatest of all English satirists, and his personal life has engaged almost as much attention as his work. The sanest of men, he died mad, partly from physical causes and partly because life's seeming irrationality tore his mind with indignation and contempt. Much of his work has to be heavily footnoted for readers today, to explain allusions that are no longer readily apparent. But his *Gulliver's Travels*, in essence an ironic and biting attack upon human nature, has so much action and excitement that it has often been read as a straight narrative without its sarcastic and even morbid undercurrents being apparent. Essentially, as his journals, sermons and kindly actions prove, he was a good though proud man, burning to set his world right—and there was much that needed putting right.

Swift was born in Ireland of English parents, and died there; but his place is less among the kindly humorists than with the earnest reformers and critics of life. At an uncle's expense (his father having died before Jonathan's birth) he went from Kilkenny School to Trinity College, Dublin. His dependence, then and after, infuriated him; he felt a dæmon of intellectual power in him—without position or prospects. He went as secretary to the vain grand gentleman, diplomatist, and elegant literary trifler, Sir William Temple, at Moor Park, near Farnham in Surrey. Life with the servants rankled in this ambitious student, and long years after he was sarcastic about the *ménage*. King William, on a visit, offered him a captaincy of horse. Certainly

the red coat might not have been such a torment to him as the clerical garb became; for, in 1694, having taken his M.A. at Oxford, he took holy orders and became prebend of Kilroot, near Belfast, at £100 a year—a fair average "hedge-parson's" salary to use his bitter words. He loathed this even more than Moor Park, to which he returned at his own request. There he had his love affair with Hester Johnson, the dark and beautiful daughter of the housekeeper; they still show you "Stella's cottage" at the gate, near Waverley Abbey. If they ever married, he never would have it publicly announced; and nobody cared to cross his will. Before he became Dean of St. Patrick's, Dublin, Esther Vanhomrigh fell in love with him; she is the Vanessa of his verses, and he was a wonderful hand at elegant, glassy-clear couplets in which affection was salted with just and worldly knowledge.

When Temple died, Swift edited all his literary remains with a dedication to the King; but Dutch William had little use for letters, and no preferment came that way. It must be admitted that the public men of the time were long blind to the age's strongest mind and character. The Whigs were indifferent, and he left them. He obtained appointments in Ireland, but his heart was all the time in London with his fellow wits from whom he was long cut off.

Shocks for the Conventional

He struck out for himself in 1704, with the amusing *Battle of the Books*, overthrowing his modern rivals in favour of the ancients; and in the same year with the dangerous and delightful *Tale of a Tub*—the characters, Peter, Jack, and Martin, standing respectively for the Catholic Church, the Calvinist, and the Anglican Church. It shocked many, including the very conventional Queen Anne; but it established him as a potent fighter whom it was worth conciliating. His own droll and audacious pen had done for him what no "influence" had really attempted to do. He never forgot that. His swarthy face and bright blue eyes lit up whenever he recalled how he made himself "his own man. Now let the reader who last saw *Gulliver's*

DEAN SWIFT

Satirist and letter-writer, Dean Jonathan Swift was born in Dublin of English parents. He
became known at the age of thirty-six with his "Battle of the Books" and "Tale of a Tub,"
both of which were published in the same year, but it is "Gulliver's Travels," published in
1726, on which his fame rests. A devastating satire on human nature—Swift prefers the nature
of the horse to that of man—it is also a grand story and a favourite with children.

Travels (or half of them) in childhood read the whole again, including the merry *Voyage among the Laputans*, to realize the fertile invention, the purpose, and the powerful, clear prose. Swift is a supreme instance of disappointed idealism and good sense turned to gall. Read, deliberately, his *Thoughts on Various Subjects* for a taste of his trenchant quality:

> Since the union of divinity and humanity is the great article of our religion, it is odd to see some clergymen in their writings on divinity wholly devoid of humanity.

Or his lovely verses of compliment to Stella and Vanessa, the prayers he used in Stella's last illness, or his serious and statesmanlike *Project for the Advancement of Religion*. As often happens, this earnest mind being more pious, and not less, than others, he was angered more than they at the lukewarmness or inconsistency of those professing the Faith; and, being utterly without fear, he said so with the cutting-edge of an incomparable pamphleteering style. But he did it differently from his rivals, indirectly, with irony, the smile and "simplicity" hiding his wrath. Surely the most terrible innuendo in all controversy occurs in his *Argument Against Abolishing Christianity*, sarcastically directed at the sceptics and worldlings of the day. One can see those dangerous "arch, blue eyes" shining with sinister humour as he writes this withering sentence on the frigid Church as it was then:

> Nor do I think my fears wholly imaginary, that abolishing Christianity may perhaps bring the Church into danger I desire I may not be mistaken. I am far from presuming to think that the Church is in danger at present, but we know not how soon it may be in danger *after the Christian religion is repealed*.

The fantasy of a Church automatically carrying on after there is no religious message, is terrific. Yet careless readers might easily pass over that concealed land-mine without noticing the peril! Conventional people, from Queen Anne and the bishops down to the drinking peers and the rake-hells of the town, merely felt perplexed and uneasy under this man's piercing scrutiny. But those who have the relish of irony—depth masquerading as innocence—never lose it; though the liquor is too dry for some tastes which prefer froth and sparkle.

Addison and Steele

There is nothing of Swift's turbulent disgust of men and their institutions in the placid calm of Joseph Addison (1672-1719) who, with his friend and colleague Sir Richard Steele (1672-1729), wrote essays that are a natural growth of the fashionable politeness of manners. Born in the rectory at Amesbury, Wiltshire, he obtained a scholarship in Magdalen College, Oxford, and went to the university at fifteen. At twenty-two he addressed a poem to Dryden, and the older man became his literary sponsor. He followed his success with some verses to the King, who awarded him a pension of £300 a year on which to travel. When King William died the pension stopped (pensions were bribes or retainers in those days) and Addison cut short his travels, taking a shabby lodging up two flights of stairs in the Haymarket, London.

Fortune liked Addison: when the Battle of Blenheim was fought, the Lord Treasurer instructed him to celebrate it, and he did so to such purpose that he was made Commissioner for Appeals. *The Campaign* is now mainly known for one simile—that of Marlborough riding the whirlwind and directing the storm. So starved of real poetry was "the town" that this line made a profound impression. Addison (or someone) so directed this storm of popularity that he at once became Under-Secretary of State, then Secretary for Ireland, and then, in 1717, Secretary of State. This was good going, in ten years.

His best work was done in conjunction with Richard Steele for the journals, the *Spectator* and the *Tatler*—the forerunners of such modern literary magazines as *The Cornhill* and *Blackwood's*. Addison's *Sir Roger de Coverley* sketches—gentle and kindly caricatures of the typical country squire of the period—are delicious in their

JOSEPH ADDISON

An essayist with a clear, restful style, and prim but not unfriendly personality, Addison collaborated with Richard Steele in the production of the "Spectator" and "Tatler." These little papers were forerunners of the modern commentaries on life and letters.

idyllic humour. He brought a breath of rural England to the fashionable drawing-rooms and coffee-houses. He dared to "preach" kindly and demurely; never does he greatly exercise our minds, and he only caresses the surface of emotion. However, his town and country "characters" were a totally new style to his generation, and gave a fruitful hint to the novelists who were to come. And, of course, for a hundred years the legend of Addison's correct diction exerted a spell (mostly for good) upon thousands of writers. Yet Dick Steele, his collaborator, is preferred by many for his freedom from priggishness, his sparkle and his genial overflow of spirits.

Addisonian Prose

Addison was once idolized. Dr. Johnson told aspirants to "give their days and nights" to Addison. Thackeray frankly imitated him. Macaulay's praise led G. B. Shaw to declare that Addison is "only one of Macaulay's characters." Nevertheless, he must be read, with Steele, as co-founder of the "middle" article. A Quakerish primness limits him. Many topics cannot be treated in "Addisonian English" at all: it is sweet, pure, restful, but to us whose emotional compass is far wider it sounds like a harpsichord or spinet with only a few notes. An example of his style, from his essay on "Westminster Abbey" which appeared in the *Spectator* of March 30, 1711, may be given:

> After having thus surveyed this great magazine of mortality, as it were, in the lump, I examined it more particularly by the accounts which I found on several of the monuments which are raised in every quarter of that ancient fabric. Some of them were covered with such extravagant epitaphs, that, if it were possible for the dead person to be acquainted with them, he would blush at the praises which his friends have bestowed upon him. There are others so excessively modest, that they deliver the character of the person departed in Greek or Hebrew, and by that means are not understood once in a twelvemonth In the poetical

RICHARD STEELE

Steele was the originator of the "Tatler" under the name of Isaac Bickerstaff. A humorist, he had a sentimental strain.

quarter, I found there were poets who had no monuments, and monuments which had no poets. . . .

We have so far dealt with only one of the dramatists who flourished in the period of changing tastes which followed the Restoration, and, as we have mentioned, Dryden was but one of many men who found in the new freedom which followed the removal of the Puritan ban on stage performances an opportunity for creating new kinds of entertainments.

When Charles II returned many new companies sprang up; the theatres no longer followed the Elizabethan model—the stage was now at one end of the hall, cut off by a proscenium arch, which meant that greater spectacle could be given. The early masques were remembered and scenery and properties, as well as lighting, were part and parcel of the new theatre; while from France, the returning Cavaliers had brought back the rhymed drama, and for the first time a definite division between tragedy and comedy appeared. The latter offered an unrestrained opportunity for wit at the expense of anything—folly, vice or virtue

William Wycherley (1640-1716), a native of Clive, near Shrewsbury, had spent his early years in France before going to Oxford and making some pretence at studying for the Bar. Early in 1671 he had his *Love in a Wood* produced at the Theatre Royal; it was a play which, for all its author's youth, showed the whole air and spirit of a hardened man of the world. The piece was dedicated to the Duchess of Cleveland, mistress of the King, whose favours the author was subsequently to enjoy. It is on two comedies—*The Country Wife* and *The Plain Dealer*, both dealing with marital infidelity—that Wycherley's fame principally rests. They abound with witty and scintillating lines and, for all their bawdiness, situations which possess a real insight into the mechanics of the stage and dramatic presentation. Wycherley's end as a writer was rather comic. He married the Countess of Drogheda, who took care during her

lifetime to keep her husband closely guarded at the domestic hearth. At seventy-five, a widower, he married a young girl to spite his heir—an act typical of the man.

William Congreve

Head and shoulders above his rivals was William Congreve (1670-1729) whose reputation as the greatest English master of comedy may be denied by some; even so, it is difficult to pick any dramatist who can rival in quality the three great plays—*The Way of the World, Love for Love* and *The Old Bachelor*—upon which his reputation largely rests. He wrote five in all, and tradition has it that the indifferent reception of *The Way of the World* determined him to write no more. Congreve anticipated the technique of a much later school of dramatists in introducing the play of conversation. In an age when plots were involved and often difficult to follow, the action of his comedies consisted largely in the tossing of the conversational ball to and fro among the characters. His prose is easy and gracious and not in the least stagey, and even today, when the topicality of many of the lines has been lost, can captivate an audience. *The Way of the World* is a play which should be read by all students of English literature and one, moreover, that can be read with perfect enjoyment and understanding at a sitting. Among the contemporaries of Wycherley and Congreve it is only necessary to mention in passing, Sir John Vanbrugh (1664-1726), author of *The Provok'd Wife*, among others; Sir George Etherege (1635-1691), whose *Love in a Tub* marked the beginning of Restoration comedy; and George Farquhar (1678-1707), an Irishman whose best and much-revived work was *The Beaux' Stratagem*, which marked the change of the Restoration stage into respectability.

Towards the end of the seventeenth century English life had settled down after the excitement and social disturbances consequent upon the Restoration, and the weight of public opinion began to weigh against the coarse, witty production that had become the mainstay of the stage. Gradually opinion came to favour sentimental comedy (as opposed to the comedy

WILLIAM CONGREVE

Master of Restoration wit and perhaps our greatest writer of comedies, William Congreve was the author of "The Way of the World" and "Love for Love."

ALEXANDER POPE

A leader among eighteenth-century men of letters, Alexander Pope made his reputation with his versified "Essay on Criticism" in 1711. His works include "The Rape of the Lock," in which a trifling subject was treated in a mock-heroic vein; "The Dunciad," satirically attacking political and other opponents as dullards; and the "Essay on Man," a quasi-philosophic poem. On the whole his subjects are intellectual rather than emotional. But the feeling of triumph and contempt that accompanies the verbal rapier thrust is much in evidence.

of manners) which, with tragedy, was to be exploited by the great actor-managers of the eighteenth century.

With the name of Alexander Pope (1688-1744) we enter the forecourts of the eighteenth century. Pope's work has experienced the complete cycle of praise, neglect, and balanced appreciation. Not only does Pope testify the love of neatness, order and style which predominated during his lifetime, but also the emergence of literature from dependence upon the generosity of a patron, or group of patrons, to dependence upon the "bookseller," whose function it was to publish, as well as to sell, books.

Poet with a Dangerous Pen

We may see from portraits what kind of a man Pope was. The dark, intelligent eyes seem to demand sympathy, while the petulant mouth is that of a man hypersensitive to criticism and prone to see an affront when none was intended. Born off Lombard Street, London, Pope was the son of a prosperous linen merchant. His studies appear to have been haphazard, but before he was twelve he had acquired some knowledge of Greek and Latin.

Excessive study was soon to undermine his health and produce a physical deformity—upon which his enemies were later to make much play. Pope himself spoke of "that long disease, my life," and there is little doubt that his misshapen body exercised an embittering influence on his mind. Added to which he was a Roman Catholic in days when members of that religious minority were virtually debarred from public life. There was nothing for the puny, sickly Alexander to do in life but read widely, practise the art of rhyme, and stay at home and take his diet. His father retired to Binfield on the edge of Windsor Forest with his fortune of £20,000 locked in a box, from which he took guineas as needed. Banks were then in their infancy, and Charles II had not long before seized bank funds. At sixteen, Alexander was writing smooth verse—a feminine, careful variation of Dryden, whom he hero-worshipped. By twenty-one, he had written the rhymed Essay on Criticism, of which John Ruskin rather audaciously said that

it has, "in the strictest language, and within briefest limits, every law of art, of criticism, of economy and of policy."

At twenty-four Pope began his translation of Homer, a thirteen-year task of love which brought him £8,000, and with the proceeds he bought a villa at Twickenham which is now a convent school. Here Pope lived in constant pain. The few hours not to be given to medicine and rest or devoted to literature, were spent in laying out his flower beds or adorning the grotto (now gone) with red spar, Cornwall diamonds, Spanish silver, and Vesuvius lava. It was at Twickenham that the Scriblerus Club met, the leading members of which were, besides Pope, Swift, Congreve, Gay, Arbuthnot, Bishop Atterbury and Thomas Parnell. Pope had become a firm adherent of the Tory Party, and was thus involved in the rough political backwash of the period, although he was not in the least fitted temperamentally to bear the criticism (often extremely offensive from our modern viewpoint) levelled against him.

Boudoir Epic

Pope's most popular poem, which appeared in its first form in 1712, was the Rape of the Lock, inspired by the current story of William, fourth Baron Petre, who had cut off a lock of Miss Arabella Fermor's hair and had found the liberty much resented. In mock heroic vein, the poem has been generally judged a masterpiece of airy, frothy fantasy, with exquisite finish. "Elegant" is perhaps the best word to describe this as well as other works by Pope.

A literary quarrel with Joseph Addison inspired Pope to the famous Epistle to Dr. Arbuthnot, a masterpiece of venomous abuse which, it must be added, owed more to imagined insults than anything else. In similar vein is his attack upon poetasters, critics and booksellers in the burlesque, The Dunciad, said to have been suggested to him by Swift. Yet for all the poisonous insults which the little man could pour out in such delicate, ordered verses, he had (like Swift) a tender side. A girl who had cherished a violent passion for him died by her own hand—no fault of his—and he wrote a beautiful elegy, *Verses to the Memory of an Unfortunate Lady*. Tender passion, too, is felt in his *Epistle of Eloisa to Abelard*, and something more besides in *The Universal Prayer* and *The Dying Christian to his Soul*, and in the noble *Essay on Man*.

Furious dispute has raged about his right to be called poet. Time has delivered judgment. It is not that he is a mere wit, critic, and consummately clever verse-builder. Nor is it Lord Byron's "Neither time nor distance, grief nor age can ever diminish my veneration for him who is the great moral poet of all times, climes and feelings, and stages of existence . . the most faultless of poets." Rather is it the verdict of the French critic, Sainte-Beuve, "that sober, delicately perfumed flower which is Pope."

Pope, then, whether bard or not, was a master of smooth reasoning and deadly effective ridicule. His brief (partly unjust) "character" of Addison pillories that famous contemporary "more in sorrow than in anger"; and that is the sting in it.

Whether Pope could rise into the lofty imaginative sphere is settled in the affirmative by the closing lines of *The Dunciad*—that field of pillories—an apostrophe to the goddess of Dullness:

In vain, in vain—the all-composing hour
Resistless falls: the muse obeys the power.
She comes! she comes! the sable throne behold
Of Night primeval and of *Chaos* old!
Before her, *Fancy's* gilden clouds decay,
And all its varying rainbows die away.
Wit shoots in vain its momentary fires,
The meteor drops, and in a flash expires . . .
Thus at her fell approach and secret might
Art after *Art* goes out, and all is night . . .
Religion blushing veils her sacred fires,
And unawares *Mortality* expires . . .
Lo! thy dread empire, CHAOS! is restored:

ADDISON WRITES TO A FRIEND

In this letter Addison asks a friend to inquire for a volume of the works of Statius, the Roman poet, and to look for a passage in the "Achilleis" in which Achilles' mother, seeking for a place to hide her son, is compared to a bird searching for a place to build her nest.

Light dies before thy uncreating word;
Thy hand, great Anarch! lets the curtain
fall,
And universal darkness buries all.

For most men of the eighteenth century,
such was the finest poetry yet written. Its
rhetorical force and intellectualism ravished
the coolest judgments, and in their (erroneous) opinion placed him alongside Milton:
for the Elizabethans, with their wild natural
notes and erratic tastes, were little valued
(though Pope himself edited Shakespeare
as our "great original").

Voltaire on the English Scene

The French philosopher, Voltaire, in his
letters on England after staying among the
London celebrities, summarizes piquantly
the verdicts then current and unquestioned.
"Mr. Pope is, in my opinion, their most
elegant, correct poet; and at the same time
the most harmonious (a circumstance which
redounds very much to the honour of his
muse). He has mellowed the harsh sounds
of the English trumpet to the soft accents
of the flute. . . .
"The first English writer who composed
a regular tragedy, and infused a spirit of

elegance through every part of it, was the
illustrious Mr. Addison. Since his time the
drama has become more regular, the audience more difficult to please, and writers
more correct and less bold. I have seen
some new pieces that were written with
great regularity, but which, at the same
time, were very flat and insipid. The
shining monsters of Shakespeare give infinitely more delight than the judicious
images of the moderns.
"Mr. Congreve's comedies are the most
witty and regular, those of Sir John Vanbrugh most gay and humorous, and those
of Mr. Wycherley have the greatest force
and spirit.
"I never found so much wit in one single
book as in Samuel Butler's *Hudibras*.
Humour when explained is no longer
humour. Whoever sets up for a commenta-
tor of such smart sayings and repartees is
a blockhead. This is the reason why the
works of the ingenious Dean Swift, who
has been called the English Rabelais, will
never be well understood in France. Swift
is Rabelais in his senses, and has the judgment in which our giggling rural vicar is
wanting. True humour, whether in prose
or verse, is his peculiar talent."

"THE BEGGAR'S OPERA" AT THE THEATRE ROYAL
This design by Hogarth embellished a ticket for Gay's musical play, "The Beggar's Opera."

COVENT GARDEN SCENE

A contemporary impression of life in the early eighteenth century is given here. St. Paul's, Covent Garden, is seen in the background; the chair carrying the drunken roisterers home is preceded by a link boy, whose job it was to carry a torch.

So much for Voltaire's comments on the English literary scene. A member of Pope's Scriblerus Club was John Gay (1685-1732), a young Devonian, who left haberdashery in the City, and wrote playful pastorals which led Swift to make the suggestion: "Why not a Newgate pastoral?" (Newgate was the great London gaol). Out of this was born *The Beggar's Opera*, which made Gay the pet of the town and the Duchess of Queensbury's lap-dog.

We should not quite neglect the thinkers of the period, among them Bishop Joseph Butler (1692-1752), whose *Analogy of Religion* was long a university text-book and stand-by of Gladstone, and whose sermons on human nature are solid and original; Bishop Berkeley (1685-1753), whose *Theory of Vision and of Ideas* puts him high among philosophers, and whose dialogues on belief are in an inimitably limpid and attractive prose; and William Paley (1743-1805), whose clearly written *Evidences of Christianity*, an attempt to refute deism and defend miracles, was a school classic for generations.

Test Yourself

1. Why was the age of Queen Anne known as Augustan?
2. Write a short account of the life and writings of Daniel Defoe, naming as many of his books as possible.
3. What were the chief characteristics of Swift's writings?
4. Who were the two authors whose names are associated with the *Spectator* and the *Tatler*?
5. What kind of drama was written during the reign of Charles II?

Answers will be found at the end of the book.

DR. SAMUEL JOHNSON

One of the wisest men of letters of his own and subsequent ages, Dr. Johnson was the compiler of the first English dictionary. His "Lives of the Poets" shows perspicacious judgment, especially in his interpretation of typical eighteenth-century writers. While praising the greatness of Shakespeare he was inclined to think him barbarous.

CHAPTER VII

DR. JOHNSON AND HIS TIMES

DR. SAMUEL JOHNSON was a struggling hack journalist while Alexander Pope, Joseph Addison and Jonathan Swift were finishing their literary careers. A change of atmosphere was taking place, not easy to define, but unmistakably reflected in the fashions of the period. Writing became graver, and thought stronger. The career of Edmund Burke, for instance, would not have been possible in Queen Anne's time. In the sphere of political and economic thought, Adam Smith and David Hume took the place of Lords Shaftesbury and Bolingbroke; in literature the gracefulness of Addison was replaced by the profundity of Johnson; no previous painter placed the practice of art in England on so solid a basis as did Sir Joshua Reynolds, nor depicted the life of the people so truly as William Hogarth. Something of the masculinity, even brutality, at the root of the English character at the time appeared in the books of the novelists, Henry Fielding and Tobias Smollett, and in the harsh realism of the grim poet George Crabbe.

New Men at Work

In the midst of the order and urbanity of the eighteenth century were forces at work that would dissolve them. The discontent that was to culminate in the French Revolution was gathering strength and bringing a desire for freedom. Meanwhile, William Blake was drawing and rhyming; Robert Burns giving lays and songs to his Scottish countryside; William Collins and Thomas Gray were infusing a freer lyrical note into poetry; William Cowper, self-banished to the country, brought back a fresh, vigorous, natural note in his verse and his lovable letters; and Oliver Goldsmith, although retaining the artificial couplet used by Pope, gave it a rustic sweetness and pathos in *The Deserted Village*.

Compared with the bold experiments in verse which were to come with Wordsworth, Coleridge and Shelley, the poets of the period lacked fire and any kind of a message, the exceptions being Robert Burns and William Blake, although the latter is not a typical product of his own or any other age.

The poets had beauty of form and expression, but in that century of low emotional temperature and busy intellect they languished because their messages were not urgent enough to defy their time. For that reason, it is a prose master, Edmund Burke (1729-1797), who is the power and the poet of those decades; and he was fighting like a man inspired *against* certain elements in the coming democracy. This part of the eighteenth century was a decorous, "rational" and literary lull before the storm. The future innovators, romantics and reformers, were at this time boys or very young men, but exposed to the atmosphere created by the new European currents of revolutionary thought.

Edward Gibbon (1737-1794), meditating on the Roman and Byzantine Empires, absorbed in embodying diligent research in stately prose, averted his thoughts from the approaching tempest clouds. His short *Autobiography* is the perfect expression of that static time, and is a gem of stately and dignified diction. David Hume (1711-1776), of Edinburgh, sceptic, historian and essayist, an idol of Paris salons, did not foresee the French Revolution and its consequences, though his corrosive thought (like Voltaire's, and like Jean Jacques Rousseau's cult of the noble savage) expressed in easy prose, was helping its birth. The man of the town and letter-writer, Horace Walpole, *did*, on the contrary, foretell the upheaval!

Boswell's Theme

Dr. Samuel Johnson, "chairman" and dictator of the London wits, holds a symbolic position in that interval of history. Born in 1709 and dying at seventy-five, he was a great personality, as may be seen from the lively, crowded pages of James Boswell's celebrated *Life of Johnson*.

There have been four literary "dictators"

in our history: Ben Jonson, Dryden, Dr. Johnson and, in a lesser degree, Thomas Carlyle. Their talk, though it swayed their listeners immensely, is of less moment to us now; it is their writings that should count for us. Johnson's *Lives of the Poets*, his best work, was composed amid pain when he was seventy; it contains judgments which time has disallowed, others which it has upheld. It has many a page of force and brilliance, even on obscure writers.

The son of a Lichfield bookseller, whose unwillingness to part with his treasures drove him to the verge of bankruptcy, Samuel Johnson showed, as a youth, the great physical strength, quickness of intellect (nurtured by his browsing among his father's books) and curious apathy and indolence which were to be his characteristics as a man.

Johnson's Early Life

His father's financial position growing steadily worse, Johnson just managed to enter Pembroke College, Oxford, on the strength of promises from a wealthy neighbour. The promises held little substance, and he resided at the university in acute poverty for only two years, during which time his grotesque bearing, tattered gown and dirty linen were barely redeemed in the eyes of his contemporaries by his scholarship and that ascendancy in conversation which was to increase with the years. Someone, taking pity on him, left a pair of good boots outside his bedroom. With a cry of offended pride he hurled them away.

Having to leave Oxford penniless, he tramped to Market Bosworth, Leicestershire, to be a school usher, a kind of inferior assistant teacher. He then turned translator to a Birmingham bookseller and married an elderly widow, Mrs. Porter, and with her money tried to set up school, but too few pupils came. In March, 1736, he set out for London with the very different, ebullient David Garrick, who took to the stage and became the greatest actor-manager in London.

And now began over a quarter of a century's drudgery for the booksellers and the *Gentleman's Magazine*, while often he and Richard Savage, the dissipated poet who claimed to be the son of an earl, wandered footsore the London streets, unable to hire the meanest shelter or to buy a penny loaf. (Garrick was doing well; therefore Johnson would not apply to him.) For his noble poem, *London* (in the Dryden-Pope manner) he got ten guineas, and followed it with a greater, *The Vanity of Human Wishes* (1749). His tragedy, *Irene*, meanwhile failed on the stage. Between 1750 and 1752 he wrote the whole of the periodical, *The Rambler*, except for four papers; then a hundred and three numbers of *The Idler*. These papers propagated his personal views on life

First English Dictionary

He was meantime toiling at the first English Dictionary. Three years was the time set him, but it took him seven. He was to receive £1,575 on completion, poor pay when he had to remunerate out of it the several copyists who worked with him in Gough Square. When it came out—a mild sensation—it had flattering notice from Lord Chesterfield, to whom Johnson had unavailingly applied for help. To Chesterfield, Johnson wrote his famous, crushing retort:

> Seven years, my lord, have now passed since I waited in your outward rooms, or was repulsed from your door; during which time I have been pushing on my work through difficulties, of which it is useless to complain, and have brought it at last to the verge of completion, without one act of assistance, one word of encouragement, or one smile of favour. Such treatment I did not expect, for I never had a patron before.

That last quiet lash of the whip proves how subtle Johnson could be.

To the end, the starving habits of his overworked youth showed in his immoderate haste in eating, and in his repeated libations of tea. He was overbearing at times in conversation, but would suddenly laugh and unbend; he sheltered in his house a peevish old doctor, a blind old woman, a negro and others, and he was a benefactor by stealth. His memory colours

JOHNSON AT THE "MITRE"

Johnson's shrewd observations on every matter likely to arise in conversation between learned and unlearned men were recorded by his biographer, James Boswell, who often enticed Johnson into arguments merely to collect his rejoinders. In this picture Johnson is seen with Goldsmith (left) and Boswell at the Mitre Tavern off Fleet Street.

Fleet Street and its courts and St. Clement's Church still. Readiness and penetration were as marked in him as an enormous knowledge of books and men; and he was often startlingly acute and right in the midst of wrongheadedness or prejudice.

It is untrue to say that Johnson always wrote in ponderous, latinized prose; with his solidity and prejudice went energy and point. Few read his prose story, *Rasselas*, today. It was written in a week, to pay his mother's funeral expenses; yet it can command respect still. It came out a few days before the French philosopher, Voltaire's *Candide*, and men often contrast them, giving the preference to the Frenchman; but mistakenly, if the test is the mood in which we lay it down, and its whole social and mental effect. Hilaire Belloc,

comparing these two works, says: "I am much better *fed* by the style of Johnson than by that of Voltaire. Voltaire's is like the blows of a hammer chiselling out a marble statue of great perfection, but Johnson's is like the rhythmical swell of deep water." Johnson puts the great deal he has to say into the antithetical form, than which no better medium perhaps has been discovered for condensing and preserving a conclusion:

To live without feeling or exciting sympathy, to be fortunate without adding to the felicity of others, is a state more gloomy than solitude: it is not retreat, but exclusion from mankind: Marriage has many pains, but celibacy has few pleasures.

With his pen, as in the animated preface to Shakespeare, he was compendious and downright: with his tongue, he could be crushing; in his deeper relations with others, he was humane and, as his wife said, "the most sensible man I ever met." Johnson's feet were planted firmly on earth, its duties and tasks—which he himself fulfilled. He clung to tradition and piety and morals, hating whatever was subversive or sophist. Reared in abject poverty, he had no sentiment to waste on over-articulate complainers: "foppish lamentations," he called them. He disliked the Scots, till his journey to the Hebrides, when his Edinburgh hosts and still primitive clans royally received him; he distrusted the French (the only continental nation which England then knew) all his life. He feared Hume, Voltaire, Rousseau and their schools as much as Burke, with, however, less political insight than he.

With that "great *power* rather than mere writer," Burke (presently to be discussed), his relations are revealing. He might have succumbed to jealousy of another massive intellect so near his conversational throne, especially as Burke was "a vile Whig" and had his admirers. But Johnson was magnanimous, Burke a courteous listener, and both emerge triumphant from the ordeal. The truth is, Johnson revered intelligence, books and bookmen—and little else on earth. He would load his worst enemy with praise for a good line or even for one sound literary opinion.

Johnson as Poet

Students who have savoured and enjoyed Dryden or Pope should proceed to Johnson's similar versifying of *The Vanity of Human Wishes*. There are noble, memorable thoughts and thought music in it. He sees man "in ignorance, sedate, Roll darkling down the torrent of his fate." And to readers he extends this advice:

Deign on the passing world to turn thine eyes,
And pause awhile from letters to be wise.

The rather gloomy tone of his meditation

and the dignity of its expression satisfy the leisured person in an armchair. Johnson was, besides a great talker, lexicographer, biographer and critic, a *poet*. The whole impact of the man's character is felt behind such strong rhymed criticisms as his prologue to *Irene*, which Garrick spoke at the opening of Drury Lane Theatre in 1747:

When Learning's triumph o'er her barbarous foes
First reared the stage, immortal Shakespeare rose;
Each change of many-coloured life he drew,
Exhausted worlds, and then imagined new:
Existence saw him spurn her bounded reign,
And panting time toiled after him in vain.

Then Jonson came, instructed from the school,
To please in method and invent by rule;
His studious patience and laborious art
By regular approach essayed the heart;
Cold approbation gave the lingering bays,
For those who durst not censure, scarce could praise;
A mortal born, he met the general doom,
But left, like Egypt's Kings, a lasting tomb.
The wits of Charles found easier ways to fame,
Nor wished for Jonson's art or Shakespeare's flame;
Themselves they studied, as they felt they writ,
Intrigue was plot, obscenity was wit;
Yet bards like these aspired to lasting praise,
And proudly hoped to pimp in future days.

Only the practitioner in composition can recognize the inner successes of such rounded, compressed structure and shape, and he salutes Johnson. As he himself said:

"The blaze of reputation cannot be blown out; but it often dies in the socket." He still burns brightly in his socket.

Of Johnson's illustrious company the most remarkable was Edmund Burke (1729-1797), called by Matthew Arnold, "our greatest English prose writer, as I think"; and by Thomas De Quincey, "the supreme writer of his century"; "with an understanding," says Macaulay, "stronger than everything except his own fierce and ungovernable sensibility." Though he belongs to politics and social philosophy more than to pure letters, none the less he triumphs also in sheer force of expression and new true ideas. At least we should note the versatile art and rhetoric, the pathos and scorn, in *Reflections on the French Revolution* (1790).

His father was a Dublin attorney, with fifteen children, of whom all but four died in their youth. Edmund, the second son, was delicate, and was taught at home and at his grandfather's country home before he was sent with his two brothers to study under a Quaker master at Ballitore. Then, at Trinity College, Dublin, he took his degrees, and when twenty years old, he came to the Middle Temple, London, to study law. But far more than law he studied history, philosophy and poetry. Soon he began to feel his talents and strength. A raw young Irishman with a slight brogue, in outer aspect he already deserved Johnson's comment: "If you took shelter with him from a shower, you would soon say: 'This is a remarkable man.' "

Burke's Guiding Idea

Quite early his guiding idea came to him —that our rights *and* duties are born with us, and inherent in us as creatures and as members of the great human family (past, present and to come). Government can never be planned on paper by theorists, and imposed upon all: it must grow up from the soil, the individual and family, the marriage vow and kinships, the village and region. So the great human adventure of living together—in freedom *and* order—is a matter of instincts, affections, implicit and unspoken bonds of blood, belief and tradition, which all demand to be respected,

E.L.L.—D*

EDMUND BURKE

Both as writer and parliamentarian Burke showed his love of liberty and justice. His idea of mankind as morally one organism was well ahead of his age.

if trouble or even disaster is to be avoided.

Pride and sensitiveness were always traits in Burke, as much as humanity and chivalry. Prime Minister Rockingham took him, when aged thirty-five, as private secretary, and then, with political influence, he entered Parliament for Wendover. In one year, the ministry fell, partly because it followed Burke's conciliatory line towards the American colonies, against the king's stubbornness. New York State, in admiration, nominated him as its agent. When forty, he spoke more of his mind on "the present discontents." In a population of eight million there were but one hundred and sixty thousand electors, mostly nominal, and when two great families disputed the County of York the fourteen-day election cost, in beer and bribes, £300,000—at least a million in our money. Once the king asked for half a million to make good a deficit in the Civil List, and men wondered what had been done with the missing money. The anonymous letter-writer, Junius, thundered criticism from the columns of the *Public Advertiser*. "Liberty" Wilkes stirred the mobs of Middlesex. The revolt of the American colonies was imminent, gruesome reports came from India of cruelty and corruption, the French Revolution was brewing; and Burke was the chief voice of England at this crisis of her fate. Burke's view of private virtue and good faith as the cement of any community, of *man* as morally *one* organism—"that mysterious incorporation of the human race"—is now the view of biology, anthropology, and the best history; but he was years ahead of those sciences.

Goldsmith and Sheridan

Like Burke, of Irish origin, but otherwise very different, were Oliver Goldsmith and Richard Brinsley Sheridan—Goldsmith (1728-1774), feckless, much loved, prodigal and therefore poor, with the endowment of mellow and tender humour; Sheridan (1751-1816), with wit as hard and brilliant as a diamond, a man about town, clever orator, theatre speculator and chronically in debt. *The School for Scandal*, *The Critic* and the other Sheridan plays still read well, besides acting well, and contain delicious characterization and satire. Irishmen have been notable in stage comedy. There had been George Farquhar; and there have been since, J. M. Synge, G. B. Shaw, Oscar Wilde, St. John Ervine, Lady Gregory, Lord Dunsany and Sean O'Casey. They can see our English life with just that slight margin of detachment which gives a new slant.

Goldsmith was a fool in life, but a sage when he wrote. His true, unobtrusive triumphs were these—he infused into the conventional Pope couplet, into the pastoral poem, *The Deserted Village*, and into *The Traveller*, a surprising sweetness and tender grace which only Cowper equals; he gave the essay one degree more human pliancy and resonance than Steele and Addison did in the *Tatler* and *Spectator*; he restored naturalness to artificial sentimental comedy in *She Stoops to Conquer* and *The Good Natured Man*; and gave us our first domestic novel, *The Vicar of Wakefield*.

Goldsmith, of English descent but born in Ireland, was more Irish than the stage Irishman. Though he was the butt and the pet of Johnson's circle, he showed, in his poem, *Retaliation*, a very keen sense of the characters in that circle.

Ignoring the amateurish plot of *The Vicar of Wakefield*, the German Goethe and others have felt it to be a portion of the hymn of nature made audible to all hearts. For Goldsmith exploits in it much of his own simplicity; he could laugh at himself exquisitely in print, though he was vain in company. His transparent lightness and ease belong rather to the earlier part of the century with its French *esprit* than to Johnson's graver school or Fielding's coarse Homeric romance. Take up the essays, *The Citizen of the World* or those from his shortlived magazines, recalling his harum-scarum adventures (from school usher to doctor and historian), read *The Strolling Players* especially, and observe what delicacy and sparkle he has. Whatever he touched, even hack compilations, he made "as interesting as a Persian tale." He died, £2,000 in debt, despite his good earnings in the end, for money burnt a hole in his pocket. "Was ever poet so trusted before?" asked Johnson.

Theatre and Novel

It is a surprising fact that from the accession of King George I, in 1714, until the 1860s the English stage produced no great plays with the exception of those by Goldsmith and R. B. Sheridan. It became the turn of the actor, rather than the playwright, to draw the crowds. David Garrick and Mrs. Siddons were names that usually guaranteed a full house; they wasted their great histrionic gifts upon trash or rewritten and mutilated versions of the old masterpieces. One of the reasons for this deterioration was the fact that until the nineteenth century Drury Lane and Covent Garden enjoyed the exclusive right of presenting what was known as the legitimate or regular drama, the monopoly proceeding from patents issued to them by Charles II in 1660.

A figure of considerable importance in the development of the novel was Samuel

OLIVER GOLDSMITH

Goldsmith is chiefly known for his novel "The Vicar of Wakefield." The story is told that Goldsmith wrote it while deeply in debt, and called for aid from Johnson; when the latter had read it through he immediately realized its merits and advanced Goldsmith money against its publication. "She Stoops to Conquer" is Goldsmith's best-known play.

Richardson (1689-1761). Son of a Derbyshire joiner, he was apprenticed to a London printer, and printer and astute man of business he remained. Richardson has recorded how his first discovery of his own mastery of the sentimental vein was in writing love-letters for maidservants when a boy. When established in considerable comfort in London, he industriously wrote, largely in letter form, *Pamela* (1740),

Clarissa Harlowe (1747-1748) and *Sir Charles Grandison* (1753-1754), long, elaborate and subjective. The sieges to ladies' and gentlemen's hearts were continued in several volumes, and exactly hit contemporary taste, and Richardson was admired for his knowledge of the female heart. To the French his psychological insight made a special appeal.

He suffers by comparison with a robust

SCENE FROM "PAMELA"

Samuel Richardson was the English writer who introduced a strong vein of sentimentality into eighteenth-century novels. His "Pamela" found popularity from the day of its publication, and was followed up by "Clarissa Harlowe" and "Sir Charles Grandison." These stories, written in the form of a long series of letters, greatly influenced French novelists.

contemporary who disliked and satirized his work as namby-pamby. This was Henry Fielding (1707-1754), a man of good family, educated at Eton and Leyden, a keen reader of the classics, a justice of the peace who reformed Bow Street methods, and a journalist. In 1742, his lively *Joseph Andrews* set out to parody Richardson's goody-goody *Pamela*. In it, Fanny is bewitching, Joseph's innocent virtue diverting, Parson Trulliber and his pigs a startling vignette of one sort of vicar, Mrs. Slipslop sheer pantomime. The glory of this tale, however, is Parson Adams, simple, comic, sublime: as complete a portrait as Chaucer's parson, or some of Shakespeare's characters, and better than Sir Walter

Scott's Dominie Sampson or Goldsmith's Dr. Primrose. Fielding is as roughly eighteenth-century English and earthy as Hogarth the painter. In 1743 he published *The History of Jonathan Wild the Great*, in which he gave an ironical estimation of the life of a thief and receiver who had been hanged at Tyburn. Fielding was a *bon viveur*, and understood low life as well as high. Generous himself, he saw that good impulses frequently move those whom society condemns. This is the theme of *Tom Jones* (1749), his greatest novel.

A lesser man, but a notable story-teller, is the Scotsman, Tobias Smollett (1721-1771), who served as surgeon on a man-o'-war, and vividly described the naval press-gang, flogging, scurvy, sea-chanties, and the pigtail days of the old fighting, swearing, sometimes sentimental Navy, when Smollett himself—Sawbones—perhaps cut up wounded sailors, without anæsthetics or antiseptics, in the cockpit. A diet of rum and salt beef can be sensed in his narrative *Roderick Random* (1748). In *Peregrine Pickle*, written three years later, his rogue hero follows disreputable ways till he marries the virtuous Emilia; but the plums of this reckless story are Commander Trunnion and Bo'sun Pipes, and a telling picture, evidently from experience, of cruelties in pre-Revolution France. These rollicking books are not for squeamish tastes, but *Humphry Clinker* (1771), written in the form of letters, is less boisterous. Captain Marryat's sea stories (*Jacob Faithful, Peter Simple* and *Mr. Midshipman Easy*, written during the 1830s) were much influenced by Smollett's Lieutenant Lismahago and Commander Trunnion. A greater novelist than he learned some of his English and his narrative art from Fielding, Smollett and Sterne—namely, Charles Dickens.

Laurence Sterne (1713-1768) was a strange, eccentric humorist. As a clergyman, he was a pulpit draw. Descended from a bishop, son of a soldier, born in Ireland, brought up in various barracks, finished off at Cambridge, given a stall at York Minster and the living of Coxwold—he was a subtle and puckish exploiter of sentimentalism and innuendo, cultivating extreme French "sensibility" in the new mode popularized by Rousseau, shedding (alleged) tears over a beaten donkey and invoking the Recording Angel to witness other minor episodes.

Sterne's "Tristram Shandy"

He sees himself as Yorick, the man of feeling, and *The Sentimental Journey*, with all its faults of taste and dubious sincerity, contains lively passages of clever observation on the roads in pre-revolutionary France, and a number of very un-parsonlike reflections and encounters.

His style, despite its dashes and dots and asides—token of a restless self-consciousness, with a hint of pruriency—is extraordinarily expressive, pure and animated. His *Life and Opinions of Tristram Shandy, Gent* (1760-1767) was both original and instantly popular. The story consists of episodes, digressions, queer syntax, bawdy sentiment and sly side-comments. From this spiced dish there stand out My Father, My Uncle Toby (veteran of Marlborough's campaigns), Doctor Slop, the Widow Wadman, and Corporal Trim. Readers new to it sometimes think it is wantonly disjointed, but Sterne was one of the first to feel that the orderly sequence of events in most novels may not be true to the fluidity of life and the human mind with its myriad jostling moods. Thus he pioneered for much later subjective novelists like Marcel Proust in France, and James Joyce and Virginia Woolf. He is the father of impressionism in fiction because he uses words to suggest a desired effect instead of an exact descriptive fashion. Try first the short story of Le Fevre in *Tristram Shandy* and make the endeavour to enjoy him.

TOBIAS SMOLLETT

Smollett's novels, among them "Roderick Random" and "Peregrine Pickle," are largely drawn from his own experiences as a naval surgeon in a man-o'-war.

RICHARD SHERIDAN

Playwright and Member of Parliament, owner of Drury Lane Theatre and intimate friend of the Prince of Wales (afterwards George IV), Sheridan enjoyed a brilliant career. His first comedy, "The Rivals," was produced in 1775, and there followed "The School for Scandal" and "The Critic," in which the writer caricatures authors, actors, patrons and audience. Sheridan's plays are very actable: the dialogue is full of wit and sparkle.

That counsel applies to the reading of all classics—not to be put off by an initial weakness of response in oneself. The good things of life and literature ask time, preparation, and second and third acquaintance.

Inimitable Jane Austen

Jane Austen (1775-1817) has a small world, but it is perfectly seen. Her delectable, demure comedies *Pride and Prejudice, Emma, Sense and Sensibility, Persuasion* and *Northanger Abbey* are, for some, acquired tastes; but men as masculine as Scott and Kipling have been Jane-ites and have been enthralled by her sly humour and fidelity to reality. Jane Austen obtained all her experience of life at Bath, Winchester and the Hampshire village of Chawton where she lived. She possessed an unerring eye for the foibles, snobberies and hypocrisies which can be observed in a small community no less than in a city. *Pride and Prejudice* is a book that every student of literature should read. It tells the story of a heroine, Elizabeth Bennet, who refuses to marry a rich suitor because of his disrespect to her family, and of her sisters. We have the impression of being witnesses of actual happenings as we read this book. Her style is quiet and its effectiveness lies in the use of small, significant details and the precise use of words.

But this is not to say that the tone of her work is mild. She is a clear-minded woman with a sharply critical wit which gives verve to her dialogue and descriptions, and, in her selection of the relevant facts to move her tale, she shows herself to be an artist in realism unmatched by her contemporaries in her own quiet field.

Elegant was the favourite eighteenth-century word. By that word was meant balance, proportion and polish—whether in the trim symmetrical architecture of Nash and the brothers Adam, the furniture of Chippendale, Hepplewhite and Sheraton, the gracious music of Corelli, Arne, Boccherini and Handel, the painting of Reynolds and Gainsborough, Raeburn and Romney, the rounded prose periods of the Scottish historian, Dr. William Robertson, the rational candour of David Hume (in his charming miscellaneous essays), the stately Latin cadences of Edward Gibbon, the scholarly, well-bred air of Gray's letters, Cowper's lovable chit-chat, and even the aristocratic polish of Lord Chesterfield or the worldly affectation of Horace Walpole. But beneath the surface elegance of the educated or the fortunate, there was much vice, squalor and ignorance. Gin-shops and press-gangs, foul sewers and public executions denoted an underlying brutality.

So urgent was the hunger for escape into the ideal that it produced three astounding literary forgeries. James Macpherson (1736-1796), originally a schoolmaster, then tutor, gave out that he had scoured the Celtic Highlands and discovered the dream poetry of one Ossian of the third century. Dr. Johnson and Gray were not taken in. Europe was deceived, and none worse than

JANE AUSTEN

She might be called the writers' novelist so many have admired the "little bit (two inches wide) of ivory" on which she worked. Macaulay loved "Mansfield Park"; Disraeli read "Pride and Prejudice" seventeen times. "The big bow-wow I can do myself . . ." said Scott in praising her, "but the exquisite touch is denied to me."

Napoleon, whose dispatches have traces of "Ossian's" declamatory rhapsody.

Strange frauds were perpetuated by the brilliant boy, Thomas Chatterton (1752-1770), son of a poor Bristol schoolmaster. He imitated ancient ballads and deceived a few men who should have known better; his claim to a minor niche is based on an immature but exceptionally, promising poetic gift, displayed at its best in his *Songe of Ælla* and his *Ode to Liberty*. Penniless, with his fine, youthful hopes seemingly shattered by two months in London, he took poison in his attic home in his seventeenth year. But the boldest of the forgers was William Henry Ireland (1777-1835), who forged Shakespearian manuscripts which for a time misled many collectors whose greed blinded them to all possible errors. He had the effrontery to "find" a new play by Shakespeare, *Vortigern*, which was produced by Kemble and laughed off the stage.

Among the minor poets of the period who repay an evening or so of reading were E. Young (*Night Thoughts*), Robert Blair (*The Grave*), Kirke White (*Clifton Grove*), John Philips (*Cyder*), George Dyer (*Grongar Hill* and *The Fleece*), and George Dodsley (who published Dr. Johnson's *London* and was himself a capable and prolific writer). One contemporary of these men even published an epic about the sugar cane! These minor poets had their day's boom, and Thomas Percy's popular *Reliques*, a collection of ancient English poems, were the genuine precursors of the coming naturalness. London little heeded all this, it would seem. Many able men seemed untroubled by idealism and deplored "enthusiasm." Nevertheless, these two qualities were to become a great force in the poets of the coming century.

Thomas Gray and William Collins

One could read all the poetry of Thomas Gray (1716-1771) in an evening—and it would be an evening happily spent. It would include, besides the famous Churchyard Elegy (so English, so meditative, so artistically finished) the *Bard* and *Progress of Poetry* odes, which some admirers put almost with Milton for sublimity.

For those who have never encountered the *Elegy Written in a Country Churchyard* we may reproduce the first three verses which form such an effective prelude to this great, reflective poem:

The curfew tolls the knell of parting day,
The lowing herd wind slowly o'er the lea,
The ploughman homeward plods his weary way,
And leaves the world to darkness and to me.

Now fades the glimmering landscape on the sight
And all the air a solemn stillness holds,
Save where the beetle wheels his droning flight,
And drowsy tinklings lull the distant folds.

Save that from yonder ivy-mantled tow'r
The moping owl does to the moon complain
Of such as wand'ring near her secret bow'r,
Molest her ancient solitary reign.

Gray's verses are very fine, if ornate, and (with those of William Collins) mark the first definite break from the too regular convention which had hypnotized everybody for over seventy years. Gray, a retiring bachelor scholar, rebelled against the conventional literary forms, but in a gentlemanlike way. He *made* or distilled fine verses, and his carefully decanted still wine tastes insipid now that we know the inspiring freshness of the Romantics who were very soon to be on the way —Wordsworth, Coleridge, Shelley, and Byron.

The same is largely true of the verse of William Collins (1721-1759). The true lyrical gift is seen here struggling against the age. The fairy horn of romance can be distantly heard through the artificiality. Once, the authentic chord did sound, in his *Ode to Evening* in which the very spirit

Elegy, written in a Country-Churchyard.

The Curfew tolls the Knell of parting Day,
The lowing Herd wind slowly o'er the Lea,
The Ploughman homeward plods his weary Way,
And leaves the World to Darkness & to me.

Now fades the glimm'ring Landscape on the Sight,
And all the Air a solemn Stillness holds:
Save where the Beetle wheels his droning Flight,
Or drowsy Tinklings lull the distant Folds.

Save that from yonder ivy-mantled Tower
The moping Owl does to the Moon complain
Of such, as wand'ring near her secret Bower
Molest her ancient solitary Reign.

Beneath those rugged Elms, that Yewtree's Shade,
Where heaves the Turf in many a mould'ring Heap,
Each in his narrow Cell for ever laid,
The rude Forefathers of the Hamlet sleep.

The breezy Call of incense-breathing Morn,
The Swallow twitt'ring from the straw-built Shed,
The Cock's shrill Clarion, & the ecchoing Horn,
No more shall rouze them from their lowly Bed.

For them no more the blazing Hearth shall burn,
Or busy Huswife ply her Evening Care.
No Children run to lisp their Sire's Return,
Nor climb his Knees the envied Kiss to share.

Oft did the Harvest to their Sickles yield,
Their Furrow oft the stubborn Glebe has broke,
How jocund did they drive their Team a-field!
How bow'd the Woods beneath their sturdy Stroke!

Let not Ambition mock their useful Toil,
Their homely Joys, & Destiny obscure;
Nor Grandeur hear with a disdainful Smile
The short & simple Annals of the Poor.

GRAY'S "ELEGY"

The "Elegy, written in a Country Churchyard," which is seen in Gray's handwriting above, was written between 1742 and 1750 and sent to Horace Walpole. The latter passed the manuscript to his circle of friends, and a pirated edition appeared before Gray himself had the poem published. Gray lived a quiet and retiring life at Cambridge, where he was a fellow-commoner at Peterhouse. Gray's other poems include "The Bard" and "The Progress of Poesy," in which he clearly shows himself as inclined towards the subject matter and beliefs which so greatly occupied the poets of the romantic revival soon to come.

of twilight in South England is perfectly invoked: finer as mood and landscape than Gray's evening elegy, but without that longer poem's human associations or its musing on mortality:

> Now air is hush'd, save where the
>   weak-eyed bat,
> With short shrill shriek, flits by on
>   leathern wing;
> Or where the beetle winds
> His small but sullen horn.

A more eager and powerful kind of genius, however, than Gray or Collins is Robert Burns (1759-1796), idol of his countrymen. The vivid appeal of his lyrics has been like that of Nature itself, lines such as:

> We twa hae paidled in the burn
> Frae morning sun till dine,
> But seas between us braid hae roared
> Sin' Auld Lang Syne

are full of the half-forgotten feelings of vanished childhood. *My love is like a red, red rose* recalls the first fine careless raptures of many Elizabethans:

> O my luve is like a red, red rose,
>   That's newly sprung in June:
> O my luve is like the melodie
> That's sweetly played in tune!

> As fair art thou, my bonnie lass,
>   So deep in luve am I,
> And I will luve thee still, my dear,
> Till a' the seas gang dry.

> Till a' the seas gang dry, my dear,
>   And the rocks melt wi' the sun;
> I will luve thee still, my dear,
> While the sands o' life shall run.

> And fare thee weel, my only luve,
>   And fare thee weel a while!
> And I will come again, my luve,
> Tho' it were ten thousand mile!

Finer pathos, never far from young love, beats in the lines to Mary Morrison, beginning "Yestre'en when tae the trembling

string." Such love-lyrics are as spontaneous and natural as any in literature.

Burns was not an untaught child of nature. His memoirs of himself and family, in strong nervous prose, evince a close study of good models. He read widely in Shakespeare, Pope, Thomson, Gray and earlier Scottish poetry. His poetry is not naïve dialect, but reveals a mastery of language varying from Ayrshire to standard English. Nor was he a child of the French Revolution: he called himself "a Pittite up to a point," was in favour of a strong Navy, and himself a militiaman; his last flicker of fun, on his death-bed, was "Dinna let the awkward squad fire ower my grave!" Boy and man, he was overworked on his father's and his own small hungry farms: "A mill-horse round," he calls it. The streaks of brightness in this worried struggling existence were: his Nature-worship (he walked by the woods just to hear the wind roar like the sea), his fleeting passions for one country wench after another, and his exultant power of expression—especially in Scots vernacular.

Humour and Passion of Burns

His richly emotional and vigorous intellect revolted against the then cast-iron social barriers between man and man— barriers as hard in proud, poor Scotland as in more feudal England; and against "holy Wullies" or sly hypocritical elders. He discovered this equalitarianism not from political theory but from experience: and it is expressed in *The Jolly Beggars* and *A man's a man for a' that*.

The perfume of his loveliest songs would evaporate if they were turned from the vernacular into correct literary English. The charm adheres to a delicately hung verbal fabric, saturated in locality and tradition, inherited from older folk poetry, into which he poured the riches of his humour and the great emotional force of his personality. This explains the immediacy of his fame and its enduring quality. His countrymen instantly greeted him as of their bone, flesh and idiom, and at the same time more splendid than anything they knew—than *The Lament for Flodden* or *The Braes of Balquhidder* or *Auld Robin*

ROBERT BURNS

Greatest of Scotland's poets, Robert Burns endured a hard and impoverished life which led to his early death in 1796. The poems of his first volume were written in his few leisure hours at farms at Lochlea and Mossgiel, and include "The Cottar's Saturday Night," "The Address to the De'il," and the lines "To a Mouse" and "To a Daisy."

"THE JOLLY BEGGARS"

This is an artist's view of Burns's "The Jolly Beggars," in which an ale-house gathering of maimed and sordid vagrants sing, frolic, and barter their rags for the drink that makes them happy. The painter, however, has purged the scene of its earthiness.

Gray. He eclipsed his sources. When he tried conventional English (except in his clear and manly memoir of himself) he is not so original. Even the once-praised *Cottar's Saturday Night* is not his best work. His own tongue, racy of Ayr and the Lothians and Border, best conveyed his pungent satire, humour and realism. His abounding fun, passion and love of freedom hastened the advent of naturalism and romance.

Thomson and Crabbe

The Seasons by James Thomson (1700-1748) is not to be compared with Burns for vividness. The vision was there admittedly—the vision of the changing skies, of snows, storms, effaced tracks, the birds that "give their wild notes to the listening waste," of Nature visiting "the lonely heart with dreams of good," of harvests and rustic life; but it is dimmed by the attempt at Miltonic blank verse, a Ulysses bow which only John Milton could bend. His *Castle of Indolence*, in the Spenserian stanza, recaptures much of its true romantic quality. He wrote *Rule, Britannia.*

Nowadays George Crabbe (1754-1832) attracts much interest for another kind of natural truth. Son of a small harbour official, he had an eye for the sombre, sordid corners of the East Anglian village seaport where he was born, with its stench of rotting wharf, seaweed, fen, docks, charlock and darnels, and oyster-beds. He was not afraid of ugliness and sordid places and people, and his audacity leaves a mark on the mind. Painting and poetry can exploit even "ugliness" for purposes of beauty and interest. Crabbe loved his drab birthplace, "its effluvia strong and peculiar, half saline, half putrid, association of ideas has it agreeable."

Bog, and marsh, and fen
Are only poor to undiscerning men.

WILLIAM COWPER

Cowper's first volume of poems was published in 1782 when he was fifty-one years old and included "Table Talk." The second volume, which appeared in 1785, contained "The Task" and "John Gilpin." His poems—many of them about everyday trivialities—have simplicity, humour, tenderness, and an almost womanly sensibility. They were an escape from his fear of damnation, which, thanks to his Calvinist upbringing, became an obsession with him. This feeling is expressed in "Hatred and Vengeance" and in "The Castaway."

William Cowper (1731-1800) gives pictures of the flat Ouse country that are not so stark and uncompromising as Crabbe's, but they ring true. His enchanting collected letters have never been surpassed for charm and style. He was a genuine forerunner of the coming lyrical outburst, a truly original poet, an honest observer and a fine mind. Because he suffered from intervals of despairing madness he confined himself to the seclusion of a country home with his good angel Mrs. Unwin, for whom he wrote *The Task*. His use of the rhymed couplet is free and effective. His innocent, retired world at Olney reminds us of the Rev. Gilbert White (1720-1793) and his exquisitely observed world of Selborne and district, described with loving accuracy. The *Natural History of Selborne* is among the most refreshing gossip in our literature.

Blake the Visionary

Drastic general changes of thought and opinion at certain junctures are in the air. Of this, perhaps the most astounding proof is William Blake (1757-1827), mystic, and forerunner of a liberating century. Artist, engraver, poet, living in obscure London streets, unknown to the literary world, esteemed slightly mad, he recalls the unpremeditated songs of certain Elizabethans. Born and bred in London, he rarely left it, seldom took walks, and lived entirely in his inner world of imagination. Pictures, sculptures, poems—even moving words— had more reality for him than for any other. His drawings and engravings are those of a titanic visionary, slightly "touched." His mystic prophecies and myths have this wild, dreamlike apocalyptic quality: half of them are even yet not fathomed.

It was no surprise for him to see clusters of angels in a tree at Peckham Rye, or spirits among the haymakers. He demanded that life should be a free, astonishing thing. He made his "world" out of the Bible, Shakespeare, Swedenborg and other mystics, newspaper reports of the Revolution and the American War, popular songs, Westminster Abbey, London streets and cries. And his poems, *Songs of Innocence* and *Songs of Experience*, have directness and simplicity like the questions of

a child, at once simple and inimitable.

Father, O father! what do we here
In this land of unbelief and fear?
The land of dreams is better far
Above the light of the morning star.

He was the extreme and violent antithesis of his earth-bound period. He thought its sanity idiocy and its religion blasphemy, and he, more than any other, rose against the pressure of the material world. A great lover of children, animals, of home, of common people, he possessed a daring prophecy and a literal belief in Christ's code of compassion which disconcerts some professing followers:

A robin redbreast in a cage
Puts all heaven in a rage . . .
A horse misused upon the road
Calls to Heaven for human blood . . .
Each outcry of the hunted hare
A fibre from the brain doth tear;
A skylark wounded on the wing
Doth make a cherub cease to sing . . .
The strongest poison ever known
Came from Caesar's laurel crown.

Sturdy Prophet

He was an *enfant terrible* in thought, uttering aloud whatever was in his fearless heart. Living a self-sufficient life on his wages, he was a bold and consistent adventurer into ideas. His prophetic books are too cryptic for other than special students; but fortunately he has simpler sources of delight—lyrics fresh and delicate, or unworldly and elemental, some richly Elizabethan, others Celtic in spirit.

When Blake told friends that King Alfred or any great person had visited him, Mrs. Blake would look at him awestruck and confirm the story. We see this amazing dreamer—a sturdy, half-Quakerish revolutionary, with rapt forehead, carrying home his nightly pint of porter.

And there is his

Tiger! Tiger! burning bright
In the forests of the night,
What immortal hand or eye
Framed thy fearful symmetry?

WILLIAM BLAKE

A painter and poet of remarkable mystic qualities William Blake is a unique figure in the history of English literature. The utter simplicity of thought in some of his "Songs of Innocence" is contrasted with the profound and prophetic knowledge expressed in such writings as "The Marriage of Heaven and Hell" (a prose work) and "The Song of Los."

In all our lyric poetry there is no voice so clear as his.

Before going up into the enchanted hill-country of the great Romantics, there remains one other strange poet—or rather poem, for it stands alone in his work—the *Song to David* of Christopher Smart (1722-1771) who ended in a madhouse. Though educated at Durham and later a Fellow of Pembroke College, Cambridge, and a leading scholar of the day, he was involved in hackwork and debt, spending his last years within rules of the King's Bench, held there by his creditors. It is believed that his masterpiece was inscribed with charcoal and nails on the walls and windows of his cell. "I do not think he ought to be shut up," said Dr. Johnson. "His infirmities were not noxious to society. He insisted on people praying with him; and I'd as lief pray with Kit Smart as with anyone else. Another charge was that he did not love clean linen; and I have no passion for it."

Mad Christopher Smart

Smart fell in love as a boy with a girl of family; and ten years later, when she married, he began to drink. In his prison he was inspired to thanksgiving, and formulated a plan by which he might become "by the grace of God the Reviver of Adoration among Englishmen." It is an utter escape from all that the century had stood for. This outburst of religious praise has the dreadful march and logical directness of abnormality finding link and series where the normal mind does not. Its exultation is as irresistible as an unexpected rush of song from a nightingale; never were all living creatures celebrated with such wild yet reverent love:

> He sang of God—the mighty source
> Of all things—the stupendous force
> On which all strength depends;
> From whose right arm, beneath whose eyes
> All period, power, and enterprise
> Commences, reigns, and ends.

> The world, the clustering spheres He made,
> The glorious light, the soothing shade,

> Dale, champaign, grove and hill,
> The multitudinous abyss,
> Where Secrecy remains in bliss,
> And Wisdom hides her skill.

And so, through eighty-six impassioned stanzas of sustained praise, he sang of stars, the flushed skies, the flowers of the earth, the temple bells, the life-force in whale and lion and horse and eagle, "the northern lights a-stream," and so up to an astonishing climax whose joy and impact surpass that of most hymns.

Wesley's Hymns

The fact that it took the world a generation or two to recognize two of the most wonderful poets of their century warns us that we cannot label a whole half-century with one description. Always there are "sports" and original aberrations. Men, and periods, are liable to be caught unawares by the gods—of the earth beneath or the heavens above. Something demonic in the universe enters and disturbs the reign of skill and commonplace. So it was in the hundreds of remarkable hymns of Charles Wesley (1707-1788), whose truth overleaps denominational barriers and re-captures the fire and directness of the early Church hymnists. This dynamic and influential side of literature is unaccountably omitted from most surveys, and so a major clue to the age is missed. After all, Dryden, Pope, Cowper, Whittier and Newman composed noble hymns which are still living. It is the great number, as well as the flamelike quality of the hymns written by Charles Wesley (brother of John) which single him out.

For a fair amount of personal background to this period, read Boswell's *Life of Johnson* and John Bailey's *Dr. Johnson and His Time*. Follow (or accompany) this with Bailey's lives of contemporaries like Richard Savage and Thomas Gray; also those on Dryden and Pope. If you can, get his *Preface to Shakespeare*. Read Burke's long *Reflections on the Revolution in France*, marking the significant passages for future reference; and the sentences that reveal his profounder attitude to life and human society. Also his *American Affairs*.

Next, look at Goldsmith's short and witty character sketch of his famous friends, in *Retaliation*. Then, certainly, the lovable poem, *The Deserted Village*; and *The Traveller*, with its glimpses of foreign peoples seen through a vagrant's eyes. *The Critic*, by Sheridan (being less often acted than *The School for Scandal*), demands to be read for its caustic portraits. Follow with *The Rehearsal*, a farce which is ablaze with wit, and cleaner than Restoration comedy.

Take time over an easy perusal of Gibbon's short dignified *Autobiography*, a gem of the ornate style; "it may boldly be pronounced perfect," said Augustine Birrell. Gibbon took great pains over it. Of letters, perhaps the best in the English language are Cowper's small domestic news in a master's hand; a close second are Gray's letters. Let these be read at the same time as their poetry, and do not omit Cowper's rhymed poems, such as *Conversation*. The above affords a fair idea of the classic style of the century. Then advance into the other side, the pre-Romantics— Blake, Smart, Collins, Burns, especially the poems alluded to.

Test Yourself

1. Who was the outstanding literary figure of the eighteenth century? What was the reason for his pre-eminence?
2. Why do modern thinkers consider that Edmund Burke was ahead of his time?
3. Write a short essay on the development of the novel during the eighteenth century. Who were the outstanding exponents of this form of literature?
4. Name three eighteenth-century poets who were the forerunners of the Romantic age of poetry.

Answers will be found at the end of the book.

THE DISTRESSED POET

Hogarth held a mirror to many aspects of eighteenth-century life. Here he paints a poet in his garret, his wife mending his trousers, the milkmaid dunning him for payment.

WILLIAM WORDSWORTH

William Wordsworth ranks with Shakespeare and Milton as one of the three great English poets of all time. He began writing at an early age and, with Coleridge, published the "Lyrical Ballads" in 1798, in which he first gave proof of his theory that the language of poetry should be a selection of the language ordinarily used by plain men.

CHAPTER VIII

THE ROMANTIC REVIVAL

THIS well-marked departure from previous styles did not spring abruptly from a void: we have seen in the previous chapter how its coming was heralded by significant tendencies and events.

Like other periods of change and new ideas, the eighteenth century produced bold experiment and exciting successes. Charlatans and imitators vied with men of great originality and genius. It was not time for high polish or excessive refinement; men were shaken and stimulated by world events and ideas; diction became less leisurely; emotions became larger, more spacious, and often consciously dramatic.

Seeing Life Anew

The subjects of authors changed. One man would choose the depths of humble life, seeing dignity or mystery in the manhood of a beggar or ditcher; another would soar into Utopias of the soul and proclaim "the world's greatest age begins anew"; yet another found his solution in weaving sensuous word pictures from "faery lands forlorn." Poetry of enormous strength and profundity will inevitably show certain weaknesses from which self-controlled, revised verse is free. The crystal-clear trickle from a man such as Gray is different from the mighty gush of verse from William Wordsworth. But it is captious and useless criticism to fasten upon these differences in order to criticize either poet. More especially is it false to belittle a man's work by making fun of his beliefs and his mode of life. A great man exhibits plenty of sides that can be made ridiculous by the pen of a "smart" biographer; great ideals look silly when burlesqued. But to mistake such facile attacks for serious criticism is a grave error and an obstacle to real culture.

Like most "revolutions," at first it was not clear what it was really seeking, nor what it was that it wanted to supersede. It said, in the persons of Wordsworth and Coleridge (in their famous youthful *Lyrical Ballads*, 1798) that it desired to get rid of the vice of an unreal and artificial mode of writing, stereotyped for nearly a hundred years, and to use the common language of life. Soon the manifesto widened and deepened, for both men had philosophic and questing minds. Soon it was clear that they—and especially Wordsworth—were resolved to express the deepest passions of the human heart, of man as man. This is how Wordsworth achieved the force and pathos of his verse, recalling some of the noblest passages of Shakespeare. Shelley attained the piercing pathos of *The Cenci*; Coleridge many a profound touch in *The Ancient Mariner* or suggestion of subtle half-tones in *Christabel*:

The night is chill; the forest bare;
Is it the wind that moaneth bleak?
There is not wind enough in the air
To move away the ringlet curl
From the lovely lady's cheek . . .

Romance in its Obvious Sense

This goes far beyond reform of mere diction; it is a different land from that of the ballad-collectors of the previous fifty years, or Horace Walpole's escapades into the "Gothic," or the infatuation with medieval "properties," old armour and tapestry, secret passages, obsolete words, and the other fashions which (it must be owned) so obsessed Sir Walter Scott in his early manhood.

Sir Walter Scott (1771-1832) was gathering strength with the help of the learned peasant John Leyden; he was producing his *Border Ballads* and translating from the German legends which caused a rustle in the nerves. Percy's *Reliques* and Thomas Chatterton's imitations all assisted. Scott's fluent versification in *The Lay of the Last Minstrel, Marmion, The Lady of the Lake* and *Rokeby* fell upon receptive and thirsty ground. And his few mystical songs, *Proud Maisie* and *Coronach*, had a wild pathos new to most ears.

All this, so far, was surface disturbance

only. Coleridge in *Kubla Khan* and Wordsworth in *Lines Written above Tintern Abbey* and the early *Prelude* knew a more genuine stir of soul. One notices a new flight of imaginative sensibility; mountains and ocean, the sleep or movement of great cities, the supernatural, the hidden life of the peasant, the worth and destiny of man— became springs of joy, release and wonder.

Wordsworth's Creed

That is not to say that Wordsworth's weapon was the bludgeon. One can appreciate the delicate sentiment of his *Intimations of Immortality*, in which gentle melancholy avoids any of the morbidity or over-lush emotionalism with which the subject has been coloured by lesser men:

> There was a time when meadow, grove,
>   and stream,
> The earth, and every common sight,
>   To me did seem
>   Apparell'd in celestial light,
> The glory and the freshness of a dream.
> It is not now as it hath been of yore;
>   Turn wheresoe'er I may,
>   By night or day,
> The things which I have seen I now
> can see no more.
>   The rainbow comes and goes,
>   And lovely is the rose;
>   The moon doth with delight
> Look round her when the heavens are
> bare;
>   Waters on a starry night
>   Are beautiful and fair;
>   The sunshine is a glorious birth;
>   But yet I know, where'er I go,
> That there hath passed away a glory
> from the earth.

It was in vain that William Hazlitt, in an irascible moment, sneered at Wordsworth's discovery of a divine value in anything human—in "beggars, leech-gatherers, Botany Bay convicts, meek daughters in the family of Christ," and so forth. That was the whole point of the new revelation; it was an extension and deepening of religion, a democratic or rather Christian faith in the affections such as had not been felt since Shakespeare—and *hardly by him*. "Leave city complexity," they seemed to say, "and social distinctions, oppressive convention, enfeebling artificialities in life or creed for the great natural world, 'the heavens—a spectacle as old as the beginnings,' where Providence has planted us, and where there is a Soul answering to our soul, a Presence that disturbs us in the sunset and sunrise, in the round ocean and the living air *and the deep heart of man*." While Wordsworth deliberately taught this, as literally as he studied mathematics, and his soul "dissolved in love and vision," Shelley sang:

> From the temples high
> Of man's ear and eye,
> Roofed over sculpture and poesy . . .
> Beyond our eyes
> The human love lies
> Which makes all it gazes on paradise

and Coleridge was saying "we receive what we give, and in our hearts alone doth Nature live." Nature, once the despised hinterland of urban civilization, is now the poet's guide to beauty and truth.

Influence of the French Revolution

William Wordsworth (1770-1850), born at Cockermouth, schooled at Hawkshead in north Lancashire, was of tough northern stock. From the days when schoolboys were boarded out among the sturdy independent villagers, he had liberty to roam the countryside by day and night. His father died when the boy was fourteen, and at seventeen Wordsworth was sent to Cambridge (all this and much else is passionately described in that autobiography, *The Prelude*—the story by which best to approach Wordsworth), and after taking his degree at twenty-one he went to France, drawn by revolutionary stir and the doctrines of fraternity and freedom. There he began writing verse, but it was not yet his inspired or masterly work. Living in a topfloor in seething Paris, he heard the mobs and wild meetings, and struggled to be an orator with the rest: but his uncles and guardians stopped his money and forced him to return home. Those days haunted his dreams ever after; he would wake from sleep addressing "unjust tribunals," or manning barricades. He never forgot the greeting, "Citizen!" he had exchanged with men: the human equality he saw in the freeholders of North England and Scotland was different, but was as much in his blood.

His habits were always Spartan. He was an enthusiastic walker, he had read intensively, but his library was not big or well kept, although his mental self-confidence was immense. He never lost that early hold on the brotherhood of all men, the rights of the poor, the evil of man's inhumanity to man. Wordsworth, when he saw the French Revolution devour its own children, and Napoleon's iron reign begin, went on singing Liberty—not the wild abstraction, but a concrete liberty for England, Switzerland, Spain, Italy and the oppressed peoples: liberty for the family, the district, the Church, opinion, and Parliamentary discussion.

How were other poets, meanwhile, reacting to the earthquake? Scott turned aside to write of the romantic past; Byron expressed the general passion of unrest in vehement verse; Shelley gave it vaguely idealized, ethereal voice; John Keats and Leigh Hunt took evasive action: Robert Southey preferred legendary "escape," epics like *Thalaba* and *The Curse of Kehama* and good prose studies of Lord Nelson and John Wesley, and Coleridge his few magic valleys, with some unprecedentedly deep interpretation of literature and thought, especially of Shakespeare.

Plain Living and High Thinking

One of the most remarkable things in literary history is the swift rise of Wordsworth's influence, till he stands near to Shakespeare and Milton, "but in a kind unborrowed and his own." After neglect, parody and misunderstanding, it is now seen that he went forward to a different and a more metaphysical comprehension of the meaning of life than had ever existed in English poetry. The words are those of Herbert Read, who adds that he was no mere product of his own or the preceding period: he took a deeper breath, and wilder leap into the "dark abyss" of thought, and returned to face the world

with a faith as daring and important as any since Milton's. The history of that revealing experience is told in the impassioned *Prelude*, which has fair claims to be regarded as the greatest poem of the age; it is the only poem at any rate (as Read truly considers) which stands in relation to the modern age as Dante's *Divine Comedy* stands to the Middle Ages. We should banish the former flat notion that he is only a "nature" poet. He is also humanist, philosophic, religious, daring to tread his own path: strong minded and independent. *Man* was his main subject:

> . . . I bend in reverence
> To Nature and the power of Human minds,
> To men as they are men within themselves.
> . . . My theme
> No other than the very heart of man,
> And Grandeur on the very humblest face
> Of human life.

"The humblest face of human life"—note the words; for in humble life, he thought, lay the poet's opportunity. In the simple dalesman, not in the sophisticated townsman, were to be seen and grasped "the primary laws of our nature." In him he found the dignity, fortitude, love, filial affection, resolution, independence and sense of duty which (with similar qualities) he held to compose the moral nature of man. The simple countryman lives close to Nature and is the better for it. For, in Wordsworth's belief, Nature herself (or, if you like, God in Nature) acts through our physical senses to influence the mental and moral worth of man:

> The eye—it cannot choose but see;
> We cannot bid the ear be still;
> Our bodies feel, where'er they be,
> Against or with our will.

> Nor less I deem that there are Powers
> Which of themselves our minds impress;
> That we can feed this mind of ours
> In a wise passiveness.

He practised what he believed. With a faith in the essence of the human soul and the common run of men, which is deeper and more Christian in mood than any predecessor has shown, he dealt with shepherds, wanderers, beggars, the leech gatherer, the sailor, the carrier, the idiot boy, the outcast, children, dalesfolk and townsfolk; cities in revolution or asleep, the hills in storm or repose. Though he saw savage deeds in Paris—"Defenceless as a wood where tigers roam"—still

> . . . In this time
> Of dereliction and dismay, I yet
> Despair not of our nature, but retain
> A more than Roman confidence, a
> faith
> That fails not.

This courage he passes on to the reader, for, like ourselves in later wars, he had seen "human nature faithful to herself under worst trials," and that nature was "my haunt, and the main region of my song." He remade faith in existence for many of the disquieted and agnostic because he penetrated far below labels and appearances. He saw himself as a priest in the wilderness, announcing "our sublime dependences," knowing that "wisdom is often nearer when we stoop than when we soar." No Bastille, he declared, is deep enough to exclude the light of goodness; and he knew, because he had witnessed "man suffering amid awful forms and powers . . . under a long-lived storm of great events." So hope was no passing mood for him, but a duty; his Deity "fills the veins that branch through every frame of life, making man what he is, creature divine." He looked outward and perceived "all things lay bedded in a quickening Soul, and respired with inward meaning."

He is our greatest exponent of the idea of Divine immanence in man and Nature: he embodies this in *The Prelude* and *The Excursion*, in the greater sonnets, and in the *Immortality* ode which Emerson called the intellectual high-water mark of the century. About man's heart and the Power behind Nature, he has not merely said some of the most intense things: he

kept on saying them in various ways. Wordsworth detested classifications and artificiality. Again and again he brings us back to

> Life, human life, with all its sacred
> claims
> Of sex and age, and heaven-descended
> rights,
> Mortal, or those beyond the reach of
> death . . .
> The dignity of individual man . . .

"individual man, no composition of the brain, but the man whom we behold with our own eyes," so as to see

> . . . into the depths of souls,
> Souls that appear to have no depth at
> all
> To careless eyes.
>   . . . I hear
> From mouths of men obscure and
> lowly, truths
> Replete with honour . . .
> Theirs is the language of the heavens.

The Creator knows and loves men "who are unregarded by the world," and thousands of us are often "pious above the intention of our thought, devout above the meaning of our will"—"God being with them when they knew it not." Underneath all politics he saw that "by love subsists all lasting grandeur: that gone, we are as dust." Besides his social vision, he is our profoundest thinking poet. "He re-created by supreme Divinity," says Mark Rutherford.

Poet of the Mature Mind

Of late years, too, in reaction from both stiff classicism and vague romanticism, a good part of the reading world more than ever values his plainness, his pure and bare style, his intense veracity, the mountain rapture we reach after the climb. Even when didactic or dull (and that is not so often) he is burningly sincere, and he has more, perhaps, to teach us than any other modern observer of life. He was that rarest thing among poets, a complete innovator, looking at things in a new way. If his vision seems familiar in our day, that is only

DOVE COTTAGE, INTERIOR
Dove Cottage, at Grasmere, was Wordsworth's home for more than fifty years and he left it only for occasional tours abroad. It is now a national monument.

because he first had it. But it is not yet accepted by all.

George Saintsbury says: "When Wordsworth writes

> The sounding cataract
> Haunted me like a passion;

or

> Our birth is but a sleep and a forgetting;
> The soul that rises with us, our life's star,
> Hath had elsewhere its setting
> And cometh from afar.

even Shakespeare, even Shelley, have little more of the echoing detonation, the auroral light, of true poetry."

We may say of him, in words of his about a reaper whom he heard one day singing while at work and long remembered:

> No sweeter voice was ever heard
> In spring-time from the cuckoo-bird
> Breaking the silence of the seas
> Among the farthest Hebrides.

He is the poet of the mind's maturity, and remains when many others fail us. He was very unequal, because his mind could only be raised by the white heat of profoundly inward passion and vision; but then he gives us our bearings. Our language owes him gratitude for the purity of his style.

Drowsy Titan

Samuel Taylor Coleridge (1772-1834), Wordsworth's "other self," was the most subtle influence of his generation: a poetical interpreter to the hardier Wordsworth, the pioneer of a deeper outlook on belief (thus helping to form the Christian socialist movement after he had gone); perhaps the most comprehensive critic we have had; a good political journalist; and, as poet,

SAMUEL TAYLOR COLERIDGE
Coleridge was poet, journalist and lecturer, and he influenced a number of writers, including William Hazlitt. His work is both thoughtful and wildly imaginative.

master of as exquisite fantasy as any in our language. He could do everything but manage his own affairs. Yet this drowsy Titan has left us only a hundred or more pages of the true elixir; he could manage thoughts and words consummately, but not his own life, and he was wrecked in a mist of opium (which also wrecked De Quincey, Crabbe and Francis Thompson).

Coleridge and his Friends

Left an orphan, he went to the Bluecoat School, Christ's Hospital (where he met Charles Lamb), then to Cambridge whence he escaped to enlist in the 15th Dragoons under the name of Comberbacke, but an officer learnt the truth and had him discharged. With Southey and others he planned an unselfish model republic in America: he called it "Pantisocracy," and it died for want of funds. Coleridge knew a Bristol bookseller, Cottle, who, in 1796, gave him thirty guineas for a small book of poems; he sent others to a London paper. Here began his historic friendship with Wordsworth, and he visited Germany

and was secretary to Sir Alex Ball in Malta in 1804-1805. Five years later he quitted the Lakes, leaving his wife and children with Southey, and remained in London, lecturing, and working for the *Morning Post* and projecting great schemes which he had not the means to put into operation. His exploring mind passed through several religious and political phases, and he knew the Greek and German philosophies; and some of his prose, *Confessions of an Inquiring Spirit* and *The Friend*, chart his voyagings of thought, though in an eloquent, oracular manner which hasty readers will find baffling. His last home was at Highgate—a plaque inset in a wall shows the spot—where he died as late as 1834, a white-haired, sweet-faced, much-speaking sage. Shelley finely portrays Coleridge:

Oft hast thou turned from men thy
   lonely feet,
With mountain winds, and babbling
   springs,
And moonlight seas, that are the voice
Of these inexplicable things,
Thou didst hold commune, and rejoice
When they did answer thee. . . .
Thine own soul still is true to thee,
But changed to a foul fiend through
   misery.

And Shelley added in 1820:

You will see Coleridge; he who sits
   obscure
In the exceeding-lustre and the pure
Intense irradiation of a mind
Which, with its own internal lightning
   blind,
Flags wearily through darkness and
   despair—
A cloud-encircled meteor of the air,
A hooded eagle among blinking owls.

Thomas Carlyle watched this amazing conversationalist (or rather monologist) weaving his spells of theory and imagery to an entranced, half-comprehending circle—clouds rolling between "sunny isles of the blest and intelligible." But Hazlitt's rapturous essay, *My First Acquaintance with Poets,* is better: "It was as if I heard the music of the spheres. In passing from subject to subject, he appeared to me to float in air, to slide on ice. ... I would swear that the very milestones had ears, and that Harmer hill stooped with all its pines to listen to a poet as he passed!" Hazlitt's picture of him in *The Spirit of the Age* is unforgettable. Coleridge's knowledge of Greek and German philosophies, of theology and poetry, and his eloquence, made him legendary in his lifetime. He rescued English thought from the imputation of prosaic provincialism, for in his mind were most of the other wisdoms of the world.

It is only too easy in our day to neglect all of Coleridge but *The Ancient Mariner*, that wonderful hallucination of the southern seas; *Christabel*, pure music and pure mystery; and *Kubla Khan*, a glimpse, and no more, of a strange world where:

. . . twice five miles of fertile ground
With walls and towers were girdled round:
And here were gardens bright with sinuous rills
Where blossom'd many an incense bearing tree;
And here were forests ancient as the hills,
Enfolding sunny spots of greenery;

but it is unwise to forget his odes on *France* and *Dejection* and *To the Departing Year;* his superb poem on *The Garden of Boccaccio*, and the strange arresting fragments—pure gold. Why do many readers overlook them? Because, possibly, this poet's voice is like Cordelia's, "soft, gentle and low." He has not the thunder and rhetoric of Byron; the pure, lyrical flow of Shelley; the hard white flame of

COLERIDGE ADDRESSES A MOUNTAIN
Lines of verse written in Coleridge's own hand, with his neat signature attached.

intense vision of Wordsworth; nor the love-passion in Rabelaisian form, of Burns. Instead, however, it is of "imagination *all* compact": it is even too rare and delicate for some palates.

'Tis a fire that few discern
And very few feel burn—
And the rest may live and learn.

There is an exaltation or spirituality of the senses which is peculiar to some dreams, to some childhoods, and to Coleridge. He brings the secrets and floating melodies of sleep, of slight alienation, out into the day-light of simple wording in his best poems, which have sometimes the strange indefi-niteness of apparitions. Many moderns have followed Coleridge into the sub-conscious, away from poetry's normal purposes—and Coleridge himself would have disapproved of the tendency. He would have liked to write poetry of the order of Shakespeare, Milton or Words-worth; but could not. He wrote what was in him—the poetry that is his.

Shelley's Life and Poetry

Into twenty-nine years (1792-1822) Percy Bysshe Shelley crowded his wonderful lyrical achievement. They were years of repeated emotional stress, of exile, of idealism and regret—and all of it, whether personal or political suffering, he trans-muted into rich and ringing song. Eldest son of Sir Timothy Shelley of Horsham, Sussex, he was brought up among sisters; this may have enhanced his extreme consti-tutional sensibility. Quite early his imagi-nation was fired by the wild mystery novels of Mrs. Radcliffe, which influenced many minds, and by a popular scientific lecturer. At Eton his nerves suffered under the fagging and roughness; at Oxford he tried to stagger the dons with a youthful pam-phlet on the necessity of atheism. If Shelley were not himself a lovable creature and exceptionally gifted, there would be a temp-tation to call much of his conduct priggish and perverse. "Sent down" from the university, he contracted an unhappy run-away match, continually changed his abode (York, the North, Wales, the Thames

PERCY BYSSHE SHELLEY

Shelley's stormy life, which included exile in Italy, is reflected in his eager, restless lyrical poetry. His social outlook was revolutionary.

Valley, Switzerland and Italy); his ill-suited wife, Harriet, committed suicide, and Shelley fell in love with a daughter of William Godwin—Godwin, the novelist-philosopher-oracle who loomed large in his day, and who, for a time, sponged on Shelley when the young rebel and wanderer had his allowance restored. Throughout all his brief life's aberrations and muddles Shelley kept a certain innocence or integrity, wrapped in his impossible ideals and Utopian dreams. Hence he fascinated most who knew him, including Byron, whom he characteristically tried to "rescue" from a dissipated life in Venice. (A glimpse of this friendship can be had in the exquisite, genial narrative, *Julian and Maddalo*.)

Shelley's vague negative message is hinted in some of his titles, *The Revolt of Islam*, *Prometheus Unbound*, *The Cloud*, *The Sensitive Plant*; while *The Cenci* deals with the risky theme of incest. Shelley's flights and raptures often end with a wail at his powerlessness—"I faint upon the thorns of life, I bleed"; he feels that "rarely, rarely comest thou, Spirit of Delight" and that he had been too like the wind, "tameless, and swift, and proud." His most glorious clouds, lit with the sunrise, have this lining of suffering. He sings of Love—and its defeat; of wild desire and its "Evermore unrest." Technically, for thrilling music and perfect execution he can hardly be over-praised. But he has little to teach anyone. In his letters he humorously owns that those who go to him for solid meat will be disappointed; he deals in moonlight, he says. It is a true self-criticism. Still, there is no resisting him at his exciting best, when the speed, tone and fiery purity of his words show him to be inspired, as it were, by his mood. Whether that is the highest kind of poet is doubtful. Virgil, Milton and Wordsworth were not driven by their moods.

Shelley lived much in Italy, bathing in Mediterranean coves, sailing in Venice or watching sun and storm on the Apennines, reading the Greeks, and hymning the perfectibility of man. Distinction and ethereality are the breath of all he wrote; he could not be clumsy in style, and we are his debtors for the atmospheric charm of *Lines written among the Euganean Hills*, and *Epipsychidion*,

As clear as elemental diamond
Or serene morning air;

the *Hymn of Pan*, the *Hymn of Apollo*, *The Skylark* and the *Hymn to Intellectual Beauty*. Shelley has the gift of striking nearly all tastes from the beginning: he is the young prophet of aspiring, idealist and repressed youth. Gradually, we learn that he is elemental rather than human and material:

... the young Spirit
That sits in the Morning Star.

His friend, Lord Byron (1788-1824), is a heavier weight; more tangible and worldly, more scenic (even theatrical); and in his

day enormously better known in England and through Europe, whose "public orator" he was—"The grand Napoleon of the realms of rhyme." A comparison is instructive. Shelley lived amid abstractions, and by sheer imaginative force made them seem real to us: the spirits of Beauty, of Love, of Evil, of Tyranny or Liberty took shape and colour; became intelligible forms, fair humanities, objects of his adoration, hate, or fear. He was made that way, a bard, utterly crediting his own emotions and mental imagery—not an author or thinker. Byron was far more worldly, a mighty hitter, the man of affairs (in both senses of the phrase).

Byron's Early Life

In 1790 a profligate captain in the Guards abandoned wife and child in London. He was John Byron; his wife was Catherine Gordon of Aberdeen, whither she returned with the lame boy to live on £130 a year. While at school, George Gordon (as he was known) learnt that, by the death of a great-uncle, he was lord and owner of Newstead Abbey, Notts. His temperamental mother became horrified at the lad's lameness, summoned quacks and doctors, and, of course, drove the consciousness of deformity into him. Her alternate caresses and scoldings prefigured the capricious world's later treatment of him. Perhaps the one comparatively happy phase of his fevered life was at Harrow School and at Cambridge, where his interests were Oriental history and a few friendships. He kept bulldogs and a bear in his rooms: the bear he introduced to others as a "Fellow of the College." At nineteen he published *Hours of Idleness*, which an Edinburgh reviewer churlishly ridiculed. He retorted with the ferocious *English Bards and Scotch Reviewers*, in the manner and couplet of his gods, Dryden and Pope. Having attained his twenty-first birthday, he took his seat in the House of Lords in March 1809, and sailed in the following July for Lisbon. He rode through the south of Portugal and Spain to Cadiz, whence he sailed to Gibraltar; from there he proceeded to Malta and Greece. His genuine love for Greece and hatred for her

Turkish oppressors is given eloquent expression in *Childe Harold's Pilgrimage* which he wrote out of his experiences as a traveller. He did not at first think of printing the poem, but when the first stanzas were published Byron "woke to find himself famous." For three years he was lionized in London.

The *Giaour* (1813) further captured the public fancy; more cantos of *Childe Harold* followed, and rapidly *The Bride of Abydos*, *The Corsair* and *Lara*. All have at their centre a projection of himself—the darkly handsome, mysterious and rebel hero who appealed to young men as what they wanted to be, and to young women as what they wanted to meet. In 1815 he married Miss Anne Isabella Milbanke: in a year the union was dissolved. One daughter, Ada he loved to the end—at a distance. He was hissed and abused by the mob for his marital unhappiness ("in one of their periodical fits of virtue," Macaulay says); and angrily spurning the islanders—for

BYRON AT SHELLEY'S FUNERAL

Both Byron and Shelley were self-exiles in Italy. Shelley and his friend Edward Williams, were drowned in the Gulf of Spezia; Byron was among those who attended the burning of Shelley's body near Via Reggio.

little he understood himself and the poetry of the future. Tod ly we may wonder why "the world" deserted Scott's lively open-air and daylight verse for Byron who lived in an emotional dusk of his own passions and exotic background. The fact is that people wanted a change from English and Scottish scenes. Neither poet is, as such, in the first flight, but both serve well as purveyors of vivid emotion to vast numbers (Macaulay is, as we shall see, another such mediator to the many).

Byron Against the World

Another reason for Byron's vogue was his vendetta with the scheme of things— "I have not loved the world, nor the world me"; and he left it his "one curse, forgiveness"—and thousands of readers feel hotly for a Titan who hits back. Thousands even liked the touch of pose. Europe particularly liked this brilliant, outcast Briton for his outspoken misanthropy, forceful satire and volcanic wit. *Don Juan,* a story with many scornful digressions in which the poet wreaks his wrath on society, was just the serio-comic epic for them. The conversational verse gathers speed for Juan's adventures, soars to lofty thoughts, and drops to earth with a flippant jest. He had not a good ear for words, and was sometimes vulgar and slovenly; but the world forgives everything for picturesque force, striking colour, and candour. For many years, from the critics in France to Brandes in Denmark, romanticism was synonymous with Byronism. It is little wonder that, when he died at Missolonghi, where he had joined the Greek insurgents in their fight against the Turks, Tennyson, then a boy, repeated dazedly "Byron is dead!" and Arnold wrote "Our souls had felt his thunder's roll." His intensity had made a universal impression. No other had lamented, rebelled, or scorned in such a *timbre.* No

which he was as admired on the Continent as much as for his stirring and Mephistophelian verses—he lived dissolutely at Venice, Ravenna, Pisa and Rome, and drew considerable sums for his exciting poetic "novels." It is a pity that Byron the man has outshone Byron the poet. Idolized in France and Germany, he is undervalued in Britain. With all his stormy wilfulness he had a divided mind. Rebel and mocker, he lauded Dryden and Pope, sneering at the "Lake" poets—thereby showing how other had shown Europe to itself, in such a diorama of romantic pictures; it was a new *genre*, before there was descriptive journalism, or a Ruskin, or a cinema, or popular conducted tours. The centenary of his death in 1924 was celebrated more on the Continent than in Britain. But many here then read him again, and discovered that in the great poem, *Darkness*, he reached the sublime, and in the companion, *Dream*, a sincere pathos; they grieved over the death of Haidée by her island shore; shivered at the wreck, and heard

> . . . the bubbling cry
> Of some strong swimmer in his agony;

and quailed at the curse in *Cain*, which is dreadful oratory rather than essential poetry.

Byron's heroic pose and his flippant manner often masked his deep feelings—he loved liberty and hated oppression; nor was his passion for mountains and the sea a pretence. His two big poems are a series of vivid drop-scenes, with gorgeous "effects." Like an actor-manager of genius, he exploited a magnetic, vain, defiant and melancholy personality with skilful limelight and tireless versatility. He took "the pageant of a bleeding heart" through France, Greece, Italy, Rome, the Alps, the Rhineland, Waterloo—and the sea; with interludes of storm, love, battle and banditti.

Scott as Poet

In poetry he supplanted Walter Scott (1771-1832) till Scott constructed another and greater legend with the Waverley novels, dealt with in the next chapter. Scott's own life was a romance, and a great one. In eighteen years, from 1796 to the publication of *Waverley* (his twenty-fifth to forty-third year) he was the national minstrel. He was also quartermaster of the Edinburgh Light Horse, and his power of drawing military scenes was fed from experience. Rising at 5 a.m. he would light his fire, look round his garden and stables, and then write till 10 a.m. and breakfast. By then he had "broken the neck of the day's work." Two more hours of composi-

tion and he was "his own man"—riding, coursing or fishing; then the evening was for friends and chat. In 1805 *The Lay of the Last Minstrel* took the general taste, followed by the Homeric *Marmion*. These have probably been spoiled for many by being imposed as school tasks. That is not the fault of the poems.

Now began his fatal land hunger. He wanted to be a laird, worthy kinsman of his clan chief, the Duke of Buccleuch. He was spared the vices of some poets; but this aristocratic infatuation wrought in the end quite as much mischief, and brought down through other people's folly and bankruptcy "one of the soundest pieces of manhood made in that century." Clarty-Hole, one hundred acres, the nucleus of the pseudo-Gothic "seat," and Abbotsford on the Tweed, were the beginning of his punishments, nobly faced as his great *Journals* show. A complicated failure in the publishing world in 1826 threw upon Scott the personal responsibility for £130,000. He had left his interests in the hands of incompetent partners and until a few weeks before the crash had no warning of the true position. When the blow fell he refused to resort to the bankruptcy court—an expedient which under the circumstances many men would not have thought dishonourable—and spent the rest of his life slaving at his writing desk in an effort to pay the creditors in full.

Scott's galloping, fresh-air rhymes have many a martial, human and natural touch. And his short songs have a ballad-like simplicity and atmosphere: *Proud Maisie* is the genuine water from the rock, a miracle worthy of Shakespeare or Burns:

> Proud Maisie is in the wood,
> Walking so early;
> Sweet Robin sits on the bush,
> Singing so rarely.
>
> "Tell me, thou bonny bird,
> When shall I marry me?"
> —"When six braw gentleman,
> Kirkward shall carry thee."
>
> "Who makes the bridal bed,
> Birdie, say truly?"

—"The grey-headed sexton
That delves the grave duly.

" The glow-worm o'er grave and stone
Shall light thee steady;
The owl from the steeple sing
Welcome, proud lady!"

We swing to his opposite with John Keats (1795-1821), a wonder even in our amazing literary story. Within twenty-five years, such thought, development, art and vision! It is still hard of belief. At fourteen he was apprenticed to a surgeon in Moorfields, and at twenty-one put forth modestly his first collection of not very good verse, and next year *Endymion*, which was less ill received. He had formed himself on Lemprière's classical dictionary, on Shakespeare, Spenser, Milton, Dryden, with some influence from Byron and Wordsworth, and especially on Chapman's translation of Homer; he was, too, considerably influenced by Leigh Hunt's friendship. Consumption was in the family, and it gained on him. Backward medicine actually "bled" him and so hastened his end. He was haunted by the apprehension of death before he had "garnered this teeming brain." Every good judge, reading him, feels that some further perfection of vision and form was about to emerge. This youth's death was a disastrous loss to English literature, and the manner of it—the journey to Rome, and his death in the arms of his friend, Joseph Severn—is tragedy in the high manner. The centenary tributes in 1921 included some from India, farther Asia, the Slav countries, Scandinavia and America; and this despite the insuperable difficulties of rendering his verbal magic in any other tongue. Phrase, sensation and thought in him are singularly indivisible.

Richness of Keats

How can one tell readers, new to Keats, what it is that will grow upon them? A few suggestions can be offered tentatively —bloom, richness, luxuriance, the patient birth of the right epithet, a quiet fruition, a luminous ripeness of word and phrase ("I look on words like a lover"), an extreme receptiveness to the immediate touches of Nature through ear and eye, and the courage of his senses. Unlike Shelley, Byron and Wordsworth, he was not shaken by the political uprisings around; he had no "causes," only the cause of perfection of sensation, tone and form, the peculiar genius of making perfect pictures—

The village maids, with fearful glance,
Avoid the ancient moss-grown wall;
Nor ever lead the merry dance
Among the groves of Cumnor Hall.

And many a traveller has sighed,
And pensive wept the Countess' fall,
As wandering onward he has spied
The haunted towers of Cumnor Hall.

Finis

IMITATION OF THE BALLAD

Above are seen the verses which conclude Scott's "Cumnor Hall," a poem based on the supposed murder of the Countess of Leicester by her husband, who loved Queen Elizabeth.

stationed and immobilized. He is the poet of stillness, of sunny Nature in Attica or Tuscany; the absorbed dreamer over the Grecian Urn or the Nightingale; the weaver of a spell—or a tapestry—out of Isabella and her tragic Basil, or the legend of St. Agnes' Eve. We read him not with excitement as we do some others, but with calm acquiescence and with pauses to savour a perfect line or a picture. His ambition was to seek the primal things of Nature :

> Seek as they once were sought, in
>   Grecian isles,   .
> By bards who died content on pleasant
>   sward,
> Leaving great verse unto a little clan.
> O, give me their old vigour, and un-
>   heard
> Save of the quiet Primrose, and the
>   span
> Of heaven and few ears,
> Rounded by thee, my song should die
>   away
> Content as theirs,
> Rich in the simple worship of a day.

The present spectacle sufficed him; he did not "look before and after, and pine for what is not"; for him this visible world abundantly existed. So the intent clearness of his gaze gives us the crystalline picture of the Eve of St. Mark, and Fingal's Cave —a new sort of graphic, pictorial poetry to which we owe the earlier Tennyson, Rossetti and the pre-Raphaelites; and, far below these, the "art's sake" and "the fleshly school." His own contemporaries did not really understand him. Perhaps we should not blame them, for there was little time to do so before his death at twenty-five.

Keats and the Critics

Perhaps it should be said here that he was not "snuffed out by an article": he was much too big to worry about hostile criticism; Lord Jeffrey in the *Edinburgh Review* (the autocrat of reviewland) gave a whole essay of praise to *Endymion* while the poet was still half-formed. Jeffrey says he was "exceedingly struck with the genius and the spirit of poetry which breathes through all the extravagance. They are so

flushed all over with rich light that it is impossible to resist the intoxication or shut our hearts to the enchantment." He knew "no other book which he would *sooner employ as a test* to ascertain whether anyone had in him the native relish for poetry." How strong and inquiring a mind Keats had, judge from his letters collected by Buxton Forman. In flexible English which sometimes has a Shakespearian smack, they show he was still finding his truer self, reacting even against his loved master-influences, making an original philosophy, and feeling "immortality like an awful warmth round the heart." We do not know what we lost when that wondrous mind was quenched. It must content us that we have his gold-tinctured grain in many a verse freighted with beauty which can almost be handled; and that his astounding intuition (without scholarship) made him free of other times—ancient Greek, medieval, Elizabethan. He looks back to all these, and forward to Tennyson, moments of Browning, the pre-Raphaelites and to more than one poet in our day. Rudyard Kipling's short story, *Wireless*, shows how the prodigy of Keats has fascinated a modern.

Aristocrat of Prose

Another man who turned away from the prevailing ordeals and currents, to live with the great men of Greece, Rome, Italy, France and England, was Walter Savage Landor (1775-1864), classicist, republican, aristocrat, master of statuesque prose. He was a man bursting with prejudice and wisdom, with magnanimity and ungovernable tempers, with the pride of Lucifer and the hospitality of a gentleman. Here again is a "character" who has enticed many pens, and he is believed to have suggested the impetuous Boythorn in *Bleak House* to Dickens. His distinction is his resolve to say things grandly, tersely or delicately; he sought for the right phrase, he says, "morosely" and habitually. Aware that he would be caviare to the generality, he declared with the confidence that has often been the mark of genius—and sometimes of the less gifted: "I shall dine late, but the company will be fit though few." And again:

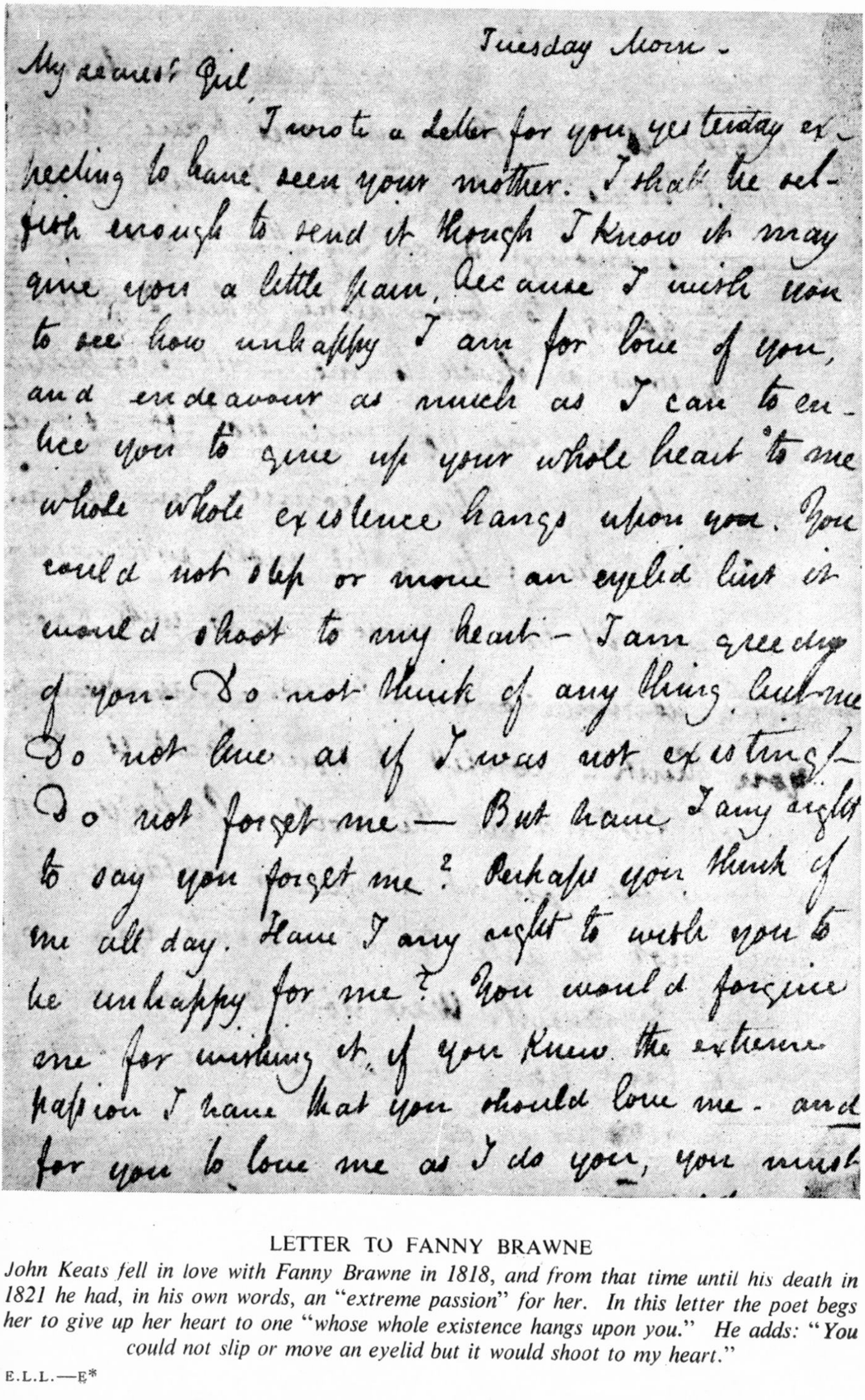

Tuesday Morn -

My dearest Girl,

    I wrote a letter for you yesterday expecting to have seen your mother. I shall be selfish enough to send it though I know it may give you a little pain, because I wish you to see how unhappy I am for love of you, and endeavour as much as I can to entice you to give up your whole heart to me whole whole existence hangs upon you. You could not slip or move an eyelid but it would shoot to my heart - I am greedy of you - Do not think of any thing but me. Do not live as if I was not existing - Do not forget me - But have I any right to say you forget me? Perhaps you think of me all day. Have I any right to wish you to be unhappy for me? You would forgive me for wishing it, if you knew the extreme passion I have that you should love me - and for you to love me as I do you, you must

---

LETTER TO FANNY BRAWNE

John Keats fell in love with Fanny Brawne in 1818, and from that time until his death in 1821 he had, in his own words, an "extreme passion" for her. In this letter the poet begs her to give up her heart to one "whose whole existence hangs upon you." He adds: "You could not slip or move an eyelid but it would shoot to my heart."

E.L.L.—E*

I strove with none, for none was worth
my strife;
Nature I loved, and, next to Nature,
Art;
I warmed both hands before the fire of
life—
It sinks, and I am ready to depart.

He saw himself proudly as an Ancient.
And he wrote like an old Roman, though
he behaved like an Olympian schoolboy.
He once threw an Italian servant out of an
upper window. The range of his *Imaginary
Conversations* is enormous, and such a high
level of noble, firmly knit prose is impressive in the mass. *The Pentameron, Pericles
and Aspasia*, and most of his verse, are a
fine dry wine, a vintage for matured tastes.
He is an author's author. But do not look
to this elaborate stylist for humour, drama
or human interest.

Friend of the Romantics

Leigh Hunt (1784-1859), the friend of
Shelley and Byron, of Keats and Lamb,
was editor of his own *London Journal*, the
Indicator and the *Liberal*; a charming light
essayist on any topic from Shakespeare to
Shops; he was imprisoned for a libel on
the Regent, whom he had merely called "a
fat Adonis." Considering what he might
have said, this was not libel but a compliment. Hunt was gifted likewise in rhyme.
Few poets have had a better-informed
appreciation of music. Consider these few
lines from his *Concert*:

There was Handel arrayed
On Olympian thunders, vast lord of
the spheres,
Yet pious himself, with his blindness
in tears,
A lover withal, and a conqueror, whose
marches
Bring demi-gods under victorious
arches;
Then Arne, sweet and tricksome; and
masterly Purcell,
Lay-clerical soul, and Mozart universal
But chiefly with exquisite gallantries
found,
With a grove in the distance of holier
sound. . . .

Or Marcello, that hushed the Venetian
sea;
And strange was the shout, when we
wept, hearing thee,
Thou soul full of grace as of grief, my
heart-cloven,
My poor, my most rich, my all-feeling
Beethoven.

Not always, however, was his taste so
flawless. He suffers from his diffuseness.

John Clare, Countryman

It is instructive to look back into eighty-
year-old histories of our literature, and
find a paragraph only devoted to names
which have, since then, risen and eclipsed
others to whom pages were assigned! Such
has been the rise of John Clare (1793-1864),
the rustic labourer poet, thanks to living
vindicators like Edmund Blunden. Clare,
born in abject poverty in a roadside
tenement on the edge of Deeping Fen,
minded horses, did odd jobs, learned his
letters, picked up Thomson's *Seasons* and
began to write verses, then came on *Paradise Lost* and *The Tempest* (he could not
have done better). At Helpston his family
lived in *one quarter* of "a narrow hut in a
plain covered with stagnant pools and
overhung by mists" and yet, looking back,
he could say:

The old house stooped just like a cave,
Thatched o'er with mosses green;
Winter around the walls would rave,
But all was calm within,
The trees are here all green again,
Here bees and flowers still kiss,
But flowers and trees seemed sweeter
then:
My early home was this.

He is perhaps best of all poets at suggesting
the tiny detail of Nature—nests and eggs
of wild birds, insects in the pools, markings
on leaves, "and full many in a nameless
weed, neglected, left to run to seed," when
in hot July "e'en the dew is parched up
from the teasel's jointed cup." He had the
eye of a countryman; and delighted, like
a pre-Raphaelite painter, to show the
slightest object in nature. His Muse:

. . . sits her down
Upon the molehill's little lap,
Who feels no fear to stain her gown.
And pauses by the hedgerow gap.

He is far more sensitive and poetical than Bloomfield, "the Farmer's Boy," or Stephen Duck, "the Thresher Poet." When he lamented leaving his old home, he missed chiefly

. . . its yellow furze,
Molehills and rabbit tracks that lead
Through beesom, lin and teasel burrs,

and this strange peasant, who at last was sent to an asylum (though local aristocrats pensioned him, too) could write piercing lines like this on the Enclosure Act:

It levelled every bush and tree and
levelled every hill
And hung the moles for traitors,
though the brook is running still,
It runs a naked stream cold and chill.

He gives no broad impressions, as Wordsworth and Keats can (and even Thomson and Cowper); he saw the kite and crow, but not their landscape and the horizons. His unhappy love for Mary Joyce, and his final years in Northampton Asylum, are part of his pathetic story.

The Romantic period is not over: we have so far seen only its high lights in poetry. There remains its prose masterpieces. Meanwhile, in this crowded stage,

Thomas Campbell would be quite overshadowed, despite his *Gertrude of Wyoming* and *The Pleasures of Hope*, were it not for a good many short poems which have a popular ring—*The Battle of the Baltic*, *Hohenlinden*, *The Pilgrims of Glencoe*, *The Soldier's Dream* and *Ye Mariners of England*. He is the romantic patriot.

Tom Hood

A word of affection is due to Thomas Hood (1799-1845), who was wittier in rhyme even than Canning of *The Anti-Jacobin* (who gave us *The Friend of Humanity and the Knife-Grinder*), or James and Horace Smith, once famed for their parodies of contemporary poets in *Rejected Addresses*. Hood's shorter triumphs are *The Song of the Shirt*, *The Bridge of Sighs*, *Eugene Aram* and *I Remember*—not only very adroit and fighting verse, but marked by pathos; for he says

There's not a string attuned to mirth
But has its chord in melancholy;

while his verses on Autumn remind us of Keats's rich ode. *The Plea of the Midsummer Fairies*, *The Haunted House*, and *Hero and Leander* can give delight still. He was a soldier in the new ranks of humanitarianism. So, in a rougher idiom, was Ebenezer Elliott with his *Corn Law Rhymes*. James Hogg, the "Ettrick Shepherd," whose gifts were discovered by Scott, has the fairy note in *Dalmeny*, *The Queen's Wake* and other poems.

Test Yourself

1. Write a four-hundred-word account of the lives and works of William Wordsworth and Samuel Taylor Coleridge.
2. Who was the "rustic poet" who wrote of the countryside and lore of his native Northamptonshire.
3. Write a short essay on Byron's life and character.
4. Name the poet, a famous character of his day, who is believed to be the original of Boythorn in Charles Dickens's *Bleak House*, and who wrote *Imaginary Conversations* and *Pericles and Aspasia*.

Answers will be found at the end of the book.

CHARLES AND MARY LAMB

Charles Lamb is, of all English essayists, the one who most endears himself to readers by the charm and humour of his personality. He knows our feelings from the gay to the poignant. He did not marry, but devoted his life to his invalid sister, Mary, who also had literary talent. They lived together in London and enjoyed a wide circle of friends.

CHAPTER IX

PROSE OF THE ROMANTIC PERIOD

WITH the growth of the towns and the gradual industrializing of vast districts an increasing proportion of the population lost all touch with the life of the soil. This resulted in a conscious seeking after what had been lost; the spirit of the countryside and of nature was eagerly sought for in literature. The high tide of this era produced remarkable prose and the new forces released were carried on into the next generations, known, not very appropriately, as the Victorian age. We get some of the finest prose of those years in Shelley's *Defence of Poetry* and his lovely and distinguished letters, which have some characteristics of his verse—the smooth, swift, easy, action of an Arab racer. Wordsworth also wrote some wise, calm pages on the Lake country, on poetic philosophy, and other themes. Southey is a master of graceful prose, though not conspicuously romantic. The letters of Byron are very well worth reading for their force, wit and freedom. An epoch which included, besides these, De Quincey, Borrow, Hazlitt, Lamb, Peacock, Hunt and Scott's Waverley Novels is admittedly one to astonish. Prose was altered, deepened and enlarged.

We must begin with the widest spread of these influences, the Scott of that immense romantic canvas, the Scottish and medieval novels. The poets (including himself) have opened door and window to the "wind on the heath," and the mysterious voices "from behind the hill." No one did more than Scott, or so much, to push that door and window wide open through the popular medium of straight narrative which appealed equally to high and low. The stage coaches in and about the 1820s carried copies of each new Waverley Novel to all parts of the country, and they were translated for European readers. It was as if people were parched for this new kind of entertainment, unsatisfied by the efforts of Horace Walpole, Mrs. Radcliffe, "Monk" Lewis and other mystifiers of the skull and cross-bones school with their ghosts, clank-ing chains and cruder effects. Here was a larger mind and firmer hand at work, a true "wizard of the North," at first anonymous and unidentified. These big, roving and crowded tales, moreover, had humour and character. Story after story poured (often more than one a year) from the unknown writer. Who could he be? When would his genius stop? Everyone, from royalty to the market-woman in Paris, from wise critics to seamstresses, doted on "the Scotch novels." Southerners toured the road over the Border for a glimpse of the Grampians and the haunts of Rob Roy, or to the Solway Firth to see if there were another Meg Merrilees. "See Scotland first" would have been the watchword of the railways, had there been railways.

Romance lies in the remote and dimly known. Scotland with its wild landscape, history and clansmen was abundantly romantic to the public of Scott's day.

Author of "Waverley"

The stories were a blast of crisp, fresh air which was appreciated equally in Britain, Germany, America and Italy. Scott's wide reading in history and ballads, and his antiquarian research, enabled him to create his background effortlessly and to concentrate on the lively relation of his story with a genial and sympathetic humanity. He understood the racial characteristics of the Scots and the English, holding the balances well.

Always in his work, through the pleasant mists of romance or hearsay, the facts of history marched—hard and indisputable, joined on to the real business of human life, like solid telegraph poles stretching through a mountain mist. He found the novel (despite the fact that one Clara Reeve sold ten thousand copies of a thriller on the day of publication) in poor repute, and he left it a respectable institution. That was done by his wide knowledge of all sorts of men and women (he was a lawyer, county sheriff, a lover of the countryside and a

141

clubbable townsman); by his common sense (of which he had a full share); and by his knowledge of great literature (he wrote lives and criticisms of the poets and novelists). Add his phenomenal industry and fertility, and the marvel becomes explicable. From the moment when *Waverley*, his first work (rescued from a drawer where it had long reposed) appeared in 1814, fiction came to be divided into those novels that were by Scott and those that were not. No other author, unless perhaps Dickens, has ever won so much of the public's time and revenue as he. And though he never exploits self (the pronoun "I" occurs only in his gossipy, leisurely prefaces), everyone felt the personality of a big, robust, and sane mind in every page. People then did not notice, as we do, that his heroes and heroines were often stiff as shop-window models; readers filled their lungs with northern air, their mind's eye with the pageantry of other times, and they recognized the truth of his portraiture of people like Dandie Dinmont, Fairservice, Dominie Sampson, the Laird of Ellangowan, Meg Merrilees, Old Roebuck, Bailie Nicol Jarvie, Rob Roy, Flora McIvor, Edie Ochiltree, Di Vernon, Dugald Dalgetty, Peter Peebles, and at least two or three hundred more real folk.

Sir Walter's Popularity

It is a blunder to suppose that no one now reads Scott. His centenary brought fine, full-length studies from the late Lord Tweedsmuir (John Buchan) and Dame Una Pope-Hennessy, and tributes from J. B. Priestley and the late Sir Hugh Walpole. He had been a life-long arm-chair favourite of Hazlitt (whose prejudices were conquered), Lord Macaulay, J. A. Froude, Andrew Lang, George Saintsbury, Augustine Birrell and other sound judges of life and reading. Today we can avoid his mistakes; but we are unlikely to produce a *Guy Mannering, Heart of Midlothian, Old Mortality, Rob Roy*, or *The Antiquary*—the novels here recommended to a beginner— human pictures of a sweep which inspired to emulation such men as Alexandre Dumas in France, Jokai in Hungary, Sienkiewicz in Poland—even Victor Hugo, Théophile

Gautier, Leo Tolstoy and Honoré de Balzac thought that Jeanie and Effie Deans and Diana Vernon were great imagined women, and that Scott was the modern Homer. Scott's comic characters differ from those of Dickens and some other novelists in this: they have at the core of them a solid, human dignity. His poor men and women stand firmly on their own feet, and speak up for themselves. They have equality of opportunity, as have Shakespeare's men and women, and even Fielding's. That is because Scott, in life, met people of all sorts on level, manly terms. Cardinal Newman professed a devotion to him; Tennyson called him "gentleman—heart, blood, and bone." Most men have greeted the worth in him and his work; Goethe said: "All is great— material effect, characters, and execution." The dash and range, the bustle and mixing of all types and classes, the tireless invention, the daylight sanity over everything, with the landscape, atone for occasional clumsiness or loose ends.

Hazlitt and Others

A more prosaic Scotland, in which the first looms and engines are heard, comes into the canvas of John Galt (1779-1839) in his *Annals of the Parish*. Scott, besides being royally generous in his verdict on Jane Austen and lesser writers, admired the Irish stories of Maria Edgeworth (1767-1849); and *Castle Rackrent* is only one of her many lively, now old-fashioned pictures. On the other hand, Mary Mitford (1787-1855) who sketched Berkshire life in *Our Village* remains fresh. She aimed at tragic drama, and was acted; but these efforts are now forgotten.

The Cromarty stonemason, Hugh Miller (1802-1856), is a model of "the pursuit of knowledge under difficulties." Self-educated, he won creditable fame as editor, and was author of *Old Red Sandstone* and *My Schools and Schoolmasters*, which had quiet realist charm. This highly strung man died by his own hand.

What Scott was in creative tale-telling, William Hazlitt (1778-1830) was in criticism and the roving combative essay. Steadily his star has mounted, from the time when his superficial contemporaries dismissed him as paradoxical, quarrelsome or a radical. Hazlitt, too, like "that rogue Sir Walter" (as he affectionately called Scott) was rich in reading and experience, saturated with literature but still more with life, and with the same vehement interest in the passing show. If he has not Lamb's subtle flavour and ability to distil a dreamy prose idyll, he is more solid and athletic and various, and he has left us (in *Winterslow, The Round Table, The Plain Speaker* and in his many volumes of criticism) golden essays in appreciation; warm, generous, frank, and acute. He and Lamb need not be compared, being dissimilars; but they go gallantly together.

Hazlitt can securely be put into any young man's hands for his salty knowledge of life and affairs, and his "depth of taste," to use the words of John Keats, who added: "If I am damned, let it be by Hazlitt." He is a shrewd guide, despite periodical tantrums, and pounces upon the very heart of an author, a poem, a book, or a play. And he was as vigorous and

WILLIAM HAZLITT

Painter, theologian, dramatic critic and essayist, Hazlitt's virtue as a writer was to be able to get to the heart of any matter and to express himself in lively, unpedantic and varied prose. "We can none of us write like Hazlitt," said Stevenson in later years.

stirring when he describes *The Fight, The Fives Players, Going a Journey, New Books* (or old), first nights at the theatre, editors, scholars, lords, politicians, actors, city men, famous poets he met and knew, and hundreds of topics. He has a sharp, idiomatic, familiar style; and a mind that was challenged by every incident. His prose does not charm or haunt us as does that of Lamb or De Quincey. Nearly everything about him is good except his temper; he was crossed in love twice, and in political idealism often; yet how readable and infectiously enthusiastic he can be, when his "hurry of the spirit" greets some favourite company, masterpieces, or landscape.

Hazlitt began in youth as a painter (and tells us all about this, as about everything else personal), and tramped England and the Louvre to see the Old Masters. He knew countless plays and romances almost verbatim, with glow and gusto. Still, writing came with difficulty. With his characteristic emphasis he says: "I could not write a line. I was brutish, inarticulate. ... To be able to convey the slightest conception of my meaning was the height of an almost hopeless ambition." Another master of animated moving prose (not unlike Hazlitt in some ways), J. A. Froude, also had a struggle to acquire the style which he, too, succeeded in making famous. He wrote in the days of his apprenticeship: "Oh! how I wish I could write. I try sometimes, for I seem to feel myself overflowing with thoughts, and I cry out to be relieved of them. But it is so stiff and miserable when I get anything done. What seemed so clear and liquid comes out so thick, stupid, and frost-bitten that I myself, who put the idea there, can hardly find it for shame if I go to look for it a few days after." To any reader aspiring to write, one would say: "These things are written for our instruction—and encouragement." If two such masters were once baffled and self-despising amateurs, why despair? A Macaulay, apparently born with his style full grown, writing at twenty-three the famous Milton essay, and hardly improving on it afterwards, is very exceptional.

The pains of forming a style seem to have been spared for Leigh Hunt (already discussed as poet). He is of lighter calibre, but always sweet and agreeable. All his essays show an eagerness to pass on to others his delight in nature, the poets, home, streets and shops, people and flowers and the small compensations and small change of life. "Everybody happy?" seems his greeting as he enters the room; "if not, why not? Let me catalogue your blessings and pleasures for you." He asks to be accounted "one who loved his fellow-men," and he expressed it in pleasant and healthy chit-chat, bright as a country brook. Hunt is one of the most amiable miscellanists we have, and set the fashion of the modern "middle" for the popular taste, on anything from *Pleasures of the Imagination* to *Thieves, Ancient and Modern*, from Chaucer to cheerfulness. Perhaps, after all, the Hunt philosophy is profounder and truer to the conditions of our existence than many graver writers and systems. Life largely consists of trifles and our reaction toward them; and the readiness to be kind and pleased may be more to the point than many of the rarer difficult virtues.

Our Greatest Essayist

Charles Lamb (1775-1834) had all this— and much else—in him. He was more complex, subtle and deep than most of the clever men and mixed with very ordinary neighbours who came for cards, grog, and supper to his and his sister's lodgings. He was not only an essayist, poet and critic— he was a personality; and his artful, wandering essays are peeps into his life, mind, and humour. In him, and in De Quincey and Hazlitt, prose broke new intimate ground: their talk of self was deliberate, part of a compelling and shaping art. They could put themselves on paper, sure of interesting us. Many previous essayists and even autobiographers (except Goldsmith) were gay and witty, but were playing at being human. Lamb's carefully matured talk with the pen (in his unique letters, too) comes straight from the depths of his mind, and as Hazlitt finely said, "his jests scald like tears." His domestic tragedy (a sister who, in madness, had killed their mother while he was barely of age) deepened and

LAMB'S HANDWRITING

*In this letter to a friend Lamb touches on his and Mary's reading, gives Hazlitt's address
and extends an invitation. Lamb's handwriting is careless, and appears to be somewha
lacking in character. It gives little indication of a great personality.*

sobered him. His humour was no surface play, but the flower plucked from the nettle of peril and awe. "He comes swaying, a grave and sensitive youth, out of a great darkness," as J. B. Priestley says. He had to watch and tend Mary always. "To live such a life is to walk the world without a skin. Compared with this, the troubles of a roaring Thomas Carlyle, who could contemptuously dismiss the 'rickety tomfool,' were mere thistledown."

His writing was at once a disguise and a revelation. His whims mask an exquisite sanity, a balance of many and dangerous forces. He clung to whatever was homely, reassuring, friendly and bright—especially the bustle of London streets, the lights and faces around him, anything known and familiar. Here is his heart talking:

"Sun, and sky, and breeze, and solitary walks, and summer holidays, and the greenness of fields, and the delicious juices of meats and fishes, and society, and the cheerful glass, and candlelight, and fireside conversations, and innocent vanities, and jests, and *irony itself*—do these things go out with life?"

At first he imitated the old seventeenth-century writers, Fuller, Burton, or Browne; he steeped himself in the Elizabethan comedy and tragedy. The resulting vintage was his very own; there is hardly a grace of style which he has not shown.

How quietly and magically is the past evoked in the nostalgic *Mackery End, Hertfordshire* or the gentle melancholy of lonely living in *Dream Children*, or the dream of bereavement and after-life in *The Child Angel*. The same tones are revealed in poems like that *On an Infant dying as soon as born*, or *On an Infant sleeping*, but his humorous verse, such as the *Farewell to Tobacco*, has the tart flavour of quince. Few men have plumbed Shakespeare in spirit as he did; he saw the depth in the wry jests of the Fools, and in real life he brought this intuition to bear to such purpose that solemn, logical, literal people—such as Carlyle—found him a puzzle. Most of his judgments anticipated the best in our own day. There is not a grain in him of the formal nonsense of the schools, nor is there a division between heart and head.

Thomas De Quincey

Thomas De Quincey (1785-1859), a member of the Lambs' circle, is another sort of dreamer, and, as prose master, an astonishing virtuoso. He is great only in patches, but there he is not surpassed and may never be surpassed. Though son of a Manchester merchant, he was a sort of changeling and truant. He ran away from Manchester Grammar School, slept out in the Welsh hills, was recaptured and sent to Eton (all this he tells in his wandering, charming autobiography) and later went to Oxford, where already he began the opium habit to dull his stomach pains. Then he settled at Grasmere to be near his revered prophet Wordsworth, his admired Coleridge, and the boisterous Professor Wilson ("Christo-

pher North"). He drew them all in his indiscreet *Reminiscences of Lake Society. Blackwood's Magazine* found him a treasure, but a worry; for he was always behindhand with his contributions—a born procrastinator. His stormy or pathetic passages may be called fantasias, ecstasies or dreams; but unluckily they are embedded in garrulous, facetious, or unimportant (though very proficiently written) matter. It is by *The Confessions of an English Opium Eater* that his melodious style is best known; but there is also much the same indefinite power and romantic reverberation in *The Spanish Military Nun, The Flight of the Kalmuck Tartars*, the solemn rhapsody on *The Afflictions of Childhood*, the exciting evocation of speed in *The English Mail Coach* with its climax on "the passion of sudden death" in the fatal collision with the pair of lovers in their gig, the superb harmonies and eloquence of *Joan of Arc* and *Dream-Fugue*. Baudelaire, a "decadent" in France, translated De Quincey and the great American short-story writer, Poe; indeed *Levana and Our Ladies of Sorrow* beats Poe on his own ground of mystery plus passion.

Art of Murder

Phantasmagoric is the word for De Quincey's most typical pages; you overhear, in this supple accomplished prose, the mysterious solemnity of certain emotions. Suddenly, the smooth narrative parts asunder, arch opens beyond arch, the vision of something for ever flying, for ever escaping, is revealed; and time stands still. His rhythm approaches music—various and indeterminate, close to the infinite of pure feeling. G. K. Chesterton spoke of his "wonderful vistas and perspectives of prose, which permit one to call him the first and most powerful of the decadents; those sentences that lengthen out like nightmare corridors, or rise higher and higher like eastern pagodas"; and there is sinister pleasantry in *Murder Considered as One of the Fine Arts*. Opium in his case, as in Coleridge's and Francis Thompson's, seemed favourable to single hours of miraculous exaltation of mood, but fatal to the completion of great artistic *wholes*

They gave us unfinished symphonies which tantalize us with a sense of loss. However, not everyone likes magicians and their spells. The reader is warned that he will not carry away from De Quincey much that is solid—any more than from Shelley.

William Cobbett (1763-1835), born at Farnham, farmer, soldier, agitator, had a gift of sappy, idiomatic English. His *Rural Rides* are deservedly famous; they form a breezy log of the shires as they appeared to an expert farmer's eye. And he wrote much colloquial prose on household economy and advice to young men. "Racy of the soil"—a phrase often used inapplicably— is strictly true of this shrewd and candid character. He derives from the Romantic spirit really—with his rural republicanism his English and patriotic democracy, his unconventional outspokenness. "Peter Porcupine" was his self-chosen and reveal ing title.

George Borrow (1803-1881) was born in Norfolk, but had Celtic blood. He was a queer original, an eccentric nomad who mixed with gipsies, distributed Bibles while the Romanys squinted with ridicule, and described the fisticuffs of the Flaming Tinman. He had a genius for wild and casual friendship, although the veracity of his anecdotes is suspect. A first-class linguist, he began by translating Swedish, Danish, Dutch and German poetry for the magazines. His best-known works are *Lavengro* and *The Bible in Spain*, the former being an autobiography enlarged by a free use of imagination, and the latter, an account of his wanderings which caught the public's fancy and brought him fame.

THOMAS DE QUINCEY

A writer of great originality, Thomas De Quincey's outstanding work is his fantastic and revealing autobiography, the "Confessions of an English Opium Eater."

Test Yourself

1. Scott was considered the outstanding novelist of his time in England and Europe. Write a short essay giving the reasons for his popularity and his hold on every type of reader.
2. Hazlitt and Lamb were two outstanding essayists of the Romantic Revival. Write a brief account of the differences in their style and approach to subjects.
3. For what work is Thomas De Quincey best known?
4. Name the novelist who, after living with the Romanys, wrote novels about them.

Answers will be found at the end of the book.

EVERY INCH A POET

To the Victorian poet laureate, Alfred Tennyson, fell the heritage of the Romantic Revival. His poetry is richly varied in style and subject and full of word pictures either romantic in feeling or accurately drawn from nature. He is best known for "The Idylls of the King."

CHAPTER X

VICTORIAN POETRY

VICTORIAN literature possessed both variety and virility, mirroring the multitude of ideas and social trends in this astonishingly distinguished time—from 1820 to 1900. There was no longer one powerful tide of public interest and emotion, but several clashing currents, such as religion, the growth of science, social change, the advance of popular education: when these waters met, the resulting sea was full of voices. Science, in particular, assumed a great importance; doubt and division of mind coincided with great industrial inventions; the immense growth in population and extremes of wealth and poverty resulted in political unrest on the one hand and attempts to justify existing circumstances on the other.

It was not at all certain when Queen Victoria came to the throne in 1837 that there would be a throne at all in a few years. Reform Bills (aimed at broadening an electoral system under which the great majority had no vote), the Chartist Movement (revolving round a monster petition calling for Parliamentary reforms), quarrels between the new industrial magnates and the old land-owning class, the machinery-breaking Luddites (who sought to oppose the introduction of new inventions), and intense religious secularism, all kept the nation in ferment behind its growing capital and resources.

Age of Grim Individualism

Yet "the hungry 'forties" were as hungry for knowledge as for bread. Men who could not read had the news-sheets, pamphlets and books read to them. Other towns besides London published literature —Norwich, Bristol, Newcastle, Halifax; colporteurs trudged the northern moors and manufacturing towns with pack-mules carrying cheap reprints. Popular self-educators became a vogue. Though it was still possible for the fortunate to talk of "the lower orders," "the deserving poor," "paupers," "females," and "hands," ine-

qu,

qualities were mitigated somewhat by organized charities, "ragged schools"—and the chance for a pushful artisan to "get on," and become a small master, with the toil of his and his neighbours' children. A grim individualist opportunism ran side by side with rebellious agitation. The Blanketeers' marches (drawn in Mark Rutherford's *The Revolution in Tanner's Lane*), fierce unemployed demonstrations, are one side of this scrimmage for money and power. The other side concerns itself with more comfort for a working minority, and real wealth and leisure for ground-rent owners and big manufacturers who gave us our Black Countries together with some better things.

More literate people, some with leisure and culture, dictated a modified literature. Not that the great Victorians echoed the crowd. Most of them either denounced the abuses of the time or its Philistines. Much Victorian literature is the literature of protest; the rest is the deliberate praise of something better by contrast. It struck out on a line of its own. It is vital to remember this.

New Questions—New Paths

Though the prophets and priests of great vision had ceased—Wordsworth, Shelley, Byron — the coming men — Tennyson, Browning, Carlyle, Ruskin, Arnold—had viewpoints quite of their own. The lovely, pictorial influence of Keats was apparent in the early verse of Tennyson; but Tennyson soon grew out of it, as Browning said farewell to Shelley quite early. They and others struck unexpected waters out of the rock and poured new rivers of poetry over the world. Literature was coloured by the theological, social, scientific and political questions disturbing England. It aimed at solutions—or at steadying formulae; either faith or resignation, either wisdom or escape. It played with a vast variety of subjects. Tennyson, for instance, seems not one sort of poet, but two or three (pictorial, or lyric, or humorous, or speculative); and all of them good, and Browning did remarkable things in three or four styles.

Literati studied and brought to great excellence the idyll, the song, the dramatic monologue, the character study, and the short poem on classic subjects with a reference to modern life. The short lyric was never written so much or so well since the days of Queen Elizabeth. Especially it went back through many poets to recapture the days of legend, chivalry, history, other men and times. The workmanship was better than at any previous time, if sometimes at the cost of sweep of inspiration or wild music like Shelley's *Prometheus* or *Hellas.* The Victorian age continued the previous one by extending the imagination (which Wordsworth, Byron and Shelley had directed on nature and history) to exploring the complexities of society, questing moods, and varied human individualities. Robert Browning was thus a novelist in verse, and Alfred, Lord Tennyson was so occasionally. Thomas Carlyle wrote novelistic character-pieces under the name of history. Even Lord Macaulay was delighted that his instalments of history beat the novels of the season, and his fellow historians, J. A. Froude and J. R. Green, carried the vivid, intimate method a step further, continuing the same technique of dramatizing detail and the familiar. This same humanism in the air accounts for the immense popular vogue of Dickens, Thackeray, Trollope, George Eliot, Charles Reade, and the Brontë sisters. Their work mirrored society.

Great Victorians

More than that, the later nineteenth century believed in itself and in its scientific and other knowledge, but it is a shaky and chastened laugh that comes from the modern critic. If we possess churchmen like Cardinal Newman, Richard Church, and Edward Pusey; scientists as big as Charles Darwin and T. H. Huxley; poets as massive and versatile as Alfred Tennyson and Robert Browning; novelists like Charles Dickens and W. M. Thackeray; prose men as capable as John Ruskin, Froude and Walter Pater—why, let us

have their names. These men felt that they had a clearer concept of creation and destiny than any preceding age, thanks to the advance of scientific theory; and so, despite much that was perplexing, they could stride out confidently. They were all for change, yet against breach or revolution. They believed in progress as something consonant with God's method.

This, then, is the celebrated "Victorian compromise"; it merely means a tendency (with exceptions). The age was, like ours, inhabited by many minds. There can be no doubt that our own outlook today—probing, even suspicious—owes much to the courage with which the so-called Victorians pioneered. Yet at first they did not know what to make of their geniuses. A detailed literary survey of 1887 actually gives nine lines to Browning, among some nonentities, and two thousand to Tennyson! Another accords ten pages to Thackeray, and not a line to Dickens. Arnold is not mentioned in either.

Tennyson's Early Life

Alfred Tennyson (1809-1892) was third son of the rector of secluded Somersby in the Lincolnshire Wolds, who himself prepared his sons, Frederick, Charles and Alfred for Cambridge. All three made ventures in poetry, and even published. Frederick's had vigour, Charles's many sonnets are still read and enjoyed; it is the youngest's work which posterity enjoys. The family were dark and gipsy-like in appearance, and were long remembered in the district. The rector must have been remarkable: the walls of his study, said gossip, were covered "wi' 'eathen gods and goddesses wi'out cloas."

At nineteen, Alfred followed his brothers to Cambridge, and later there joined "the Apostles," so named because there were twelve of them, including his closest friend, Arthur Hallam, "the master bowman of the group." Two years more, and the Somersby home was broken up by death, and Tennyson's outlook was so poor that for ten years his engagement to Emily Sellwood was broken off: then the success of *In Memoriam* made it possible for them to marry; and at forty-one he was made

Poet Laureate, borrowing for the event the court dress of Samuel Rogers which Wordsworth had previously worn for a like occasion. His 1842 volume was a marked advance on the work of 1830-1832; for here, in *Ulysses*, he combined his early melody with the heroic spirit, and *Locksley Hall* had both that and a sense of landscape new in English literature.

Our Best Landscapist

"The spirit of *place*"—that is his unique contribution. He was more English, in a regional, recognizable sense, than any other poet whatever. His "long gray fields at night," his "rank wood-walks drenched with dew," his cloudy wolds, low sandy shores, marshes and dikes, compose a landscape such as everyone sees when walking or riding in England. The weather is utterly English weather. His poetry is saturated with the lights, aspects, and little things of the three or four countrysides that were in his blood. For exactitude of tone and touch in these things, no other poet has come anywhere near him Whatever his limitations, that particular distinction is his for ever.

Tennyson, who was an "instinctive," not an "intellectual," touched contemporary life at more points than anyone else: for his friend and peer, Browning, had a roving commission through time and space. Tennyson, in faultless verse, precipitated newly accepted ways of thought; Browning arduously experimented, and created an audience to like his outlook and his different verbal music. Tennyson owed much to the Latin poet Virgil, but a debt to Virgil is like a debt to Nature. An island, English Virgil no doubt, without the scope of the Roman—though J. R. Green, the historian, called Virgil "the Tennyson of the old world," while T. H. Huxley and the astronomer, Lockyer, said Tennyson alone among writers understood the drift of science. Tennyson called Virgil a "lord of language": certainly he was one himself. The English are wedded to old gardens, stately lawns, lonely granges, meres, glimpses of plantation and downland, cornfields rippled by wind and shadow, glebe, hall and park. To all this side of the English soul Tennyson is the Pied Piper: he is the voice and very mirror of our characteristic landscapes and their human associations. He brooded on them till "I grow incorporate into thee." A. C. Bradley, the Shakespearian scholar, says: "If a man who had derived great happiness from observing nature were condemned to lose all poets but one, Tennyson's is the poetry he would wish to keep." That is, he is our best landscapist—and one does not forget the early Milton, nor Collins's *Evening*, nor Wordsworth's prospects, nor Keats's vignettes of southern dells and temple-crowned mountains, nor Shelley's storms and sun in the Apennines. Tennyson alone gives us these perfections in single poems, single stanzas, often in single lines or even in evocative phrases.

Voice of His Age

"No mind that is free, and above fashion," says G. K. Chesterton, "can feel anything but contempt for efforts to discredit his greatness." He was not one poet but four, each of them very good: the poet of romance and landscape; of faith and science and their interaction; of rich character and comedy in the dialect pieces; and of patriotism and statesmanship. Conventional intruders into criticism have tried to be amusing about a man who believed in the reconciliation of religion and knowledge, in moderation, the British race, responsibility and empire, the Fleet and Forces, the Crown and free Parliament, the gentleman, woman's modesty, the peasant, a well-kept countryside, the country house, the immortality of the soul, the classics and style. They confuse these things with wax fruits and the antimacassar. It puzzles conventionalists when they come across a poet who has a sense of morality, duty and proportion—who does not drink, drug, steal anyone's wife, or live disreputably. He does not conform to their naïve specifications. Others are reduced to picking on weak lines, and console their inferiority with these.

When all is said, what a heritage of strength is left. Anyone deeply read in Tennyson can remember a host of such lines as the following:

Wet sands marbled with moon and
cloud

When the long dun wolds are ribb'd
with snow.

The happy birds that change their sky.

By ashen roots the violets blow.

Four gray walls and four gray towers.

Bright Phosphor fresher for the night.

The quarry trenched along the hill
And haunted by the wrangling daw.

Far as the wild swan sings, to where
the sky dips down to sea and sands.

Gray old grange, or lonely fold,
Or low morass and whispering reed,
Or simple stile from mead to mead
Or sheepwalk up the windy wold.

The plunging seas draw backward from
the land
Their moon-led waters white.

There all in spaces rosy-bright
Large Hesper glittered on her tears;
And, deep'ning through the silent
spheres,
Heaven over heaven rose the night.

There are thousands of such perfect precise
pictures in his work. And there are other
evocative lines like:

Tears from the depths of some divine
despair.

Lay a great water and the moon was
full.

God made Himself an awful rose of
dawn.

That friend of mine who lives with
God.

But he was noble, too, in exquisitely completed wholes, in such bewitching colour

and reverie as *Œnone, The Lotus Eaters,
Mariana in the South, Memory*, and so on.
These carry further the secret of Keats, of
conveying a magically clear pictorial effect.
All his life he was a keen, sympathetic
observer of nature, down to insects, larvae,
and moss. And behind his amazingly sharp
senses and matchless dream-faculty, he felt
the philosophic wonder inscribed on his
statue outside Lincoln Cathedral:

Little flower, I pluck you out of the
crannies,
Root and all, and all in all . . .
But if I could understand what you
are,
Root and all, and all in all,
I should know what God and man is.

His critics may be disconcerted to know
that in America the anarchic poet-philo-
sopher, Walt Whitman, called him "Boss of
us all"; Edgar Allan Poe lectured on him
as the greatest modern poet; Ralph Waldo
Emerson and Carlyle hailed his new subtle,
ringing music.   While many poets are
admired when we most agree with them,
his *The Lady of Shalott* is of unimpeachable
beauty, whether we believe in it or not!
Such a work should be preserved, like the
New Forest or the Trossachs, on aesthetic
grounds alone: "a thing of beauty is a
joy for ever." The words he uses are the
sole possible ones in their only possible
place. A misquotation of him is fatal: all
is branded with his seal, for he let nothing
imperfect leave him. A mass of his dis-
carded poetry exists, which is yet beautiful.

He had also a fine understanding of
humanity. His northern countrymen are
conceived with as much breadth of sympathy and richness of humour as those of
Chaucer and Burns. "Doän't thou marry
for munny, but goä wheer munny is!"
says his northern farmer, new style.
Another, dying, wonders "what God
A'mighty's a-doin', taking me: and Squire,
he will be mad." This is the yeoman who
boasts that he "stubbed Thornaby waste."
There is also *Owd Roä, The Entail, The
Spinster's Sweethearts* and *The Northern
Cobbler*. These, too, from the most fastidious of poets, the most subtly and sensi-

tively organized of the Victorian romantics!

A note of passionate humanity is in him, as in Browning, but more wistful and yearning; it makes vivid and intimate his handling of Greek myth—*Ulysses, Tithonus, Tiresias* and *Œnone*, and this has been the cause of the comfort he has brought to sorrow. None of his generation has such a human attitude to death. Shelley longed for the infinite; to Wordsworth death is the return to the Spirit that dwells in nature; to Browning it is the "one fight more, the best and the last"; to Arnold it is to be met with resignation. But to Tennyson it was this:

> O that 'twere possible,
> After long grief and pain,
> To find the arms of my true love
> Round me once again.
>
> Ah Christ! that it were possible
> For one short hour to see
> The souls we loved, that they might tell us
> What and where they be.
>
> Ah, sad and strange as on dark summer dawns
> The earliest pipe of half-awaken'd birds
> To dying ears, when unto dying eyes
> The casement slowly grows a glimmering square.

Such words, cried suddenly in the open air (says Oliver Elton) "give the actual fugitive essence of the south of England with the perfumed exhalations of its earth and its plaintive or happy melancholy." There are tracts of Lincolnshire fen and wold and sands, or downland in Sussex and Hampshire, where, in spring or autumn, you may feel the elusive soul of his typical poems.

Doubt and Faith

Arnold Bennett in *Clayhanger* depicts the Orgreaves, a typically intelligent provincial family in the 'forties, discovering *In Memoriam* with a shock of joy in evening readings. It was a cardinal document of that period, with its ardent curiosity, its hope grappling with doubt, its rare sensitiveness to all the phenomena of nature and human sorrow, its variation of key and consummate execution, and its perfectly cut stones from a cunning lapidary. Its allusions to evolution preceded Darwin's *Origin of Species* by nine years. Until his death at a great age Tennyson retained his powers; he was a sage, quoted in Parliament, pulpit, Press and novel. When very old he wrote the wonderful lyrics:

> Once more the Heavenly Power
> Makes all things new,

and

> When the dumb hour, clothed in black,
> Brings the dreams about my bed,

and the swan-song *Crossing the Bar*. He was waiting, "A spirit nearing the dark portal," for "the silent Opener of the Gate." What will live of Tennyson are minute flashing pictures of park and wold and weald, a plaintive corner of garden landscape, with kiosk and sun-dial, seashore and marsh, a woodland brook—seen through an enchanted crystal; the words playing the same tune on us as the scene might have done itself.

Robert Browning

This art rather spoilt most readers at first for the audacious innovations of Robert Browning (1812-1889), the Danton of poetry. He was reared, like Macaulay, in a bookish and well-to-do home at Clapham. The elder Browning was a clerk in the Bank of England, and knew not only the ancient and modern classics but divined what was in his son, to whom public schools and universities were then closed because the Brownings were dissenters. The fact may have strengthened his originality of mind. Certainly Browning senior (like Milton the elder) devoted the youth to letters as a calling, and used his savings to that end. For these years he had a private tutor, attended lectures at the University of London, visited Russia and Italy, and gathered immense worldly and aesthetic knowledge. At twenty-one, he published

ROBERT BROWNING

Among the Victorian poets Browning alone is the equal of Tennyson. His verse is rugged, lively and full of dramatic flashes. Beyond other English poets he is interested in the psychology of individual men and women, and is specially successful with the type of poem which is a monologue intended to display a character.

Pauline—a Fragment of a Confession. Though he is under the dominion of Shelley, he has his creed already—that there is nothing of first importance in life except the growth of the soul. At twenty-three he had written the remarkable *Paracelsus*, with this youthful majestic comment:

What fairer seal
Shall I require to my authentic mission
Than this fierce energy? this instant
  striving
Because its nature is to strive?
        Be sure that God
Ne'er dooms to waste the strength he
  deigns impart.

Be sure they sleep not whom God
  needs:
        I go to prove my soul!
I see my way as birds their trackless
  way,
I shall arrive! What time, what circuit
  first
I ask not: but unless God send his hail
Or blinding fireballs, sleet or stifling
  snow,
In some time, His good time, I shall
  arrive,
He guides me and the birds. In his
  good time.

That is like something from the Greeks.

Actually it was from a wonderful boy. In 1846 he married the poetess Elizabeth Barrett. She was an invalid and he practically carried her from Wimpole Street to the church in Euston Road, without the knowledge of her relatives. The two went to Italy, where a son was born, and where they revelled in the historic glories of Florence and other cities. "Open my heart and you will see, graved inside it, 'Italy.'" On Elizabeth's death he came back to England, but later returned to the Venetian palace of his son, and died there.

Realist, Not Optimist

The time is long past when knowledgeable people called Browning "difficult" or "optimist." He is neither. He can be blunt, sudden, surprising. As for the other charge, no man explored further into the murky recesses of fraud, scamp, conspirator or worldling, or had a firmer understanding of the basenesses as well as the altitudes of human character. In one of his poetic plays there passes by, at a crucial moment of evil, a little weaver-girl, Pippa. In terrific contrast to the guilty lovers, she is made to sing in their hearing her little impulsive song of sunny holiday, "God's in His heaven." This innocent ditty precipitates one crisis after another in the story. Believe it or not, ignorance has torn this little wild bird-note from *her*, and fastened it on the dramatist as *his* view of the universe! What would become of Shakespeare or Dickens if such an ineptitude were applied to them? With a pitying smile for such aberrations, we pass to the almost Shakespearian range of people Browning dramatized from within like a great novelist of the Human Comedy in verse. Literary taste, like running water, clears itself as it advances. It now rejoices in Browning's word music—its counterpoint, its harmonies, its discords resolved and unresolved, its dazzling changes of pitch: he is, what he called a cathedral organ, "a huge house of sounds." Where Tennyson brooded in delicious dusks, and enlarged the sensuous and exotic range of lyric, Browning's less leisurely and more trenchant brain ranged for new effects. Read the dazzling *Waring* to see what incredibly graphic impressionism can do

to express the very soul of Adventure.

Rodin, the great French sculptor, often left a lovely carved figure, at the base, "in the rough," joined on to the original stone: Browning sometimes chooses to do the same. He had a different end in view from most poets, and did things not possible in any other style. By all means start with the simple pieces—the Cavalier Songs, *The Pied Piper*, *The Patriot*, and *How they brought the good news to Aix*; but these are no more than *apéritifs* before the feast. Every poem of his was done in a special, deliberately chosen form and tone. He rarely repeated a style.

No one—not even Browning, before it or after it—ever wrote such realism of love as *A Lover's Quarrel* and *A Serenade at the Villa*; nor again anything quite like *The Heretic's Tragedy*, beginning with "John, Master of the Temple of God," with its weird choruses and creepy prose directions; nor such sharp wood-cuts as there are in *By the Fireside*; nor such odd exultation as in *A Grammarian's Funeral*. He is good to read in despondent hours; because tonic virtue goes out of him and we are infected by his leonine energy. The sight of so much activity, courage and masculinity makes for health in us. When we grasp his clue explicitly in *Childe Roland*, with its magnificent climax of fortitude in a forlorn hope, we may feel we can never be cowards again. Landor said of him: "Since Chaucer was alive and hale, no man has walked along our road with step so active, or with tongue so varied in discourse." People of low vitality and high pedantry-index shrink from this throbbing contact; but they are just the people who most need his battery cure.

Drama of the Mind

Browning did not set up for a thinker, teacher or systematic philosopher—despite the Browning Societies. He is, instead, the dramatist, the listener-in to others as they excuse or explain themselves; he is an entrepreneur who gives them a stage, a prompter who sets them off confessing or justifying. It is their processes and emotions that we hear; not results or formulae. Right through the twenty thousand lines of

CHARACTERISTIC VICTORIAN

Once a school inspector, Matthew Arnold developed into a very thoughtful poet whose manner is calm and temperate and akin to the classicists rather than the romanticists. He was outstanding as a critic of literature and sought to establish in England a body similar to the Académie française through which, he hoped, a higher standard of literature and thought might be maintained. Among his poems are "The Scholar Gipsy" and "Thyrsis."

the crime epic, *The Ring and the Book*, he sets others talking, and we hear their heart's dialogue while he, off-stage, manages the lighting. And so nearly everywhere: he does not give us final judgment crystallized, but the very activity of thinking, the flux of man's passions at work inside. As poet, spectator, and interpreter, it was not for him to judge and define life, but to portray it—to dramatize human souls in all their variations.

"Then he is not so unlike Shakespeare Dickens, Chaucer, and Tennyson, after all?" Exactly. The "views of existence" which students used to cull from his poetry were not his, speaking as Browning: they were in the character. He tells us this in *Shop*. People, he there says, complain that Shakespeare does not walk upstage and disclose himself, his private creed and views. If he had done so, says Browning, "The less Shakespeare he." That was Browning, for once in person, asking to be left alone by fussy imputers of this or that belief in him. Again, he sketches a poignant situation, and ends thus:

> Here, Robert Browning, you writer of plays,
> Is a subject made to your hand.

In *At the Mermaid*, he claims the same right of artistic and spiritual sanctuary as Shakespeare. Of course, biographers and commentators have tried to get behind these defences; and he has been dramatized in *The Barretts of Wimpole Street*—as Lamb has in *Charles and Mary*, and Shakespeare in *The Dark Lady of the Sonnets*. He showed us life as an adventure and challenge, not as a scheme. He could not explain evil (of which he knew more than his softer critics); but he could defy it. He thought that a good fight helps to hallow a cause, and the game is greater than the score. In truth, we do not know the score; the Scorer is God. "On earth the broken arc: on heaven the perfect round": we shall be judged by purposes unsure and immature, by "All I could never be, all men ignored in me." "Other heights in other lives, God willing." Art is a contact, a vitamin and experience, not a belief-test.

Its purpose is to stretch our minds, not to deliver neat explanations. It is impossible to give here a fair conception of Browning's abounding variety in *Men and Women*, *Dramatic Romances*, *Dramatic Lyrics*, and *Dramatic Personae*—the fantastic contrasts of character and age in *The Flight of the Duchess* (with its exciting mountain country), *Cleon, Karshish, Fra Angelico, A Grammarian's Funeral, Bishop Blougram's Apology, Sludge the Medium, Abt Vogler*, the astonishing vision in *Saul*, or of their miraculous articulation—a gift of tongues. If challenged as a musician, he could come into court with a hundred stirring lyrics as confidently as Sophocles with the *Coloneus* chorus. Drama and lyricism are one in him.

Arnold, a Thoughtful Poet

Different from those twin brethren is Matthew Arnold (1822-1888), son of the great educationalist, Dr. Arnold of Rugby. He himself became a school inspector, and his reports to the Board reveal an interest as deep as his father's in pedagogy. Imagination in him was chilled by six things—his sad inability to believe, the ugliness of much in contemporary society, the grind of school inspecting, his unsleeping critical faculty, his digressions into scriptural polemics, and his almost messianic sense of responsibility for a mission to a vulgar age. With more in him of his own vagabond *Scholar Gipsy*, or more abandon like that of Tennyson or Browning (neither of whom he admired), he would have made more mark than he did as the gentleman, scholar and civil servant with an aching heart and refined agnosticism. Still, his searching criticism cleared the air in many ways, and his poetry—mostly in the minor key—suits more than one modern mood. He strove against English insularity, excess and Philistinism; and commended the classic modes against eccentricity or lawless romance, French lucidity against German confusion. Of his prose it is requisite to read at least his *Essays in Criticism*: and most of his verse with its quick sensitiveness to the intellectual tendencies of the age, its wistful resignation. His gods were the Greeks, Oxford, culture, "sweetness and light," the Alps, and "the cheerful silence of the falls." A high, clear silver music as of water from the mountain tarn, a music like Grieg's—that is his characteristic. His poetry is most meditative, aspiration rather than hope. *The Scholar Gipsy* is of a more rich and complex beauty than anything else of his: the upland and Thames Valley setting draw us back to it again and again. There is also charm in certain stanzas in *Thyrsis*, in *Switzerland*, *Resignation*, and *The Forsaken Merman*. He reaches a fine height of stoic vision in *Dover Beach* and in *In Utrumque Paratus*, which is like a starry night with a touch of frost.

His friend and fellow Rugbeian, Arthur Hugh Clough (1819-1861) also felt the strain of life without secure belief, and fell back on duty, endurance and conduct. He, too, after declining Oxford posts which implied belief, became head of University Hall, London, a students' place of residence, and later took a position in the Education Office. His Highland story in hexameters, *The Bothie of Tober-na-Vuolich*, has an open-air holiday spirit.

Rubá'iyát of Omar Khayyám

Most people who recite bits from *Omar Khayyám* little suspect what a crusted eccentric wrote it, Edward Fitzgerald (1809-1883). In a battered silk hat and disreputable old clothes, this recluse scholar and wit idled about Woodbridge harbour in Suffolk; or in his craft, the *Scandal*, sailed the Deben River to Lowestoft and Aldeburgh with his boatman "Posh," with bread, cheese, and bottled porter. He was the complete East Anglian, even being educated at Bury St. Edmunds and Cambridge. He loved his fellow Suffolk poet, Crabbe, and befriended Crabbe's son; entertained famous contemporaries, Tennyson, Thackeray and Carlyle, who knew his powers while the villagers merely thought him crazy. So lacking in news was he that in writing to Carlyle eight months after the death of Mrs. Carlyle, he sent her his compliments. His letters and his dialogue *Euphranor* are prose of a fine vintage.

The *Rubá'iyát* is not so much a translation as an original *tour de force*. Of its first edition only two hundred and fifty copies were printed: two hundred of these were given to Quaritch, the bookseller, who sold them at a penny each! Rossetti and Swinburne bought theirs at this price. Now a small library has grown up round its four hundred and four lines. Tennyson, who tells us of his Lenten fare when staying with Fitz, and how tame doves would settle all over his host, says of *Omar*:

> Your golden lay
> Than which I know no version done
> In English more divinely well;
> A planet equal to the sun
> Which cast it, that large infidel
> Your Omar; and your Omar drew
> Full-handed plaudits from our best
> In modern letters.

His wise yet crochety letters shed welcome light on this hermit, who acclimatized other Persian poems which ought to be better known. It is odd that melancholy fatalism and voluptuous word-music should have such a vogue, a hashish dream varied by sceptical epigram.

Quite a different *Earthly Paradise* is presented by William Morris (1834-1896) to whose many-sidedness Bernard Shaw (who spoke with him from soap-boxes in the 'seventies and 'eighties on Socialism) pays animated tribute. Morris was an innovator in furniture, interior decoration, printing and illustration; he really knew the medieval age better than most, and the Icelandic sagas which he Anglicized in *Sigurd the Volsung*. Born to wealth, he was educated at Marlborough and Oxford, where he met Burne-Jones the artist; both had meant to be clergymen, but they were attracted by the pre-Raphaelite painter, Rossetti, who cultivated medievalism. Morris played many parts in life—poet, artist, manufacturer, socialist, public speaker, decorator, translator, and business man. The thirteenth century, whatever its shortcomings, had for him the ideal workshops, when every labourer was an artist and craft-proud, and his quality of work was protected by the guilds. He loved Chaucer, and revived something of him in *The Earthly Paradise* and *The Life and Death*

BROWNING'S WIFE, ELIZABETH BARRETT

Elizabeth Barrett was a poet in her own right before her marriage with Robert Browning with whom she eloped, against her father's wishes, to Italy. Her "Sonnets from the Portuguese" hold a high place in English literature; "Aurora Leigh" is a novel in poetic form which won immediate success on its publication in 1857.

of Jason. From romances he turned to the stark Scandinavian sagas, and after visiting Iceland he published his own version of some. Morris knew the Rossettis, but his note was very much his own. He hated the ugliness of the industrial revolution, and fought it with every weapon he had. He was, at bottom, quite practical and English—an aesthete who successfully made things and even made money thereby. His medievalism is simple and fresh, not mere retrospect; as became a working artist and song-smith.

Pre-Raphaelite Rossetti

Dante Gabriel Rossetti (1828-1882), son of an Italian political refugee, induced a group of young painters, like himself—Holman Hunt, Millais, and Ford Madox Brown—to abandon formalism and go back to the Italian Primitives. He turned his back on the burning questions of the day which so exercised Tennyson, Browning, Arnold and the prose prophets, and retired into a visionary world of symbols and colours. But his intense and egotistical personality drew Swinburne and others to him.

In 1860 he married Eleanor Siddal, whose face is seen in many of his canvases. In two years she died from an overdose of laudanum, and in his grief Rossetti buried the manuscripts of his poems in her coffin: seven years later the grave was reopened and the poems retrieved, and by these he became most widely known, and by the *Ballads and Sonnets* (1881). He put much poetry into his paintings, and much painting into his poetry; which, though hybrid art, in his hands is often memorable. His sonnet sequence of love, *The House of Life,* is rich in sensuous resonance and loaded associational music. So are the marvellous *Monochord* and *The Belfry of Bruges.* His *Blessed Damosel* summarizes his manner and the ideas of his circle. He could also write very fine poems of simple cast like *Jenny* and *The Burden of Nineveh,* but he preferred a mystical Romanticism, melancholy in tone, suffused with a sunset splendour. Something of his masters, Coleridge, Shelley and Keats, mingles with this noble but "literary" poetry.

After a disturbed career at Eton and Oxford, Algernon Charles Swinburne (1837-1909) migrated to London, where he produced *Poems and Ballads* (1886), a volume of amorous amoral poems written in intoxicating metres which could not fail to shock English readers of his day, but some of which seem a trifle absurd now. Moxon, the publisher, would have nothing more to do with him afterwards. His *Atalanta in Calydon,* however, opened the eyes of the informed to the lyric measures possible in our language. He tried drama repeatedly, especially on the theme of Mary Queen of Scots, in *Chastelard, Bothwell* and *Mary Stuart;* then three more which, despite their occasional poetic beauty, showed little sense of the theatre.

Much of his knowledge of the dark places of passion came from reading Baudelaire and other neo-pagans, but he clothed it in a resonant chant which, with its rush and swing, had a sensuous appeal to heady youth. He was a variation of Shelley in his paeans to liberty and revolt, the winds, and the sea in its protean moods.

He loved the Northumberland and Suffolk coasts, though he lived long in the Isle of Wight (in the house at Bonchurch, afterwards occupied by Alfred Noyes) and at Putney, in the care of Theodore Watts-Dunton. His father threw him in childhood to swim in the waves, and from his love of the sea he was known as "Sea-mew."

Swinburne's Word Music

His ideas are rickety, but his style is more virile and noble than commonly made out—not languorous, but Saxon, like this: "I have lived long enough to have seen one thing, that love hath an end." His paganism ends in sadness and frustration, though its pretext was joy. Thousands have had an inebriated Swinburne phase. He is, too, a dazzling *improvisatore,* "a reed through which all things blow into music," and little else. Kipling owed much to him, and both were in debt to the Bible and its short forceful English words. That is the one strength of Swinburne—style. In later years he tended to give imposing echoes of his first inspirations; the complex harmonies and rhapsody exceeded the substance and sense. Poetry had to turn and

ALGERNON CHARLES SWINBURNE

The poet is here seen caricatured by the Victorian cartoonist, Ape. Swinburne came to fame at the age of thirty after the publication of his "Atalanta in Calydon."

find some other way, as certain imitators discovered, of whom it was brightly said:

The lyrical cry isn't in it,
And the high gods spot in a minute
That it isn't the genuine thing.

Newcomers to him should begin with *The Garden of Proserpine, On the Downs, By the North Sea, Itylus, Dolores, Heartsease County, In a Garden* and *In the Salt Marshes.*

A few women poets deserve notice here. Elizabeth Barrett (Mrs. Browning) had something of the Brontës' verve and passion, and something more—European travel and ideas. Her swift, glowing story, *Aurora Leigh,* should be read as a poetic novel, for it beats most novels for intensity; Arnold Bennett came upon it with surprise and called it a feminine David Copperfield, vivid as Dickens, while Robertson Nicoll wrote: "I have ever regarded it as a touchstone. Those who like it are always catholic in their tastes, and not tied to the dogmas of any school or faction." It is strange that it has left no successor. She possessed a sure ear for rhyme and vocabulary, and had every quality except control. From this fault the *Sonnets from the Portuguese* are happily free. So are *Cowper's Grave* and the *Romaunt of Margret.*

Christina Rossetti

Christina Rossetti (sister of D. G. Rossetti) was a thoroughly Anglicized Italian. Her lyrics have a lighter voice and movement than his, as in her *Goblin Market, A Pageant* and other poems. Some of her best work is devotional (partly in prose, in which she was an adept) in *Time Flies* (1883) and later in *The Face of the Deep.* She has humour often, and pathos more often. Her truest strain is the religious, unspoiled by craven fear: the seventeenth-century poets do not surpass her *Sleep at Sea* and *Birds of Paradise.* Like all instinctives, she had a keen sense of the visual beauty of the world, and its fun; so she could give us verses like an air by Glück. The pressure of a tremendous faith circles all these songs, and to this they owe their firmness and conviction. She pruned away all that was unneeded, like a sure artist.

Here a word upon the intense verse of Emily Brontë. (The sisters' prose is commented on in a later chapter.) She was a feminine Blake or Shelley, tethered to her beloved dark moorlands, which said to her:

Few hearts to mortals given,
On earth to wildly pine;
Yet few would ask a heaven
More like this earth than thine.

and her reply:

We would not leave our nature home
For *any* world beyond the tomb!
No, mother, on thy kindly breast
Let us be laid in lasting rest,
Or waken but to share with thee
A mutual immortality.

"TO MY MOTHER ON HER BIRTHDAY"
Above is depicted the manuscript of Christina Rossetti's poem, written when the author was a child of twelve.

She vehemently clung to life and to "the distant, dreamy, dim blue chain of mountains circling every side." And yet she was strangely drawn beyond, too. She seems to have had a great mystical experience very early, and thereafter desired to recapture it. It appears to have been a love of the Absolute, personified for her by a human apparition, and in poem after poem expresses desire for "That glorious world" of which she once had close apprehension. Her work shows more spiritual courage than any other woman's.

Patmore and Thompson

Coventry Patmore (1823-1896) is the greatest religious poet since the seventeenth century, with Crashaw and Vaughan; a more magnificent one, and more interesting prophet than even the literary seem as yet to realize. Himself a sensitive proud man, he was devoutly audacious, and dared to be mystical-amorous like the humble, fervid southern singers of the Christian experience. Beginners will not find him in *The Angel in the House*, but in his odes, in *The Unknown Eros* and *Amelia*, which link him with the intrepid contemplatives of all times and countries. The odes are the best free verse there is. They are filled with a great rejoicing wind, yet every phrase projects a thought. He hardly belongs to the lesser Victorians but to the austere, ecstatic, and fiery seers of the love-union between divine and human.

Francis Thompson (1859-1907) with whom he is sometimes remembered, has a catholic vision like him, but it is not of so pure and erect a flame. He often clogged his mystical verse with ecclesiastical imagery, but his supreme poem, *The Hound of Heaven*, broke free of this, and calls to mind the work of Donne and other seventeenth-century poets. But his simple strain is also memorable:

> She looked a little wistfully
> Then went her sunshine way:
> The sea's eye had a mist on it,
> And the leaves fell from the day.

Frederick W. H. Myers, a lifelong seeker for evidence of personal survival

STEVENSON, THE ROMANTIC
As a poet R. L. Stevenson is best known for his "Child's Garden of Verses."

(on which he wrote a volume containing some startlingly eloquent prose) is known and still quoted for his greatest poem, *St. Paul*. He was a Virgilian and Dante scholar, and the biographer of Wordsworth.

John Keble's *Christian Year*, however, attracted a more staid, devotional circle than any of the works mentioned above. It was a book of pious professorial verses with a feeling for nature and was popular in Victorian homes.

Novelists' Verses

Robert Louis Stevenson (1850-1894) is a striking figure among the later romance writers. Here, only his verse is touched upon. His whole life was a gallant struggle against ill-health, which began in babyhood in Edinburgh and the Pentlands. His gift to all other children was *A Child's Garden of Verses*, utterly simple, exquisitely imaginative. But his consciously brilliant knack of phrase is present in his Scots vernacular poems, too, his South Sea ballads (Samoa was his home from home), *Christmas Morning at Sea* and *Heather Ale*. Much of his verse, though mannered and "made," is stimulating and companionable.

The novels also of Charles Kingsley (1819-1875) and his essays, are memorable. He was rector of the moorland Eversley in North Hampshire, social reformer, "Christian Socialist," novelist, a lecturer on history. He wrote several really fine ballads, like *The Three Fishers*, *The Last Buccaneer* and the *Sands of Dee*. His *Andromeda* (1858) has almost the only good continuous hexameters in English, with certain lines of noble lift, "chanting of Order and Right, and of Foresight, Warden of Nations" in the deep blue abysses of Hellas. *Hypatia* is one of his finest character studies.

A life begun and ended in misfortune was that of James Thomson (1834-1882), and this explains his *City of Dreadful Night*, that elaborate manifesto of pessimism. His father was stricken with paralysis, and the

LEWIS CARROLL
Author of the "Alice" books and the nonsense verse, "The Hunting of the Snark."

home was run by the mother, who was a melancholy but pious member of the Irvingite faith. A beautiful girl, too, with whom he was in love, died. In Ireland he became a henchman of Charles Bradlaugh, the secularist, and to his *National Reformer* Thomson contributed. When he quarrelled with his patron, and lost the means of living, he had a second harvest of verse less gloomy than *Insomnia* and *The City of Dreadful Night*. His lighter mood is expressed in his *Idylls of Cockaigne, Sunday Up the River* and *Sunday at Hampstead*, as well as in the later *At Belvoir* and *Richard Forest's Midsummer Night*. On June 3, 1882, after four terrible weeks of "intemperance, homelessness, and desperation," he died in University College Hospital, whither he had been carried from the house of his blind friend, the poet, Philip Bourke Marston.

There was a group of ill-starred gifted men, called decadents, about that time— Richard Middleton; Marston; Wilde; John Davidson (author of *Fleet Street Eclogues* and *The Runnable Stag*) who disappeared mysteriously over a cliff; Lionel Johnson, scholarly, stylistic, reserved— and maimed by his habits; Arthur O'Shaughnessy, who gave us the pretty, but decadent poem, *The Music Makers*.

We are ungrateful if we forget W. E. Henley (1849-1903), the rather berserker friend of Stevenson and of able Andrew Lang: his verse has (when it is not bullying in tone) a force and lightness that can still stir the blood. Lang, too—"Andrew with the brindled hair"—was a scholar with a light touch, equally good at criticism and folk-lore.

Now we come upon T. E. Brown (1830-1897), Manxman, master at Clifton, who still deserves a wider circle of friends; those he has are devoted, and included Quiller-Couch (see his *From a Cornish Window*). He spoke out his feelings more frankly and tunefully than is considered "the thing" today: a virtue, surely, not a defect, in a poet. Here is a little outburst of finer pantheism:

What moves at Cardiff, how a man
At Newport ends the day as he began,

He was a Gael, with the gifts of pathos and humour, both blended in his tales of the Isle of Man and its people.

John Addington Symonds, accomplished poet, is also known for his Italian studies, his life of Shelley, and his Renaissance learning. The double role was also Arthur Symons's; and his exquisite prose itself, in sensitive criticism of men or appreciation of "the spirit of place," will please whoever comes upon it.

Nonsense (with sense concealed in it) was a speciality of the same Victorian time which was otherwise so keen upon belief, morals, effort, and eloquence. There are still people who pull from a pocket the treasured parodies and translations of C. S. Calverley, with their tincture of classic grace which acts as preserving salt. R. H. Barham's macabre fun in *The Ingoldsby Legends* is a pleasant shiver for the young. Canning diverted thousands; and Hood is an adept at two-edged pleasantry—as Lamb is in his letters. Lewis Carroll (1832-1898), mathematician at Oxford, author of *Alice*, gave us *The Hunting of the Snark*; and Edward Lear's *Nonsense Verses* have had, in our day, a sort of continuation in the *Clerihews* of E. C. Bentley, in Belloc's *Bad Child's Book of Beasts*, in Max Beerbohm's barbed, caressing wit, in A. P. Herbert, Owen Seaman, and other *Punch* jesters. Your "light" men often have learning, and experience of life. Puck can put a girdle round the earth. W S. Gilbert (1836-1911) brought comedy to millions, who, but for the Savoy Opera, would never have gone near a theatre. Gilbert—whose fun has created the term "Gilbertian"—is even more popular in *Bab Ballads*.

HUMOROUS VERSIFIER

R. H. Barham, author of the grotesque and amusing verses, "The Ingoldsby Legends."

At Weston what adventure may befall,
What Bristol dreams, or if she dream at all,
Upon the pier with step sedate
I meditate—
Poor souls, whose God is Mammon—
Meanwhile from Ocean's gate,
Keen for the foaming spate,
The true God rushes in the salmon

Test Yourself

1. Tennyson and Browning were the outstanding poets of the Victorian era. Write a brief essay outlining the main characteristics of the verse of each.

2. Give a brief account of the life and career of William Morris.

3. Name the outstanding women poets of the age.

4. Who were the authors of *The Blessed Damosel* and *Atalanta in Calydon*?

Answers will be found at the end of the book.

ENGLAND'S BEST-LOVED NOVELIST

*After a childhood of considerable hardship and some success as a journalist Dickens was
launched on a lucrative literary career in 1836 with the publication of "The Pickwick Papers."
Thanks to his boisterous sense of humour and his facility for inventing characters, unexcelled,
except by Shakespeare, Dickens's novels enjoyed enormous popularity in his own day, and
many of his characters are as much alive as are most living celebrities.*

CHAPTER XI

VICTORIAN PROSE

WE put De Quincey's prose fantasias in the Romantic period; for, though he lived well into Victoria's reign, he drew his inspiration from the ancients, and Wordsworth and Coleridge. But Thomas Carlyle, an "oracle" and *enfant terrible* of the Victorian time, was nearly contemporary with De Quincey, too, and met Charles Lamb. Men's lives and work overlap. Carlyle was a victim of self-torment and of what we, today, would call neurosis. His personal doubt and troubles are told with almost brutal frankness in a life by J. A. Froude—a book that scandalized a generation which, perhaps wisely, would rather not have heard the facts.

Carlyle's Background

Carlyle was born in the Scots border village of Ecclefechan in 1795, child of a stonemason father and a peasant mother, who taught herself to read and write so that she might answer her son's letters. Looking back on his boyhood existence and its friends, Carlyle wrote with one of his occasional moods of piercing pathos: "they are gone now and vanished all: their bits of thrifty clothes, their struggling effort, their little life: it is all away. It is all melted into the still sea; it was rounded with a sleep." It was intended that he should be a minister, but after going to Edinburgh University he rejected the Church in favour of teaching. In 1826 he married witty, temperamental Jane Welch, with whom he eventually established a home in Chelsea upon small means supplemented by fees earned by lecturing on German literature. His fondness for German influenced his own style, sprinkling it with clumsy, portmanteau phrases, and a preoccupation with philosophic shades of meaning. Before he came to London, Carlyle had already written some of his best essays, including *The Diamond Necklace*, perhaps the most perfect of his works. Carlyle did not write with ease—one can tell the pain with which his thoughts were born from his writings—but in his first years in London he wrote his *French Revolution*. Having finished the first book in six months he lent the manuscript to the economist, John Stuart Mill. While there it was used by a careless housemaid as firelighters. Told of the hideous mishap, Carlyle (usually so explosive) was silent, set himself grimly to rewrite it, and took a year doing so. When the history was published in 1837 it created a sensation and founded the reputation the author was to enjoy till his death in 1881. It is a formidable work to read all at once—most of Carlyle's works are; but it is full of vivid pages and readily quotable sentences. To him history was not dead, but a living lesson. He unfolds the lives of Robespierre, Mirabeau, and Danton with uncanny insight into their souls and secret thoughts. He re-creates incidents like the taking of the Bastille with breath-taking realism.

His Social Outlook

Carlyle was a radical and a social critic. Unfortunately, his work is not polished, but rough hewn and sometimes contradictory. His *Sartor Resartus*, a satire upon social customs and conventions, is sometimes brilliant, but is to most people unreadable with its tortuous obscurities and twisted phrases. Then, again, his choice of a ruthless Prussian king for his most ambitious history (*History of Frederick the Great*) has made him a favourite in Germany to this day, but has done his name much harm in Britain, France and America. He possessed, along with his sympathy for the oppressed, a Teutonic weakness for Strong Men—Fuehrers—to tell the mob its way, overlooking the four deadly facts that (*a*) the great man is not ever big enough for the task; (*b*) he cannot guarantee a good successor; (*c*) the world often only recognizes the really great man after his death; and (*d*) the many are in the long run wiser than any individual and frequently reverse their dictators' policies.

AGGRESSIVE VICTORIAN

The outstanding essayist of the early Victorian era, Thomas Carlyle, was educated for the ministry, but rejected these plans when his belief in Christianity was assailed. After a period of teaching he devoted himself to writing, his "French Revolution" and his "History of Frederick the Great" being his major undertakings.

Just because he had lost theological belief—and could not accept political optimisms instead—he was a fierce *moralizer*. But he over-simplified here, too. "Moral progress is everything," he said, "material progress is nothing." The first is true, the second is too bald as it stands. Material improvements may help goodness by helping health and intelligence.

What remains of Carlyle for us? Vivid pictorial evocations of what men and women in the past felt at the *Commune* and the fall of the Bastille, the pathos of the French king's escape, the life in an old monastery, or during the exciting Diamond Necklace affair, or at the battles of Naseby or Dunbar. He had an almost Highland "second sight"; a clairvoyant power of guessing what was in a man—and especially at what was *not* in him! He sees men and events by flashes of lightning. He had pathos and tenderness at call; wild humour, but humour never got into his philosophy, which was a Teutonic idealism unaware of the complexity of things.

Contrast in Life and Style

Sharper contrast there could not be than between him and Thomas Babington Macaulay (1800-1859). While Carlyle's life was a struggle against the spirit of the age, Macaulay *was* that spirit—prosperous, competent, philanthropic, materialist in some ways, even tempered and complacent. He rose by merit in the Government, in Indian administration, as War Minister, as historian and essayist and versifier, from being a briefless barrister. It is piquant to think of these two actually meeting sometimes at a *soirée*. Carlyle considered Macaulay a "sounding brass," while Macaulay, unable to fathom his brother Scot, discreetly does not refer to him. It is interesting to picture the two—Carlyle, uneasily peering behind the veils of mystery; Macaulay content with the foreground and the learning in his great library; Carlyle feeling the weight of this world and the beyond; Macaulay confident that rational debate and work can solve everything; Carlyle declaring that we moderns were "shooting Niagara"; Macaulay sure that, as trade figures showed, we were going

from strength to strength as a nation.

Today we endorse neither. Our aim should be to disengage the sound deposit from each. To youth in the last seventy years, the page in Macaulay which is not a burst of sunlight is at least a projection from an astonishingly clear magic lantern.

Born in Clapham, son of Zachary Macaulay, the slave emancipator, one of the Clapham Sect, he was, as a boy, a prodigy of reading, talk and letter-writing; the pride of his sisters and hope of the family. He studied law, but soon turned to politics as a Whig, one of several clever Cambridge young men, and twice winner of poetry prizes, and a contributor to magazines. His memory staggered Thackeray and other contemporaries. If *Paradise Lost* were destroyed he could have repeated it. His taste was eighteenth century and Latin: his mind was closed to Carlyle and the German school. There is not a sentence in his works which any one has to read twice to understand, though some we read again for their sonority or lucid statement. At twenty-five, that style (steel at its best, tin at its worst) was at his command, and his famous youthful essay in the *Edinburgh Review* on Milton contains this among other remembered passages (on the rise of Christianity):

> God the uncreated, the incomprehensible, the invisible, attracted few worshippers. A philosopher might admire so noble a conception; but the crowd turned away in disgust from words which present no image to their minds. It was before Deity embodied in a human Form, walking among men, partaking of their infirmities, leaning on their bosoms, weeping over their graves, slumbering in the manger, bleeding on the Cross, that the prejudices of the synagogue, and the doubts of the academy, and the pride of the portico, and the fasces of the lictor, and the swords of thirty Legions were humbled in the dust!

Such a panorama as his has always been a people's resort; as J. R. Green's *History* was later. The obvious, temporal side of

Macaulay is not the half of him: he had the romance and zeal of history in his blood and can stir us with the trumpet of rhetoric and the spell of names in which many a sentence culminates—the eagles of Rome, the temple of Tarpeian Jove, the choir of York and the majestic towers of Lincoln, the city of a thousand masts, or the pillars of Hercules. Some are little more than a muster-roll of names: but they are charmed names.

The moment it was known he would speak (and his orations were prepared compositions, just as his writing is oratory) Parliament filled as it did later for Disraeli or Churchill. Every one understood him: he is the common man in an uncommon degree—a Philistine, but with genius, erudition, clarity and fire. Of prejudice (chiefly Whiggish) he had his share, and we allow for it. His superbly militant *Lays of Ancient Rome* and the *Armada* express his spirit.

Froude, the Historian

Prejudice, too, biased J. A. Froude (1818-1894); but Froude's was for Henry VIII and the harsh Tudor policy. He started life in a home too High Church to admit into its library a *Pilgrim's Progress*; quite naturally, in reaction, he was later to write a classic on Bunyan! His brother persuaded him into the Church and into writing lives of the saints; again, not unnaturally, Froude reacted into scepticism—retaining, however, morality and Theism and a Christian sympathy. His *Nemesis of Faith* caused more than excitement; it was burnt in hall, he had to resign his Fellowship, his archdeacon father "cut him off," and he had to sell his books. No wonder that, ever after, he stood for charity as the true orthodoxy.

Because his wonderfully simple style is likely to be a lasting attraction, readers should, avoiding the controversial books, approach him by way of these papers in his *Short Studies on Great Subjects*: "A Fortnight in Kerry," "Sea Studies," "A Twelfth Century Bishop," "Representative Men," "Lives of the Saints," "Divus Caesar," "Job," "Homer," "England's Forgotten Worthies," "The Science of History," "The Philosophy of Catholicism," "Times of

LORD MACAULAY

Macaulay's style as an essayist was based on that of the classical school; his prose is lively, lucid and dignified. Every schoolboy of fourteen knows his verse.

Erasmus and Luther" and "Cheneys and the Russels." Then they will see a style surpassed by few others, for the soft play of life and natural colouring. Carlyle was his "master," but the pupil kept out all trace of Carlylese. He is much more like Hazlitt or Dryden in his easy, distinguished flow, light yet weighty, ripe like very good talk.

Newcomers will find him immediately interesting in the chapters in his *History* on the Pilgrimage of Grace and the bridals of Anne Boleyn; in Grenville's fight in the *Revenge* in *Short Studies* (this set Tennyson on his poem), and many an ocean passage in *Oceans* and *The English in the West Indies*. His mellow prose can rise into a fine glow or thrill us with a splendid scene. He has left also the noblest word-portrait of his intimate friend, Cardinal Newman, from whom he parted in thought.

Another severer beauty marks the renowned prose of John Henry, Cardinal Newman (1801-1890)—refined, supple and gracious. The inexperienced think he has been over-esteemed. There are selections of his varied work, and his idyllic papers on *The Early Benedictine Centuries*, which have a very similar proportion and continuity to his own masters, Virgil and Cicero; indeed, he read some Latin classic to begin every day. Matthew Arnold (among others) idolized his urbanity and charm, and called his work "a miracle of intellectual tact." His *Apologia* is effective always, ironic and beautiful in pages. His *Dream of Gerontius* (set to music by Edward Elgar) is but one of his exquisite poems, all in the minor key, and of searching character. His sermons (on *Immortality* and the *Second Spring*) used to be known almost by heart by some men of affairs and literature. His transition to the Catholic Church was a major spiritual event of the time, with reverberations felt long afterwards.

Versatile Ruskin

A very different artist in prose is John Ruskin (1819-1900). Many of our fathers were "brought up" on Ruskin—on his long, elaborated, often beautiful sentences on Gothic and Romanesque architecture, his long-drawn rhapsodies on mountains, clouds, Turner the gorgeous and at one time neglected painter; his economics, social sermons and ethics. The only child of a well-to-do wine merchant, he never went to school, but till he went to Oxford he had a cultured home; and his father read to him "all the Shakespeare comedies and historical plays again and again; all Scott and all Don Quixote." In summer, boy and parents visited the old halls and castles of England, then the Rhine and Switzerland. His mother was strictly evangelical, and father and son acquiesced. She read the Bible with him from Genesis to Revelation—and began over again. By all this, Ruskin acquired backbone to thought and style, which might else have been lacking. She wanted him to be a preacher. A preacher he became—but not of her kind. Today we are said to fight shy of eloquence; but it is a good thing,

even if Ruskin is too liberal of it. Here is a tiny characteristic example of his manner, on Venice:

It lay along the face of the waters, no larger, as its captains saw it from their masts at evening, than a bar of sunset that could not pass away; but for its power, it must have seemed to them as if they were sailing in the expanse of heaven, and this a great planet, whose orient edge widened through ether. No foulness, nor tumult, in those tremulous streets, that filled, or fell, beneath the moon; but rippled music of majestic change, or thrilling silence. And around them, far as the eye could reach, the soft moving of stainless waters, proudly pure. Ethereal strength of Alps, dreamlike, vanishing, in high procession beyond the Torcellan shore; blue islands of Paduan hills, poised in the golden west. Brightness out of the north, and balm from the south, and the stars of the evening and morning clear in the limitless light of arched heaven and circling sea.

At any rate, the man who wrote hundreds of pages of such word-symphonies cared enormously for English and expression. A promising beginning with this deliberate if mannered charmer of the ear would be with *Sesame and Lilies* and then *Modern Painters* which was for years the cultured classes' guide to Europe.

Aesthete and Historian

Walter Pater (1839-1894) was another idol, but of the aesthetes and hedonists His writing is more "precious" and hothouse; still, his *Marius the Epicurean*, his appreciations and studies of the troubadours contain exquisitely "made," enamelled prose, of which the most quoted is his fanciful passage on Mona Lisa's smile. He is a good interpreter of Wordsworth, Coleridge, and Lamb.

"You are a jolly, vivid man," Tennyson told J. R. Green (1837-1883), known best as author of the wonderfully full yet readable *History of the English People*, the best

annals of their kind. President Woodrow
Wilson, in American literary lectures, said:
"A patient scholar and rare artist; but his
writing is pitched in one key. It is a very
fine and moving key. Many an elevated
strain and rich harmony commend it alike
to the ear and imagination; it is employed
with an easy mastery: but it is always one
key." This is not true of Green's gaily-
coloured *Stray Studies* on his Italian, Alpine
and English holidays seeking the health that
never was captured. He was an East End
parson for years till the work was too
much for him.

One cannot leave these years without
allusion (it can be no more) to the striking
and noble *Ecce Homo* (Behold the Man)
which brought fresh air into the rather
stagnating theological dovecotes. It was
the work of the famous historian, Sir John
Seeley, author also of *The Expansion of
England* and *Natural Religion*. Another
sturdy, unconventional adviser to the age
was Walter Bagehot, banker, editor of the
Economist, historian of Lombard Street,
writer on the Constitution, *Physics and
Politics*, and a very stimulating critic indeed
when he writes on men of letters. He was
a favourite of Augustine Birrell, who carried his free-and-easy method further. The
inventor of the miner's Davy lamp, Sir
Humphry Davy (1778-1829) was widely
lettered, and his *Consolations of Travel* are
readable still. He was the discoverer and
financer of Faraday. Another scientist who
wrote lucidly on religion was Professor
Henry Drummond, who was able to lend
original and singular charm to difficult
subjects in *Natural Law in the Spiritual
World* and *The Ascent of Man*. He was a
power for good with thinking youth.

Statesman and Playwright

Tory Prime Minister, romantic, cynic,
courtier to Queen Victoria, novelist—
Benjamin Disraeli was not merely charlatan
or vulgarian in his political novels. Beneath
his Oriental, childlike love of glittering
verbal trinkets and his oracular affecta-
tions, the man could diagnose and
prophesy—and even, at moments, prescribe. Rush through the jeweller's shop
passages, and *Sybil* will prove itself a

powerful and intelligent novel. If interest
survives, the others can be tried—*Coningsby,
Tancred* and the rest.

The name of Oscar Wilde (1854-1900)
was for years in disrepute in Britain and
America, although his work was always
popular on the Continent. This eclipse was
due to his imprisonment for immoral
practices, but in recent years his personal
misfortunes have been forgotten and his
work read and acted without prejudice.
Son of an Irish surgeon, Wilde came under
the influence of the aesthetic movement
which, with its dictum of "art for art's
sake," was a rebellion against the more
Philistine aspects of the age. Brilliant in
conversation and with an exquisite sense
of the colour and feeling of words, his
prose works consisted of *Lord Arthur
Savile's Crime and Other Stories*, and the
sensuous collection of fairy stories, *The
House of Pomegranates*. But it is for his
witty, artificial plays that he will chiefly be
remembered—*Lady Windermere's Fan, A
Woman of No Importance, An Ideal
Husband*, and *The Importance of Being
Earnest*. Wilde excelled in the epigram,
fundamentally based upon taking some
accustomed phrase or statement and
inverting it: "Nothing succeeds like
excess"; "One should always choose one's
enemies carefully."

The Child's Eye of Dickens

Beginning with Dickens and Thackeray
let us now consider the long line of distinguished Victorian novelists.

Can anything fresh and true be said
of Charles Dickens (1812-1870)? Just
possibly. A main clue to him surely is this
—that he absorbed, in his profoundly
impressionable and unhappy childhood, an
intense emotional view of the strange world
of grown-ups. In *Oliver Twist*, his first
romance of Cockaigne, and in *David
Copperfield*, his most characteristic and
semi-autobiographical novel, he saw life
from a secret peep-hole in childhood's
land; he continued to stare at that incalculable race of adults with the eye of youth
—so swift to notice grimace, oddity,
hypocrisy or villainy, and he drew them
with the exaggerated curves and angles

CRUIKSHANK TITLE-PAGE

The title-page of Dickens's collected sketches, published under his pseudonym, Boz.

which an imaginative schoolboy would put secretly on to the fly-leaf of a book—Squeers, Pickwick, Mr. Dick, Sam Weller, Mr. Micawber (and Mrs.), Jingle, the Cheerybles, Peggotty, Nancy, the Artful Dodger, Bumble, Oliver Twist, Barkis, Pecksniff, Dick Swiveller, Chadband, Mrs. Gamp, Betsy Trotwood, Tulkinghorn, and a hundred others. How utterly he understands the souls of all Copperfields—bewildered, homesick, credulous, amused—sent like a parcel on coach journeys to school or strangers, and taken in charge by ostlers and waiters! Notice how naïve and vehement, from the heart, are his loves, hates, and scorns; and his pity for all the desolate and oppressed. One hears his big heart beating in that sometimes untidy, high-spirited, always effective style. Being a very human being ("Papa is in love again!" said his children when they saw him with sad, bent head at table), his feelings flooded everything he wrote; and in his tales he enjoyed everybody (as they enjoy themselves—realists forget that). He even liked Uriah Heep and Mr. Pecksniff.

Always do we hope, as they depart, that they will come back and make another grimace or string of characteristic remarks, as in our pantomime and melodrama days. Simple people still talk of these vivid apparitions as if they are alive. His fictional names have given us a fresh list of adjectives for people we know: can a novelist achieve more? So intense is his imagination that gas lamps, windows, and doors seem to us invested with personality, as they were to him.

40,000 Pickwicks

Dickens was son of a clerk in the Navy Pay Office and himself worked in a blacking factory. All this misery and his Micawber-ish father, are in David Copperfield. Charles had a sketchy schooling, and at fifteen went for a year into a lawyer's office, leaving to be a reporter (the best and most rapid ever known, he claimed) on The True Sun. He trained to be an actor—a useless training, except for his final readings of his work here and in America. In 1833 his first Sketch by Boz got into the Monthly Magazine (it was "Mr. Minns and his

Cousin"). Three years later came Pickwick Papers: four hundred copies of the first printing were ordered, but forty thousand of the fifteenth. The rest of his life consists in dates of his books, the purchase of Gad's Hill and the spirited public readings in Britain and America, which netted about £45,000. "He acts better than any Macready in the world," said Carlyle, "a whole theatre performing under one hat."

Exuberance and Breadth

He carried on the gusto of the robust narrative tradition of Fielding and Smollett; he gathered all his experience in their sort of pre-railway, pre-lighting world. He sees dark foggy streets of London—from Lambeth to Wapping and the Isle of Dogs—by the jigging of naphtha-flares; he hears the nocturnal and diurnal street cries as an imaginative, fearing, wondering child does; he hears, from gutter and hovel, the invincible Cockney joke, the endearment, the sudden straw-blaze of a quarrel. He was a summary of the people, in his instinctive knowledge, his traditional roots, and his ignorances. He spoke from the private lives of the masses, and blazed a trail of romance. To critics who complained that Pickwick and others began by being purely ludicrous and then became serious and sympathetic beings, Dickens replied that this is exactly what takes place in life where odd encounters ripen into friendships.

He was right. No one leads us into the mazes of his queer, convincing, warm invention so easily, with one trait first, and then the fuller creation. His nerve was untiring, his own belief really engaged (he laughed or wept as he wrote top-speed). He never puts us off with externals; all is felt. Besides, life itself is often comic, fantastic and melodramatic. He impressed the Russian Turgenev, and Daudet in France; Joseph Conrad called him "the master" and vowed he had met Lady Dedlock and other Dickens people; he has influenced William de Morgan, H. G. Wells, Pett Ridge, Barry Pain and W. W. Jacobs.

W. M. Thackeray (1811-1863) also had deep human tenderness, but expressed differently and on a less exuberant scale. Dickens floodlights the crowd, Thackeray

SCENES FROM THE "PICKWICK" PAPERS

Above may be seen illustrations by Phiz of two famous incidents from "Pickwick Papers" –
the composition of Weller's Valentine, and Mrs. Bardell's fainting fit.

one or two classes and the individual. His easy, sparkling style recalls Steele, Addison, Goldsmith and the Queen Anne classics. With these he had a strong affinity of temper; and *Henry Esmond* is written wholly in their idiom.

Thackeray's Novels

Thackeray was born into a competence, in India; went to Charterhouse School and the University, studied in Weimar (where he saw Goethe), tried art (he was as amusing with pencil as with pen), idled a good deal, adored the eighteenth century and knew his London and West End thoroughly. Only a downward turn in his affairs forced his indolence to other literature than *jeux d'esprit*. *Vanity Fair*, when it appeared, astonished, shocked, or pleased by its unwincing honesty in the portrayal of Becky Sharp and her "superiors"; it is "a novel without a hero," unless Dobbin was that hero. More sympathetic was *Pendennis*; it has the aroma of all adolescence and young manhood. The opening, with the Major at the Club, is masterly, but so are Harry Foker, Captain Costigan and his daughter, and Warrington. We seem to be intimates in his circle while the peep-show lasts.

He was an inconveniently emotional man with a tragic domestic life, manfully borne; he half betrays, half curbs his sense of tears in things. At his best, his reticent pathos is very telling, not least in exquisite light verse like *Vanitas Vanitatum*, *The Mahogany Tree* and *Bouillabaisse*. He began with dashing burlesque like Fielding, with a sentimental dash of Sterne. But he soon saw the larger chart of society spread before him—from Pall Mall, however. He probably saw more through wide open eyes than Scott with his telescope or Jane Austen with her microscope. It was only in self-mockery that he called his characters "puppets."

He is perennially interesting; his style has a perfect gossiping ease, equal alike to pathos, sharp statement, parody and high jinks. Saintsbury calls it "flutteringly alive" and intimate. The Brontës, away in moorland Haworth, revered Thackeray as "The Great Master." Tennyson and Fitzgerald placed him high; Trollope, in his auto-biography, did not hesitate to put Thackeray first of living novelists. He left no disciple, unless it was George Du Maurier in *Trilby*. Israel Zangwill says: "One feels that Thackeray was a greater master than Dickens, in that he took himself less seriously and had the finer sense of proportion. Yet he lived with his characters quite as much as his great contemporary." That, however, is a thorny subject.

A novelist whose stock has steadily risen after a long period of eclipse is Anthony Trollope (1815-1882). His mother was a competent novelist before him; Trollope, after an unhappy youth, became an important Post Office official—he is said to have invented the pillar box. His *Autobiography* should be read by any would-be author with romantic ideas. He wrote for money and devoted a certain period of the day to it, writing two hundred and fifty words every quarter of an hour, and calculating new books in so many hours of work. It was his self-revelation of these workaday methods that did much to disillusion and even disgust that section of the public which regards writing as a matter of genius.

World of Anthony Trollope

Trollope disdained inspiration and the method worked well—with him. Explaining the success of one of his novels, he said: "The story was thoroughly English. There was a little fox-hunting, and a little tuft-hunting, some Christian virtue and some Christian cant. There was no heroism and no villainy. There was much church, but more love-making." Trollope's virtue lies in his eye for character; his careful and fascinating depiction of the mid-Victorian upper class against its peculiar background. We watch the unfolding of character, the thousand subtle indications of desires and prejudices, all told in even prose and naturalistic dialogue (Trollope's books lend themselves to being read aloud), and without the partisan enthusiasms to be found in Dickens or the satirical flavour of Thackeray. His books on ecclesiastical life (of which he had no personal experience) are the best known—*The Warden, Barchester Towers, Framley Parsonage* abound in delightfully drawn cameos—the hen-

WILLIAM MAKEPEACE THACKERAY

Thackeray's position as a novelist has always been overshadowed by Dickens's humour and fertility of invention, but for purity of prose and well-balanced characterization he is preferred by some. "Vanity Fair" and "The History of Henry Esmond" are his best-known novels.

pecked Bishop, Dr. Proudie, and his dominating wife, the worldly Dr. Stanhope, the sly and pushing Mr. Slope, the proudly humble Mr. Crawley, perpetual curate of Hogglestock. Among his other works may be mentioned *Orley Farm*, *The Claverings*, and *The Way We Live Now*, with its superb study of Mr. Auguste Melmotte, the prototype of every city swindler.

A more purposeful social critic and reformer than Dickens was Charles Reade (1814-1884), son of an Oxfordshire squire, with private income and Fellowship (he was later Vice-President) of Magdalen; early on, he was a non-practising barrister with ambition to be a dramatist which was never successfully fulfilled. He earnestly

documented all his stories, so that they read like "our special commissioner" exposing some abuse. This stiffened the joints of his art. When he wanted fisherfolk for his novel, *Christie Johnstone*, he went to sea with them, suffering agonies of sickness. *It is Never Too Late to Mend* depicts prison life and its object was reform. *Hard Cash* demanded a change in lunatic asylums. Even *The Cloister and the Hearth*, that fine canvas of the Reformation time, is tendentious in places. An angry realist, he wished to influence legislation. It is dangerous to challenge his most surprising statements, for he took pains to ascertain facts. But whether he was wise in this may be doubted. He never knew that "the actual is not the true," and some facts "affect us as a lie." He tended to loud-pedal the pathos and the violence.

Another novelist reformist was Charles Kingsley (1819-1875) whose poems have been dealt with. In *Yeast, Alton Locke*, and *Two Years Ago*, he was a Christian socialist, and his belief was that if working men strove to get into the class above, and did so, there would be no permanent improvement in any class. Kingsley's goodness of heart, exuberance of style, and love of natural objects are everywhere visible as in his book for young children, *Water Babies*. His multifarious activities embraced *Chalk Stream Studies*, sermons, history, lectures, literary criticism, poetry, hunting, fishing, pastoral work. His best-known novels are *Westward Ho!* about the Elizabethan buccaneers, a lively tale for boys but not very good history; and *Hereward the Wake*, a tale about the Fens in Saxon days.

We can still find on bookshelves an occasional novel of Lord Lytton, first known as Edward Bulwer (1803-1873). He was a Byronic man of fashion, and a fashionable writer who has "gone out." He started writing in his 'teens, then joined a band of gipsies, one of whom he married. In 1827 he married (unhappily) one of his own circle, and he wrote her remunerative "revelations." He lived expensively and had to work hard at romances, and at politics, in which he reached Cabinet rank and was a good orator. He was buried in Westminster Abbey. *Eugene Aram* and *Paul Clifford* were early studies of crime; *The Last Days of Pompeii* and *Rienzi* are imitations of Scott. What most attracted him was the preternatural, as in *Zanoni*.

Three Literary Sisters

The Brontës, Charlotte (1816-1855), Emily (1818-1848) and Anne (1820-1849), those "daughters of debate," had for father the Rev. Patrick Brontë, an Irishman who had dabbled in verse. He became, in 1820, vicar of windswept Haworth (grey stone cottages on the dun Pennine moors) and moved there with his five girls and one boy, Branwell, at first the idol of the home, its sorrow. All of them were wrapped up in each other and their intense studies and wanderings over the vast heathery tracts in all weathers. Two girls died at their grim boarding school, and all this was remembered by Charlotte and Emily when they found themselves novelists.

Oddly enough their fame rests only on five novels—four by Charlotte, and one by Emily, for the lovable Anne's two little efforts hardly count. The two inspired sisters could appropriately have been classed with the previous Romantic age—for there is something Byronic, Shelleyan or Blake-like in them at times. They contrast sharply with the complete self-possession and ironic commonsense of Jane Austen, and with the serious, sometimes photo-graphic George Eliot, who were also more objective in drawing the male half of the human race.

Many heads have been turned by the Brontë legend; the sisters have been a cult about which very good and very bad books have appeared. Picking a careful way to the truth, we may say they had genius, Celtic blood, and a sullenly romantic environment which emphasized their peculiar and very personal and vivid gifts, which could only feed upon their narrow and intense experi-ence, filled by a background of dream. What they brought into fiction was what Carlyle brought into history, a blast of mysticism from the North. They really did initiate. Charlotte reached highest romance through lowest realism, fusing the lowly materials of a struggling governess into graphic adventure of soul and body. Seeing the sensational in the commonplace they wrote, as it were, in their blood.

Emily's fiery poems have been noticed; with them goes *Wuthering Heights*, which Chesterton, with pardonable exaggeration, said "might have been written by an eagle." Poem and tale throw light on each other. Arnold wrote that her soul:

Knew no fellow for might,
Passion, vehemence, grief,
Daring, since Byron died;

and Emily is now less an authoress than a great real character. Charlotte's tense and trenchant work should be approached by

ANTHONY TROLLOPE

Popular in his own day for his Barsetshire novels Trollope suffered an eclipse after his death, and it was only later generations of novel readers who realized the worth of his realistic, vivid stories, with their shrewd insight into every type of character.

way of the forceful *Shirley* and *Villette,* taking her best novel—that strange blend of the romantic and the grim—*Jane Eyre*—for later reading.

George Eliot

The Brontës lived richly in the high places of the mind. So did George Eliot (1819-1880), but it was a very different mind. The author of *Adam Bede, The Mill on the Floss, Silas Marner, Scenes of Clerical Life* and *Felix Holt* (the most attractive stories to begin with) was, when not writing novels, a critic, translator, social theorist, a moral rationalist, and serious oracle. She had a brain and used it from precocious childhood. Born in Warwickshire, she "remem-

bered in tranquillity" that unspoiled district near Coventry where her father farmed. At seventeen, motherless, she kept house, and was proud of her butter and cheese making, yet found time to study French, German, Italian, the classics and some science. She had musical and religious instincts, though the latter encountered the scepticism in the air. It was not till her friend, G. H. Lewes, suggested fiction to her that she found her calling. This gave her sage humour and cool grasp of character their chance. A time came when the artist and tale-teller in her did not blend in her last books with the theorist and thinker. She has too little ease and melody of style, but she has most skilful lighting and

shading and an almost Shakespearian sense of rustic bar-parlour gossips. Being unsentimental, she could draw women better than most novelists. Her first work, anonymous, was mistaken for a man's; much later, people thought Hardy's *Far from the Madding Crowd* was by her; there was the same daylight sanity and technical competence. The better brains of her generation ranked her perhaps excessively high; yet her human creations continue to deserve the epithet, "great." Tragedy, pathos, analysis, domestic incident, crusty humour; at least she gave these in her better work, with well-designed incident and plain credible characters. In *Middlemarch*

THE BRONTËS AND THEIR HOME

Emily and Charlotte Brontë wrote their novels in the bleak Yorkshire parsonage where their father (centre) was vicar.

A book of lasting popularity is *Cranford* (based on Knutsford, in Cheshire), by Mrs. Gaskell (1810-1865). She came of the Unitarians of Manchester, who have produced some able people. Another couple of *Cranfords* and she would be high among English novelists. Nevertheless, how very good is *Sylvia's Lovers*, about Whitby and the Yorkshire Moors in the time of the press-gangs; and *North and South* and *Mary Barton*, concerning the workers in the manufacturing North, whom she knew at first hand.

Writers who deserve mentioning are Mrs. Oliphant, a pleasing and easy depicter of Scottish life; Mrs. Craik, authoress of *John Halifax, Gentleman*; Mrs. Henry Wood, with the sentimental *East Lynne*; Charlotte Yonge, whose *Heir of Redclyffe* made a stir; Thomas Hughes, of *Tom Brown's Schooldays*; Wilkie Collins (1824-1889), precursor of detective stories with his clever stories, *The Moonstone* and *The Woman in White*. Indeed the ingenuity and complexity of the plots of Collins's novels have given them a new public in modern connoisseurs of detective fiction.

Then there is Dr. John Brown (1810-1882) with his delightful *Rab and His Friends*, which has had successors. We can only hail in passing, William Black (1841-1898), and the rich southern moorland air of R. D. Blackmore's (1825-1900) *Lorna Doone*, though he wrote well about other regions in *The Maid of Sker* and *Cripps the Carrier*; Sir Walter Besant (1836-1901) for *All Sorts and Conditions of Men* and *The Children of Gibeon*, and for his enthusiastic book on Richard Jefferies.

John Inglesant is still a strangely attractive story, with its moments of greatness (a word never to be used lightly). Its remarkable author, J. H. Shorthouse (1834-1903), was a Birmingham business man of wide culture, and he gave up ten years to this evocation of a past period in history, about 1670, concerning the Little Gidding sanctuary of the good Mr. Ferrar and

(1871-1872) she gathered her powers to build one of the century's finer novels of English country life, and the interaction of families. Her sympathy for her characters softens her inexorable determinism. She attempted to stretch the novel-form to include new themes and penetrate new aspects of character.

family, and the musing religious quietism which reigned there.

In 1844 there appeared something quite distinctive in travel books: *Eothen* by Alexander Kinglake (1809-1891), strangely beautiful and individual in its power to convey the hot colouring, the smells and sounds of the Near East. It is still of outstanding merit. Alone, or with native convoys, he traversed the Balkans, Turkey, Cyprus, Palestine, Egypt and the Lebanon and Syria, with many wayside adventures. It will be read long after his *Invasion of the Crimea* (1863-1887) which, though spirited even to violence, is diffuse.

One of the greatest historical minds— who, it happens, has left little but suggestive memoranda—was Lord Acton (1834-1902). He formed other minds by his strong ethical outlook:

> Judge not according to the orthodox standard of a system, religious, philosophical or political, but according as it promotes, or fails to promote, the delicacy, integrity and authority of Conscience.

At the age of twenty-nine, T. H. Buckle (1821-1862) had a working knowledge of nineteen languages; yet had been too delicate to go to school or university. His father left him enough to study upon, and Buckle early had the idea that we find the key to an age in its averages, not in its "great" exceptions. In this belief he is with Macaulay and against Carlyle. So he wrote *The History of Civilization in England*, which was widely translated. The toil killed him, and at Damascus he died exclaiming: "My book! I shall never finish my book."

Stevenson and His Contemporaries

Robert Louis Stevenson (1850-1894), whose life in detail—from ailing childhood to gallant manhood—is known to all, from his essays, poems and confessions, was the son of a lighthouse engineer, and he sailed many a rough sea and imbibed vivid impressions. He read omnivorously, and set about forming a style; but too much has been heard of his imitations. In truth, he was bigger than a copyist. Though influenced by Meredith's pranks with words, by Hazlitt, Dumas, Scott and many others, the resulting technique was Stevenson's own, pictorial, expressive, alert. His *début* was with *Treasure Island* in a boys' periodical, and it took adult fancy, too. Then he delighted an avid public with *New Arabian Nights* (1882), *Kidnapped* (1886), *The Black Arrow* (1888) and *The Master of Ballantrae* (1889). These were not overwritten, as a few of his otherwise delectable essays are.

In criticism and observation of life, he had his share of wisdom. At his death he was working on *Weir of Hermiston*, which has the elements of a still greater work. Coming out of the roots of his life, the Lord Justice Clerk is a grand creation showing assurance and judgment. In his essays and some of his brightly stylized tales, he inclines to the over ornate, but in *Weir* and parts of *The Master of Ballantrae* he was a master, not self-conscious in manner and striving for literary perfection, but finding and using matter and psychology equal to diction and artifice. His pictures of Edinburgh—its winds and wynds—of the Pentlands in all weathers, of south Europe, and travels in France and across America, are brilliant examples of the writing craft. Then came the *Vailima Letters* and the thunder of surf and the offshore wind of *South Sea Islands Nights Entertainments*. At his burial F. W. H. Myers spoke of "the thrilling, the unique voice" silenced. J. M. Barrie and Arthur Quiller-Couch, Augustine Birrell and Sidney Colvin are only a few of a great band of Stevensonians; and what colour, zest and artful effects he gave us. He has been a lead and stimulus to writers like Stanley Weyman, A. E. W. Mason, Quiller-Couch and P. C. Wren.

A leap to his opposite brings us to George Gissing (1857-1903). Still, one thing they had in common was a great love of letters and story. Gissing should first be read in *The Private Papers of Henry Ryecroft*, a rich diary of meditation written when he had retired to the peace of a cottage on the Exe; and afterwards in Greece.

He had an unhappy life as student at Manchester, and an unfortunate marriage

STEVENSON AMONG HIS SAMOAN FRIENDS

Stevenson's romances, such as "The Master of Ballantrae" and "Kidnapped" were written with knowledge and imagination. He drew on his Scots background even when, for the sake of his health, he made his home in the South Sea Islands, where he is seen here.

did not help matters. No one faced the disease of his time with franker realism —*Workers in the Dawn* (1880), *Demos* (1886), *The Nether World* (1889), *New Grub Street* (1891). Because he offered no facile solution and did not mix humour and pantomime with his photography, as Dickens did, he has never been popular. After *Ryecroft* we know the man behind the honest, truthful, if grey novels of the suppressed under-middle classes of the grim London of the 'eighties. These give no rein to day-dreaming, and, unlike so many novels of the twentieth century, are without hope or vision of social betterment.

By himself stands the ironic, original, enigmatic Samuel Butler (1835-1902), who said and wrote the most shattering things in a demure, casual manner that has fascinated critics, including Bernard Shaw, who confesses to "stealing" from him. *The Way of All Flesh* is a fierce side-attack on his own upbringing, and on his father, "Mr. Pontifex." It is not fair; but Butler was many other things before he was just. More amusing and suggestive are *Erewhon* (Nowhere) and *Erewhon Revisited*. The freedom of his thinking and expression releases originality and enterprise in the reader; yet he puzzles and disturbs also.

He was unjustly treated by scientists whose names he deflated, but he warded off popularity by his prickly shyness. "Above all," he said, "let no unwary reader do me the injustice of believing in *me*. In that I write at all I am among the damned. If he must believe in anything, let him believe in the music of Handel, the painting of Giovanni Bellini, and the thirteenth chapter of St. Paul's epistle to the Corinthians." He was a rebel in the succession of Swift, full of crotchets, but gifted with piercing insight and wisdom. His *Alps and Sanctuaries*, illustrated by himself (for like Thackeray, Hardy and Belloc he could draw), is a charming log, prototype of Belloc's roguish and happy *Path to Rome*, or Norman Douglas's *In Old Calabria* and *South Wind*. It is one of his few happy books.

To Victorian youth, W. Harrison Ainsworth (1805-1882) was a prize-book author, like Ballantyne later. But a re-reading of *The Tower of London*, *Old St. Paul's*, *The Lancashire Witches* and *Jack Sheppard* discloses something violent in the incident and tawdry in the style.

Meredith, Analyst of Foibles

Two conspicuous names remain, Meredith and Hardy. While "penny plain" Trollope was in full production, George Meredith (1828-1909), who was more "twopence coloured," began to strike and perplex a small circle with the curious eastern tale, *The Shaving of Shagpat*. George Eliot called it a new Arabian Nights, with poetic genius: Stevenson and others became admirers when he added *The Ordeal of Richard Feverel*. Yet nineteen years passed before the public asked for a second edition, though it has the brilliant character of Sir Austin, the love idyll of Richard and Lucy, and the two boy characters. Meredith is fascinated by human foibles and tracks them with more than Richardson's perseverance. Meredith was the son of a tailor, and was too sensitive on that score. It comes out in *Evan Harrington*, who is a tailor's son always wanting to forget the fact. *Rhoda Fleming* is more free from these class preoccupations. *Beauchamp's Career* and *Harry Richmond* show a poet's outlook, a restless

page crowded with simile, and the cosmic spirit. *The Egoist*—perhaps his best book —is the psychological comedy of an insufferable baronet in search of a wife. His verbal agility fatigues sometimes, and in place of humour he gives us the cactus of flickering, philosophical wit. As storyteller he is too impatient of material he cannot transfigure poetically. He harnesses winged horses to his prose, and goes too fast and high for the average pedestrian. He could draw fine women: his heroines (who seem, however, princesses in disguise) are seen in their setting of beechwoods, hills and country houses.

When he inherited a legacy which made him more independent, he says: "I took it into my head to serve these gentlemen (the critics) a strong dose of my most indigestible production." The packet, labelled "indigestible," included *The Amazing Marriage* and *One of Our Conquerors*. He there subtly dissects the deceits of the human mind, but a reader may well feel that the effort demanded of him has not been quite rewarded. In poetry, he began with swiftly intelligible and dancing lyrics, notably the long *Love in the Valley*, young love with a south English setting, answering the lyric chapter on that theme in the early scenes of his novel, *Richard Feverel*; contrariwise, the analysis of mood in the novels has one counterpart in the sonnet sequence, *Modern Love*. His philosophy of paganism, *Poems and Lyrics of the Joy of Earth* (1883) in frequently hard and cramped diction, conveys the idea of Nature's medicinal virtue. For him, the downs, woods and winds are doctor and nurse for our fevered nerves, and will finally take us into their breasts.

Into the earth that gives the rose,
Shall I with shuddering fall.

Thomas Hardy

Thomas Hardy (1840-1928) always let man monopolize mercy, and denied it to the Creator. His literary force and selection of incident make the illusion possible. He sees man as "slighted and enduring." If Meredith is Pegasus, Hardy is a patient draught horse that pulls a full load along

MAX BEERBOHM'S MEREDITH

George Meredith, caricatured above, was journalist, poet and novelist; "The Egoist" and "Diana of the Crossways" best illustrate his style and mystical philosophy.

LATE VICTORIAN NOVELIST AND POET
Trained as an architect, Thomas Hardy took to writing novels about the English countryside.
He writes of simple people striving in tragic circumstances towards goals they cannot reach.

the long Wessex roads. But he arrives.

Unlike his Victorian contemporaries, who survived the 1870-1880 epidemic of doubt and maintained an optimistic spirit whether they looked on the bright or the dark side of things, Hardy took a very sombre view of man's life on earth. Having a philosophic cast of mind, he sought an explanation for the tragic patterns which so often, it seemed to him, formed the lives of individuals; and he found his explanation in the hypothesis of God as being not all-powerful and beneficent, but a blind Will existing in and through the universe, powerful to create, but unconscious of its own creations. In a poem he asks:

> Has some Vast Imbecility
> Mighty to build and blend,
> But impotent to tend,

Framed us in jest, and left us now to hazardry?

Again of this Power or Will he writes:

> . . . Like a knitter drowsed,
> Whose fingers play in skilled unmind-fulness,
> The Will has woven with an absent heed
> Since life first was; and ever will so weave.

This outlook is surely the extreme of pessimism. Better for man there should be no God at all than for Him to be a "Pur-blind Doomster," creating man in jest, or —more terrible still—as the unknown by-product of a blind activity.

This core of his outlook Hardy manifests in some of his early lyrics and *The Dynasts*

(1906), an epic-drama in which he shows the schemes and strivings of the great ones of the Napoleonic epoch against the belittling background of the Universe and its soulless deity, the Immanent Will.

In some men such a belief would lead to cynicism and sterility. In Hardy it leads to pity for his fellow-man, interest in the natural world, and love of being alive. It is as though he were to conclude: "Yes, we are the sport of the gods; but we are also men tied by our common fate and capable of compassion. Life itself for us is its own justification. However much we get hurt there are still the simple pleasures of life like cider, dancing and lovemaking." And these (in his own words) are "great things to me."

In his greatest novels (which, we should not forget, were written in the last century) Hardy writes of simple men and women who, having some dominant aim such as desire for power in *The Mayor of Casterbridge*, desire for education in *Jude the Obscure*, desire for married happiness beyond her unfortunate past in *Tess of the D'Urbervilles*, are frustrated by adverse circumstance and ill luck, and find a fate tragically different from their hopes. He has been accused, not without substance, of loading the dice of Destiny against his players; to one of Hardy's outlook, however, the play of chance leading ironically to disaster is a legitimate part of life's picture, and when it occurs we are moved by compassion for the figures whose characters in combination with misfortune have brought about their tragedy.

There is, however, another side of Hardy the novelist—the Hardy of Egdon Heath, of the lush English water meadows, of the rolling southern counties. In him nature is ever the background of man; and the moods of nature, described in words as truly as Constable described them in paint, become a symbolical accompaniment to the moods of his characters.

Read first *Far from the Madding Crowd*, *The Mayor of Casterbridge*, *The Woodlanders* and *The Return of the Native*. Other characteristic work can wait—*Tess*, *Jude*, *Two on a Tower*, though a dip into *Wessex Tales* will tell a good deal. His conspicuous gift to us is his rich sense of the physical world, of nature and landscape conferring a deep and solemn beauty on his drama. The dark downland, with shepherd's huts and barrows, rises against the sky, smooth as a sea-wave, but eternal and solid, sheltering in its folds quiet villages whose smoke rises by day, whose lamps burn in the dark night. There is something pastoral, timeless, of the Old Testament in this noble setting. In the valley, his rustics gather at the inns, the malt-house, farm-kitchen or fair, and exude their slow humours in the language which Shakespeare, George Eliot and Scott loved, but loved and understood no better than Hardy.

These peasants of his are the last sanctuary of sanity and content. They can laugh and act and suffer, but theirs is the power to sink into Nature and become part of her silence and solemnity. This is a Wordsworthian trait; so is Hardy's passion for ordinary souls. Both poet-seers make their human being symbolical of the long life of earth. Both are occasionally maladroit, for a few lines—and it does not matter. Some solid and permanent substratum makes both a restful world in themselves.

Test Yourself

1. Give a brief account of the difference in style and thought of Thomas Carlyle and Thomas Macaulay.
2. Name four plays of Oscar Wilde.
3. Write a brief sketch (roughly two hundred words) about each of the three outstanding novelists of the Victorian age—Dickens, Thackeray and Trollope.
4. Mention three outstanding women novelists of the Victorian era together with the name of a work of each.

Answers will be found at the end of the book.

GEORGE BERNARD SHAW

For over half a century this Irishman held and enlivened the English stage. His total life was a brilliant offensive against the ruling ideas of his age, and, being a dramatist, he presented the conflict in his plays. Among his best works are "Arms and the Man," "Candida," "Man and Superman," "Heartbreak House," "Back to Methuselah," and his tragedy, "St. Joan."

CHAPTER XII

FROM 1900 TO THE PRESENT DAY

As we leave the past and approach the present, the problem of forming sound judgments grows acute. A trained literary critic will place Shakespeare, Wordsworth and even Tennyson in a perspective that will find agreement with the great majority of readers, no matter what their individual tastes may be. But by saying "*even* Tennyson," one suggests that doubt and difficulty have already begun to attack the critic. Time is the great distiller and purifier, but its laboratory methods are deliberate and slow. There is still some cloudiness in the essence that survives from the work of the great Victorians. That cloudiness is bound to make a slight obscuration in our angle of vision. So in these matters of taste, of preference, in relation to the modern novelists and poets, it is suggested that the reader shall bring a personal tolerance by which those differences of vision may be allowed for. Only thus may the critic and the reader remain on good terms.

Now the first thing to be realized is that the twentieth century, like any other century, is only an arbitrary measurement. By saying this, the writer shows himself up as a useful example of what has happened to the processes of thought during the past forty years. We are all tinctured with relativity today. That is to say, we can no longer believe that things, ideas, morals, exist or have existed as it were in a vacuum, unassociated and uninfluenced. So now, he cannot make a clean cut and see see the twentieth century as something that began about half a century ago. No new copy books were handed out to the historian, the theologian, the philosopher, the poet and the scientist. Harvests are being reaped to-day that were sown at various times during the reign of Queen Victoria.

This belief is so much a part of our everyday environment, that it can be taken for granted, without further argument. That being so, we can see together how one great event right in the middle of the last century, the publication of Darwin's *Origin of Species*, was like a boulder rolling down the mountain of human thought and plunging into the lake of human life. The ripples are still spreading out, wider and wider. It is to be noted, too, that they are affecting a surface that is still restless from the disturbance created by the discoveries of Copernicus and Galileo in the sixteenth and seventeenth centuries.

Industrial Society

And before Darwin's disturbing of the balance in the world of religion and philosophy, economic problems had already begun to assume their modern aspect, arising out of the sudden increase in populations, the drag of populations from the soil to the cities, and the entirely new and rootless activities imposed on those populations by the advent of the machine. The unshakable British Constitution was certainly shaken in the 'forties of last century, and we were within an ace of a political revolution that would have made the social background of Dickens's, Thackeray's, and Trollope's novels totally, instead of only partially, unfamiliar to the children of our generation.

But these are matters of wider scope, the impersonal influence of events and social forces upon the growth of writers and literature. Here it is intended to survey the outstanding figures that were moulded by, and took a hand in moulding, those nation-wide and even world-wide affairs. But the reader needs always to bear in mind that moving background, swinging its vast tides to and fro upon the shores of humanity, cleansing them, and throwing up strange treasures, and sometimes horrors, from the unfathomed deeps.

One fact stands out before all others. Things were no longer deemed to be static. The long decades of prosperity in this country, while our coal and iron were over-capitalizing what had formerly been that picturesque old family concern, the British

Empire, had lulled us into a sense of false security. Too much, no doubt, of Queen Victoria's get-rich days shows them to be seething with unrest, new ideas, moral protests, passionate religious and aesthetic reactions. Indeed, the poets and novelists of that time were much more violently rebellious than are any in our time. We are a gentle, mealy-mouthed lot in comparison. You have already learned about Thomas Carlyle (in Chapter XI), about Cardinal Newman and John Ruskin. These are only three of the admonitory prophets who belaboured that hard-faced generation of money-makers. Two schools of critics, the religious and the social, never ceased from their crying in the wilderness as they watched the growth of industrial society and saw it tending more and more to the practices of Babylon and the worshipping of the Golden Calf.

"Art for Art's Sake"

This rush for riches drove out both prophets and artists. They no longer had a place in this over-accelerated society. In consequence they behaved as uprooted folk always behave. They became self-conscious, superior, neurotic. They became aesthetes and highbrows. Mrs. Humphry Ward's first novel, *Robert Elsmere*, published in 1888, gave a portrait of one of these bewildered young priests who could see no place for his vocation in a world of much profit and little loss—except the loss of everything of spiritual worth. This book was so near the truth that even the Prime Minister, Gladstone, had to review it. We see today how Mrs. Ward's book was a more popular exposition of the protests uttered by her uncle, Matthew Arnold, that specimen of the stoical, austere English professional class that looked with abhorrence on the new commercial society, and contemptuously dubbed it "Philistine."

And parallel with *Robert Elsmere*, one may cite Walter Pater's only novel, *Marius the Epicurean*. Though this novel was laid in classical times, it dealt with the contemporary problem of the man of sensitive taste confronted with a world whose values were revolting to him. Gradually a whole school of writers emerged whose chief aim was to find a means of escape from a society that they despaired of reforming from its inveterate materialism. Allying themselves with their counterpart (but much more articulate fellow artists) in France, they evolved systems of "art for art's sake," and deliberately over-accented the significance of symbolism in art, confusing it indeed with secrecy. The influential critic, Arthur Symons, was their spokesman. His *Studies in Prose and Verse* (1904) and his *The Symbolist Movement in Literature* (1899) are useful aids to an understanding of what was happening in English letters at the turn of the century.

French and Russian Influence

The influence of France on English writers at that time was enormous, especially in the matter of technique. Formerly the English novel, and indeed the English poem, had been loose and spontaneous in its growth. The picaresque, or episodic style of writing, was for long the fashion. It seems to be our nature to work in that rule-of-thumb way, and in spite of the efforts of Matthew Arnold to impose a Classical Academy of English literature, comparable to the *Académie Française* whereby certain standards of composition should be set up and maintained; and in spite still more of the example of a number of our leading novelists since then to borrow the forms imposed upon the novel by French masters such as Flaubert and Guy de Maupassant, our writers of tales still go the way of the "rolling English road" that G. K. Chesterton followed with such vitality and gusto.

But with that French influence there emerged another. It was in the 'nineties that a group of writers, with the famous critic, Edward Garnett, as their impresario, first began to read, and to imitate, the Russian novelists. And at that time it was Dostoevski who was the chief mentor. Here was a massive, turbulent genius who used the form of the novel in a new, closely introspective way, just suitable for the painful need that was felt by English writers. Here was a novelist whose method could be exploited to trace the mental and

INFLUENCE OF RUSSIAN WRITERS

English writers, particularly those of Edward Garnett's circle, were influenced by four Russian novelists of the nineteenth century when the novels, stories and sketches of Leo Tolstoy (top left), Feodor Dostoevski (top right), Anton Chekhov (lower left) and Ivan Turgenev (lower right) were translated for the first time.

W. B. YEATS: A MODERN ROMANTICIST

First and foremost a lyrical poet, whose distinctive qualities may be found in such collections as "The Wind Among the Reeds," much of Yeats's finest work is included in the poetic plays which he wrote for the Irish National Theatre, Dublin, of which he was a co-founder in 1899. As an essayist he was a penetrating and witty critic.

emotional adventures of men and women deprived by an increasingly departmentalized society of any worth-while form of external adventure. Alongside this widening of the scope of the novel, there came into our literature the influence of Turgenev, and later of Chekhov, to show how that exploration of the adventures of the human soul within its own solitude could be expressed in forms of exquisite structure. New sensibilities: new shapes; these were what the Russian writers brought us. Outstanding amongst translators were Aylmer Maude, and Edward Garnett's wife, Constance, who has put into English the works of Dostoevski, Turgenev, Chekhov, and Tolstoy, as well as books by other and lesser Russian writers. Through those translations, the Russian influence is enormous even today. At the turn of the century it was predominant, just as twenty years later the Russian ballet and Russian music burst like a red sunrise from the east of Europe, heralding the storms that have surely followed.

New Philosophers

In the arts, as in philosophy, the heavy, static German influence was at last broken. A new, fluid way of thought began to catch up with the orientations of the men of science, who by now had broken away from the dogmas of a strict rationalism, and were beginning to question the authenticity of matter itself. In philosophy, Bergson, Croce, and Santayana (in France, Italy, and America respectively), and F. H. Bradley in England, began to split the atom of appearance, and to show how reality is an ever-receding non-absolute. Alongside them, the great William James in New England (brother of Henry James the novelist) brought these abstract researches in the realm of mind down to practical, ethical problems, setting up a system of thought called Pragmatism by which values are related to necessity. Such a philosophical power chariot has had its dangers. In the hands of inexperienced or reckless drivers, the machine can run wild, and endanger not only the driver but the rest of society.

We are concerned here, however, with

literary events. But it is difficult not to turn aside to the other arts, to the sciences, to politics and economics, in our survey. For note one thing; the isolation of the men of letters was over. With the gradual breakdown of the prosperity of the middle decades of the nineteenth century, people began once more to look for non-material values. It was a case of "the devil was sick, the devil a monk would be." And by the end of the century, society was very sick. Unemployment, the decay of standards of work in the crafts, the growth of trades unionism on the one hand and the growth of cartels on the other, all these factors were throwing false stresses on society as a whole. And to this were added the questionings and revolts consequent upon the discoveries of science and the changes of habit which they had brought, with their mechanisms, into the old way of life that had gone on since Roman days.

So the twentieth century came in like the Severn bore, rushing with such force that there was no time to control it, or to prevent many ancient institutions (so many of them noble and beautiful) from being overwhelmed. That process is accelerated today to the point of madness. None of us sees the way clearly. None of us can prophesy.

On that flood there rode three figures, G. B. Shaw, H. G. Wells and Rudyard Kipling. These were writers who once more brought their art into every man's life, and gave the writer a power comparable to that of the statesman and the prelate. But before dealing with them and with their contemporaries, Barrie, Bennett and Galsworthy, let us look at some of the figures representative of the more distinctly aesthetic manifestations that merged the nineteenth into the twentieth centuries.

The Celtic Twilight

Outstanding among these are the poet, William Butler Yeats, and the novelist, Henry James. Yeats (1865-1939), the son of an Irish artist, has been the most influential poet in English literature since Browning died in 1889. That influence has been not so much technical, or even literary, as purely aesthetic. Yeats, by his whole life and by his complete devotion to the art of poetry, has maintained a standard, a sort of poetic procedure, from which he has never swerved. With his keen mind and his susceptible imagination he has followed many paths, some of them into dubious country and dark places; but he has always returned to the main road of poetry, the richer for his odd experiences. Beginning as a singer of what was called the Celtic Twilight, his early work was lyrical, and celebrated the Irish fairies and folk lore, many of his verse-plays being dramatizations of the national legends. But as he matured his nature demanded something more concrete and more intellectually founded. He turned to politics, and to the practical project of founding a national theatre (the Abbey Theatre, Dublin, run in partnership with another dramatist, Lady Gregory, and others such as J. M. Synge).

Mysticism in W. B. Yeats

In addition, he turned to a more cosmopolitan field of inquiry, taking up a study of oriental religion, and coming under the influence of Madame Blavatsky, who introduced him to much semi-mystical speculation that might have sunk him as a poet. But his native genius triumphed even over this vague stimulant. In spite of the wanderings of his curious intellect, the poet in him had a simple integrity that was never deceived. His activities and whims were many. He was always willing to follow a mood. During the last year of his life he said to the writer: "The young English poets of today have forgotten one essential. They never trust to luck." That may sound capricious. In fact, it is profound, and comes from the acuteness of instinct, which is the source of poetry. Such a course is the only one to prevent stagnation of the soul.

Yeats made a system out of such caprice, and in consequence he never grew old as a poet. Indeed, in his last period, he was ahead of the younger generation of English poets of the 1930s, a greater rebel than them all, while knowing fully—which they did not—what he was rebelling against. He was rebelling against the tyranny of Time, that merciless leveller. In his later books, *The Tower*, *The Winding Stair*, and *Last Poems*, we see his poetry purged of facile beauties and the glamour of the Celtic mythology. It is bare, almost harsh and cryptic, making gestures of magnificent defiance. Here is an example, in a small poem called *Death* :

> Nor dread nor hope attend
> A dying animal;
> A man awaits his end
> Dreading and hoping all;
> Many times he died,
> Many times rose again.
> A great man in his pride
> Confronting murderous men
> Casts derision upon
> Supersession of breath;
> He knows death to the bone—
> Man has created death.

GEORGE MOORE

Moore's early style as a novelist was an imitation of the French realists; "A Mummer's Wife" and "Esther Waters" are examples.

Compare that with one of his early lyrics, and you will understand how this poet's genius profited from the storms and changes through which he lived during his seventy eventful years, marching triumphantly

abreast of them, a standard bearer to
the poets that came after him. Here is an
example of his early work:

> Down by the salley gardens my love
>   and I did meet;
> She passed the salley gardens with little
>   snow-white feet.
> She bid me take love easy, as the leaves
>   grow on the tree;
> But I, being young and foolish, with
>   her would not agree.
>
> In a field by the river my love and I
>   did stand,
> And on my leaning shoulder she laid
>   her snow-white hand.
> She bid me take life easy, as the grass
>   grows on the weirs;
> But I was young and foolish, and now
>   am full of tears.

In addition to the several volumes of his
poems and plays, the writer recommends
his prose book, *Autobiographies*, which
introduces the reader into the world of
artists and writers who flourished at the
beginning of the century.

Conscious Artistry of George Moore

Read also the autobiographical books
of the Irish novelist, George Moore (1852-
1933), *Confessions of a Young Man* and *Hail
and Farewell*. They relate how this son of
an Anglo-Irish squire, with a small patri-
mony, went to Paris and played the dilet-
tante in the art studios there during the time
when the masters of the Impressionist
School were flourishing: how he came back
to Dublin and took a hand (a mischievous
one) with Yeats in the setting up of the
Irish School; how he quarrelled with people,
and how as a writer he perfected the art of
spying through the keyhole of his contemporaries. He was an odd, untrustworthy
figure, beginning as an almost illiterate,
horsy squireen who spoke of his "father's
serfs," and gradually evolving a prose style
that ran as smoothly as a billiard ball over
the green table. His early novels were direct
imitations of the French realists, such as
Zola and Huysmans. *Esther Waters* and *A
Mummer's Wife* are the best examples of

HENRY JAMES

*Henry James, though an American, was an
interpreter of late nineteenth-century English
social life and manners.*

this direct transportation of the French
technique across the Channel. But they are
living books, because Moore had a tenderness of touch, the tenderness of the indul-
gent sensualist, especially in his portrayal
of women. The two heroines of these books
are living women, unforgettable and
haunting.

From this harsh realism he soon moved
on to a more subtle inquiry into the world
of human emotions. *Evelyn Innes, Sister
Teresa*, and *The Lake* show him exploring
the almost mystical values of music and
religion, but here again, as indeed through
all his books early and late, his contact was
a sensuous one, from outside and never
from internal experience. He was a chronic
sympathizer, even when his sympathy took
the form of betrayal and derision. By the
time he wrote his novel on the life of Christ,
The Brook Kerith, he had evolved his later
prose style, a fugal one that ran without
colour like a stream of never-pausing
waters. It is monotonous, but it has a
hypnotic beauty, just as the sound of running water has. Its last manifestation took

the form of a series of loosely connected reconstructions of old Irish folk tales, called *A Storyteller's Holiday*. They are quite magical in their deliberately low-toned counterpoint, running on and on until the reader surrenders and floats willingly downstream. Nevertheless, they have a most sincere (if Moore can ever be called sincere) value as a marvellous impressionist picture of the period, comparable to the canvases of Manet, the French artist whom Moore so much admired.

American in London

Moore was something of an uprooted creature, but not nearly so much so as Henry James. This large, monumental figure, booming and soliloquizing his way through the drawing-rooms and hotel salons of Europe during the 'nineties and the first two decades of our present century, summed up in his career one of the unique cultural problems of that time. That problem is pithily expressed in a phrase from Somerset Maugham's novel, *Cakes and Ale*. "Henry James turned his back on one of the great events of the world's history, the rise of the United States, in order to report tittle-tattle at tea parties in English country houses." Why he did that is more analytically explained by the admirable American literary critic, Van Wyck Brooks, in his long history of the decline and fall of New England culture, that last flower of the old English stock transported in Elizabethan and Caroline times to flourish round the tea-tables of Boston. No high-brows have been more austere than those intellectual aristocrats, whose president was Emerson, and whose ambassador was Longfellow. They produced a noble harvest of poets, novelists and historians, scholars and philosophers. And now their culture has been diffused and diluted, into the general stock of modern America. They were a survival from Europe, and the less vital of them believed that they had no place in the new, aggressive American consciousness springing out of the Middle West and the pioneer States.

Henry James was the greatest example of these defeatists. He fled to Europe, as one or two others have done since. But like all uprooted plants, he had no reservoir on which to draw, and gradually he withered upwards, his work growing more and more attenuated and remote from life. The miracle is that it achieved so much upon so little sustenance. Settling in Paris in 1875 (but rather as a swallow settles), he made the personal acquaintance of the masters whom he proposed to model himself upon: the Goncourts, Flaubert, Zola and Turgenev, with Flaubert's pupil, Guy de Maupassant. Here he met George Moore, in many respects a similar rootless plant. When they both came to England, it was with the same mission, to reorganize the technique of the English novel, to give it shape and definition, and to cure it of its characteristic looseness of plot, ease of writing, and lack of selectivity.

Subtlety of Henry James

James's early novels are based on this theme of self-education in art, being morbidly concerned with the struggle of the artist towards self-expression, and the discovery of a healthy place in a society that persists in remaining indifferent to the claims of the creative muse. *Watch and Ward*, *The Tragic Muse*, and *Roderick Hudson* are examples of this pursuit, the central figures in each of them being concerned with some form of artistic or cultural self-discovery. The style in these is not remarkably idiosyncratic, but already the author's character shows its bias towards a tortuous method of emotional analysis. His nerves seem already strung up to that pitch of intense sensitivity that led him, in his later work, to a masterly indecisiveness, so that not only was he reluctant to bring the plots of his novels to a crisis, but he could hardly bear to commit himself to the completion of a sentence. His parentheses have become famous. Not only do they string out his novels upon a chain of qualifications, but also in the record of his conversation with friends, and also in his letters, they have immortalized him so that the memory of his personality is a grotesque parody of the man.

It was inevitable that a man of such a temperament, always a traveller and repudiating his native elements, should become

he recorder of appearances and sophistica-
tions rather than of solid worth. Manners
meant more to him than morals. Yet he
made a puritanism, and a singularly
mirthless puritanism, out of this obsession.
His preoccupation with social values and
niceties became almost ritualistic, and his
snobbery was elaborated into a religion

Henry James, although his native language was English, was a self-conscious
import into our English life. Still more
exotic was his disciple, Joseph Conrad.
Such a career is unique in any literature.
Conrad's surname was Korzeniowski, his
father being a small Polish landowner,
whose liberal sentiments got him into

POLE WHO ENRICHED ENGLISH LITERATURE
*Son of Polish parents, Joseph Conrad spent years in the English merchant navy before
devoting himself to novel writing, and life at sea is reflected in many of his stories. But his
main interest is in character, particularly in "difficult people" who in some sense (like
Conrad himself) feel cut off from their fellows. The bust is by Epstein.*

whose inner shrine he tended with exquisite
precision.

Representing his style at its prime,
before it began to parody itself, are the
novels, *The Bostonians* and *Washington
Square*. His most popular work, perhaps,
is *Daisy Miller*. For his later work try
The Golden Bowl. To realize his background
one might well first read the autobiography
of his contemporary, Henry Adams, and
follow this with the two volumes of his own
letters, in which both his style and his
predicament are fully revealed.

trouble with the Czarist regime. Exile
resulted in illness and death, and the boy
was early resolved to remove himself to
spheres where freedom was the first consideration. From the inland forests he
went to sea, and from Poland he came to
England. Born in 1857, he first saw the sea
in 1874, by which time he had begun to
read books in English. Four years later he
was a sailor before the mast on an English
ship. The story of his subsequent career
at sea is told in one of his most enjoyable
books, *A Personal Record*, which is

recommended as an introduction to this great artist. While an officer in our mercantile marine, he wrote his first novel, *Almayer's Folly*. This was reported on favourably by Edward Garnett—quick to discover and befriend men of talents. Garnett saw his book through the press, remaining always a valuable adviser and introducing him to other writers, such as Henry James, Galsworthy, Ford Madox Hueffer (with whom he collaborated in the novel, *Romance*) and W. H. Hudson the naturalist and master of a perfect prose style. He learned from them all; but later he copied the trick of relating his stories in an indirect way through the narration of a fictitious observer, as though the method of direct observation were too blatant to capture the subtleties of character aimed at by the novelist. This proxy for his own self took the form of a sea captain whom he called Marlow, and the reader has, in many of the novels, to approach the action and the characters through the memory and sensibility of Marlow, whose yarning was often extremely leisurely.

Conrad's Magnificent Prose

Conrad's work is marked throughout by a romantic pride. He wears an aristocratic mantle of aloofness, and that dignity which characterized his personal habits also touched his work with a distinction that cannot be overlooked even by the most careless reader. His prose was like the music of a cathedral organ, achieving sonority after sonority, with shifts of key that only occasionally betrayed the fact of his foreign origin. He has a habit of opening a paragraph with a simple statement that helps the narrative along. But from here he builds up a sort of soliloquy on that fact, adding clause to clause until the paragraph has become a spiritual adventure such as one would expect from a poet rather than from a novelist. There is not space here to give an example of this device, for Conrad worked in amplitude. But here is an extract from *An Outcast of the Islands*, the sequel to *Almayer's Folly*, which will show how he builds up his prose music, and also will reveal his habit of turning the mundane

to the significant and even transcendental

She had taken up her burden already with the intention of pursuing her path. His sudden movement arrested her at the first step, and again she stood straight, slim, expectant, with a readiness to dart away suggested in the light immobility of her pose. High above, the branches of the trees met in a transparent shimmer of waving green mist, through which the rain of yellow rays descended upon her head, streamed in glints down her black tresses, shone with the glow of liquid metal on her face, and lost itself in vanishing sparks in the sombre depths of her eyes that, wide open now, with enlarged pupils, looked steadily at the man in her path. And Willems stared at her, charmed with a charm that carries with it a sense of irreparable loss, tingling with that feeling which begins like a caress and ends in a blow, in that sudden hurt of a new emotion making its way into a human heart, with the brusque stirring of sleeping sensations awakening suddenly to the rush of new hopes, new fears, new desires—and to the flight of one's old self.

In such prose, superb but not quite the prose of an Englishman, he told his tales of the sea, the tropics, and the wild places of the human soul. Try first *Chance*, the book that brought him fame. Then take *The Mirror of the Sea*, a collection of sketches that will lead to the rest of his short works, the crown of which is, in the writer's opinion, *The Shadow Line*. Then enjoy his more ambitious works such as *Lord Jim* and *The Arrow of Gold*. And to learn something of his agonies while composing, one may read the letters (almost every one of them a cry of pain) which he wrote to Edward Garnett continuously from the time when he settled in Kent, as a professional novelist, until his death in 1924.

We come now to six figures whose names will be long associated with the first three decades of our century, and without whose prolific contribution to the stage and novel the significant literature of our time would be reduced indeed. They are Shaw, Barrie, Wells, Kipling, Bennett and Galsworthy. It may be, of course, that time and posterity will remove some of these figures from the front of the picture, replacing them with one or more of those already discussed, or indeed by some name still little known or little considered by literary historians. The fact that they have played so large a part in moulding the manners and morals of our age may suggest that, their purpose achieved, they are doomed by the very obviousness of their aims. Nothing is so fatal as successful prophecy.

It is sufficient, however, to realize today how much these six writers have done in their own lifetime. It is impossible to say who is the most important of them. That depends upon the reader's own bias.

George Bernard Shaw

Let us take them in order of age. George Bernard Shaw was born in Dublin in 1856. Like Wells, he was self-educated (is there any other form of education?). In 1876 he came to London and began to teach English to the English, a profession which he never dropped. He was fed on Karl Marx; and, by his friendship with Sidney Webb, Edward Carpenter and William Morris, he soon learned to arm himself formidably for the long war against British *laissez-faire*, narrow-mindedness, vested interests, flesh-eating habits, and Philistinism towards the arts, the sciences and life in general.

Although practising and celebrating the art of reason, he had something of the mystic in his nature. That is why he could call poverty "a crime." He felt that in his blood and not with his brain. His lifelong habit of mind was one of extreme fastidiousness; physical, mental and moral. His asceticism may have been more sanitary than catholic, but it was nevertheless a determinant throughout his life. It found a dogma in the philosophy of Nietzsche, and a technical expression from the plays of Ibsen and the dialectic of the drawing-room conversation of intellectual Dublin. He began as a very readable critic of art and music, and then of the theatre.

The years of moral breakdown in Britain following the Boer War gave Shaw a chance to put his preachings into practice. He used the newly created Stage Society, and afterwards the management and production of J. E. Vedrenne and Granville Barker, to produce his play, *John Bull's Other Island*. From that time the English stage was Bernard Shaw. Everybody knows that, and his plays became known to everybody of intelligence. Through them, and the prefaces written to emphasize them, he mocked the British public, whipped it with cold Irish derision, accused it of complacency and stupid sentimentalism, ridiculed its foibles and traditions. But his most savage audacities never made it lose its temper with him. He remained an idol, in spite of the fact that much of his teaching was accepted in his lifetime and incorporated into the life of the nation. His lifework was crowned in 1925 by the award of the Nobel Prize for literature. He was among the greatest journalists and public speakers of our time. The charm of his Irish voice, the rapier-like speed of his repartee, the laughter and clear logic working simultaneously, gave his oratory a power that is already legendary. He may have scoffed at fantasy, and the elusive qualities of poetry. But the clarity of his prose style, and the dance and sparkle of his dialogue, are the voice of poetry. Further, there occur in his plays moments when the argument becomes incandescent, and throws a ray of light into regions of the soul far beyond the comprehension of the purely logical mind.

Creator of Peter Pan

Since Freud opened a window into the scullery of the human soul, it has been difficult to take the voluminous work of J. M. Barrie quite seriously. Born in 1860, he was famous at the age of thirty, through *My Lady Nicotine* and *The Little Minister*, his fourth and fifth novels.

The latter being successful also as a play, he took to writing for the theatre, with even greater success than that which he had won as a novelist. *Peter Pan*, in 1904, put him among the creators of a universal symbolism, along with Hans Andersen and Defoe. The child who refused to grow up

J. M. BARRIE

The delicate fantasy of J. M. Barrie's plays may be seen in " Dear Brutus," "Mary Rose," "Quality Street," and "Peter Pan."

may be said to stand for Barrie himself. This shrewd Scotsman insisted upon maintaining the emotional world of childhood intact, and refused to free himself from his mother's apron strings.

He made this refusal into a philosophic principle, elaborated in the book *Margaret Ogilvy* (1896), a biography of his mother. Thus, to the end of his life and his lifework, he kept up the queer, irrelevant and often fantastic realism of the child. It was hedged around by a dark forest of fear, shapeless and primordial. That forest came up to the very doors of his house of life (see the play *Dear Brutus*). Against this background of unresolved childhood terrors, his humour was shadowed by bitterness and often by a debilitating tearfulness, which makes us tend today to underrate him.

Voice of Rudyard Kipling

Next in order of age comes Rudyard Kipling, born in India in 1865, and dying in Sussex in 1936. Those two geographical poles mark the extreme locations of his work and temperament. The work of Kipling, the Anglo-Indian, has run like a scarlet thread through the pattern of the British literary scene during the past half-

century. Blatant imperialism shouted with a loud voice round the turn of the last Victorian years. The voice was Kipling's. In verse that rarely rises to the height of poetry, and in short stories remarkable for their mastery of plot, succinct expression, and economy of material, he sang the slogans of the makers of empire, and advocated the White Man's Burden. But at the same time he criticized "muddied oafs and flannelled fools," summing up in his phrase our addiction to professional sports. His novel, *Kim*, presents a startlingly un-European view of the Indian scene, anticipating by many years E. M. Forster's *Passage to India*. While in general his politics and racial doctrines belong to a phase of British history which we dare hope will be modified by our recent bitter national experience, there is another side to Kipling represented by his devotion to Sussex. From it we realize that he was not brought up as a Philistine. There was a touch of the aesthete and the mystic in him. Read his exquisite poem, *The Way through the Woods*. And re-read *Kim*. Here is a Kipling who has escaped from *The Barrack Room Ballads*, an artist as temperamental and subtle in his effects as the Russian, Chekhov.

Masefield's Revival of Narrative Poetry

Kipling introduced into polite verse the language of the barracks. Another poet, John Masefield, came after him to enlarge this experiment by writing long narrative poems in the vernacular of the sailor and the peasant. Born in 1878, he was trained for the merchant navy, but took to a wandering life and to literature. At the age of twenty-four he published *Salt Water Ballads* and followed this with books of short stories and his first novel, *Captain Margaret*, while a play, *The Tragedy of Nan*, was produced by Granville Barker in 1909. Then *The Everlasting Mercy*, a narrative poem published serially in *The English Review*, made him both famous and notorious: famous because of the fervour and passion of the poem; notorious because it contained words hitherto taboo on the printed page—at least, since Elizabethan days. He brought

POET OF EMPIRE

Rudyard Kipling's stirring verses had a great vogue at the end of the nineteenth century;
his novels include "Kim"; his short stories "Plain Tales from the Hills" and "Soldiers Three."
The illustration is a photograph of a portrait by Sir Philip Burne-Jones.

E.L.L.—G*

poetry once more into popularity, and might well be called the Chaucer of our day, but without the humour of that master. His output is large, but success (he is now Poet Laureate and has been honoured with the O.M.) has not clouded his faculty of exalted enthusiasm. His style, especially in his prose, has become more sparse and laconic, but he employs it still to show the sufferings of the under-dog.

"The Old Wives' Tale"

Those sufferings have also been the concern of Arnold Bennett and H. G. Wells. Bennett used them to demonstrate a theory of the art of fiction. Wells used them to feed his own indignation over the wrong turning taken by the machine age. For him, they were the symbol of all that was unscientific, unethical and uneconomic in a world that the genuis and application of the chemist, the engineer and the biologist might by now have made into an earthly paradise.

Arnold Bennett was born in 1867 at Hanley, in the Potteries, an industrial district which he has portrayed in minute detail in his finest novels, one of which, *The Old Wives' Tale*, is certainly among the great novels of this century. He was the son of a solicitor, but early went into journalism, editing first a paper for women. After his first novel, *A Man from the North* (1898), he gave up journalism as a regular profession and set about the more risky one of pure letters. From 1900 to 1908 he lived in France and married a Frenchwoman. The fruits of this sojourn are shown not only in the technique of *The Old Wives' Tale*, but also in the setting of the second portion of it, where he gives a most realistic picture of the siege of Paris during the Franco-Prussian War. This book, a long, ambitious work, was written in five months after years of preparation and the study of such French masters as Flaubert, Balzac and Zola. He lived the life of the detached literary artist until 1914, publishing by that time his other novels of the Pottery Towns, *Clayhanger*, *Hilda Lessways*, *These Twain*. In addition, he wrote under the pen-name of "Jacob Tonson" a weekly critical essay for

The New Age that brought him a second reputation as one of the shrewdest critics of the day. His pose as a man of almost Philistine common sense, with a touch of provincial contrariness, could not hide the sensibility and dignity of his prose style.

The 1914-18 war involved Bennett in propaganda work for the Government. During this period he met politicians, soldiers, big-business men, and public figures hitherto outside his range of experience. Especially he attracted the notice and admiration of Lord Beaverbrook, whose friendship drew him more and more into the world of affairs. He became, very consciously, the man of the world, a part which his financial success enabled him to fulfil. But he remained a generous-hearted artist and a discriminating critic. His weekly article in one of Beaverbrook's newspapers was the most authoritative literary criterion for a decade. He died in 1931, largely as a result of consistent overwork.

Much of his work was ephemeral because of its theme. He lacked, perhaps, a central purpose (apart from his noble devotion to the art of writing), and after his first enthusiasm for portraying the country and society of his early years, he seemed to lose his way in eccentric literary enterprises, such as writing a huge novel, full of detail, about the running of a hotel (*Imperial Palace*).

This may be because he lacked the fire of genius, such as burned out another writer from the Midlands, D. H. Lawrence, who also wrote one of the great novels of this century, *Sons and Lovers*. To read two great books together is instructive. The cool deliberation of *The Old Wives' Tale* and the untidy fervour of *Sons and Lovers*, reveal the extremes of literary inspiration and method. One is left with the conviction that Bennett was a larger man than one's first impression suggested, and that the overtone of his prosaic method and theme was one of poetry. It might startle some readers if it is suggested that Bennett, the registrar of the lives of petty middle-class shopkeepers in the dreary industrial Midlands, was possessed of the manners and ideals of the Age of Reason, and might have enjoyed life in the eighteenth century.

H. G. Wells claimed to be, above all, a man of Reason. But how much more he was! No English writer of this century, or indeed of any century was more vital and prolific. Since he published his first book, *The Time Machine*, in 1895, he wrote some two or more books each year as long as he lived. One of them is an *Outline of World History* that well might have been the major achievement of a historian. It is a book that is ridden by Wells's particular demon. All the bees in his bonnet buzz there. But it is a wonderful survey of the story of the human race in its gradual climb from the slime to the laboratory, an uninterrupted progress in spite of the delays occasioned, in Mr. Wells's opinion, by religions and heroes. It is as though Voltaire had compromised with Tolstoy, after co-opting Rutherford and Darwin.

Herbert George Wells was born in Bromley, Kent, in 1866, the son of a professional cricketer. His childhood was one of chronic half-poverty, and this experience coloured the whole of his view of life. His purpose was consistently to show where the "little man," the John Citizen, has stood in the modern world of industrial expansion, of machines, of vast organizations of capital and labour, of applied science, and of the surviving influences of dogmatic religion and feudalism.

H. G. Wells and the Little Man

Examination of his books reveals that almost every one of them has a central character who is a sort of economic innocent, blandly and pathetically moving from the cradle to the grave unaware of what is going on around him, yet feeling in his struggle to exist the increasing competition of the dangerous world. Kipps, Mr. Polly, Bert Smallways, are typical examples. These generous, ill-educated, bamboozled men and women move through the world as Wells saw it, rather like the child Pippa through Robert Browning's great poem, *Pippa Passes*, by their very unawareness setting the conscience of the world to restless self-questioning. Should these things be: the poverty, the ignorance, the squalor, ugliness, waste, clumsiness and superstition?

H. G. WELLS
A prophet of his times, H. G. Wells in his middle years was popularizing the scientist's views, methods and discoveries.

Wells answered the question with a flood of eloquence, calling for a complete reorganization of human society under the administration of reason, science and goodwill. Amid the multitude of his books, the enormous range of subject matter, this simple question-and-answer emerges as his main motive, stated from the data of his childhood in the so-called prosperous decades of the nineteenth century.

After working in a draper's shop (see *Kipps*), he became a pupil teacher. Then he graduated in science at London University, continued teaching and wrote his first book, a textbook on biology. Science and socialism soon claimed him altogether, or almost altogether, for there was an element in Wells's character that was uncapturable. It was the artist in Wells; sly, puckish, humorous, sensuous and childlike; the leaven in the lump. He was a founder member of the Fabian Society, but its dreary statistical methods were inadequate for this exuberant creature of genius, and after writing such tracts for it as

This Misery of Boots, Socialism and Marriage and *New Worlds for Old,* he broke away from it and remained for the rest of his career a *franc-tireur,* moving along the snowclad summits of science, like Excelsior, luring the masses to follow him with his vision of a world set free by technique instead of politics.

It is needless to list here the huge number of his books. They consist of the early scientific romances such as *The Invisible Man, When the Sleeper Wakes, The First Men in the Moon;* the sociological novels such as *Love and Mr. Lewisham, Kipps, Tono-Bungay* (surely his greatest book), *Mr. Polly* and *Ann Veronica;* studies in general philosophy such as *First and Last Things, God the Invisible King, Joan and Peter* and *William Clissold.* Latterly he had concerned himself almost entirely with the problem of the reorganization of society, a problem overshadowed in his last year of life by the invention of atomic warfare and the despair of man which it aroused in him.

But the mere listing of his work tells nothing of his genius; nor does it recall how his amazing prophecies have come true. More and more he emerges, as time recesses him and his contemporaries, as the most representative voice of the world in transition from the iron age of the nineteenth century to the chemico-physical age of the twentieth.

Never did he cease to call his fellow men to the habits of reason rather than of passion. But what an appetite for life he has always enjoyed!

Creator of the Forsytes

Let us turn now to the last of the six literary figures whose massive output of work, much of it on a high level, lends them a stature beyond most of the writers of our time. John Galsworthy (1867-1933) belonged, like Conrad, to the circle of Edward Garnett—that most discerning of critics and fosterer of talent whose retreat in the lovely wooded hill country on the borders of Kent was known to so many of

JOHN GALSWORTHY
Galsworthy drew on the life and emotions of the English middle-class for his novels and plays.

our leading men of letters both before and after they became established. In Britain Galsworthy gained fame both as dramatist and as novelist—fame temporarily clouded, perhaps, by the rise of new fashions and problems; but in Europe his fame has been even more exalted.

At the core of all drama is conflict—opposition between man and man, or the struggle against obstacles towards some goal. As a dramatist, Galsworthy was interested in showing us that type of conflict in which both parties are convinced of their own righteousness. The struggle between capital and labour is presented in *Strife,* between the new rich and the old aristocracy in *The Skin Game.* Galsworthy's mind, trained in law, shows both the virtues and the weaknesses of both sets of protagonists and both, in the main, act according to their lights. If the struggle leads to disaster for the innocent, no one can be blamed for the outcome. The only villain in the piece is man's own nature—for its insufficiency of tolerance and love. In *Justice* he stirs the imagination by his presentation of the law-breaker, his trial and his punishment. We are made to recognize that bare justice and consciousness of right are not enough. Galsworthy has no explicit solutions for the problems he raises; he simply holds a lamp in the dark places and seeks to increase the sum of our humanitarianism.

But Galsworthy's chief claim to fame is as a novelist. His *Forsyte* books, consisting of the two omnibus volumes, six novels in all, have become a sort of sociological testament for foreigners who are curious to know what England is, how it functions, and wherein lies the secret of its power. These tales, the backbone of his lifework, are so well known that they hardly need describing. The reader need only be reminded of the graphic picture they give of the commercial, upper middle-class world whose tough, ruthless, and dynastic code of life dominated our politics, trade and culture throughout the latter half of last century, and is only just beginning to relinquish its hold on this one. Its power is breaking before the advance of bigger combinations of forces, and therefore Galsworthy's stories already belong to the historical past so far as concerns their sociological aspect. But these books, in common with the rest of his novels and his plays, have something more than that. It is a rich, emotional glow, expressed in a nostalgic and dignified prose. Latter-day critics ignore this, and have underrated him. His noble faculty for sympathy with man and beast gives dramatic as well as moral strength to his work, and has made his influence as a playwright comparable, or at least complementary, to that of Somerset Maugham, another writer unduly neglected by the critics in spite of his enormous success.

Maugham's Detachment

Both are novelists who seek to hide from their readers their own emotions, Galsworthy with a cloak of stoicism, Maugham with one of cynicism. Both are concerned to portray the go-getters, the hard-faced money worshippers and makers of Empire. But Maugham deals with a later stage of that dynastic regime, when decay has set in around the outer fringes of it. In one of his most successful plays, *Our Betters*, the very title sets the keynote of derisive irony with which this writer excoriates his own social class. Maugham, like Galsworthy, has shown a mastery of the short story, and in this form both rank with Wells and Kipling. But the most self-revealing work by Maugham is his *magnum opus, Of Human Bondage*. It is one of the great novels of our century. *Cakes and Ale*, a novel about novelists, contains a cruel portrait of Hugh Walpole, and a kindly one of an older writer whom the author assures us is not Thomas Hardy. The heroine of this book, Rose Driffield, is a memorable creature, who will live along with her sister weak-woman, Manon Lescaut, created by the French priest, the Abbé Prévost, and with Thomas Hardy's Tess of the D'Urbervilles.

On Galsworthy's death in 1933, his mantle was divided between Hugh Walpole (*died* 1944) and Francis Brett Young. Hugh

SIR HUGH WALPOLE
One of the most popular novelists of his day, Hugh Walpole found his material in clerical life, in history, in the life of childhood and in the psychology of abnormal people.

W. H. HUDSON
*Great naturalist author of "A Shepherd's
Life" and "The Purple Land."*

Walpole's *Fortitude*, had a romantic glow,
but as he became more successful he settled
into literary habits, either of neurotic irri-
tability bordering near-melodrama, as in
his long *Herries* saga, or of sadism, as in
the novels, *Mr. Perrin and Mr. Traill* and
Portrait of a Man with Red Hair.

Francis Brett Young worked with a more
deliberate literary artistry, out of a character more open and buoyant. His novels
such as *The Portrait of Clare*, have a quality
which reminds us of the English water-
colour painters. Most of them are set in his
native Worcestershire, where, after training
as a doctor, he settled after the first World
War. He also published a long verse
epic relating the history of England, *The
Island* (1944). He died in 1954.

Hudson the Naturalist

Now let us turn again to the circle of
Edward Garnett, which gives such a shape
to the history of literature during the
opening decades of the century.

Besides Galsworthy, there were W. H.
Hudson, Walter de la Mare, W. H. Davies,
and Edward Thomas, all of whom have in
their work the quality of permanence.

W. H. Hudson was born of American
parentage in the Argentine in 1841. His
boyhood there is described in *Far Away and
Long Ago*, written in old age, and one of
the most beautiful autobiographies in the
English language. This book alone would
stamp him as one of our greatest prose
masters. But it is of a piece with all his
work. He wrote principally of nature, and
especially of birds, of which he had an
intimate and exact knowledge. By some
magic of his own, he even had the ability
to express their songs in his prose, differen-
tiating one finch from another. Not birds
only, however, were the source of that
delight and absorption which filled him in
his contact with nature, and which saturated
his prose as the September sunshine satu-
rates our countryside and makes the autumn
days timeless and almost heart-breaking in
their beauty. Nothing escaped his observant
eye. In his collection of essays, *Nature in
Downland*, the tiny flowers, dwarfed from
their original form by the age-long cropping
of the sheep on the bare South Downs, are
differentiated by him with a most exciting
exactitude. Exciting, because in all his
writing he had a faculty of at once catching
the reader's interest, and keeping it; and
this although his interest in human nature
is often perfunctory.

We can discover, however, a semi-
mystical strain in him, which emerges most
in his romances (they can hardly be called
novels), *The Purple Land* and *Green
Mansions*. In the latter there is a character,
half-human and half-dryad, called Rima,
who inspired the sculptor, Jacob Epstein,
when he was commissioned to carve the
memorial to Hudson in Hyde Park. Possibly the most perfect of Hudson's work is to
be found in *A Shepherd's Life*, but this is a
matter of personal choice. He died in 1922,
and his fame has grown steadily since then.
for he was neglected in his lifetime.

Nature Poet

Edward Thomas, a London-born Welshman (1879-1917), killed in the first World
War, had a literary career, the significance
of which would have appealed to his wry
sense of humour had he survived. Setting
out with high ambition, he found himself
too sensitive to push his way to the front

in the world of letters. A diffident man, he was a firm critic, and in spite of his shyness and somewhat under-vitalized nature made a considerable reputation as a reviewer. He wrote hack-books to add to his income (topographical books and biographies), but in spite of the weariness of this occupation he perfected his style as an essayist. Not until after his death was it discovered that under the name of Edward Eastaway, he had also been practising the art of verse, under the stimulation of his friend, the American poet, Robert Frost, who had settled in England and was one of Garnett's discoveries. Thomas's poetry catches from Frost's a quality of laconic understatement. His rhythms are elusive, delicate, melancholy, like a robin's song in autumn. But gradually the originality of mood and tone comes home upon the reader and remains there with a haunting persistence. It is this posthumous work that will remain.

Poet and Super-tramp

Of the poets whom Garnett knew and proclaimed, there remain de la Mare and Davies. About these two there is surely complete unanimity of opinion amongst critics, no matter what their views and prejudices may be. Here are two immortals. W. H. Davies had a picturesque career, which he has described in a book called *The Autobiography of a Super-tramp*, written in 1907 in a cottage near Sevenoaks, lent him for that purpose by Edward Thomas. This book, with its preface by Bernard Shaw, brought in a steady competence in royalties for the rest of Davies's life (he died in 1940). It is a masterpiece of artful candour and simplicity. Davies, son of a Welsh sailor from Newport, refused to be caught up in the industrial machine, so he became a tramp, both here and in America. In Canada, he lost a foot train-jumping. He was then about thirty-five. This put an end to his roving. He came home, and limped the streets of London, singing, or selling boot-laces, sleeping in a Lambeth dosshouse. From this place he published, at his own expense, his first book of poems, *The Soul's Destroyer*. It would have wasted his pennies, had he not sent a copy by post to Bernard Shaw, with the request that if

the famous man liked it he could pay for it, if not, he could return it! Shaw paid for it, and introduced it to the leading critics, among them Thomas and Garnett.

Davies was instantly recognized as a creature of genius. A Civil List pension was given him by Mr. Asquith, and from that time (1905) until his death he continued to sing his unique song. He has been called a nature poet. But that is nonsense. He never knew an oak from an elm. The substance of his muse consists of a sparrow, a robin, sunshine, the moon and the snow. The second aspect of him consists of his recollections of human society as seen by an outcast. Prostitutes, tramps, children, working folk, sailors, figure in his simply constructed lyrics. He was not a scholar. He had shrewd and impeccable taste, especially in Elizabethan song writers. But he could not sustain the mental effort of reading an epic. Yet his own work is always recognizable, stamped with his personality.

EDWARD THOMAS

Edward Thomas's literary work included essays and criticisms, but it was his poetry that won him recognition.

W. H. DAVIES

Davies won quick fame in literary circles with the publication, in 1908, of his "Autobiography of a Super-tramp"; his collected poems appeared in 1929.

It has a summer-day, joyous and brave vitality, even when it is presenting a tragic theme. Davies the man was exactly like his work; simple, with a touch of innocent cunning, truly innocent of soul, and generous as a sailor. His emotions were completely uninhibited, and in conversation tears of sympathy or sheer delight would suffuse his large brown eyes. His poetry has the same characteristics.

Terror and Fantasy

Walter de la Mare was Davies's junior by three years. He had indifferent health, and was always a man of the study. His scholarship was wide and out-of-the-way. He was a geographer of the other side of the moon. The ordinary, everyday things were for him significant of another world, and out of the commonplace he produced the occult. This affects his prose and his poetry in a queer, oblique way, throwing slant lights, of insight, of terror, of fantastic humour, of desperate solitude, across the scene of his universe, making the unreal

real, and the real fabulous. There is always a beauty of the earth or of divine and human love. He seems always to be saying:

> The night was cloyed with flowers
> In the darkness deep and sweet,
> When, at the window of the World,
> I heard the dancing feet;
> And viol and tambour
> Made musical the air,
> While yet a voice within me cried,
> "Beware!"

His prose is rich and odd, like that of the masters of the later seventeenth century. *Henry Brocken, The Return, The Memoirs of a Midget* are examples of his use of the novel form. What a weird, yet exquisitely beautiful thing he makes of it. His technique as a poet is subtle, making infinitely important the inversion of a phrase, or the stress upon a single syllable. Look, in the collected poems, at such a gem as *The Bottle*, or the now famous dramatic lyric, *The Listeners*.

Rupert Brooke and Others

This poet and others mentioned are of an older generation, luminaries of the opening decades of the century. Coming after them was the generation of poets of the war of 1914-18, of whom Rupert Brooke was the most popular. He was for long with John Masefield, the best-seller among modern poets, and indeed became a legend. That legend, together with the appeal of his richly emotional verse, extravagant in the Elizabethan way, while being nobly mannered in the Cambridge mode of his time, shone like a star above the literary turmoil of the 'twenties. He died on foreign service in 1915. The 'forties and the 'fifties almost ignore him, and he has had no influence on the latest generation of poets. But his verse has a fine sense of form, and his phrases are always lit by imagination. He has, perhaps, something in common with the Caroline poet, Andrew Marvell; the same clarity of image, the same suave pleading and the same charm of personality. After him came Wilfred Owen, who was killed in action before being able to realize the

JOHN MASEFIELD

John Masefield, who followed Robert Bridges as Poet Laureate in 1930, published his first poetry in 1902. This was "Salt Water Ballads," reflecting his early years at sea. Much of his verse and prose since then has the same invigorating atmosphere. "Reynard the Fox," a narrative poem, "The Tragedy of Nan," a play, and "Odtaa" and "Sard Harker," both novels, are among his best-known works. The first part of his autobiography, "In the Mill," tells of his early life and work in Canada.

greater range of his literary gift. His poems are desperate and tragic. Their form is most interesting to the craftsman, with their experiments in assonance (the rhyming of vowels), and in internal rhyme (the rhymes hidden in the middle of lines).

Siegfried Sassoon, Robert Graves and Robert Nichols are three poets who have survived and made a mark in the between-the-wars world. Sassoon has the gift of being both idyllic and satiric; Robert Nichols has eloquence and intensity of feeling; Robert Graves, both in prose and verse, is a deliberate word-master who can turn his well-disciplined technique to various uses. As a narrator of a complicated mass of facts in a simple way, he is a master, as, for example, in the novels *I, Claudius* and *Claudius the God*. In verse he harks back to that quaint old poet, John Skelton, once tutor to Henry the Eighth.

This survey is hardly the place to discuss the poets of a still younger generation. They are legion, for a revival of poetry, both the reading of it and the making of it, has been apparent for the past seven or eight years. Two young poets of both promise and accomplishment were killed in the second World War, Sidney Keyes and Alun Lewis, and their names should have made their mark in literature, had not another sacrifice been demanded of them.

Bridges's "The Testament of Beauty"

Turn now to one or two survivors from Victorian times, and one or two distinct individualists: of the former, Robert Bridges and his friend Gerard Manley Hopkins. Bridges was a country gentleman and doctor, who early gave up his profession to devote himself solely to letters. His poetry is exquisite in form, and wholly lyrical. He works in a sort of pastel, or tempera, a technique that compels austerity of touch and coolness of colour in its devotee. His long poem, *Eros and Psyche*, for example, might be a wall decoration by the French artist Puvis de Chavannes. But what he lacks in sensuous heat, he makes up in mental vigour. Although he was made Poet Laureate after the trifling Alfred Austin, his nobility of spirit never brought him to the notice of the general public until, in the eighty-fourth year of his life, he published his major work, *The Testament of Beauty*, a vast philosophical poem, written in a classic quantitative metre and indulging in quaint fads with spelling. This poem has some beautiful landscape work in it, in the English school of water-colours, and its verbal graces are manifold.

Discovery of Gerard Manley Hopkins

Hopkins was a Roman Catholic priest, who left his manuscripts to Bridges. They remained unpublished between 1889, the year of his death, and 1918. Why Bridges allowed this lapse of time is perhaps to be explained by the strange form of the poems. Both poets were technical experimenters, but in opposite directions, Bridges towards lucidity, Hopkins towards the cryptic. The curious thing is that Hopkins's tricks with English prosody immediately found favour with the poets of the 1920s and his influence was marked, often with deplor-

WALTER DE LA MARE
Both as poet and novelist, Walter de la Mare displayed his love of the eerie and fanciful. Many of his poems are loved by children.

ROBERT BRIDGES
Created Poet Laureate in 1913, *Bridges published his major work, "The Testament of Beauty," in* 1929 *when he was eighty-five years old. The portrait is by William Strang.*

able result, on the outward form of much verse written by young poets who violently rejected his religious faith and his emotional writings. At his best he was a mystic and a devotee. At his worst he was a self-torturer and poseur, a verbal fop wearing his verse with a difference. He has been called a "great" poet; but it is to be doubted if eccentricity of manners (and technique constitutes a poet's "manners") is ever the sign of greatness.

Flamboyant Chesterton

How different was another poet, Gilbert Keith Chesterton, who later came to Catholicism. This rollicking figure, with his two friends, Hilaire Belloc and Maurice Baring, might be called one of the Three Musketeers of the Roman Catholic Revival in this country. Each of them is a literary character of distinct originality, standing in his own manner for the maintenance of the great Roman tradition. Such a definite purpose has given these men a firmness and

sense of form. As essayists and critics they take the European view. The paradox is that Chesterton was also a Little Englander. But then he is a master of paradox, indeed, paradox is often a master of him, becoming in his later work a literary device too easily introduced. In spite of this fault, he is a master of the essay, he is a poet with a magnificent gift of rhetoric and invective, and he is a literary critic of inspired insight. His first book was a study of Robert Browning, published in 1903, when he was thirty-one. He followed this with a book on Dickens, whose wild inventiveness and fantasy were qualities that he himself possessed in abundance. He believed in the Golden Age (for him it was probably in the fourteenth century when the Craft Guilds flourished and men worked with their hands), and this romantic faith coloured his political beliefs. He was a Distributionist. But then he was a bit of everything, except a dry economist and rationalist.

Creator of Father Brown

G. K. Chesterton lived hugely, in a sort of absent-minded consciousness of the whole universe. There is a legend that while on a lecture tour in the Midlands, he sent a telegram home to his wife: "Am in Loughborough; where should I be?" And of course, all the time he was in paradise; a paradise of shrewd benevolence and delight in what was going on around him. As poet, novelist (see *The Napoleon of Notting Hill, The Man Who Was Thursday, The Flying Inn*), thriller writer (*The Innocence of Father Brown*), dramatist (*Magic*), and religious writer (*Lives of St. Francis of Assisi* and *St. Thomas Aquinas*) he stamps his work recklessly with his personality, and the reader has to peer round the giant figure to see what is behind it. He died prematurely in 1934.

In comparison, his friend Belloc, surely a colourful enough writer, appears to be a sober and austere figure, an example of the Catholic-born as compared with the enthusiastic convert. Half French (see the charming account of their childhood by his sister, Mrs. Belloc Lowndes), Belloc's outlook was wholly European. For him the

Rhineland marked the outer bounds of civilization. Born in 1870 in France, he was educated in England, served for a year in the French army, and then did brilliantly at Balliol. He sat in Parliament from 1906 to 1910, but by that time he had already published his masterpiece, *The Path to Rome*, a travel book whose title has a double significance. He had always been a savage critic of bureaucracy and the control by the State of man's conscience and good taste. Some would say that his book, *The Servile State*, published in 1912, was prophetic of what was to come in Europe; a political development which he hated. Both his prose and his verse are richly formal, in the high Roman manner of Gibbon. His essays reflect every aspect of his rich mind (*On Nothing*, etc.) and his verse shows his humour. His historical writing has a religious bias, but it also has dignity and insight (*French Revolution, James II*). He died in 1953.

Maurice Baring (died 1945), beginning as a rich amateur of letters, who worked in the Diplomatic Service, was born in 1874. He, too, was converted to Rome, a spiritual experience which he describes in his autobiography, *The Puppet Show of Memory.* He wrote much on Russian literature, and his poetry is sensitive, orthodox work. In his novels he emerges, through a prose style laconic and deliberately low-toned, as an artist of exquisite if melancholy sensibility, resigned to the tragedy of the hopeless conflict of the human soul with an indifferent and crushing environment. His novel with the odd title of "*C*" shows this aspect of him; a gloomy aspect, in mood much like the later Latin poets who suffered in the shadow of the decline of Rome. His story *The Coat Without Seam*, shows a way of redemption from this pessimism. He, too, was a graceful essayist (*Lost Diaries*).

Poets without Hope

With a similar temperament given towards renunciation of the world, the poet, T. S. Eliot, like Henry James an American by birth, has for three decades been the monitor of the younger poets, both in form and mood.

In form he owes much to Browning and Walt Whitman, a compromise between free verse and metrical shapes marking most of his poetry. Cautious, arid of temper, his literary personality has been summed up by the American critic, Van Wyck Brooks, who said that he was a Christian "with little faith, less hope and no charity." Hating his homeland, he became a naturalized Englishman. But he does not seem to love us much more than the land of his birth. His poetry moves from one stage of desiccation to another, as some titles of his major poems suggest: *Waste Land, Ash Wednesday, East Coker, Burnt Norton, Dry Salvages.* His plays, *Murder in the Cathedral, Family Reunion* and *The Cocktail Party*, have done much towards the renewal of verse-drama in Britain—a surprising development since it has had no stage successes since the seventeenth century.

A different sort of pessimism marks the character of A. E. Housman, the poet who has made fame on so slight an output. He was born outside Shropshire county in 1859, and lived until 1936. His early

HILAIRE BELLOC
A belletrist of astonishing diversity. He was an essayist, critic, historian, biographer, novelist, poet and writer of ferociously amusing verses for children.

GILBERT KEITH CHESTERTON

Chesterton was a prolific journalist as well as an imaginative essayist, critic, poet and novelist. His studies of Browning, Dickens and Shaw, his allegorical novels, his creation of Father Brown, the detective-priest, and his rhetorical poetry are among his many and varied achievements. Paradox was his favourite literary device.

ambition to be a great Latinist was interrupted by his failure to take an Honours degree at Oxford. This minor disaster is said to have turned him into a misanthrope; but how could such a trivial symptom be a cause of a life-long stance? Besides, he achieved his ambition after all, going later to Cambridge as Professor of Latin and making a European reputation as a scholar This career he pursued with a savagery worthy of a political cause. Alongside this, he wrote a collection of poems which he published in 1896 under the title of *A Shropshire Lad*. Marked by the gloom of the *fin de siècle*, and simple in form, they came like folksongs upon the heart of the public. And they remain there, augmented a quarter of a century later by *Last Poems*.

Virginia Woolf

In this survey of English literature since 1900 nothing has been said of work done by women writers, or by many men who are likely to survive as Time may select: such poets as Edmund Blunden and Andrew Young. Generally, the women writers have not been pioneers, apart from Dorothy Richardson and Virginia Woolf. The former, with her continuous novel, *Pilgrimage*, in twelve volumes, was the first novelist to explore the potentialities of psychology as an instrument in the hands of the artist. This ambitious book shows the interior life of the mind and spirit, upon which the incidents of physical experience, the *outside* world, impinge rather like meteors plunging into and out of the atmosphere, making a momentary incandescence. Virginia Woolf, a more charming and coherent handler of words, worked in a more miniature way—but in similar fashion. She considerably influenced our novelists during the 'thirties, and along with Katherine Mansfield, the short-story writer, who died prematurely in the 'twenties, is likely to be regarded as the most finished artist among women writers at least during the first half of the century.

The pioneer work done by Virginia Woolf is as much in matter as in manner. She has been called a miniaturist, but that does not always mean an artist of small scope. With her astonishing faculty for seeing microscopic significances in odds and ends of habit, appearance and temper, she was able to indulge her tendency to allow herself to drift on the stream of consciousness with a deceptive air of sheer indolence. But that faculty saved her from formlessness. Every facet of the passing welter of life was caught by her, a drifting wealth of symbols, shreds of actuality that she spelled afresh into the alphabet of the mind and the soul. Her daring experiment in fiction, a prose-poem called *The Waves*, shows in a most accentuated form this control of a nervous tendency by a mind highly trained and disciplined. Here, from *The Waves*, are the thoughts and sensations of a young girl as she travels home for her summer holidays:

"I sit snug in my own corner going North, in this roaring express which is yet so smooth that it flattens hedges, lengthens hills. We flash past signal-

VIRGINIA WOOLF

The outstanding woman writer between the wars, she was a novelist and critic of rare sensibility.

TWENTIETH-CENTURY POET AND ESSAYIST

Thomas Stearns Eliot, born 1888 in St. Louis, U.S.A., became a British citizen in 1927. His poem "The Waste Land" has been the most influential work on the poetry of our time.

boxes; we make the earth rock slightly from side to side. The distance closes for ever in a point; and we for ever open the distance wide again. The telegraph poles bob up incessantly; one is felled, another rises. Now we roar and swing into a tunnel. The gentleman pulls up the window. I see reflections on the shining glass which lines the tunnel. I see him lower his paper. He smiles at my reflection in the tunnel. My body instantly of its own accord puts forth a frill under his gaze. My body lives a life of its own. Now the black window glass is green again. We are out of the tunnel. He reads his paper. But we have exchanged the approval of our bodies. There is then a great society of bodies, and mine is introduced; mine has come into the room where the gilt chairs are. Look—all the windows of the villas and their white-tented curtains dance; and the men sitting in the hedges in the cornfields with knotted blue handkerchiefs are aware too, as I am aware, of the heat and rapture. One waves as we pass him. There are bowers and arbours in these villa gardens and young men in shirt-sleeves on ladders trimming roses. A man on a horse canters over the field. His horse plunges as we pass. And the rider turns to look at us. We roar again through blackness. And I lie back; I give myself up to rapture; I think that at the end of the tunnel I enter a lamp-lit room with chairs, into one of which I sink, much admired, my dress billowing round me. But behold, looking up, I meet the eyes of a sour woman, who suspects me of rapture. My body shuts in her face, impertinently, like a parasol. I open my body, I shut my body at my will. Life is beginning. I now break into my hoard of life."

Her genius of sensibility has been matched only by that of E. M. Forster, whose *Passage to India* is already mentioned in this chapter. Mrs. Woolf was the daughter of Leslie Stephen, the eminent Victorian critic and editor of the Dictionary of National Biography. She spent her formative years in the company of the finest and most representative minds of the latter years of the nineteenth century. E. M. Forster, too, sat at the feet of the Gamaliels of his time. A student at Cambridge in the days when the Hellenist, Lowes-Dickinson was an influence at King's College, his mind was shaped toward a classical coolness and aloofness. With all his later enthusiasm for humane conduct, his rebellion against orthodoxy of thought and conduct, his defence of the underdog and the down-trodden, that detachment has never left him. He is the most fastidious literary critic of our time. His Clarke Lectures at Cambridge, published under the title of *Aspects of the Novel*, should be read along with Virginia Woolf's *The Common Reader*, to show how, beneath a fastidious air of culture (what the irreverent would call intellectual snobbery) there moves a strong current of primitive, almost animal vitality. Forster has his appetites, and it is this which distinguishes him from Henry James as a novelist. Sudden, dark floods of passion sweep over the exquisite cultivations of mind and manners in his novels, and in crises where James tended to fade out in pompous qualifications, Forster's critical moments are submerged in a sort of hot, tropical vagueness which leaves the reader as bewildered and terrified as are the characters in the book. Especially to be recommended is the novel, *Howard's End.*

Aldous Huxley

Aldous Huxley, born in 1894, grandson of T. H. Huxley, Darwin's great publicist nearly a century ago, must be included with Virginia Woolf and Forster as the third star in a constellation of excessive sensibility. He, too, was reared on an undiluted cultural diet from birth. On his mother's side he was related to Matthew Arnold and Mrs. Humphry Ward. Is it not to be expected that he should find everyday life somewhat disgusting? Happy and confident in the fields of literature, where he moves as a critic with the assurance and grace of the two others who have been discussed, he loses both grace and confidence when he descends to a contem-

LOW'S CARICATURE OF ALDOUS HUXLEY

Huxley is a delineator of fashions and manners. His "Point Counter Point" (1928) paints unbalanced lives; and his later novels reflect the war between his sympathetic understanding of over-subtle types and his sense of their moral inadequacy.

plation of hot flesh and blood, the men and women of his own time. In the cynical twenties of this century he revolted especially against the gaiety and vulgarity that followed the horrors of the first World War. *Antic Hay, Those Barren Leaves, Point Counter Point, Brave New World* and *Eyeless in Gaza* show him as a latter-day Savonarola ordering a bonfire of vanities.

In addition, his preoccupation with mysticism on all levels has produced such varying works as *The Perennial Philosophy, The Devils of Loudon* and the controversial *Doors of Perception* in which he describes his experiments with the drug mescaline.

Following these writers in a still later generation is Rex Warner, a young novelist and poet whom some critics have spoken of as an English Kafka—an Austrian novelist whose characters wander and suffer in an allegorical world that is terrifyingly irrational. But Rex Warner is surely more native in his sources. Here, too, is detachment, but it is that of an artist craving to find a means for reducing the over-abundant material of modern life to some degree of pattern and formality. His withdrawal is, therefore, rather aesthetic than moral. Like Kafka he seeks an allegory for the interpretation of events and emotions. His work is yet in its early stages, but it is already recognizable as a distinctive, personal creation. His novels, *The Wild Goose Chase, The Professor, The Aerodrome* and *Why was I Killed?* with his volume of poems called *Poems and Contradictions*, have made him one of the most interesting writers of the period of the second World War.

Working apart from this group of fastidious spirits, there have been contemporaries of wider scope and sometimes more robust vitality. Eminent among these by reason of intellectual force and artistry is Sir Compton Mackenzie, prolific and versatile. He published his first novel in 1911 (*The Passionate Elopement*). *Carnival, Sinister Street, Guy and Pauline,* the long fiction-sequence, *The Four Winds of Love,* and his later comedies, such as *Whisky Galore* or *The Rival Monster,* all show the unflagging intellectual curiosity and sympathy of this author. His stories are always warm and teeming with events and discussions, and the discussion is as dramatic as the event.

Rose Macaulay, too, is a writer for whom intellectual problems are as real as those of emotional life. She has the historical faculty in her veins, as her name should imply. Her novel, *They Were Defeated,* is her finest work, for it has shed a quality of acid contempt for the rest of humanity which somewhat sours her writing. This novel is an historical evocation of the Cambridge of the Platonist revival at the end of the seventeenth century, and may be placed alongside *John Inglesant,* the Victorian novel by Shorthouse, which portrayed Oxford during the same picturesque period in English history. As an essayist she again reveals an extreme sensitivity of approach (*Minor Pleasures of Life* and *Pleasure of Ruins*). She died in 1958.

Test Yourself

1. Name three novels of each of the following writers: (*a*) Henry James; (*b*) Joseph Conrad; (*c*) George Moore.

2. Both John Galsworthy and H. G. Wells are known for their novels about ordinary English people. Write a brief account of the work of each, remarking on the type of character each portrayed.

3. G. K. Chesterton was an "all-rounder" as a man of letters. Name a novel, a thriller, a play and a biographical study written by him.

4. English writers, in the latter part of the nineteenth century and beginning of the twentieth century, were influenced by two groups of foreign writers, Russian and French. Name three novelists of each group.

Answers will be found at the end of the book.

THREE MODERN WRITERS

Sir Compton Mackenzie (above), one of the most popular writers of our times; Rose Macaulay and E. M. Forster (below). Forster's first story appeared in 1905 and his works have exercised a considerable influence on many of his younger contemporaries.

FAMED FOR THEIR ORATORY

The Earl of Chatham (upper left); his son, William Pitt (upper right), Prime Minister during the Napoleonic wars; Gladstone (lower left), Liberal Prime Minister of the Victorian era; and Lloyd George (lower right), leader of the country during the first World War.

CHAPTER XIII

GOOD SPEECH

"WHY must I say *offen* instead of *of-ten*?"

"Is *neether* or *nighther* correct?"

"Please, Miss, is it *wich* or *which*?"

"Will the lecturer kindly pronounce the following words . . ."

"Does the speaker recommend *envelope* or *onvelope*?"

Queries such as these are often put to anyone who talks about speech. They afford an illustration of some of the many variations in the pronunciation of English which are current today. The man-in-the-street—if he notices speech at all—only notices pronunciation and he is not aware that this is but one of a number of elements that make up his means of vocal communication with his fellows.

Is he concerned with being understood by all and sundry? Generally speaking he is not. The average man's speech is often of the take-it-or-leave-it variety: " That is the way I do it and what right have you to interfere?" We have no right to interfere but we may, without offending him, try to interest him in what speech is and how the mechanism works. Differences of pronunciation, as will be shown, have their place in the spoken language, but some examination of what speech is and why certain things are considered good and others bad is desirable. There are many people who look for guidance in this respect and if they can be given information which has a sound scientific—that is to say physiological and psychological—basis they will be greatly helped.

Speech is a human activity and its foremost aim is communication. Many animals have the power of conveying their needs and of indicating their emotional states by sound-signals. Man has extended the use of sound and developed a speech mechanism which is not only more definite, but is capable of great subtlety of expression; and which, moreover, can be used as a medium for conveying abstract thought. Man is gregarious and he depends upon co-operation. If this were not so, he could supply his intellectual needs by thinking, his bodily needs by the action of his muscles, and his emotional needs by cries, groans or expletives. He prefers to share his thoughts and feelings, so for speech a listener (or listeners) is required as well as a speaker. If the listener is one who is intimately acquainted with him, all is well: they will talk the same language with possibly the same variety of pronunciation and choice of phrase. In effect they will understand each other. If, on the other hand, our speaker finds himself in a district where his type of speech is not acceptable, let alone understood, he may experience great difficulty in conveying his ideas to the people there. He may, too, find that the people are unintelligible to him.

Speech Barriers

Differences of speech constitute one of the greatest barriers between groups of English-speaking people today. If this particular barrier is to be broken down, it must be done by providing everyone with a common language: that is, one which is readily understood by all, and which, while it retains individual characteristics, does not reduce utterance to a dead level of uniformity.

Everyone, therefore, should be equipped to the extent of being able to express himself effectively. Poor or ineffective speech gives a false impression of the speaker. It may, too, give an imperfect idea of what he wishes to convey. It sometimes comes as a shock to people to find that what they have said with earnestness and sincerity and—as far as they were aware—with clarity and lucidity has been completely misconstrued.

Man's speech is the product of his upbringing and environment and these may be good or bad. A child speaks as his family does, and because the power of speech is acquired in early life, his manner of speaking becomes, for good or ill, part and parcel of himself. His environment may produce

221

certain habits which will be a handicap to him in later life. If he has the ability to adjust himself, he may adjust his speech, too, and all will be well, but there are many who lack this ability and who require some assistance. Other problems may have psychological or physiological causes and these will be dealt with in due course.

What Is Good Speech?

Good speech is that which uses the voice and speech organs to the best advantage. The fact that these organs are part of the human body and are, therefore, subject to the same laws of healthy function as the other parts of the body is often overlooked. Good speech enables the speaker to be audible without effort, and to express himself effectively and in an agreeable manner. Pleasant voices fall more kindly upon the ear and help to make the listener more receptive to the matter that the speaker wishes to put across. The criticism that overmuch attention to the tone of the voice produces voice-consciousness, which draws attention to how the thing is being done instead of what is being said, may sometimes be true, but this is rare, and if people cared more for the effect their voices had upon others they would inevitably seek to develop a pleasant quality.

The speaker who can rely upon a voice which will fulfil its functions, which is ready at all times to convey his ideas and which he knows he can use to good purpose, is in a fair way to mastering his environment.

Good speech is not something which is overlaid as a kind of veneer; it is not a type of utterance which is turned on for special occasions; it does not consist in the elimination of all personal characteristics; and it is most emphatically not a series of tricks and dodges which enable one person to obtain the same effect as another. It cannot be "picked up" and there are no short cuts. We shall come to its foundations presently.

We have already seen that speech, to be at all effective, must be widely understood. Differences there may be, but these should not be so marked as to make the speech of one district unintelligible in another. Some

kind of standard must be accepted and adhered to which will not stifle individuality and personality.

The various aspects of speech are best considered separately and their various contributions can then be related to one another and a policy drawn from them.

In the first place sound, whether human or otherwise, is subject to physical laws. Secondly, the human instrument of sound is part of the body and is, therefore, subject to physiological laws. Thirdly, certain fashions prevail in utterance, and guidance is necessary if the individual wishes to conform to what is generally regarded as accepted. In this connexion assistance is derived from a phonetic approach. Finally, since speech is the means whereby the human being expresses his thoughts and emotions the whole of his intellectual and emotional make-up is involved and a psychological approach becomes necessary. It is not proposed that these sciences should be studied in detail. All that is necessary is a simple account of the processes that go to make human sound. This will show that there is a scientific basis for argument and that the recommendations made here have a solid foundation and are not the product of any particular fancy, taste or prejudice.

Importance of Posture

The physical and physiological processes which go to the making of human sound are so closely bound up with each other that we may take them together. Before we begin analysing them, however, it is as well to make certain that the body as a whole is in a good condition as this materially affects the sound which it will produce. A body that is over-tense will produce strained or harsh sound, a body that is too flabby or too relaxed can only produce sounds that are indistinct and weak. For example, clenched hands are often accompanied by a clenched jaw through which the sounds cannot pass easily; a bad stance, in which the alignment of the body is poor, will hinder the audibility and carrying power of the voice. Posture, then, is a first consideration and good posture is dependent upon balance and control: it should be easy but not too lax, and erect but not strained. The body that is coerced into an unnatural position will produce unnatural sounds. Exercises in movement which will develop an easy stance are most beneficial.

Physical Aspects of Sound

To make any musical sound—as opposed to a noise—three things are necessary:

1. A force to set the instrument in motion. This may be likened to the bow of the violinist which makes the strings vibrate or, if you prefer it, to the starting handle of a car which sets the engine going. In the human being this force is supplied by the breath. The chest, together with the rest of the means by which we breathe, expels air from the lungs. No sound can be made without breath, a fact which it is well to remember.

2. An instrument which vibrates and which by vibration disturbs the particles of air surrounding it so that waves of sound are transmitted through the air. The strings of the violin or the parchment of a drum act in this way. In the voice the outgoing breath comes into contact with the vocal cords, which are two membranes stretched across the windpipe, and it makes them vibrate (that is, of course, if we wish to make a sound, otherwise the breath passes out unchecked). These vibrations make what we call a note. The length and tension of the cords determine the pitch of the note produced. This is regulated by a quite unconscious process which is best left to look after itself because if we try to interfere we can do no good and may do harm. Our inner ear hears a sound, we want to make it, the vocal cords take up the required position and the sound is made. The whole process is so quick that we do not stop to analyse it, and so long as all goes well we do not bother about it at all. Our voices rise and fall in accordance with the meaning of what we are saying, or because we follow a particular pattern or tune of our own. This we call inflexion or intonation, and though the process is unconscious we can, by practice or imitation learn to control it to some extent, though and this cannot be too strongly emphasized, we can never do so by direct methods

We can to some degree help the production of notes by seeing that there is always enough breath, and it must be obvious that if the breath gives out the note will be affected, as may be seen in speakers who fade out towards the ends of their phrases.

3. An instrument which amplifies or qualifies the vibrations by virtue of its capacity for resounding. The hollow body of the violin and the hollow body of the drum reinforce the vibrations of the strings and the parchment respectively. Such an instrument is called a resonator. In the voice the vibrations set up by the vocal cords pass through the hollow spaces of the neck, the mouth and the nose, and receive the addition which we call tone. If the hollow space or resonator is open and unhampered it will have a better effect upon the sound than if there is any tension or constriction. The carriage of the neck and head naturally affects this part of the resonator, and the condition of the body as a whole will also add to or detract from its successful functioning. The essential difference between the human organ and musical instruments lies in the nature of the former: whereas in musical instruments the resonator acts as a whole, in the human voice it has a dual function. In the first place, it acts as do all other resonators in that hollow spaces will always affect sound passing through them but, and herein lies the difference, the human instrument is provided with mobile organs of articulation in the mouth which impart a particular character to the sound as it passes through. It is this capacity for movement on the part of the jaw, tongue, lips and soft palate which has enabled man to develop his power of speech.

Forming Vowels and Consonants

The interaction of the mobile organs in the mouth produces the sound-qualities which we call vowels and consonants. For example, if the tongue comes into contact with the hard palate in various ways we get consonants such as T, D, L, R and, if the nose passage is open, N. Similarly, if the mouth is open and the lips are rounded we get vowels such as OO, OH and AW. When we connect vowel-movements and consonant-movements in various combinations words result. Words strung together form phrases and sentences and so the structure of articulate language is built up. This part of the instrument can be directly controlled, and it is in this connexion that we are concerned with the problems of speech as opposed to those which are purely vocal.

The nose cavity and the hollow spaces in the bones of the face also contribute to the tone of the voice as a whole. The passage to the nose may be opened or closed and when it is open it imparts a special character to certain sounds, for instance *M*, *N*, and *NG*.

Speaking and Listening

Speech may thus be seen to consist of a stream of sound which rises and falls and which carries in it a pattern of sounds arranged in such a manner that they carry a message to the ear of the listener. The ear of the listener plays an essential part in the exchange of thoughts and ideas between two or more people. The process is partly physical, partly physiological and, of course, partly psychological. The sound waves coming from the voice disturb the air, this disturbance makes the tympanum of the ear of the listener vibrate, and these vibrations are transmitted to his brain where they are perceived as sound. If the sounds are familiar he recognizes them quickly, but if they are unfamiliar he may have difficulty in doing so.

The ear as a vital factor in speech is often overlooked. If everyone regarded himself as both speaker and listener he would become more critical of the sounds of the human voice, both those of his own voice and those of others, and he might derive great profit from this.

Some suggestions which can be put to practical use may be helpful:

1. Those parts of the instrument which can be brought under voluntary control should be tackled first. Control of these helps to bring about an automatic response on the part of the organs. We want to be able to speak without thinking of what we are doing. To achieve this we must exercise our speech organs just as we exercise our bodies. The "daily dozen" is a routine practice and we forget about our muscles when we set out to work.

2. Muscular activity and, what is just as important, the sensation of that activity help to make the organs of articulation agile and flexible. We must try to feel what our tongues and lips are doing. To look at them in the glass is useful, too, because we often think the tongue is being quite active when actually it is being very lazy.

3. For the development of tone we need a good posture, an adequate breath supply and we must see that there is no unnecessary tension in the neck and throat. Exercises of the jaw, tongue and lips, in addition to improving clarity of speech help to make better tone as well.

4. If we wish to acquire a greater variety in our inflexions we must train our ears to detect greater subtlety of sound. The working of this part of the instrument must be managed by indirect means.

Conscious control may be established over breathing, articulation and tone. The jaw must not be clenched; it should be in readiness to open and close as desired. No excessive movement is necessary, and practice should take the form of opening and shutting the mouth with ease. Dropping the jaw and then closing it and dropping it again is also helpful.

It is as well at the outset to recognize the difference between the vowel sounds we are capable of making and the letters we call vowels: *a, e, i, o, u*. For example, the letter *a* will be found sounded: *make, cat, father*. The letter *e* will be found sounded: *pen, peep*. The letter *i* will be found sounded: *fine, fin*.

Similarly the sound *EE* will be found written: *feel, beat, receive*. The sound *AY* may be written: *pay, hey, fail, great, neigh*. The sound *I* will be written: *life, height, style, light*.

Symbols for Vowel Sounds

We have, therefore, to decide upon a way of writing down sounds which will, if possible, avoid confusion with letters. The difficulty will at once become apparent as letters have to be used. The method has been kept as simple as possible and consists of indicating vowels which give an impression of length or weight by capital letters (*OO* for the sound in moon and *AY* for the sound in make) and by using small letters for those vowels which are characteristically short or light (*e* for the sound in pen, *a* for the sound in hat).

Vowel sounds may be divided into two main groups: simple and compound. The simple are those in which only one position is required and the compound those in which two or more positions are necessary to complete the sound. There are thirteen simple vowel sounds:

OO	*oo*	*OH*	*AW*	*o*	*AH*	*u*
boot	book	boat	ball	box	bath	but

ER	*a*	*e*	*AY*	*i*	*EE*
bird	bat	bed	bake	bit	bead

Some are made by rounding the lips and others by raising the tongue. You must note, however, that the vowels which have been indicated by the symbols *OH* and *AY* are really compound vowels, being composed of *OHOO* and *AYi* respectively. As it is desirable to reduce the diphthongal element they are better practised as simple sounds, the diphthong being allowed in connected speech, but never stressed in isolated practice.

The main compound vowels (diphthongs) are to be found in the words: *high, how, hoist, hue*. Then there are those which are made up of a simple vowel and a short or unstressed *er*: *poor, door, hair, hear*. Similarly, we encounter those made up of a diphthong and *er* (triphthongs): *flower, hire, lure*.

Vowel sounds may all be made with an open jaw, and it is useful to practise them as open sounds despite that when combined with consonants the jaw position may vary.

About Consonants

Consonants may be regarded as interruptions of the sound on its journey out. They are in a sense departures from and arrivals at the vowel positions. They may be divided into two main groups: those which completely close the passage and are, therefore, explosive in character, such as *T* or *P*, and those which close the passage

partially and are continuous in sound, such as *M* and *Z*. The former may be called explosives and the latter continuants. These may again be divided into those made in the breath alone (voiceless), such as *F* and *P*, and those in which there is vocal sound (voiced), such as *V* and *B*. There are many classifications, but in our one the headings suggest the nature of the sounds, and when we add the place in which they are made, we have a good basis on which to work. So the reader is advised to study the Consonant Table on page 228, and to make use of the comments tabulated, as follows:

1. In No. 7 a definite position cannot be laid down for the formation of *S* and *Z*, as a certain latitude must always be allowed for dentition. The tongue lying flat and slightly forwards will generally be found to be most satisfactory.

2. In No. 9, *CH* and *J* are really a mixture of continuant and explosive, being composed of *T-SH* and *D-ZH* respectively, but because they should not be prolonged the explosive element is the one which should be stressed.

Tone and Pitch

The terms tone, resonance and quality are all used to describe the *kind* of voice we hear. The quality of the voice reflects the state of mind and sometimes the physical condition of the speaker. Absence of tone may be due to: bad posture; stiff muscles of jaw, throat, tongue, lips; blockage in the passage between mouth and nose. Good tone is acquired by: relaxation and good breathing; co-ordination and flexibility of all muscles; sensitivity to vibration and movement. It is helpful to think of the tone as being made in the front of the face, and practising sounds with the hands cupped as a megaphone can be most useful. This is really due to psychological rather than physical causes; but nevertheless feeling vibration in front does take away the attention from the back; and it is quite true to say that sensation at the back encourages tension and is harmful, whereas sensation in the front is of the greatest possible use.

Flexibility of pitch can be improved provided that there is plenty of breath and

In Shaw's "Pygmalion," Eliza Doo-
little is a Covent Garden flower girl:
"Cheer up, Keptin: n'baw ya flahr
orf a pore gel."

Her slovenly speech and Cockney
accent are overheard by Higgins, a
professor of phonetics. So confident is
Higgins of his powers as a speech
expert that he offers to bet a friend
that he can "make a duchess of this
draggle-tailed guttersnipe."

Eliza takes him at his word and
arrives at his home next day. Higgins
tells her: ". . . The streets will be
strewn with the dead bodies of men
shooting themselves for your sake
before I've done with you."

Eliza is alarmed: "I don't want
no balmies teaching me."

Nevertheless, Higgins begins his
experiment with flamboyancy and
vigour.

SHAVIAN EXPERIMENT
Shaw's "Pygmalion" deals with better pronunciation. He would have liked also to see a

Eliza is quick to learn, but tries to keep to safe subjects when she visits Mrs. Higgins.

"There are no indications of any great change in the barometrical situation," she informs the surprised guests.

Eventually Higgins wins his bet. Eliza is accepted as one of themselves by fashionable society. Returned from the opera, Higgins' insufferable smugness infuriates her, and she attacks him. Finally she threatens to offer herself as assistant to his rival in phonetics.

IN PHONETICS
new alphabet formulated, and on his death left money to be used for this purpose.

PLACE OF FORMATION	CONTINUANTS			EXPLOSIVES		JAW
	Breath	Sound	Nose	Breath	Sound	
1. Larynx . . .	H					
2. Body of tongue and soft palate . . .			NG	K	G	Open
3. Tongue tip and hard palate. . .		L R	N	T	D	
4. Lips			M	P	B	
5. Tongue and teeth .	TH (thin)	TH (this)				Partly open
6. Lower lip and upper teeth	F	V				
7. Teeth	S	Z				
8. Teeth, with lip rounding . .	SH (hush)	ZH (azure)				Closed
9. Teeth, tongue tip .				CH (church)	J (judge)	

CONSONANT TABLE

that the neck and throat muscles are kept relaxed. Any sign of discomfort reveals that all is not well, but preparatory exercises for tone and articulation attract the attention to the right places, and then inflexions can safely be practised. To alter inflexions is to change the character of speech. We may not wish to make radical changes but simply to increase our range of expressiveness. Saying the days of the week or the months of the year, either going up and down the scale while doing so, or saying them in tones of surprise, anger, distress and so forth, will help the voice to adjust itself unconsciously and increase its flexibility. If we analyse a phrase we find that not only does the voice rise and fall but that some words are more strongly accented than others. Take any simple remark or query and change the pitch and the emphasis. Below is a sentence, which you can utter aloud, with at least four different meanings according to how you stress certain words. Try it for your-self, stressing those syllables marked with accents:

Hullo, what are you doing there?
Hulló, what are yóu doing there?
Hullo, what are you doing thére?
Húlló, what áre you doing there?

In addition to receiving a particular stress in a phrase many words have an accent or stress on certain syllables. We see this if we compare words like: phótograph, photográphic and photógraphy. There are also words which change their meaning if the accent is changed. Compare the following nouns and verbs:

cónvict	convíct
présent	presént
récord	recórd
áccent	accént
cóntent	contént

Accent, stress, emphasis, call it what you will, is partly a question of force and partly a question of length, and accent on words in a sentence is closely connected with rise and fall of pitch.

Notice the difference in meaning that exists between:

a black bird and a blackbird
a blue bottle and a bluebottle
a black berry and a blackberry.

In connected speech we do not go slowly enough to give every sound its full value. We run some of them together as in:

handkerchief
bread and butter.

Similarly the words "the" and "for" are often slid over. If we say them by themselves and then in a sentence we see the difference immediately.

Rhythm of Speech

The language we speak is made up of a series of phrases. Each phrase has its own pattern and this pattern is made by the alternating strong and weak beats, the rising or falling pitch, a quicker or slower tempo and pauses. We do not hear each word as a separate unit because if we did we should speak in a staccato, detached manner. We say a whole phrase and then another and another, and the variations of stress, inflexion and tempo help us to draw attention to the key words and so make our meaning clear. Rhythm is the element which joins all the sounds together and yet at the same time helps us to be varied and interesting.

We come next to the question of which sounds we are to choose. How are we to know what to do, and what kind of standard is there to guide us? We do not want any one group of people to be regarded as better or superior simply because they conform to something which is unattainable by others. We do not want any man, woman or child to be denied intercourse with men, women and children of any other group, and, therefore, a common meeting-ground is desirable.

It is generally agreed that there is no hard and fast standard in English which dictates that you must do this and you must

not do that. Opinions are many and varied but it is also generally agreed that there is a type of pronunciation which is regarded as acceptable among educated people. It is true that all educated speakers do not conform to the same standard but the range of divergences is not so very great. There is no value in a standard if it tends towards hundreds of thousands of people all talking exactly alike. The value lies in the fact that some kind of a standard provides a common currency which may be understood by all and which yet allows for individuality in each and every speaker.

Fashion in Pronunciation

Pronunciation is a question of fashion. It is not so much a question of right and wrong or good and bad but of the usage which prevails at a given time. Some years ago it was fashionable to pronounce herb and humour without the *h*, and to change the *NG* sound in words like interesting to *n*—making it interestin'. Today we sound the *h* in herb and humour and have restored the *ng* in interesting. Many other instances could be given but these will serve to show that fashions in speech are changeable like fashions in dress.

One difficulty particularly associated with the English language and its pronunciation is the inconsistency of its spelling. How can we lay down rules for the pronunciation of sounds when we find examples like these:

bough, through, though, rough, cough.

Letters and sounds, as we have already seen, are different things and we must keep them separate in our minds when we are thinking of the sounds of a language or we shall find ourselves in difficulties. It is not difficult to make lists of words which look very much alike and which sound different; for example, rough and cough, now and tow, wear and fear; or of words which sound alike and which look different, such as high, my, buy, fie, and go, foe, slow. Once we have learned to think in terms of sounds everything becomes easier. Practice in making lists of words and saying them aloud is very helpful. Listening to other people and taking note of their vowel and consonant values, their stresses and inflexions, create awareness of the differences which exist. The speaker who knows how to listen will soon learn to adapt himself to other methods, that is, of course, if he wishes to do so. But the point is that he who is aware of the existing differences is in a position to choose for himself and is not the slave of his own habits.

Dialects and "Accents"

Genuine dialects have their individual forms of pronunciation, vocabulary and phraseology, and as such they are languages which should be preserved. What we want to guard against is poor or slipshod speech masquerading as a dialect when it is nothing of the kind.

The word "accent" has another use in addition to that we have already noticed. It is generally accompanied by the word "bad" and may be used to denote a geographical peculiarity, in which case there is no reason why it should be eliminated unless it is disadvantageous to the speaker, or it may mean some kind of error in formation which calls for correction for reasons of health or in the interests of better tone.

Since genuine dialects are for the most part physiologically sound, those who speak them will simply require a second language in the form of a standard type of speech to make them understood by all and sundry. Those, however, who make faulty or debased sounds should be shown how to correct them and their best line of action is to try to set up new habits of speech so that the organs are being well used all the time. After a while these new habits become second nature.

We come next to the psychological aspect of the voice. The person who is inarticulate finds difficulty in being clear to other people, either because his voice is hampered by physical causes or because he lacks words in which to express himself. These often go together and attention must, therefore, be paid to both factors if this is so. Mastery of his instrument gives the speaker self-confidence; his personality is, as it were, released, and, if he knows he can

be heard and that he is pleasant to listen to, he is free from worry and can get on with what he has to say.

We have already seen that the human being grows up with his voice and his own brand of speech, and because it is part of himself he is apt to be very sensitive of criticism; indeed, many people are very resentful if it is so much as hinted that there is room for any alteration or improvement. If we are to help such people it can only be by explaining in as attractive a manner as possible that everybody is the better for a little attention to the voice, and that nobody wishes to blot out his personal characteristics. A healthy voice, it can be pointed out, will do its work better than a tired or a strained one, and a type of speech which is understood by all and yet retains its individual colour is more useful than one which is understood only by a few. We want the voice and the speech to sound natural, something which is the speaker's own, and in order to do this the speaker must be at ease. If he cares at all for the effect he has upon other people he will be interested in seeing that, as he gains in control over his voice and speech organs, he is able to make closer contact with his fellows and in general to make a much better impression upon them.

It has been noticed, too, that children who have been branded as "difficult" have gained self-confidence and have developed normally when given the means of vocal self-expression.

Speech Disabilities

Questions of psychology and physiology are so closely bound together—we have seen how freedom of the personality is largely dependent on good use of speech organs—that they cannot be separated and dealt with in watertight compartments.

Some people suffer from definite disabilities of voice and speech which are more serious than the minor difficulties that have already been mentioned. These cases require medical advice and the services of a qualified speech therapist. They cannot help themselves nor can others help them unless they have specialized knowledge, but it might be mentioned in passing that some of these disabilities might be prevented if the speech of children received proper care in their early years.

The language we speak, like the sounds we make, grows up with us. It depends largely upon our home and our school and, in later life, the kind of people we associate with. We are able to express ourselves more easily if we have a good vocabulary, and this applies to writing as well as to speaking, but the language we write is not the same as that which we speak. We use more than one type for speaking. First, there is the colloquial speech of everyday, with its contractions and abbreviations, its slang, jargon and specialized terms. If we are talking to those we know well, we don't always take the trouble to finish our sentences because we know that we are being understood. When we can't think of a word we say "um" or "er" or talk about the "what's it" or the "thingummy." This is all very well for our intimate friends but it will not do if we find ourselves on a platform. On formal occasions our speech becomes more formal, and if we ourselves are adaptable our speech takes on the degree of formality necessary to the occasion.

The spoken language has become a more important means of communication in the modern world than it used to be. This is due to the effect of the telephone, the wireless, the gramophone and the talking-film, and also that in these days of easy transport by motor and aeroplane personal contacts have become easier. We often prefer to ring somebody up rather than write a letter. We are all of us listeners, even if it is only to the nine o'clock news. This simplification of contacts has had its effect upon the words we use, the fashions in slang, the catch-phrases that come and go and it should be able to help us to arrive at a common language which we could all use and understand.

We must remember, however, that our everyday speech is very apt to be slipshod and go-as-you-please. If we have to make a speech or give a lecture we take more care, or it sometimes happens that we become over-careful and may sound precious and pedantic. We could, profitably, bring about a closer approximation between the two: something which preserves the peculiar requirements of each type but which is neither slipshod nor careless on the one hand nor unnatural and pedantic on the other. We may say that our parts of speech are voice and language: (1) The way in which we make our sounds and the kind of voice we use, and (2) the words we have at our command and their correct grammatical use.

Bad speech is not simply bad because it is ugly, but because it is incorrectly made. Good speech is dependent upon proper use of the voice and speech organs. Attention to the proper function of these organs will automatically correct many errors which are commonly associated with pronunciation, but which actually are errors in formation. Given correct function, pronunciation becomes a matter for choice in which the individual does things his own way or conforms to accepted usage because he chooses to and not because he can do no other. Inarticulate speakers acquire freedom of expression and mastery over their environment when they have learnt to master their vocal instrument and have a good supply of words at their command. Speech is a social activity, and fashions in speech change as do other kinds of behaviour. The good speaker is sensitive, critical and adaptable.

Test Yourself

1. How is the voice produced?
2. Give examples of three pairs of words in which an altered stress makes a difference in the meaning: e.g. cónvict: convíct.
3. Give five examples of words with "ough" endings, each of which carries a different pronunciation.

Answers will be found at the end of the book.

A

DICTIONARY

OF THE

ENGLISH LANGUAGE:

IN WHICH

The WORDS are deduced from their ORIGINALS,

AND

ILLUSTRATED in their DIFFERENT SIGNIFICATIONS

BY

EXAMPLES from the beſt WRITERS.

TO WHICH ARE PREFIXED,

A HISTORY of the LANGUAGE,

AND

AN ENGLISH GRAMMAR.

BY SAMUEL JOHNSON, A. M.

IN TWO VOLUMES.

VOL. I.

Cum tabulis animum cenſoris ſumet honeſti :
Audebit quæcunque parum ſplendoris habebunt,
Et fine pondere erunt, et honore indigna ferentur,
Verba movere loco ; quamvis invita recedant,
Et verientur adhuc hitra penetralia Veſtæ ;
Obſcurata diu populo bonus eruet, atque
Proferet in lucem ſpecioſa vocabula rerum,
Quæ priſcis memorata Catonibus atque Cethegis,
Nunc ſitus informis premit et deferta vetuſtas.   HOR.

LONDON,
Printed by W. STRAHAN,
For J. and P. KNAPTON ; T. and T. LONGMAN ; C. HITCH and L. HAWES ;
A. MILLAR; and R. and J. DODSLEY.
MDCCLV.

TITLE-PAGE OF JOHNSON'S DICTIONARY, 1755

Johnson's work set out to "fix the pronunciation of our language and preserve its purity."

CHAPTER XIV

THE USE AND CHOICE OF VOCABULARY

As has been shown in the first chapter, our mother tongue is rich and varied in its resources. According to the Oxford Dictionary there are no fewer than four hundred thousand words in the English language, and every year, almost every day, new words are being borrowed or created.

It has been found that a little girl of two uses a full three hundred word vocabulary in her daily chatter. Her brother, by the way, takes six months longer to get so far! At the age of eight a girl's vocabulary is over three thousand words, and she reaches the total of nine thousand by the age of fourteen.

After this the rate of progress slows down. An average adult is estimated to use about eleven thousand seven hundred words, and a more highly educated man or woman about thirteen thousand five hundred. These figures are quoted from Dr. P. B. Ballard's *Thought and Language*.

When we are grown up, we meet with new words only occasionally. Much depends upon the company we keep, the papers we read, the meetings we attend, and our daily occupation. We may skip through a dozen popular novels without encountering a solitary new word, whereas a book with real substance in it may introduce us to a score.

In many cases we can deduce the meaning of a new word from the context, but if we are interested in words for their own sake, we make a note of them and look them up in a good dictionary. This is the most satisfactory way of increasing vocabulary.

Use of a Dictionary

Studying a dictionary is not a dull business at all. It can be a most fascinating pastime. Haven't we all found that the looking up of one word generally lures one on to look up another? It can be as amusing as a treasure hunt.

You learn, for example, that the Latin word for moon is *luna* and you think of such related words as lunatic, lunacy. Then you begin to speculate as to whether there is any connexion between the moon and a person who is mentally deranged. And at once you remember the common belief that the moon exercises an unfavourable influence on unbalanced persons.

The study of Latin is an extremely valuable asset in the acquisition of a good vocabulary. It is perhaps not generally realized that a knowledge of Latin not only helps the student to understand French, Italian and Spanish, but is a necessity to the individual who desires to qualify as a doctor, chemist, solicitor or teacher of languages.

There are hundreds of these interesting discoveries to be made by anyone who looks for them. Queer things happen to words as they travel from country to country or down the centuries. Here are a few examples of words which have curious origins: assassin, bedlam, bunkum, caddie, currant, dandelion, hooligan, lady, lord. Look them up in the dictionary.

Clues to Word Formation

The primary purpose of a dictionary is to explain the meaning of a word, and incidentally to supply the correct spelling and pronunciation. But it is always worth while to notice the derivation. You may want to know the exact meaning of a word like intermittent which signifies "ceasing at intervals." Thus, we hear of an intermittent spring (of water) or an intermittent fever. But the heart of the word, *mit*, comes from the Latin *mitto*—I send. (Past tense *misi*). This clue puts you on the track of scores of other words from the same root: admit, commit, dismiss, emit, intermit, omit, permit, remit, submit, transmit, etc.

And from these we get admission, admittance, commission, emission, omission, permission, remission, remittance,

Our earliest known languages
are the Celtic group: Gaelic.
Manx, Welsh and Cornish.

7th Century.
Roman alphabet in
Written records comme

5th to 12th Centuries.
Anglo-Saxon established
by West Germanic invaders.

INFLUENCES ON THE STREAM

1st to 5th Centuries.
Roman conquest brings
Latin words to Britain.

A.D. 597.
Christian teaching
from Rome begins.

EVOLUTION OF WRITTEN

This illustration, together with that on pages 240-241, is designed to show the constant

1340—1400.
Chaucer's work establishes
literary English.

12th to 14th Centuries.
Songs and ballads
perpetuated
by minstrels.

OF THE ENGLISH LANGUAGE

1066.
Norman conquest introduces
French as tongue of the ruling classes.

1476.
Caxton sets up printing
press in England.

AND SPOKEN ENGLISH
development of the English language through the influence of invasions and discoveries.

submission, transmission, mission, missionary.

One speculates as to the difference between admission and admittance, between remission and remittance. While the dictionary is at hand it would be a good idea to get the point settled. Why do we say "Price of admission" and "No admittance except on business"?

The knowledge of a dozen or two Latin and Greek roots is invaluable to anyone who wants to enlarge his vocabulary. Some of the most useful will be given a little further on in this chapter.

Collecting Synonyms

Since the English language has absorbed words from many other languages it often follows that we have several words with the same meaning. Thus, we have atmosphere and air; altitude and height; wedding, marriage, and matrimony. The last three mean practically the same thing, but wedding is the Old English word, marriage was brought over from France, and matrimony is derived from Latin.

We say that words which have the same meaning are synonyms. Sometimes synonyms have shades of difference according to the context. For example, no one would say, "I am going to a marriage" or talk about a "marriage present," and no bride would be told to take care of her "wedding lines."

For ordinary purposes, we often have a choice of half a dozen words which mean practically the same thing. The man who wants to improve his vocabulary might make lists of synonyms. This was the method adopted by Robert Blatchford—a most accomplished journalist who was almost entirely self-taught. In his little book on *English Prose and How to Write It* he quotes examples:

Solace: comfort, console, alleviate, soothe, assuage.

Devise: design, plan, contrive, scheme, project, invent.

Integrity: honesty, probity, rectitude, uprightness.

It is a good exercise.

Think how many words we have signifying "little": small, tiny, wee, midget, diminutive, puny, minute, petty, miniature, undersized, dwarfish, exiguous, pigmy, Lilliputian.

Think of the number of words which might be used as alternatives to "see": notice, observe, inspect, scrutinize, spy, examine, glance, eye, glimpse, peep, peer, stare, gaze, and so on.

Yet—and this is very important—there are shades of difference in the meanings of each of these words for each has its own purpose, its own wealth of associations for us. You get the idea of standing on tiptoe to "peer," and the word "stare" has a suggestion of bad manners. Roget's *Thesaurus of English Words and Phrases* is well known to journalists. It is practically a dictionary of synonyms and antonyms. The simplest way to explain it is to quote an example:

Vanity: conceit, conceitedness, self-conceit, self-confidence, self-sufficiency self-esteem, self-approbation, self-importance, self-praise, self-laudation, self-admiration, complacency, *amour propre.* . . .

(Adjectives). Vain, conceited, overweening, forward, vainglorious, puffed up, high-flown, inflated, flushed, stuck-up, self-satisfied, self-flattering. . .

In a parallel column one finds the opposite words:

Modesty: humility, diffidence, shyness, coyness, sheepishness, demureness, bashfulness, self-consciousness.

Choosing Words Carefully

It often happens that one cannot hit on the exact word that is needed. There is such a word but it seems to be floating round and evading capture. We often say it is "on the tip of the tongue". We know other words very like it but they are not the perfect word to suit the purpose.

In such a difficulty Roget's *Thesaurus* will often supply the missing word, and the instant we see it we know that it is right —the inevitable word. The famous French writer, Flaubert, would lie awake all night in a kind of agony, searching for the *mot juste,* as he called it—the perfect word, the perfect phrase. R. L. Stevenson suffered the same experience. To find the right word, after a long search, gave him a thrill of triumph that reminds one of the finding of Cinderella—the one girl in the world whose foot would fit the dainty slipper! Another advantage of knowing a number of synonyms is that it enables a speaker or writer to avoid using the same word too many times in the same context.

Latin and Greek Roots

To return to a subject mentioned earlier —the value of knowing Latin and Greek roots: *Scribo* means "I write," and the past participle is *scriptum.* We have the old word scribe meaning "a writer," and the B.B.C. has made us familiar with script. But we can use a number of prefixes to ring the changes: ascribe, circumscribe, describe, inscribe, subscribe, superscribe, transcribe, proscribe, prescribe, etc., and many other words derived from all these.

Subscribe literally means "write under" and superscribe to "write over." It reminds one of the schoolboy howler in the Scripture lesson: "Then He said, 'Show me a penny' and they showed Him. Then said He unto them: 'Whose subscription is this?' They say unto Him: 'It is Caesar's'."

Let us now take a look at a few more Latin roots:

Dico (*dictum*)—I say. (Contradict, interdict, predict.)

Duco (*ductum*)—I lead. (Conduct, reduce, introduce.)

Volo—I am willing. (Voluntary, devolve, involve.)

Manus—the hand. (Manual, manuscript, manufacture.)

Pes (ped-)—the foot. (Pedal, impede, impediment, pedestal, pedestrian, pedometer, pedlar.)

Similarly, the Greek roots:

Grapho—I write; *phone*—sound; *tele*—afar; *micro*—small; *scope*—I see; *geos*—earth; *helios*—sun.

Combining these in various ways we get words like: graphic, graphite, telegraph, aerograph, heliograph, phonograph, gramophone, photograph, microscope, microphone, geology, geography, telephone, telescope, and many more.

Before we leave this subject of the value of the classics in increasing one's vocabu-

lary, it would be useful to make a list of the chief prefixes:

LATIN	Meaning	Example
A-, ab-, abs-	From, away	Absent, avert.
Ad-	To	Admit, adhere.
Bi-, bis-	Two, twice	Biped, biscuit.
Con-, com-	With	Connect, combine.
Contra-	Against	Contradict.
De-	Down	Descend, degrade.
Di-, dis-	Asunder	Divide, dissect.
E-, ex-	Out of	Exit, export.
In-with noun	Not	Incorrect.
In- with verb	Into	Inject, Induce.
Inter-	Between	Interfere.
Intro-	Within	Introspect.
Male-	Ill, evil	Malignant.
Per-	Through	Perspire, percolate.
Pre-	Before	Predict, preface.
Pro-	Forth	Proceed.
Post-	After	Postpone.
Re-	Back, again	Return, refill.
Sub-	Under	Submarine.
Super-	Over	Supernatural.
Trans-	Across	Translate.
Ultra-	Beyond	Ultramarine.

There are a number of others, but the above will be found useful in providing clues to essential meanings.

GREEK	Meaning	Example
A-, an-	Without	Atheist.
Ant-, anti-	Against	Antidote.
Arch-	Rule	Archbishop.
Cata-	Down	Catastrophe.
Dia-	Through	Diameter.
Mono-	Single	Monotone.
Peri-	Round	Periphrasis.
Poly-	Many	Polysyllable.

Here is a typical collection of words borrowed from the Greek: arthritis, asthma, apoplexy, epilepsy, paralysis, pneumonia, bronchitis, catarrh, dysentery, tuberculosis (and other names of diseases); chemistry, physics, electricity, geology,

MR. MICAWBER MAKES A SPEECH

Dickens created many characters whose peculiarities of speech are one of the delights of English literature, and none is more amusing than David Copperfield's friend, Micawber.

geography, physiology, physiography, psychology, dynamics, statics, astronomy, anatomy, mathematics, arithmetic (and other branches of learning); enigma, acme, axis, asbestos, basis, dogma, drama, emphasis, echo, idea, horizon, panacea, stigma, phantasy, chaos, cosmos, character, iris, anthracite, phenomenon, telegram, horoscope.

The derivation, supplied by most dictionaries, gives the clue to the meaning. The word panacea, for example, means a cure-all and we grasp the idea when we realize that *pan* means "all." Thus we talk about a disease being pandemic as opposed to endemic—it affects a whole people; the name Pandora suggests a gift of all things, and those who remember the old story of Pandora's box will see its significance. Then we have words like Pan-Anglican, Panislam, pantheism, pantechnicon, Pantheon, pantomime, and so on.

All this may seem dull, but it is useful to anyone who wants to discover methods of increasing his vocabulary. It is worth anyone's while to spend an occasional half-hour in dipping into the dictionary. In fact, it is said that Kipling went right through the dictionary in order to find some new adjectives. It was tedious, perhaps, but anyone who reads his stories will realize how rarely he uses the conventional word —how he strikes the imagination with his unexpectedness.

Readers of Charles Dickens will remember that when young David Copperfield first met Mr. Micawber he was addressed as follows:

"Under the impression that your peregrinations in this metropolis have not as yet been extensive, and that you might have some difficulty in penetrating the arcana of the Modern Babylon in the direction of City Road—in short that you might lose yourself—I shall be happy to call this evening, and instal you in the knowledge of the nearest way."

Mr. Micawber always talked like that. He loved high-sounding words, and the bigger the better. He would never say a thing in three words if he could wrap it up in fifteen or twenty. The man was constantly in debt but he did not use such a simple word, preferring to say that owing to circumstances beyond his individual control he was temporarily suffering from financial embarrassment!

He is a laughable figure, of course; and so is any man who uses long words when short ones would suit his purpose as well —or better. The present writer once asked a stranger the way to a certain avenue. The man replied: "As I am proceeding in that direction myself I will indicate it to you." He could have said: "I'm going that way myself and will show you." He was another Micawber. During the walk he continued talking in the same high-flown way until the avenue was reached. "That," said the stranger, "constitutes the avenue for which you enquired."

Five Famous Rules

Now the warning is fairly clear. The authors of *The King's English* put it this way: (1) Prefer the familiar word to the far-fetched; (2) Prefer the concrete word to the abstract; (3) Prefer the single word to the circumlocution; (4) Prefer the short word to the long; (5) Prefer the Saxon word to the Romance.

Does this seem rather disappointing? When we are young we often enjoy the sound of impressive words. A passage like Shakespeare's "the multitudinous seas incarnadine" gives us a thrill of elation. We find pleasure in using words like tempestuous, tumultuous, multiplicity, inexorable, inevitable, incontrovertible, magnificence, magnanimous, and so on—Latin words which we have borrowed to enrich the language. There is not the slightest objection to them—unless they are used unnecessarily. Old English—based upon Anglo-Saxon—is simple and contains many words of one syllable. Read, for example, the opening words of St. John's Gospel:

In the beginning was the Word, and the Word was with God, and the Word was God. The same was in the beginning with God. All things were made by Him; and without Him was not anything made that was made. In Him was life, and the life was the light of men. And the light shineth in darkness and the darkness comprehended it not. There was a man sent from God whose name was John. The same came for a witness to bear witness of the light that all men through him might believe. He was not that light but was sent to bear witness of that light. That was the true Light, which lighteth every man that cometh into the world. He was in the world, and the world was made by Him, and the world knew Him not.

According to *The Loom of Language* (edited by Lancelot Hogben), the passage quoted above has one hundred and twenty-four words of one syllable out of one hundred and thirty-nine—ninety per cent; but the same passage in the Latin version has twenty-six words of one syllable out of ninety-two—only twenty-eight per cent. The passage from St. John's Gospel is almost entirely Old English or Saxon. The word "comprehended" seems to be the only foreign word in the collection.

Contrast this with a passage from a speech by the Earl of Chatham:

I cannot, my lords, I will not, join in congratulation on misfortune and disgrace. This, my lords, is a perilous and tremendous moment! It is not a time for adulation; the smoothness of flattery cannot now avail—cannot now save us in this rugged and awful crisis. It is now necessary to instruct the throne in the language of truth. We must dispel the delusion and darkness which envelop it, and display, in its full danger and true colours, the ruin that is brought to our doors. Can ministers still presume to expect support in their infatuation? . . . I

15th and 16th Centuries. Age of exploration and discovery; words from abroad.

About 1650—1750.
Broadsheets and news-sheets "fix" the literary style.

INFLUENCES ON THE STREAM

16th and 17th Centuries.
Elizabethan and Jacobean drama.

1755.
Dr. Samuel Johnson produces first English Dictionary.

EVOLUTION OF WRITTEN
Many changes and developments had repercussions on language. Some are shown above;

19th Century.
School Education tends to
break down local dialect.

Early 19th Century.
Romantic Revival creates
interest in the past.

20th Century
Modern newspapers create
simple brisk style.

OF THE ENGLISH LANGUAGE

19th Century. Works of Dickens
create middle-class reading public.

20th Century.
Radio tends to
standardize
spoken English.

AND SPOKEN ENGLISH
others, occurring earlier than the 16th century, are illustrated on pages 234-235.

solemnly call upon your lordships, and upon every order of men in the state, to stamp upon this infamous procedure the indelible stigma of the public abhorrence. More particularly I call upon the holy prelates of our religion to do away with this iniquity; let them perform a lustration to purify the country from this deep and deadly sin.

My lords, I am old and weak, and at present unable to say more; but my feelings and indignation were too strong to have said less. I could not have slept this night in my bed, nor even reposed my head on my pillow, without giving vent to my eternal abhorrence of such enormous and preposterous principles.

The passage from the New Testament is so simple and homely that everyone can understand it; the speech of the Earl of Chatham is not so easy. It contains a large admixture of Latin words which give it strength and richness—congratulation, misfortune, disgrace, perilous, tremendous, adulation, ministers, infatuation, indelible, abhorrence, religion, iniquity, perform, lustration, indignation, preposterous, and quite a number of others. When the speaker became most moved by his feelings he broke into the homely Saxon: "My lords, I am old and weak and unable to say more . . . I could not have slept this night in my bed . . .".

Effectiveness of the Homely Word

The oldest and simplest words in our language are most charged with emotion. If a man's house is on fire he yells, "Fire!" He would not dream of shouting, "Conflagration!" And if he makes love in earnest he is bound to fall back on the language of his remote ancestors: "I love you!"

When Dr. Johnson wrote his letter of rebuke to Lord Chesterfield he used a great many Latin words. It was his usual style—the fashion of his century. But the strongest passage is in plain Saxon:

The notice which you have been pleased to take of my labours, had it been early, had been kind; but it has been delayed till I am indifferent, and cannot enjoy it; till I am solitary and cannot impart it; till I am known and do not want it.

Notice the beautiful rhythm of the sentences and see how the whole weight falls on that final clause which is the complete rebuff.

Writers today prefer the simplest forms of speech and avoid all ornamentation that is not really necessary. We might almost say that the modern fashion in language is to make it "stream-lined."

As a contrast to the elaborate style of Dr. Johnson, study a passage from Bunyan's *The Pilgrim's Progress:*

At last, lighting under a little shelter, Christian and Hopeful sat down until day brake; but, being weary, they fell asleep. Now there was, not far from the place where they lay, a castle, called Doubting Castle, the owner whereof was Giant Despair, and it was in his grounds they now were sleeping; wherefore, he, getting up in the morning early, and walking up and down in his fields, caught Christian and Hopeful asleep in his grounds. Then with a grim and surly voice he bid them awake, and asked them whence they were, and what they did in his grounds.

The student who is eager to enlarge his vocabulary will not find many new words in Bunyan. His style reminds one of the Bible in its homeliness and simplicity, and he uses only a small percentage of words borrowed from Greece or Rome.

Slang and Provincialisms

Certain words became fashionable and were "done to death" by the "smart set" and the "bright young things." It is advisable to avoid them. A few years ago the words definitely, actually and absolutely were dragged into almost every sentence; a few years before that, certain words of terror were made almost meaningless by misuse. Everything was fearfully, frightfully, awfully, terribly—something or other.

How can a man be fearfully nice? How can a beef-steak be awfully good? These words were employed to mean nothing more than "very."

More recently there has been a fashion of using words like divine, priceless, devastating, without any reference to their real meaning. Words used in a wrong sense and contrary to the spirit of the English idiom are called solecisms or barbarisms. It is wise to avoid them altogether. The same advice should be given with regard to those ready-made and hackneyed expressions which are spoilt by over-familiarity. It is sometimes difficult to avoid them in talking—they slip out only too readily; but in writing we can always find a substitute, with a little thought.

Here are a few examples of these *clichés:* As a matter of fact; to all intents and purposes; part and parcel; to the bitter end; the unvarnished truth; last but not least; to leave no stone unturned; without fear of contradiction; one may venture to assert; it stands to reason. There are hundreds of them, but one may search through a whole book by a good writer (like Stevenson, Pater, or George Moore) without discovering a single example.

Then there are dialect words and provincialisms, used only in certain districts at first, which gradually become adopted into colloquial speech but are not accepted as good King's English until they are fully absorbed into the language. Many of them are highly expressive—words like gallivanting, flapdoodle, tommyrot, skedaddle —which would be out of place in a leading article or from the pulpit.

Slang words, the meaning of which is well known to ordinary people, are not included in the dictionary until it is obvious that they are something more than a temporary fashion. Many of them last only a short time; others become fixed and are ultimately accepted as English.

Americanisms, too, are creeping into the language through the influence of films and American literature. We learn that corn means maize in America, and that lumber applies to felled trees. We get to know the alternative words for lift, braces, tram, railway, station, car, petrol, biscuit and sweets. In some cases we find that a new Americanism is really an old English word which was gradually forgotten over here but kept alive on the other side of the Atlantic.

Finally, we have a great many foreign expressions which are in frequent use but have not yet become naturalized. In some cases they are unnecessary and should be killed outright. There is no need to say "menu" when we mean "bill of fare," or "serviette" when we mean "table napkin"; but there are many other examples for which we cannot find an exact equivalent and we keep them because we need them.

Test Yourself

1. Write down as many words as you can signifying or suggesting "little," "big," "thoughtful," "generous," "mean," "rich." Do the same for "solace," "devise," "integrity."

2. What is meant by the *mot juste*? How would you accustom yourself to finding it?

3. Why do we laugh at Mr. Micawber's conversation? What is the chief characteristic of Dr. Johnson's writing?

4. The authors of *The King's English* gave excellent advice to the would-be writer (quoted on p. 239). How many of their five rules can you remember? Is there any rule which you would like to add? (Question 2 above may give you a hint.)

5. Would you ever deliberately use slang in writing? If so, on what occasions?

Answers will be found at the end of the book.

DR. BUSBY'S CHAIR PERSONIFYING HIS FAVOURITE SUBJECTS
Headmaster of Westminster School, Dr. Busby counted Dryden, Locke and Prior among his pupils. His prowess as a grammarian was commemorated in Sir Peter Lely's sketch.

CHAPTER XV
ESSENTIALS OF GRAMMAR AND CONSTRUCTION

IN looking at a house you see first of all the building materials which have been used —wood, bricks, stones, or ferro-concrete. But you see something more: the general plan or design, the architect's idea which has taken tangible shape. Similarly, in examining a language you notice not only the actual words of which it is composed, but also the general pattern or construction —the architecture of it. The study of the general principles underlying a language is called grammar.

In talking there must be something to talk about (a subject) and something must be said about it. If we want to tell how a young boy killed a giant with a stone from a sling, the English pattern of arrangement is simple:

> David killed Goliath with a small stone.

But the ancient Romans would arrange it as follows:

> David Goliath with a small stone killed.

Every language has its own rules about the arrangement of its words.

Living Language
The rules of English grammar are not rigid as they would be in a logical, artificial or dead language. They are constantly changing as the language evolves and adapts itself to new circumstances. A living language must continually change and grow, and English is very much alive. New words are always being invented or borrowed; old words become old-fashioned and either disappear or gain a fresh meaning. New patterns of speech emerge, new turns of phrase, new idioms. Words like farthingale and cravat still appear in the dictionary, but we scarcely ever use them and they might almost be regarded as fossils. The word broadcast—a method of sowing seed—seemed on the point of disappearing when it suddenly acquired a new meaning through wireless. And every new discovery or invention requires new words —television, heterodyne, penicillin, vitamin, gremlin, jeep.

Flexibility and Freedom
The ancient languages of Greece and Rome were highly inflected; that is to say the words changed their shape to suit the circumstances. In English a word like table can be altered by adding an *s* to show that more than one table is referred to; but in Latin the word has a number of shapes —*mensa, mensam, mensae, mensas, mensarum, mensis*. One single word can mean "You have been warned" or "I shall have been cured." Here is an example of the way words are inflected in Latin. It is not suggested that the reader should try to remember it—merely that he should see the idea. *Amare* means to love; *amo*—I love; *amamus*—we love; *amatis*—you love; *amabam*—I was loving; *amabamus*—we were loving; *amabimus*—we shall love; *amabitis*—you will love; *amamur*—we are loved; *amamini*—you are loved; *amantur*— they are loved; *amabuntur*—they will be loved; *amabantur*—they were being loved. And there are scores of others!

We have dropped a great many inflexions which appeared in Old English or Anglo-Saxon. We have other ways of expressing changes of time, for example, by means of auxiliary words like have, had, is, was, shall, will, would and should. The result of this method is to give the language greater flexibility and freedom. We can secure subtle differences of meaning by changing the order of the words—to throw the emphasis on different parts of the sentence. There is a difference between:

> I want to read a book,

and

> I want a book to read.

The first is more energetic, the second

suggests that I want to kill time—any book will do for the purpose.

There is a difference between:

She found the basket empty,

and

She found the empty basket.

In the former sentence she was surprised (or disappointed) to find that the contents had vanished.

Take a line of poetry like:

Home they brought her warrior dead;

and rearrange the words:

They brought her dead warrior home,
They brought her warrior home dead,
They brought home her dead warrior,
They brought home her warrior dead.

There are differences in the effect which all these word-patterns produce: no two are precisely the same.

Unfortunately, English education in the Middle Ages and during the Renaissance was based mainly upon the study of the classics, and when our first grammarians got to work they tried to force our own language into the same patterns that suited the languages of Greece and Rome. The rigid rules were difficult to apply: the living language refused to stick to them. Some authorities in recent years, like the late Professor Jespersen, argued that we ought to scrap the old terminology and invent a new one more adaptable to the language as we use it. They talk about double-faced verbs, split subjects, adjuncts, nexus, primaries, secondaries, tertiaries, etc. But until these new terms are adopted there is no need to worry about them.

Parts of Speech

Words are classified into eight or nine groups called the parts of speech. These are as follows: nouns, verbs, pronouns, adjectives, adverbs, prepositions, conjunctions, interjections, and a ninth class (articles) may be added. Roughly speaking:

Nouns are names of persons, places, things, materials, etc., like Cromwell, Birmingham, cabbage, velvet, tungsten.

Verbs are words which tell of things done—words of action like come, go, dance, vanish, rage.

Pronouns are noun-substitutes like he, she, you, who, I, we, they.

Adjectives are words which modify nouns—words like big, little, red, French, benevolent.

Adverbs are used chiefly to modify verbs and other adverbs—like weakly, gaily, often, now, yesterday.

Prepositions are used in phrases and govern nouns—words like over, under, in, on, of, after, followed by a noun or pronoun.

Conjunctions are used to join words or sentences—words like and, but, for.

Interjections are exclamatory—Indeed! Oh! Pooh! and indicate surprise, indignation, etc.

Articles are words like the, a, an, used with nouns, and often included with adjectives. "A" is called the indefinite article and "the" is known as the definite article.

These parts of speech can be further divided into groups, and it is necessary to examine each class in turn.

Nouns—The Names of Things

These words are all-important. We cannot speak at all without knowing the names of things. A baby begins with nouns like Mammie, Daddy, Bow-wow. A missionary entering a foreign country gets to learn the language by pointing to things and making a note of their names. Nouns are divided into three principal classes: common nouns are names of familiar things like book, man, woman, tree, star, sky, locomotive. Proper nouns are names of special things and are spelt with an initial capital letter. Thus a special man is John, Julius Caesar, Mr. Jones; a special star is Venus, Jupiter, or Sirius; a special place is Hull, Leeds, Leningrad, Iran, Indo-China. Abstract nouns are names of qualities or ideas: sweetness, acidity, justice, mercy, tyranny, perseverance, nutrition, health. A fourth class may be the names of a number of things—collective nouns or nouns of multitude—like flock, herd, regiment, squadron, flotilla, swarm, mob, audience. In English the names of the days of the week and months of the year are considered to be proper nouns, but the French treat them as common nouns and

STUDENTS AND TEACHER IN THE MIDDLE AGES

From a fourteenth-century manuscript comes this impression of a university class at work.

do not use a capital letter. It sometimes seems odd that special things like the sun and moon are treated as common nouns. We give a capital letter to Neptune but only a small letter to moon.

Nouns—Gender and Number

English nouns have gender as follows: names of all males are masculine: John, King Charles, bull, colt, lion, gander, peacock, actor, janitor. Names of all females are feminine: Mary, Queen Caroline, cow, filly, lioness, goose, peahen, actress, janitrix. Names of things with no sex are neuter: book, pen, hat, maisonette, filigree, diamond. What could be simpler? Some words, however, like cousin, person, neighbour, friend and witness may signify either a male or a female, and we say that they are of common gender. All this is extremely logical and practical.

We have two numbers in English—

singular (to signify one) and plural to signify more than one. In ninety-nine cases out of a hundred we form the plural by adding *s* or *es* to the singular. Thus, books, chimneys, days, nights, typewriters, potatoes, volcanoes, etc. Words ending in *y* often change *y* to *i* and add *es*: for example, fly becomes flies, ferry becomes ferries, and so on. There are a few exceptions, when the words don't change at all: deer, sheep, cod, perch, salmon, etc. Some change the vowel to show the plural: feet, mice, lice, men, women, geese (but the plural of mongoose is mongooses). One or two ancient words keep the ancient plural ending in "en." Thus ox becomes oxen and child becomes children. Some foreign words keep their foreign plurals. Terminus becomes termini; radius becomes radii; crisis becomes crises, cherub and seraph become cherubim and seraphim; bandit becomes either bandits or banditti; libretto becomes libretti. And there are a few tricky words like passer-by, lord justice, knight templar, court martial, man-servant, commander-in-chief, which become passers-by, lords justices, knights templars, courts martial, men-servants, commanders-in-chief. There are even words that have no plural, and plurals that have no singular; there are words that change their meaning when they become plural, e.g. copper, domino, force, iron, salt, manner, spectacle. It is hardly necessary to explain things that everyone knows. In spite of all these exceptions—and there are still others—the rule still stands: To make the plural of an English noun, add *s* or *es* to the singular.

Verbs—Action Words

These are as important as nouns. If we must have something to talk about, we must also have something to say about it. A noun followed by a verb makes the simplest kind of sentence: fishes swim, birds fly, wolves howl. Verbs suggest action or inaction—jump, run, walk, rest, sleep, strike, whistle. They are divided into two or three classes: Transitive verbs require an object. If you say:

Moses struck . . .

you want to know what he struck and so the sentence has to be completed:

Moses struck the rock.

The verb struck describes an action which passes over to something else and is therefore transitive. But if we say:

The baby smiled,

there is no need to ask what. The sense is complete, and the verb smiled is intransitive and needs no object to follow.

If this is perfectly clear we are now in a position to analyse a simple sentence.

Subject	Verb	Object
Mice	. eat .	. cheese
We .	. met	. two foreigners
Honesty	. pays	
Stars	. twinkle	

But a verb may be used either intransitively or transitively:

Subject	Verb	Object
Chimneys	. smoke (intransitive)	
Millionaires	. smoke	. Havana cigars (transitive)
The kettle	. boiled (intransitive)	

The chef	. boiled	. the lobsters (transitive)

The verb "to be" cannot be transitive because it does not suggest any action and therefore cannot have an object. It merely links words together by identifying them. For example:

John was a spy.

Here it is clear that the spy and John were the same person. It is not the object but only a complement to the subject. Compare these sentences:

The detective caught the criminal.

The detective was the criminal.

"Caught" is a transitive verb with an object; "was" is a link-verb with a complement. If we reverse the first sentence we reverse the meaning, but if we reverse the second there is no change of meaning.

Transitive verbs are said to have voice—either active or passive. When the subject is the doer of the action, the verb is in the active voice:

Subject	Verb	Object
Christian	defeated	Apollyon

If the subject is not the doer but the sufferer of the action, the verb is in the passive voice:

Apollyon was defeated by Christian.

Compare these two sentences:

Policemen collect evidence (active voice)

Evidence is collected by policemen (passive voice).

Editors of our daily papers are fond of using the passive voice. Instead of writing "I think" or "We think" they prefer to say "It is thought" or "It may be assumed." The active voice is more direct and vigorous; the passive less personal: "You were observed in Euston" tells rather less than "I saw you in Euston" or "Brenda saw you in Euston." "This book is being read" tells us less than "You are reading this book."

Tenses and Moods of Verbs

All verbs have tense, the three main classes being past, present and future:

Past Tense. I saw. You believed. He did.

Present Tense. I see. You believe. He does.

CANDIDATE FOR THE UNIVERSITY

This eighteenth-century print shows the examination of the talents and abilities of a young and nervous candidate seeking admission to the halls of learning.

Future Tense. I shall see. You will believe. He will do.

Each of these tenses has four distinct forms:

I shall see. (Future Indefinite);
I shall be seeing. (Future Continuous);
I shall have seen. (Future Perfect);
I shall have been seeing. (Future Perfect Continuous).

There is no need to try to remember all these. It is enough to get the idea and apply it to other tenses. In the present tense, for example, there is an obvious difference between "I read" and "I am reading."

People are often confused about the use of shall and will. We say "I shall" and "we shall" to express the simple idea of futurity. We say "I will" and "we will" if we mean something more. they suggest determination or the use of force. But with other words—you, he, she, it, they—the opposite rule applies. "You will" or "they will" suggest merely the future, but "you shall"

or "they shall" implies compulsion or determination. The rule can be best remembered by recalling the story of the foreigner who, while bathing in deep water, exclaimed: "I will be drowned and no one shall save me!" It sounds like deliberate suicide.

Verbs, like human beings, also have moods. The most familiar is the indicative mood which makes a statement or asks a question: I am going, I have been, You will know. The imperative mood indicates a command: Go! Speak! Jump! The infinitive mood is the essential verb like to go, to descend, to jump. The subjunctive mood expresses doubt, wish, hope, etc.: I may go, If I were you, Unless you think differently.

In passing it might be noted that they have number like nouns, and this is shown by word-endings: The man shouts. The men shout. Verbs also have person but that subject can be left for the moment. We shall return to it when reviewing pronouns.

Summarizing all we have learnt about verbs so far:

They are transitive, intransitive, or merely link-verbs.

They have moods, tenses, number and person.

Only transitive verbs have voice.

At least one verb must be expressed or implied in every sentence, for without it the thought is incomplete.

Pronouns in Place of Nouns

Pronouns are substitutes for nouns. It would be awkward if the noun had to be repeated every time in this way:

John picked up John's cap and set off, but Mary laughed because instead of putting John's cap on John's head John carried the cap in John's hand.

How much easier to say:

John picked up his cap and set off, but Mary laughed because instead of putting it on his head he carried it in his hand.

There are four kinds of pronouns: personal, interrogative, relative and demonstrative. The chief personal pronouns are these:

I, me, mine, we, us, ours (first person).

Thou, thee, thine, you, yours (second person).

He, him, she, her, hers, it, they, them, theirs (third person).

The first person is used for the person speaking; the second for the person spoken to; the third for the person spoken about. If Mrs. Jones writes to Mrs. Smith in the first person, she begins:

I shall be glad if you can meet me at Charing Cross . . .

but if she writes in the third person, she begins:

Mrs. Jones will be glad if Mrs. Smith can meet her at Charing Cross.

Note that nouns and verbs also have person. Nouns do not change their form, fortunately, but verbs do, e.g.

I am, thou art, he is, we are, etc.

I stand, she stands, we stand, etc.

Interrogative pronouns (who, whose, whom, which, what) are used in asking questions:

Who is that man?

Which is the way?

What are you doing?

Relative pronouns (who, whose, whom, which, what, that) do not ask questions but refer to some antecedent, expressed or understood:

I know the man who advised you to call.

We suspect the man whose identity card has been lost.

The people whom he saw at Liverpool have arrived in London.

An interrogative pronoun usually begins a sentence which ends with a question mark. A relative pronoun rarely comes first and is not used to ask a question.

Demonstrative pronouns (this, that, these, those) are used like this:

This is better than that.

These are nearly ripe but those are still green.

Adjectives and Adverbs

Adjectives are used with nouns to make the meaning more definite. "Boy" does not give a very vivid picture, but we can make it clearer by adding words like:

The little, red-haired Irish boy . . .

all the extra words are adjectives.

There are several kinds of adjectives. Adjectives of number: two, seven, fifty, second, twelfth. Adjectives of quality: good, bad, intelligent, stupid. Adjectives of quantity: few, many, much, more, most. Demonstrative adjectives· this, that, these, those. If we say: "This girl," the word "this" is an adjective because it is used with a noun; but if we say: "This is very pretty," the word "this" is a noun-substitute and is therefore a pronoun. Words like French, Irish, English, are sometimes called proper adjectives because they are derived from proper nouns; hence they are spelt with capital letters.

Adjectives of quality have degrees of comparison: Positive (referring to one only): wise, good, beautiful. Comparative (for two only): wiser, better, more beautiful. Superlative (for more than two): wisest, best, most beautiful.

The three degrees of "ill" are: ill, worse, worst. (Not, as the intelligent schoolboy suggested: ill, worse, dead.)

Adverbs modify verbs just as adjectives modify nouns. They tell how, when, where, or why a thing happens:

The man is dressing now. He went yesterday.

The carriage is here (or there).

The girl spoke quickly and clearly.

Adverbs also have three degrees of comparison:

Clearly, more clearly, most clearly.

Magnificently, more magnificently, most magnificently.

It should be observed that adjectives need to be chosen with very particular care. They are often a clue to a writer's ability and his sense of word values. A story-writer like Kipling or Stevenson rarely uses a commonplace adjective. He seeks to avoid the obvious and so captures the reader's interest. Everybody talks about a noble lord, a learned judge, a staunch teetotaller, a rippling brook, and so forth; but a first-rate writer avoids these ready-made expressions and prefers to find an adjective of his own. Thus, Kipling writes about a "giggling brook" and Stevenson about a "wimpling stream"; and the unexpected words give one a sense of pleasure. The choice of adjectives is a fine test of a man's originality.

Conjunctions and Prepositions

As the name suggests, conjunctions are joining words. They link together nouns, adjectives, verbs, sentences, etc.

The commonest are: and, but, or, so. For example:

Tom and John will be present sooner or later.

Many are called but few are chosen.

The preacher had finished his sermon, so he sat down.

But many conjunctions and adverbs unite to form what is called an adverbial conjunction. Thus we might say:

I found the spot and the man had been seen there.

It is rather awkward, isn't it? Better to say:

I found the spot where the man had been seen.

(Where is equal to "and there," uniting a conjunction and an adverb in one word —an adverbial conjunction. Similarly, when equals "and then," whence equals "and thence," whither equals "and thither.")

Words like: because, unless, if, and since are also adverbial conjunctions linking sentences together:

You shall not go unless you apologize.

Prepositions are placed before a noun or pronoun to show its relationship to the rest of the sentence. The preposition with the noun or pronoun makes a phrase: The aeroplane flew in the clouds, or under the clouds, or above the clouds, or through the clouds.

Prepositions are generally little words: in, under, above, through, across, below, over, past, beside, on, of, etc. We often use a phrase instead of an adjective or an adverb. Instead of saying: "The aviator fell here," we can say: "The aviator fell at this spot," and the last three words (the phrase) may be called an adverbial phrase. Similarly, "at daybreak" or "in the morning" are phrases equal to an adverb telling when: adverbial phrases of time.

Interjections—Expressing Emotion

Interjections express sudden emotions and do not really belong to the sentence in which they are found. They are words like: oh! alas! by heavens! Great Scott! well!

It is important to remember that we can never say what part of speech any word is until we know just how it is used—what part it plays in the sentence. For example, the word "well" might be a noun, an adjective, an adverb, a verb, or an interjection.

The well is dry. (Noun.)

The girl is quite well. (Adjective.)

She writes well. (Adverb.)

Tears began to well up in her eyes. (Verb.)

"Well!" she exclaimed in her astonishment. (Interjection.)

Perhaps the adjective may seem a little puzzling since it is not alongside a noun; but the sentence really means: "The girl is a well girl" just as yesterday she was sick.

Gerunds are nouns and verbs at the same time. Thus if we say: "The crowd welcomed his coming," the word coming is partly verb because it is part of the verb to come; but it is also partly noun because it is equal to saying that the crowd welcomed his arrival.

Running races is popular,

and

Buying hats is always in fashion

are two other examples of gerunds—words that come from verbs yet have a noun significance.

Participles are verbs and adjectives at the same time, e.g.

The leaves are falling.

The old oak-tree is fallen.

Here the words falling and fallen both come from the verb fall—they are participles—but are equal to adjectives and qualify nouns: "falling leaves," "fallen tree."

What Are Sentences?

A sentence may consist of any number of words, from two to a couple of hundred or more; but however long or short it may be, it must have (a) something to talk about—a subject, (b) something to say about it—the predicate. We can analyse simple sentences like this:

Subject	Predicate
Time . .	flies
Foxes .	steal geese

To take another example:

The quick brown fox	jumped over the lazy dog.

Here the simple subject is fox, and the other words (adjectives) merely enlarge the subject. In a similar way, the real predicate (the verb) is jumped, and the other words make a phrase that extends the verb, telling where or how the fox jumped. The essential sentence is "fox jumped": all the other words enlarge or extend the meaning.

Suppose we analyse a little more fully:

Subject		Predicate		
Noun	Enlargement	Verb	Object	Extension
Time		flies		
Foxes		steal	geese	
Roads	all	lead		to Rome
Wolves,	desperate with hunger	attack	men	furiously

Notice the two items which are always there—the simple subject and the verb. The other items may or may not be present.

When we join two or more simple sentences together with conjunctions like and or but, the sentence is said to be compound:

Foxes are crafty but geese are stupid.

Men must work and women must weep.

Note that the two sentences joined together are of equal importance. They are known as co-ordinate clauses. Here is another example:

Men may come, and men may go, but I go on for ever.

This compound sentence has three co-ordinate clauses, and each clause has its own subject and predicate. But if the clauses are not of equal importance, i.e. if one be the main clause and the others dependent upon it, the whole sentence is said to be complex, as in (3) below.

(1) Simple Sentence: "Scrooge hated Christmas."

(2) Compound Sentence: "Scrooge was a miser and Scrooge hated Christmas.

(3) Complex Sentence: "Scrooge, who was a miser, hated Christmas."

In this last: "Scrooge hated Christmas" is the main clause. "Who was a miser" is equal to an adjective because it describes Scrooge: it is a subordinate adjectival clause.

Another example: "When he heard the carol singers, Scrooge seized a ruler." It is clear that "Scrooge seized a ruler" is the main clause; "When he heard the carol singers" merely tells you when Scrooge performed the action. It has the effect of an adverb, telling when the thing happened. We conclude, therefore, that it is a subordinate adverbial clause.

Now let us look at a more complicated one still: "When he awoke from the dream that terrified him, Scrooge, who had never given a present in his life, bought the prize turkey that was twice as big as Tiny Tim." There are about half a dozen clauses wrapped up in that sentence, but the main clause is: "Scrooge bought the prize

THE SENTENCE

" When he awoke from the dream that terrified him Scrooge, who had never bought a present in his life, bought a prize turkey that was twice as big as Tiny Tim."

MAIN CLAUSE

Scrooge bought a prize turkey

Subordinate Adjectival Clause
that was twice as big
as Tiny Tim
Subordinate Adverbial Clause

Subordinate Adverbial Clause
when he awoke from the dream

that terrified him
Subordinate Adjectival Clause

who had never bought a present in his life
Subordinate Adjectival Clause

GRAMMAR TREE

Above may be seen a pictorial analysis of the sentence from Dickens given at the top left-hand corner. For the sake of simplicity, the main clause is likened to the main trunk of a tree. Various branches growing from the tree are used to illustrate the subordinate clauses connected with elements in the main clause and sometimes giving rise to subordinate clauses. Thus, if these clauses are analysed further, it will be seen that the subordinate adjectival clause "that terrified him" describes Scrooge's dream; that the subordinate adjectival clause "who had never bought a turkey in his life" describes Scrooge; while the subordinate adjectival clause "that was twice as big" describes the turkey that he bought. All subordinate clauses can be viewed in relation to the main clause or to one another.

turkey." All the other clauses merely add further details "When he awoke from the dream" tells when he bought the turkey; "that terrified him" describes the dream itself; "who had never given a present in his life" describes Scrooge; "that was twice as big" describes turkey; "as Tiny Tim (was big)" completes the comparison. Every one of those clauses has its own subject and verb.

Perhaps the complex sentence can best be represented by a tree with a main stem and various dependent branches.

Punctuation

It would be easy to fill pages in a discussion of punctuation but it really is not necessary. One can discover all the main rules by examining a newspaper, using

THE

ROYAL GRAMMAR

Reformed into

A more Eafie Method,

FOR THE

Better Underſtanding

OF

The Engliſh:

AND

More Speedy Attainment

OF THE

LATIN TONGUE.

Nullum Munus afferre majus meliúſve poſſumus, quàm ſi eru-
diamus Juventutem, iis præſertim moribus atque tempo-
ribus, quibus ita prolapſa eſt; ut omnium opibus refræ-
nanda & coercenda ſit. Cic.

IMPRIMATUR,

March 6. 1694.

Humph. Hody.

LONDON,

Printed by J. Heptinſtall, for J. and J. Churchill, at the
Black-Swan in Pater-Noſter-Row. MDCXCV.

ROYAL GRAMMAR BOOK

Published in 1694, this book is a very early example of those which were used for the instruction of young scholars.

one's powers of comparison, and applying a little common sense.

The full-stop or period is used:

(a) at the end of a complete sentence;

(b) to indicate that a word is abbreviated, for example: Rev., Esq., M.P., B.A., inst., Ltd., Co.

The comma is used to indicate a very short pause, as in "Bill Brewer, Jan Stewer, Peter Gurney, Peter Davy . . ." and "Friends, Romans, countrymen, lend me your ears." Note that commas are used more sparingly today than in former years. The present fashion is to use them only when they are necessary to make the meaning clear. There is a difference between:

Some men I know are very rich

and

Some men, I know, are very rich.

Most people use full-stops and commas, but they fight shy of colons and semicolons. The colon is used:

(a) to introduce a quotation of some weight justifying a longer pause than the comma provides;

(b) to introduce a list such as this one;

(c) most of all to separate statements balanced one against the other. Examples are:

Everyone knows the old saying: "If you wish for peace, prepare for war."

There is a newer saying: "Prepare for war, and you'll get it."

Shakespeare's chief comedies are these: *The Merchant of Venice, Twelfth Night, As You Like It, A Midsummer Night's Dream.* . . .

Brown is an obstinate fellow: they say the whole breed are obstinate.

The word "success" can be used in two senses: it may apply to a man who serves a useful purpose to the community; it may mean that he gets what he wants.

The semicolon indicates a shorter pause than a colon and a longer one than a comma, and its use may be gathered from the following example from Bacon:

To spend too much time in studies is sloth; to use them too much for ornament is affectation; to make judgment wholly by their rules is the humour of the scholar.

The note of interrogation is used after a direct question, as in:

What are you going to do next?

(But not in such a sentence as: "He asked what he was going to do next," for that is not a question but merely a statement.)

A note of exclamation is used to express an ejaculation or to suggest surprise: "Great Jupiter! Marvellous!" It should be used very sparingly indeed—almost never.

Quotation marks (inverted commas) are used when exact words are quoted as in the reporting of conversation: "My dear Mary," said her father. "you can't mean what you say."

A dash is used in several ways:

(a) to indicate an unfinished sentence;

(b) to add an afterthought.

For example:

"Well," said the sailor, "if that's what you think——"

It rained the whole time—a horrible week we had.

The apostrophe s, used to indicate possession, is often a source of confusion because it is sometimes complicated with the plural s. The old-fashioned rule (Use apostrophe before s when the word is singular and after the s when it is plural) works satisfactorily in nineteen cases out of twenty, but it fails when the plural is formed by vowel-changes or by adding en. We say, for instance:

A boy's cap. Boys' caps.
A lady's handbag was found.
Ladies' handbags are expensive.
A man's pipe. Men's pipes.
Women's dresses. Children's shoes.

The reason why we say: "Girls' school" is simply that "Girls's school" would sound awkward. The s in "Girls' school" is the plural: the s used to denote possession is dropped altogether. The apostrophe is also used to indicate that something is missing (i.e. deliberately left out as in an abbreviation). Thus we write 'phone, 'bus, and it's (short for "it is"). Note that the apostrophe s is never used with pronouns like ours, yours, theirs, its.

The only other punctuation mark of any consequence is the pair of dashes or pair of brackets. Two dashes or brackets can be used to mark off an idea which is additional to the main flow of the sentence (or of the paragraph) and is in a sense an interruption of it:

As I walked down the street—it was after five o'clock—I saw him leave the office.

Such additional remarks as are enclosed in brackets are said to be in parenthesis. (See this example and the many others in this book.)

Test Yourself

1. Give the feminine of: emperor, prosecutor, he-goat, ram, stallion, earl, duke and author. Give the masculine of: bride, widow, duck, goose, mare, heifer.

2. What is the plural of the following words : piano, brother, bureau, terminus, axis, phenomenon.

3. Use the apostrophe (or apostrophe s) to indicate: the rattle of a baby; cycles for ladies; brushes belonging to foxes; the tails of oxen; a nursery for children.

4. Make a list of inflexions and of other means still used in English to show: (a) plural number of nouns; (b) past tenses of verbs; (c) the comparative degree of adjectives.

5. What is the difference between "shall" and "will" to indicate the simple future?

Answers will be found at the end of the book.

OUTSTANDING WRITERS ON ENGLISH LITERATURE

Above are four of the most famous modern critics and teachers of literature. Walter Pater (top left), 1839-1894, was a friend of the pre-Raphaelite painters, a stylist and critic; George Saintsbury (top right), 1845-1933, was an authority on English and Scandinavian literature and historian of literary criticism; Sir Edmund Gosse (lower right), 1849-1928, was a brilliant exponent of seventeenth- and eighteenth-century literature; Sir Arthur Quiller-Couch (lower left), 1863-1944, novelist, taught for many years at Cambridge, edited the "Oxford Book of English Verse" and wrote: "On the Art of Writing."

CHAPTER XVI

COMMON MISTAKES IN THE USE OF ENGLISH

THE general rules of English having been explained in the last chapter, it is now proposed to consider some of the many ways in which people often go wrong. Words are sometimes misused, mispronounced, misspelt; but the commonest mistake is the tripping-up over the rules of grammar.

"I deny the allegation and I despise the *alligator!*" said a character in one of Edna Lyall's novels. He imagined that an alligator signified a person who makes an allegation. Unfortunately, it happens to be the name of the American crocodile; hence his laughable mistake.

One often hears amusing slips of this kind. A small girl explained to her mother that her letter was written with an *indelicate* pencil and a small boy went into a sweet shop and asked for two penn'orth of *cannibals.* An old lady looking at the delphiniums in the garden exclaimed: "Aren't these lovely *Philadelphians!*" Another lady spoke about the *converted* mantles needed for a *convalescent* light. Mistakes of this type are known as malapropisms or malaprops. The word is derived from Mrs. Malaprop, a character in Sheridan's play, *The Rivals,* who had an uncanny knack of choosing the wrong word. Here are a few examples:

Illiterate him from your memory.

You are an absolute *misanthropy.*

I would by no means wish a daughter of mine to be a *progeny* of learning .

I would send her to a boarding school where she would have a *supercilious* knowledge in accounts, and as she grew up I would have her instructed in *geometry* so that she might know something of *contagious* countries.

I hope you will represent her to the captain as an object not altogether *illegible.*

I have laid Sir Anthony's *preposition* before her.

Oh, it gives me *hydrostatics.*

I have *interceded* another letter from the fellow.

She is as headstrong as an *allegory* on the banks of the Nile.

I am sorry to say that my *affluence* over my niece is very small.

We will not *anticipate* the past.

O mercy! I'm quite *analysed.*

He can tell you the *prependiculars.*

If I *reprehend* anything in this world it is the use of my *oracular* tongue, and a nice *derangement* of *epitaphs.*

It is fairly easy to guess the words which the lady intended. The "nice derangement of epitaphs" should have been, of course, a "nice arrangement of epithets." The people most liable to make malaprops are (a) elderly persons whose memory plays them tricks, (b) young people who are trying to use an impressive vocabulary which they have not properly mastered. The results are often humorous, but not always; and there are some malaprops which are used unwittingly by well-educated people. The word eerie means lonely or isolated, but it is generally used to suggest the weird, the uncanny, or the supernatural. When there is only one of a thing it is said to be unique. It cannot, therefore, be more unique, less unique, rather unique, or even very unique. If it is unique it is unique, and that's all one can say about it.

If a man, suspected of having committed a crime, can prove that he was elsewhere at the time, he establishes his innocence —he has an alibi, from the Latin, meaning elsewhere. Today the word is being used for any sort of excuse: "I was late at work but I had a good alibi—the alarm clock didn't go off."

Readers of *The Pickwick Papers* will remember how Old Weller misunderstood the term. He hoped Mr. Pickwick could defend himself in a breach of promise case by proving an alibi! A hundred years ago this was regarded as a joke. Today it is liable to be taken seriously. Any natural event like the rising of the sun or the falling of the leaves is a phenomenon. That is to say, it is perfectly natural—part of Nature's phenomena. But today people talk about a "phenomenal sight" meaning something surprising or unexpected. Mr. Crummles in *Nicholas Nickleby*, referred to his daughter as the *phenomenon*.

The lady who said that the cyclist was "literally flying" down the road was mis-using the word literally. She meant meta-phorically or symbolically. One can only "literally fly" in a plane. The majority of malaprops are not humorous. People confuse two words which have some resemblance, e.g.

practical . practicable
ingenious . ingenuous
observance . observation
deprecate . depreciate
perspicuous . perspicacious
idolize . . idealize
comprehensive comprehensible

A man is said to be practical when he can do things—when he can apply his theory in practice. A scheme which is workable is practicable, but the word cannot be applied to a man or woman. The above pairs of words should be carefully distinguished, and the reader is advised to consult his dictionary whenever he is in doubt.

Before leaving this subject of misused words, one very common blunder might be noted. The word chronic means recur-ring or lasting for a long time. Many people appear to think it means serious, as when a man says: "My toothache was something chronic!"

Sounds and Spelling

The chief reason for mispronunciation of English words is that the sounds so rarely follow the spelling. Knew, new and gnu share the same sound, whereas words like present and refuse each have two different sounds. Yacht is sounded "yot" and school is "skool." Some of our proper nouns are worse. How could one guess that Cholmondeley should be pronounced "Chumley" and Earwaker pronounced "Erriker"? Some of our reformers want to

scrap our spelling and use only a phonetic system. It would save a great deal of time and trouble. They would invent a new sign to represent *th*, and a word like though would have only two letters instead of six. Popular prejudice is opposed to the change and it can evolve only gradually. A familiar passage written in phonetic spelling looks "komik to inglish ize."

Mispronunciations

Since spelling affords such unreliable clues to sound, it is small wonder that words are pronounced differently, but a standard pronunciation is being set by the B.B.C., and as millions of people listen to the broadcast news, one might expect that the correct pronunciation of familiar words would be picked up by everyone.

But it is not so. How many times do we hear the right pronunciation of a word like coupons in a year? The broadcast speaker makes it sound like "koopongs," yet at least half the people one meets still pronounce it "kewpons." It is rather difficult to explain this habit of clinging to the wrong sound when one hears the right one so often.

Here are a few examples of words which are constantly being mispronounced:

Westminster is changed into "West-minister": Admiralty into "Admirality"; accompanist into "accompanyist"; route into "rout" (instead of "root"); and so on. Casualties has its accent on the first syllable, not on the third, with an extra vowel—"casualities." Interesting is ac-cented on the first syllable, not the third. The word margarine is always being dis-puted. According to the rules, the *g* should be hard, as in Margaret; but the majority of people (including many broadcasters) make it soft—"marjarine." The Irishman's solution is the best: make it hard in winter and soft in summer!

But mispronunciations on a wider scale are due to: (a) dialect, varying according to the district in which one lives, and (b) one's station in life.

A simple word like down has half a dozen sounds in various counties: "doon" in Scotland, "dewn" in parts of Southern England, "dahn" in parts of London. No

MRS. GAMP TAKES LIBERTIES

Sarah Gamp, the disreputable old midwife of Dickens's "Martin Chuzzlewit," was renowned for her mispronunciation of the English tongue. Here she is seen with Betsey Prig at the famous tea-party, "propoging" a toast to the mythical Mrs. Harris.

English vowel has a consistent pronunciation throughout the country.

The half-educated Englishman is apt to drop the letter *h* at the beginning of a word, but it is never dropped in Scotland and Ireland. Oddly enough, the man who drops the *h* where it is needed is inclined to put it in wrongly. Thus, a London bus conductor will call out "'Igh 'Olborn" and "Hoxford Street!"

The better educated and the so-called upper classes never drop their aspirates but they do other things that are equally wrong. They are inclined to drop the final *g* and talk about the joys of huntin', shootin' and fishin'. These mispronunciations are indications of social distinction. In the East End of London, for instance, the word tame sounds rather like time, but in certain localities where "refanement" is sought, people say "What 'tame' is it?"

The young person who gets ideas of high-class speech describes her work as "tape-rating."

Other common mistakes in London speech are the substitution of *f* for *th* in numbers like three, thirty-three, etc., making three sound like "free" and so on.

The letter *t* in the middle of a word is sometimes sadly neglected, too, and one notices the same omission in the speech of certain Scottish comedians.

Mispronunciations due to dialect, whether of class or district, would take up a whole book. It is sufficient for our purpose to mention a few of the most obvious. When one is in doubt it is always possible to consult a good dictionary. Take a word like subsidence. Is the accent on the first syllable or the second? (The first is correct.) Is the word amateur pronounced "amaterr" or "amachewer"? And how should one pronounce theatre, decadent, capitalist, laboratory and horizon? How should one pronounce nautical terms like boatswain, gunwale, coxswain, forecastle?

Difficulties With Foreign Words

When foreign words invade the language they are usually pronounced correctly at first, but the Britisher gradually alters them for his own purpose. Garage and chauffeur are typical examples. In French the accent is on the second syllable in each case, but because they seemed ill-balanced to us, the accent was moved to the first syllable. In time the new words settle down as acceptable English words and become naturalized in the language.

People who have never studied Latin or Greek often give English pronunciations to names like Penelope or Calliope which are bestowed on our ships. They should be given four syllables each, the accent being placed on the second. The final syllable is pronounced like the *y* in happy.

Similarly, the Italians pronounce the letter *c* as if it were *ch*, and this applies to words borrowed from the Italian. Thus, 'cello (short for violoncello) is correctly pronounced "chello," and vermicelli as "vermichelly."

German words like *Reuter* and *Freud* are pronounced "Roiter" and "Froid."

English spelling always seems hopelessly inconsistent to a foreigner and is often a subject of mirth among ourselves. The same sound can be represented in half a dozen different ways, and the same letters can have half a dozen different sounds. For examples of the former, think of the ways in which the long *a* can be represented— pay, made, maid, gauge, weigh, café, fête, grey, eh. For examples of the latter, think of the pronunciation of words ending in *ough*—plough, though, through, rough, lough, cough, hiccough. Again, was is pronounced "woz"; war fails to rhyme with tar except in one famous county.

The most difficult looking words to spell are those derived from the Greek (phthisis, psychic, haemorrhage, catarrh), while those from the Latin (magnificent, multitudinous, enumeration, circumnavigate) are usually easy to spell.

To the majority of people the greatest difficulties occur in familiar words like friends, receive, believe, truly, sincerely, oblige. Even some of our great writers, like Jane Austen, were bad spellers.

Spelling is mainly a matter of memorizing. There are dozens of familiar words which are frequently misspelt, and these should be looked up in a dictionary and learned by heart. Any others which give the reader trouble should also be looked up, transferred to a notebook and memorized.

Common Spelling Errors

One of the commonest difficulties arises from the doubling of letters. We write commit (one *t*) but committed; begin but beginning; rag but ragging; tap but tapping; occur but occurred (but benefited breaks the rule). Another difficulty arises from the dropping of letters like *e*. Thus, receive but receiving; write but writing; change but changing. (the *e* is retained, however, in changeable). Similarly with *l* we have full but joyful, careful, grateful; till but until; fulfil but fulfilled. There is always a certain doubt about endings, *-ance* or *-ence*, *-able* or *ible*, *-ant* or *-ent*. Here are a few typical examples of the *-able* and *-ible* words:

Acceptable	Accessible
Admirable	Audible
Capable	Flexible
Delectable	Incorrigible
Indispensable	Irresistible
Laudable	Legible
Noticeable	Permissible
Obtainable	Responsible
Retractable	Tangible
Unmistakable	Visible

AT THE TIME OF WATERLOO

A hundred and fifty years ago bookshops and lending libraries sedately prospered in our country towns. The "Public Library," however, was then a commercial, not a municipal, feature, and in this Teignmouth scene was associated with the bookshop.

Some mistakes are due to slovenly speech. A schoolgirl in describing a walk in springtime, wrote about the "wooden enemies" when she meant wood anemones, and a boy wrote praising the song of the "frush."

As has been explained in the preceding chapter, the English language is based upon certain rules or general principles, but there are a great many exceptions to be considered. One has to know both the rules and the exceptions before one can speak or write good English. Perhaps the most difficult rule should be taken first, namely, the rule of concord: The verb must agree with the subject of the sentence in number and person. Thus:

I am ill; I was going.
He is ill; he was going.
They are ill; they are going.
John was successful.
John and George were successful.

But:

Either John or George gets the prize.

The verb here *must* be singular, because only one boy gets the prize, not both. So, too:

Neither Mary nor Martha wishes to go out.

The verb is wishes, not wish, because the girls are thought of separately, and not as a pair. However, when one part of the subject is singular and the other part plural, the rule is that the verb agrees with the one which is nearer:

Either the Emperor or his sons were there.

Neither the Crown Princes nor the King was there.

The same rule applies when there is a change of person:

Either you or I am . . .
Neither you nor he is . . .

Doubtful Singulars

People sometimes make a mistake through not realizing whether the subject is singular or plural. Books is a plural noun, but if the subject is "a collection of books" it is singular because there is only one collection. Similarly we should say:

This series of booklets is issued;
The flock of sheep was sold.
On the other hand, when we are speaking of a committee, the Board of Education, the Ministry of Health, or the Government, we treat the subject as plural:
The Government have decided.
The committee were sitting.
This is the usual practice, but some authorities disagree.

Collective nouns, and nouns of multitude, require the verb to be either singular or plural according to the sense. If the subject is regarded as a complete whole the verb is singular; if it is regarded as a number of separate units, the verb is plural. Thus:
The crew was loyal.
The crew were provided with life-belts.

Distributive Words

A further complication arises with distributive words like each, every, and many a one; they compel us to think of individuals separately—one at a time—and hence the verb has to be singular:
Every man is aware.
Every woman knows.
Each citizen has to record his or her vote.
The his or her is a nuisance, and people are inclined to say their—which is wrong. It is clumsy (but correct) to say:
When each candidate has finished his or her paper, he or she must remain seated until twelve o'clock.
But it is far better to say:
When candidates have finished their papers, they must remain seated.
It is wrong to say:
When each candidate has finished their papers, etc.
Similarly, it is wrong to say:
Those kind of apples.
Those sort of people.
We should say:
That kind of apple.
That sort of person.
Before we leave the rule of concord it may be mentioned that the worst mistake is to say "We was," "Was you?" "You was." Years ago it was considered correct to say "You was" and "Was you?" Examples are

found in old plays and novels. But now that the word thou has almost disappeared (except in prayers to God), we treat the word you as a plural. Hence the confusion which has spread to other words. So much for the rule of concord.

Double Negatives

The other rules are comparatively simple: Two negatives should not be used to express the same idea. We can say:
The man has no money,
or
The man has not any money.
But it is wrong to say:
He hasn't no money,
because the two negatives cancel each other out, implying that the man *has* money.

In speaking of two persons (or things) we use the comparative degree, but in speaking of more than two we use the superlative degree:
A certain man had two sons, and the younger of them said . . .
Which is the better of these two roads?
Faith, hope, and charity . . . and the greatest of these is charity.
The verb "to be" requires the same case after as before. Thus,
I am he (not him); this is she (not her); it is I (not me).
This rule is gradually giving way to popular custom. When someone knocks at the door and you say: "Who's there?" very few people would answer "It is I." The reply is nearly always "It's me." (The same thing happens in French: "*C'est moi.*")

Case after Prepositions

The accusative case must always be used (a) after a transitive verb, and (b) after a preposition.
Thus, we say:
Mary and I have been invited;
or
They have invited Mary and me.
(Many people are inclined to say "They invited Mary and I," but it is obviously wrong. They invited Mary and they invited I!) Similarly:
The man who saw me was hiding in ambush . . .

The man whom I saw was hiding in ambush . . .

He beckoned to me.

He beckoned to Tom and me (not Tom and I).

It is incorrect to say, "Between you and I." Between is a preposition and should be followed by the objective case, but this error can be heard several times a day. Almost equally common is the sentence: "Who were you talking to?" The first word should be whom, although here again popular custom is threatening to change the rule.

Certain verbs require to be followed by certain prepositions. Thus, we agree *with* a person, but agree *to* an idea. Money is divided *between* two people, but *among* three or more.

Avoiding Split Infinitives

The split infinitive is a subject about which there is considerable argument, but on the whole it is best to avoid it wherever possible. For example:

To slowly stroll down the road,

would be better expressed:

To stroll slowly down the road.

Similarly we should say:

To say at least that you are leaving.

(Not "to at least say . . .")

There are times, however, when a split infinitive is unavoidable:

"Will you ask your mother to kindly tell the baker to call tomorrow."

If you say:

"Will you ask your mother kindly to tell the baker . . ."

or

"Will you ask your mother to tell the baker kindly . . ."

the meaning is not what was intended.

Final Batch

Finally, here are a few of the commonest mistakes:

Different *to* should be different *from*.

I done it. He done it. *Done* should be *did*.

Excuse me interrupting you.

Do you object to him going now? The former should be "Excuse my interrupting you," and the latter "Do you object to his going?" These participles are equal to nouns. No one would say:

"Excuse me interruption."

Or

"Object to him departure."

The words lie and lay are always being confused. Lie is an intransitive verb—you cannot lie anything; and the past tense is (unfortunately) lay. But lay is transitive. A hen can lay an egg, and a builder can lay a solid foundation. The past tense is laid. People are wrong when they say:

I am going for a lay down.

Or

The vessel was laying at anchor.

Lay down for a bit, is wrong; but lay down your arms is right. The trouble between these two words has been further confused because some people pronounce lay as if it were lie, while others pronounce lie as if it were lay.

Test Yourself

1. Correct the mistakes in Mrs. Malaprop's phrases given on page 257.

2. Give the meanings of the following phrases: by hook or by crook; spoiling the ship for a ha'porth of tar; closing the stable door after the horse has gone.

3. What is the difference between: practice and practise; respectful and and respectable; oral and aural; literary and literally?

Answers will be found at the end of the book.

VENVS
AND ADONIS

Vilia miretur vulgus: mihi flauus Apollo
Pocula Caftalia plena miniftret aqua.

LONDON.

Imprinted by Richard Field, and are to be fold at
the figne of the white Greyhound in
Paules Church-yard.
1594.

TITLE PAGE OF "VENUS AND ADONIS"

*Probably Shakespeare's first published work, "Venus and Adonis" is a poem in six-lined
stanzas, and tells the story of the unrequited love of the goddess Venus for the youth Adonis.*

CHAPTER XVII

THE ESSENTIALS OF POETRY

WHAT is poetry? What is its purpose and its place in the history of human endeavour? What, in the hands of those whom the world as a whole has agreed to call great, are the methods and means by which it has sought to achieve its purpose and establish its place? There are many other questions of a kindred nature which surround a subject so vast, so ancient, and so all-pervading as poetry: but these three will suffice. If we can find adequate answers to these we shall arrive as near to "the burthen of the mystery" as may reasonably be expected by any inquirer.

First, then, what is poetry? It is a question which has been asked many a time since the world began and it has received a number of widely differing answers. That insatiable seeker after knowledge, or, perhaps, more accurately, that inveterate exhibitionist, James Boswell, asked it of Samuel Johnson only to receive the reply, "Why, sir, it is much easier to say what it is not. We all *know* what light is; but it is not easy to *tell* what it is." That, of course, was a mere evasion by an expert in authoritative pronouncement, and, had it not been, it is hardly to Johnson, for all his erudition and interest, that we should look for a satisfactory definition. Samuel Taylor Coleridge, attempting what he called "homely definitions of prose and poetry," declared: "Prose = words in their best order; poetry = the best words in the best order"—but that is clearly inadequate and inexact. Everyone can think of prose where the words were not in the best order, and, furthermore, it would immediately necessitate another definition, that of the word "best," since words appropriate to one purpose are by no means necessarily the best, or most appropriate, for another. What says Coleridge's friend? In the passage that is, perhaps, the most often quoted for answer, William Wordsworth wrote, "Poetry is the spontaneous overflow of powerful feelings," adding, for the sake of an elucidation that is certainly essential, "it takes its origin from emotion recollected in tranquillity."

Famous as the words are, they will hardly suffice. Anger is also unquestionably "the spontaneous overflow of powerful feelings"—that is really a general description, not a definition; and the origin of poetry is not invariably that ascribed to it by Wordsworth, even though that ascription goes deep. Do we get anything better from Wordsworth's great junior, John Keats? He called poetry a "drainless shower of light," and "the supreme of power," adding, "'tis might half slumb'ring on its own right arm." That may itself be poetry; it is, however, no great help to an understanding of its nature. Nor does the critical thinker, as supplementing the creative artists, increase that understanding: John Ruskin asks himself the question, "What is poetry?" and answers it by saying, "the suggestion, by the imagination, of noble grounds for the noble emotions." That, too, will not satisfy: poetry exists in the literature of the world which gives that definition a direct denial; that definition at once suggests the poetry that "has a palpable design upon us," which Keats declared we hate—and, though a great deal of very great poetry has been written with such a design, it is certainly not an essential ingredient.

Highest Form of Expression

We are forced away from the famous sayings, all of which, doubtless, contain degrees of truth, so that it may be that, adding all together, we can arrive near enough to the throne. "Poetry," says the Oxford English Dictionary, is "composition in verse or metrical language," and that is, probably, as close as we shall ever get in a few words. Avoiding the confusion of such loose usages as "the poetry of motion" and the like, we may understand that, in general and admitting exceptions, poetry must be metrical, however irregular or even unrhythmic. Furthermore, it must be based rather upon qualities of imagination than those of matter of fact; it must soar rather than stalk; it must divine rather than expound, illumine rather than explain; it must, in truth, deal with the things and thoughts of the spirit rather than be limited to the mundane and the obvious, with that which is permanent rather than that which is transitory. It is not necessary to agree with Robert Burton that "all poets are mad" —many, and these the greatest, have been conspicuous for their sanity—but, in general, Mr. Weller was right in declaring "poetry's unnat'ral; no man ever talked poetry 'cept a beadle on Boxin' Day, or Warren's blackin' or Rowland's oil, or some of them low fellows." It is, in brief, an art, and, like every art, subject to rules, however elastic.

Being full of contradictions and inconsistencies, it defies definition. It is, rather unexpectedly, the glory not merely of Greece but of England, whose poetic heritage challenges comparison fearlessly with that of any land or race; and it is nothing unless its quality is of the best: "*Mediocribus esse poetis*," truly wrote Horace centuries ago, "*non homines, non dei, non concessere columnae*" (To poets to be second-rate is a privilege which neither men, nor gods, nor bookstalls ever allowed.) Poetry is, in the realm of language, the highest form of expression available to man: it says, memorably—and for the most part musically—the profound and the unexpected; in the words of Shelley, "it lifts the veil from the hidden beauty of the world, and makes familiar objects to be as if they were not familiar." To this may also be added the converse, that it makes the unfamiliar to be as though it were familiar.

The Gracious Stream

All poetry is one, from the beginning of time until now. A spring gushes out of the mountain-side and tumbles down the slope in music and in vigour: later in its course it develops into a wide, smoothly flowing, gracious river—but its element is the same. It may have splashings and windings and currents, it may have broad reaches of quiet strength; it may be of crystal clearness and simplicity, it may, in places, degenerate into muddy sloth—but throughout all its varieties and vicissitudes its basic principles remain the same. So is it with poetry.

There have been poets throughout the ages who have set themselves a deliberate purpose: they have had something within them that called insistently for public declaration, something they felt they had to teach or tell—and their writing was in answer to that call. But that is not peculiar to poetry: it is found, though, perhaps, not so insistently, in prose-writers and belongs as of right to any who aspire to teach.

A poet has, in all truth, but one purpose, which may be termed self-expression; but in fulfilling that he is certain, however much of an individualist he may be, to fulfil another, namely, the exposition of the tides moving in humanity in the age in which he writes. He is, if he have any depth of vision in him—and without vision not only do the people perish but no poetry exists—the interpreter of his age: even Shakespeare, whom Benjamin Jonson declared to be "not of an age, but for all time," is continually this, however much else he may also be. And so it has always been from the earliest days when the songs rang out on the lyre to tell of mythological or ancestral deeds or glorify the prize-winners of contests, to the days of the bards giving musical expression to the sagas of their lands, to the days of the itinerant minstrels playing beside the great log-fire in the centre of the baronial hall, right down to the present when, in that dolorous period of indecision, depression and disillusion between the two world wars, T S. Eliot produced such devastatingly illuminating poems as *The Waste Land* and *The Hollow Men*.

As an interpreter, memorable, concise, gleaming—

> jewels five words long
> That on the stretched forefinger of old
> Time
> Sparkle for ever,

in Tennyson's phrase—poetry has always

had and will always have its place. A living writer who has abandoned it for prose (in itself a revealing act) has described it, sourly, as "a bygone phase in the history of the human mind": Macaulay, many a year previously, had uttered the dictum, "as civilization advances, poetry almost necessarily declines." It is true that it now has rivals once unknown, so that in all probability a Shakespeare of today would write novels, not plays, and almost certainly keep the bulk of his work to prose, not poetry. But that does not affect the truth that in poetry always lives the spirit of Youth—and that, happily, is perennial, everlastingly renewed, if not in one way, then in another. And it is in relation to this that the fullest meaning is to be attached to such an aphorism as that of Katherine Tynan: "It is only the immortal and the very young who can go on writing poetry which no one reads." The poet, in short, writes primarily for himself alone.

Sincerity, Clarity and Simplicity

Hence, first and foremost amongst essential qualities comes sincerity: without sincerity there can be no true poetry. A writer must be himself, even if, for the purposes, for instance, of dramatic expression, he creates and assumes the character of another: it must be a sincere creation and a sincere assumption. Much of that which has been, and is, put forth as poetry breaks down on this test of sincerity: whatever the theme, great or small, glorious or gray, it must be written with all the truth the writer has in him. A man may write pretty verses, full of quaint conceits, sonnets, for example, to his mistress's eyebrow, but unless there is feeling behind the prettiness, unless the basis on which the quaintness rests be real, his verses will never deserve the high name of poetry. In days of unrest, such as these of the twentieth century when all is in flux and when destruction and desolation stalk like twin avenging demons through mankind's hearts and hearths, the cry for the bursting of chains becomes dominant: but the chains of poetry have reality only in the imagination of the prisoner who confines himself within his own creation. Sir John Squire

has written the truth in a review of that notable exponent of free verse, Walt Whitman: "The 'shackles' which are talked of do not exist. No poet need use rhymes or regular lines; the only fetters he must wear if he wishes to be an artist are those of the Muse; he must see, think, and feel; he must express what he sees, thinks, and feels accurately."

There is another quality which cannot be termed essential in poetry, yet is, paradoxically, almost of its essence, namely, clarity. Even as running water should be clear, so should poetry. Being "unnat'ral," poetry can never have the simplicity, the lucidity rather, of prose: it is elliptic, elusive, and also allusive; it hints rather than states—but in the hands of the great masters it is made plain, so that there is no need for it to be obscure. That we can readily test—as, indeed, we can test so much —by reference to Shakespeare: as a dramatist he had necessarily to write words which could be understood when first heard, and in consequence there is, except for occasional lines or passages where the text is in dispute or where the meaning of the words used has altered or grown obsolete since he used them, hardly anything in the whole of Shakespeare's plays that cannot be clearly and immediately understood. The inner and fuller meaning may elude or yield itself slowly, but the main thread is there for all to grasp.

It was said of Cardinal Gasquet, "He is a man of simplicity, and successful simplicity is one of the hardest things to obtain. He is more than that, he is the very soul of sincerity." Simplicity and sincerity! What greater attributes could any poetry have?

And yet it has to be admitted that, though sincerity abides in all real poetry, simplicity certainly does not. Take *Endymion*, which has been called "a paradise without a plan" and about the true meaning of which the critics are still variously explanatory; yet that is Keats's longest work. Robert Browning is, in places, so needlessly contorted and confused that the joke passed round that once when he was asked to explain the meaning of a line he had written years before, he remarked that

JOHN KEATS

Son of a London livery-stable keeper, Keats made the most of his scanty education and pursued beauty with the help of the British Museum and a dictionary of mythology. The physical world and its richness fired his imagination and delighted his senses. His odes and sonnets will show you how he loads "every rift with ore."

"once two people knew it, God and Robert Browning, and now there is only God." Or consider George Meredith who could write so fresh, so virginal and delicious a poem as *Love in the Valley*, and yet of whose work that eminent critic, John Bailey, could also write, "The greatest appearance that Napoleon has yet made in our poetry is unquestionably to be found in that astonishing poem which is the second of Meredith's four *Odes in contribution to the Song of French History*. Unfortunately the ode is one of the extremist examples of Meredith's involved and tortuous obscurity. The first reading of it is apt to leave the reader faint and gasping, a weary traveller struggling through an impenetrable forest under a midnight thunderstorm, seeing nothing of his path but what is shown him for an instant, and only for an instant, by flashes of lightning which daze as much as they illumine." Obscurity is always to be regretted; it hinders recognition not only of the particular poet in question but of all poetry, and limits its influence. Yet its existence is so frequent as to make it apparent that poetry is not merely too diverse to admit of definition, but that through the ages it has travelled far from the simplicity of song.

Song and its "Motifs"

And yet it is as song that poetry began, endured, and will continue: all departures from song are supplementary to, and often divergent from, the one great road on which every poet from the earliest day has set foot. We must examine that road and look along some of its windings and gradients before we can attempt any conclusion as to the purpose and place of poetry in the world of today, and—not to lengthen and widen the survey unduly—we must confine ourselves to this great little island, which has been periodically throughout its noble story "a nest of singing-birds," not forgetting, however, that all poetry is one and our heritage would not be the glory that it is were it not for its forerunners in our own, in ancient, and in other lands: as Sir Henry Hadow wrote, "The continuity of human history and human civilization is not broken, but

fulfilled, by the advent of genius. The great artists are supreme, not because they are freaks or usurpers, but because they stand in the royal line of succession." That is a truth often forgotten or ignored—but it is still, and always, truth.

In the beginning poetry had three motifs only, and even today they are dominant in it, religion, battle, and love—and of these three the last is the most constant and prolific. And in the beginning, when the bards sang with passion the prowess of the heroes, the structure of our poetry "like that of almost all the poetry of primitive nations, was," as Richard Garnett observed, "trochaic and alliterative." A well-known specimen is the poem celebrating the battle of Brunanburh (A.D. 927) or, later and more anapaestic, William Langland's *Piers Plowman*, beginning:

> In a summer season, when soft was the sun,
> I shop me into a shroud, a sheep as I were;
> In habit of an hermit unholy of works,
> Wended I wyden in this world, wonders to hear.
> But in a May morning on Malvern Hills . . .

"The first conspicuous instance in our history," commented Dr. Garnett, "of Literature taking upon herself what had hitherto been the especial office of the Church." And from Langland onwards we come to Chaucer and enter the main and ever widening river of our heritage.

This river has four chief branches—though each of these has many a tributary: the four are epic, dramatic, narrative, and lyric. The first and third may blend, as an epic must needs be concerned with narration; but there has been many a short poem, the purpose of which is simply the telling of a story or incident which is in no degree epic. In a single chapter it is clearly impossible to dilate upon the qualities and differences of the four, and indeed these are sufficiently obvious to all who are in the least interested or knowledgeable; but, in weighing them, let us not forget, especially in an age inimical to long

MAX BEERBOHM'S "WILLIAM WORDSWORTH . . . AT CROSS-PURPOSES"
A famous burlesque of the poet who sought eternal truths from simple minds.

work in poetry, the pronouncement of Keats, "a long poem is a test of invention which I take to be the Polar star of poetry, as fancy is the sails, and imagination the rudder." Length by itself is clearly of no merit: the converse rather is true, since there is no one who would not prefer a short bad poem to a long bad one: "the world, we believe, is pretty well agreed," wrote Macaulay, "in thinking that the shorter a prize poem is, the better"—and many would add, "not prize poems only." Nevertheless, granted excellence, more goes to the making of a long poem beyond all questioning: just as a novel full of incidents and characters requires more sustained power than a short story, so it is essential in a poem of any length to avoid a descent into flatness; all parts cannot, and indeed should not, be pitched equally, or monotony is assured, but all should be poetic. "Prose," said Walter Savage Landor, "on certain occasions can bear a great deal of poetry: on the other hand, poetry sinks and swoons under a moderate weight of prose."

Characteristic Metres

Passing to the great, the intricate and varied subject of metre, every national tongue has the metres most familiar to its stresses and inflexions, most suited to its idioms and its syntax. The flexibility of Greek led to the usage of many metres, the five-foot iambic, perhaps, most, but closely rivalled by the swinging hexameter, which in English becomes, as Tennyson said, "barbarous." Latin, more rigorous, more severe, had its principal usage in the hexameter, less musical but possibly more sonorous, than the Greek, and the tripping pentameter; and the great lyricists, such as Horace, perfected the formal Alcaic and Sapphic, borrowing from the Greek. Similarly in English the main, the most characteristic metre is the five-foot iambic which, because of its suitability to the stresses of our tongue, has gradually come to dominate almost all our poems of length and weighty purpose—with the great exception of Spenser who wrought for the immensity of his *Faerie Queene* as cumbrous and difficult, and yet as flexible

and delicate, a metre as could well be devised, nine-line stanzas closely knit by the elaborate pattern of their rhyming sequence, but weighted by their final six-foot line, of which Alexander Pope wrote,

A needless Alexandrine ends the song,
That, like a wounded snake, drags its
    slow length along.

And it may here be noted, in passing, that this Alexandrine exemplifies succinctly the differences between languages: what best suited both Greek and Latin for length of line is heavy almost to weariness in English.

It is when we come to the Elizabethans, those chief glories of our tongue, that the full freedom of the iambic is found—and how varied is that freedom! Contrast the young Shakespeare with his ageing self: here are a few lines from the young, from *Love's Labour's Lost*:

Another of these students at that time
Was there with him, if I have heard a
    truth:
Berowne they call him, but a merrier
    man,
Within the limit of becoming mirth,
I never spent an hour's talk withal.
His eye begets occasion for his wit . . .

Regular, even and self-contained lines, it will be observed. What a contrast to these almost concluding lines from *The Tempest*:

Do not infest your mind with beating
    on
The strangeness of this business: at
    picked leisure
Which shall be shortly, single I'll
    resolve you—
Which to you shall seem probable—of
    every
These happened accidents; till when,
    be cheerful,
And think of each thing well . . .

Irregular, broken, overflowing—and mostly feminine endings, that is, five feet and a half instead of the fixed five feet. Between these two extracts lies all the realm of

Shakespeare — the work of a lifetime.

And yet, even with all that realm so newly minted Milton found it advisable to explain and apologize to the readers of *Paradise Lost* for writing in blank verse: "Rime," he observes, "being no necessary Adjunct or true Ornament of Poem or good Verse, in longer works especially, but the Invention of a barbarous Age, to set off wretched matter and lame Meeter."

Form and Subject

It is worth while to dwell upon this matter. The young and the inexpert are often wont to remark that blank verse—by which, according to common usage, is meant not unrhymed verse in general or free verse (a later favourite) but unrhymed five-foot iambic lines—is the easiest to write, since there is no difficulty about fitting sense to rhyme. That difficulty, however, is a small one compared with that of creating variety and sustaining interest: there are no rhymes to help, and each line is (apparently) the same. And yet in the hands of a master blank verse is an instrument of infinite melody, power, and range, and so intensely individual that it would not be hard for one familiar with it to name the writer of any twenty or thirty lines that were read out to him from, say, Shakespeare, Milton, Wordsworth, Keats, or Browning, even if the actual lines were not recognized. Each one of these masters, whilst playing the same instrument, has a music all his own—and so little easy is blank verse that when these five have been named, they can be seen standing out far above all their rivals. Tennyson, for all his metrical skill, never mastered blank verse; and, if anyone wishes to get his ear attuned to differences and to gaze into the pit of monotony, let him listen to a passage from, say Stephen Phillips.

Shakespeare, the most luxuriant of all poets, moving like a mighty river with an unmatched opulence and ease, yet calls to mind also the practice of the strictest and most confined poetic form, namely, the sonnet In spite of Wordsworth's adjuration, "Scorn not the sonnet," that form has fallen now upon days of neglect and disapprobation. It is too artificial—and possibly too difficult—for the young moderns who are in such a hurry and who are such exalters of liberty that they refuse to be circumscribed. And yet many of the greatest of the short poems of England are in that form, either the simpler Shakespearian form, three quatrains (rhyming *abab, cdcd, efef*) followed by a couplet summing up the whole, and summing it up, if by a real poet, with ease and power, or the compact, intricate, but indeed wonderfully effective, Petrarchan form, first an octet woven into one by its rhyme-sequence, *abba, abba,* and then a sextet, in the strict form 1, 2, 3: 1, 2, 3, *cde, cde* (though this rhyme sequence is subject to individual variation). As an exercise in poetic composition there can be none better: as a form to set down a thought and then its consequence it is unequalled. And of the difficulties there can be no doubt when it is remembered that throughout the ages since the days, at least, of Wyatt thousands of sonnets have been written, and many by poets of fame, and yet few indeed survive the test—a single weak line or even word, and the whole is lost. The really great sonneteers can be counted on the fingers of one hand, Shakespeare, Milton, Wordsworth, Keats (though, perhaps, we should add Elizabeth Barrett Browning for her special, personal, passionate contribution, her *Sonnets from the Portuguese*). Exuberant poets, like Robert Browning, never tried to compete.

English may not be a language as flexible as Greek: as to that no pronouncement can well be made, and "comparisons," we remember, "are odorous"; but at least there is in it a marvellous variety, governed, nevertheless, always and inevitably by the characteristic stresses of the language. These it is which guide unconsciously to the choice of metre: it is far easier, far more natural, for an Englishman to write any short poem in pairs of lines, four-foot iambics, followed by three-foot iambics, as, for example, Wordsworth's

A slumber did my spirit seal;
I had no human fears:
She seemed a thing that could not feel
The touch of earthly years.

than to use the trochees of Milton's *L'Allegro*,

> Haste thee, Nymph, and bring with thee
> Jest and youthful jollity,
> Quips and cranks, and wanton wiles,
> Nods, and becks, and wreathèd smiles.

The English sentence does not normally begin with a stressed syllable, but with a weak one, an "a" or a "the," for preference, and the writer wishing to invert the stress meets with an initial difficulty.

Learning from the Masters

In the hands of any master the subject chooses the metre—or rather both grow indissolubly together, body and soul; and how infinitely wide is the range! For the young aspirant there is but one way, one road to a rightness of choice, and that is to study the masters and examine the technique by which, often unconsciously but also often consciously, they have arrived at the effects of the magic by which they have beguiled the world. Some poets are the better teachers because they are the more obvious. Magic is an art, and it is an essential part of poetry—but how can magic be disintegrated into rules and precepts? Where it is most felt, it is usually least easy to reduce to formulae. Who, for instance, has analysed the music of Coleridge at his best as in *Kubla Khan* or *The Ancient Mariner*:

> Yet still the sails made on
> A pleasant noise till noon,
> A noise like of a hidden brook
> In the leafy month of June
> That to the sleeping woods all night
> Singeth a quiet tune . . .

The Ancient Mariner is crowded with such lines of unresolved, magical music. Or, to take an example of a different, graver, even greater kind—Hamlet's dying words to Horatio:

> Absent thee from felicity awhile,
> And in this harsh world draw thy breath in pain
> To tell my story.

It is practically impossible to say that second line without drawing one's breath in pain: substitute any word in the language for "harsh," and note the difference: the magic, unexplainably, is gone.

Coleridge, and on the mountain-tops Shakespeare also, rise beyond analysis: let any doubter read again that most lyrically exquisite of all dramatic scenes —intense drama, blank verse, and yet pure lyricism—the first thirty-six lines of Act III, Scene v, of *Romeo and Juliet*, with its

> Night's candles are burnt out, and jocund day
> Stands tip-toe on the misty mountain tops,

the very loveliest two lines, in the writer's opinion, in all literature. But other poets, great poets, are not beyond analysis, notably Tennyson, who is one of the most instructive of poets accordingly: occasionally he, too, has the single magical word, the one word of all others that is right as in *Boadicea*,

> Where the roaring breakers boom and blanch on the precipices,

where the reader can both hear and see the breaker in the hiss, and in the meaning of the perfectly used "blanch," and yet is not made definitely conscious of it. But more often Tennyson's is the art that does not quite conceal art, and so his work is specially available for examination and instruction. Pause and consider the three lines in *The Princess*:

> Myriads of rivulets hurrying thro' the lawn,
> The moan of doves in immemorial elms,
> And murmuring of innumerable bees.

These lines have been much praised for their onomatopoeic power, but their art, skilled as it is, is just a little too obvious, and also it lacks that delicate accuracy of observation which is Tennyson's at his best. The first of the three lines obtains its effect—obviously—by the huddling together of many little syllables, but the words really suggest a downpour and not the peace intended; in no circumstances but a downpour would a lawn become a mass of rivulets. Similarly, the mutes and liquids of the second and third lines produce admirably the sound the sense requires, but—as no one knew better than Tennyson—elms are not truly to be designated "immemorial," an adjective more appropriate to oak or yew; but the "k" of the word "oak" would have been fatal to the liquidity of the line and "yew" too heavy and strong a vowel sound also, nor do doves inhabit yews. As for the last line, lovely as it is, it is really not in the same class as verbal magic with Shakespeare's exquisite "singing masons building roofs of gold," where the triple *ing* produces the same suggestion as that which Tennyson was conveying, but quietly and without parade: it would seem to be the difference between the conscious art of the highly skilled craftsman and the careless ease of the supreme artist.

Accuracy and Felicity

Observe Nature—yes, a good maxim for any aspirant for poetic honour, but observe accurately. Tennyson was praised by Mrs. Gaskell for describing a girl's hair as "More black than ashbuds in the front of March," no one, apparently before him, having noted ashbuds at all—though let us bear in mind that Keats praised Milton for placing vales in hell, but Milton had been preceded many centuries by Caedmon. And ash-buds are not really black at all; there are almost no blacks in Nature: ash-buds in March are a very dark greeny-brown—which is not really the colour of any girl's hair. Better, by far, is Tennyson's "a million emeralds break from the ruby-budded lime." In such accuracy and such felicity lie much of the grace and charm of poetry.

All critics argue and dispute as to their favourites; but probably the quotation that is most generally given as containing the essence of poetry—if such could ever be distilled and held up for observation—is that from Keats's *Ode to a Nightingale*:

Magic casements, opening on the foam
Of perilous seas, in faery lands forlorn.

And yet it may, perhaps, be objected that for all their beauty and suggestions, there is in the words, somehow, almost an over-elaboration of phantasy for any but the most sensitively receptive reader: they are, certainly, not for the million, as all the very best poetry is. The writer would, for choice and confining his selection to the same author, prefer the magnificent simplicity of the five words in *Endymion*, "the sea-swell took her hair." In the first is elfin charm, but in the second that power of perfection that brings the majesty of Heaven into the heart of Man.

Imagery

A second maxim for the aspirant might be, "use but do not overdo imagery": beware of similes and metaphors in which from all ages poets have tended to indulge too much. When they are used, let them be new and natural to the theme, not far-fetched and incongruous. One of the most famous is Shelley's from *Adonais*:

Life, like a dome of many-coloured glass,
Stains the white radiance of eternity
Until Death tramples it to fragments;

one of the worst—"this," wrote Macaulay savagely, "I take to be the worst similitude in the world"—is poor Robert Montgomery's line from *The Omnipresence of the Deity*,

As streams meander level with their fount,

which hardly needed Macaulay to show as pure rubbish.

And that last word, "like a bell to toll me back," brings the writer from the realms of magic to the labours of the present day—though he must hastily add that he is far from suggesting by that, that all the poetic work of recent times is rubbish. It is, no doubt, true that even the emotional stresses of two vast international conflicts have not thrown up any poets whom the world at large has yet agreed to call great; but, after all, not only do such agreements take time, but also it

LAKE DISTRICT LANDSCAPES WHICH WORDSWORTH KNEW AND LOVED

These prints are contemporary with the poet's own life and show the mountain and lake scenery which inspired his work and influenced his "moral being." Above is seen Lake Ullswater: below, Ambleside Village.

must be remembered that it was not until nearly a hundred years after the close of the Napoleonic wars that Thomas Hardy produced *The Dynasts*. Great poetry normally succeeds rather than accompanies great history. However that may be, the first half of the twentieth century has given birth to much strong, interesting, and instructive work, and from that new growth is assured. Poetry, to live, cannot be static: it must always be experimenting and learning. Patrick Henry's need, "Give me liberty, or give me death!" relates as closely to poetry as it does to people; and the age of the pneumatic drill, the motor-car, and the aeroplane cannot conceivably be content merely to repeat the old.

Fashion and Originality

So much may be admitted: but we may at the same time remember that liberty is not the same thing as licence or unintelligibility as inspiration. Keats had the truth of genius in him in going to the crux of the matter when he wrote at Teignmouth on April 18, 1818, in his preface to *Endymion*:

The imagination of a boy is healthy, and the mature imagination of a man is healthy: but there is a space of life between, in which the soul is in a ferment, the character undecided, the way of life uncertain, the ambition thick-sighted: thence proceeds mawkishness, and all the thousand bitters . . .

That is the case of the world: the world is new, in a ferment, undecided, uncertain, thick-sighted—and its poetry has, as yet, hardly controlled its effervescence.

All literary history is a tale of swings, one age scorning that in which their fathers delighted. Even as the *Lyrical Ballads* of Wordsworth and Coleridge were born of a determination to return to the simple and the natural from the artificialities of the age of Boileau, from the formalism of Pope, and the fripperies of the eighteenth century, so has that same principle of the pendulum been in operation anew; and, just as the oscillations of the world in the first half of the twentieth century have been violent and confused

beyond all previous experience, so in poetry, the most sensitive of the arts. Reference has been made to Meredith's obscurity; but that is the obscurity of genius cleaving its way impatiently through the thickets of thought: that is not the deliberate cult of the incomprehensible which reigns in some of the work of many notable writers of verse today. The following, complete in itself, is by one who has been acclaimed by a number of critics as of special eminence:

By after long appearance
Appears the time all the time
Name please now you may go.

By after love time and she knows
And he says rose
Unless unless if not.

Or if if sometimes if
How like myself I was
Among the salt and minutes.

That has been described as "setting a new standard of poetic originality": but mere unintelligibility is neither new nor poetic nor original—and its standard is nothing but darkness and despair. To all aspirants after poetry one can only say, "be understood or be silent"; else, deserve Pope's words: "It is not poetry, but prose run mad." There are those who seem to imagine that anything will do; all that is needed is a pencil and paper, let the fancy stray and poetry will result. It is not so. "Artists," as has been greatly written by an anonymous reviewer, "do not blunder into beauty; and great triumphs of the pen, as of the sword, are not produced without an infinity of pains and thought, and an infinity of delight in production."

Poet's Craft

"It is the best of all trades, to make songs," sings Hilaire Belloc. Trades? Yes: poetry, like all else, is a trade to those who practise it seriously, and it needs to be worked at, slaved at, to be mastered. There is no easy road to any summit. There are, of course, tricks in all trades, or, rather, there is skill in all crafts, and poetry demands the highest craftsmanship from its votaries. We have moved far nowadays from the simple alliterative device of the Anglo-Saxons: alliteration, especially if it be concealed, hidden that is, in the centre of words and not invariably at their beginnings, is still, and always will be, an invaluable adjunct to the music of poetry; but it is not the main one and it is often overdone as in Swinburne's "lilies and languors of virtue," and "roses and raptures of vice." Consonants and their proper connexion are important, but, more important, and much more subtle, is the use of vowels, either by way of repetition or of modulation. In the great poets that use is part of the magic almost defying analysis and in most of the famous instances came naturally, not because, we may be sure, the poet laboriously worked it out, but because that alone satisfied his ear.

And here another interpolation, a very necessary one. Let all who seek to tread the mountain paths of poetry take heed; over the gateway of the Court of Poetic Justice is inscribed the solemn words, "By your adjectives shall ye be judged." How often have we not all come upon lines in which the adjectives are inserted not because they are inevitable but because they are needed to fill up; not because they elucidate but because they expand? How often has a writer been tempted to indulge in such padding?

Poetic Devices

You see the converse in the magic use of adjectives when they burst upon the reader, filling him with joyous satisfaction, as when the young Keats, studying Spenser, cried aloud with delight at "sea-shouldering" as an adjective for whales: let our adjectives be of that calibre and then indeed we need not fear the verdict of the Court.

But apart from the use of vowels and adjectives, both of which are basic, there are tricks, devices, usages, characteristics of poetic craftsmanship—call them what you will—other than, for instance, alliteration, not, perhaps, easier to do, but easier to illustrate. Let us give two examples chosen from the work of the writer of this chapter, not to magnify that but to estab-

EDMUND SPENSER

Spenser's fine craftsmanship, love of melli-fluous language for its own sake and delight in sensuous beauty make him, beyond other writers, "the poet's poet."

lish the fact that practice has preceded precept. The first is a single blank verse line from *The Silver Cord:*

> A bird, half waking, piped faint notes to dawn.

The three weighted, single heavinesses of monosyllable are intended to suggest the individual sounds of a half-wakened bird, and, it is hoped, do so unobtrusively. The second example, taken from *On the Ponte Vecchio, Florence,* also blank verse, is

> As when a wind that has soughed among the trees
> Drops, and the whole wood suddenly is still.

It will be observed that in the second line the caesura, that break in the line essential to all poetry, at all events to all blank verse passages, comes in the middle of the first foot: that is to say, abnormally early. The intention, obviously, is to reproduce the

"MR. TENNYSON READING *IN MEMORIAM* TO HIS SOVEREIGN"

This is another of Sir Max Beerbohm's irreverent drawings from his famous book, "The Poet's Corner," published early in the century. In these are satirized what might be called the weaker side of a poet's strength—airs and virtues which have become pompous.

pause that comes suddenly with the calm that follows an abrupt cessation of wind. It may be objected that here the device is a trifle obvious, to which the only answer must be that the poem in which the lines occur was written in the author's twenties, and subtlety is the growth of years.

Discover Yourself

How, it may be asked in general, is craftsmanship in poetry to be gained, how is technique, without which there can be no such thing as craftsmanship, to be acquired? Here is the advice tendered to his readers by the editor of a poetry magazine which was started in 1939: "A word," wrote this authority, "on technique. If the subject matter is up to date, technique is not worth bothering about. But don't scorn rhyme or the traditional metres—the best of the moderns have used them frequently. And if you use *vers libre* it is as well to give it rhythm and possibly form." We have moved far and fast, it seems, since for nearly half a century Tennyson held English poetry in thrall, and we are paying for that

thraldom by the violence of our reaction: we have even passed far beyond Gerard Manley Hopkins and his interesting and scholarly experiments in "sprung," that is, accentuated, metres. But to say "possibly form" is revealing. Poetry in its essence is imagination winged with form: a man can no more write poetry without form than he can play football without feet. It need not be old form; it must be some form. The editor quoted above can never have considered the truth of Ellen Terry's wit, "Before you can be eccentric you must know where the centre of the circle is."

There is, in fact, but one precept, or, rather, one pair of precepts: look into yourself and make sure that you have some emotion, some experience, some tale that is genuine to express or share or tell—and, as has been said, study the master-craftsmen who have wrestled with the same problems before you. That does not mean, copy them: no, study them, examine their difficulties and the bridges they threw across those difficulties, observe how they set about their production and then apply that study, that examination, that observation to your own individual music. Subjects, it must be repeated, choose their own metres: to write a dirge in such tripping dactyls as Rossetti's

> Say, is it dawn, is it dusk in thy bower,
> Lady I sigh for, who sighest for me?

would be no more appropriate than to go to a funeral in sports costume.

"But," inquires the poet, "what subject shall I choose?" The modern editor would assuredly reply, "Anything as long as it is up to date"; but what is up to date today is terribly apt to be out of date tomorrow —and no great poetry, no true poetry even, is ever out of date. In the ferment of the world the machine is become a god and the revulsion from all that is loosely termed "mid-Victorianism" is extreme: it has tended accordingly to a glorification of the grim and a cataloguing of the commonplace; there has been a swing away from beauty and an exaltation of the squalid. It is the most familiar of familiar objects which is constantly dwelt upon and it is the ugliness of the world from which the veil is lifted. Not so lives enduringly the spirit of poetry; and the phase will pass, as other phases have passed before.

The old world dies, the hues are sobered and the glamour less: the new struggles terribly into birth, and all the values are indeterminate. People no longer quote the classics, no longer cultivate the graces, letter-writing is a lost art, and all is subject, as Henry James wrote even before the German wars, "to the fatal fusions and uniformities inflicted on our newer generations, the running together of all the differences of form and tone, the ruinous liquefying wash of the great industrial brush over the old conditions of contrast and colour": our lives are caught in the whirl and rush, the telephone at our ears, the motor-car at our doors, the aeroplane on our roofs; we crowd into a day distances and experiences which would have sufficed our ancestors for a life-time—and appalling warfare has devastated vast parts of the inhabited globe. And yet poetry lives on.

Poets may or may not be "the unacknowledged legislators of the world" as Shelley claimed them to be; but their work exercises a profound influence upon the thought of man. And it is because of all the cataclysms and transformations of the twentieth century that poetry, the undying, is more, and not less, necessary. It will assuredly not be the same poetry as was written before the advent of the internal combustion engine, but the master-passions, love, ambition, jealousy, hate, and fear, remain unchangingly—so does the beauty of the sunset, the architecture of the clouds, the blessings of a summer's day, the greatness of endeavour, and the grandeur of love.

Poetry is no more capable of death than is the human race: poetry is no more static than the world in which that race breathes; it "alters as it alteration finds," and yet it endures. On all poets, as Wordsworth emphasized, is laid the duty of hope: it is the spirit that animates the form, and it is that, in the "brave, new world" to be, that will retain, for always, poetry, the true poetry, as the enlightenment, the solace, and the glory of mankind.

Test Yourself

1. What are the "three dominant motives of poetry"?
2. The work of an English poet is said to be "the first conspicuous instance in our history of literature taking upon herself what had hitherto been the special office of the Church." Who was the poet and what was the work?
3. What is the commonest English poetic metre?
4. Name the four English masters of the sonnet.

Answers will be found at the end of the book.

BEN JONSON

Shakespeare's contemporary, Ben Jonson, has his place in the Poets' Corner of Westminster Abbey.   His plays are more satiric, his characters more rigid, than Shakespeare's.

DRAMA

LET us begin by realizing that the general belief, inculcated unintentionally by Thomas Carlyle, that genius in any art can be acquired by taking pains is false and delusive. It is born in a person and, like the wind, it bloweth where it listeth, choosing its instrument capriciously and without regard to creed, colour or class. Shakespeare, a grammar-school boy, who never went to a university and had small Latin and less Greek, wrote *Hamlet*. A boy born in a Dublin slum, Sean O'Casey, having no more education than was obtainable in an Irish elementary school when he was a child and after some time spent as a labourer, wrote *Juno and the Paycock*. But all his learning did not enable Dr. Johnson, producer in 1755 of the first English dictionary, to write a better tragedy than *Irene*, which was received in silence and has not been revived. The poets, Byron and Shelley, Browning and Tennyson, were all ambitious to write plays, but they failed utterly. Even Charles Dickens, who had a great love of the stage, could not write a play. The Russian novelist, Tolstoy, was a bad dramatist, but the Norwegian, Henrik Ibsen, an apprentice to an apothecary, changed the mind of Europe with his plays.

Hence the first fact to be learnt and remembered is that a man is *born* a great artist: he is not *made* into one, although he may become, with some talent and perseverance, a competent craftsman. There are no rules for men of genius: they develop their own technique; but there are rules for the rest of us.

Talk: the Medium of the Playwright

Two points must be noted immediately. The first is that a man may be a writer of great quality but incapable of writing a play. Dr. Johnson, Byron, Shelley, Browning, Tennyson and Tolstoy, all of whom were men of genius, have already been named as examples of authors who, though they desired to be dramatists, failed to achieve their desire. The second is that a dramatist is a man who naturally tells a story in dialogue. It is this fact which distinguishes him from a novelist. A novelist tells a story in narrative. He may not use any dialogue or use very little, but a dramatist cannot use anything else. A novel may be composed of conversation, of description, of narrative, any or all of these, and it may take many forms; but a play is entirely composed of talk, even when there is a great deal of what is called action in it; and its form is much more restricted than that of the novel. It is this conversational character of the drama which settles whether or not an author is a dramatist. If he finds himself habitually thinking of a theme in the shape of dialogue then he is, undoubtedly, a dramatist rather than a novelist. Does he instinctively tell a story in the way many people relate their experiences in the I-said-to-her-and-then-she-said-to-me fashion? If he does not do that, then the probability is that he is not, and never will be, a dramatist.

The novelist Henry James (1843-1916) wished to write plays, but anyone who has read a novel by him with its emphasis upon descriptions of human feelings, will perceive immediately that he had few of the traits of a dramatist.

The number of authors who can write plays *and* novels is small, and it may be said even of these authors that each of them is usually better at one form than at another. In the last thirty years John Galsworthy and Somerset Maugham are examples of novelist-playwrights.

It is an undeniable fact that a man cannot become a dramatist unless he thinks in terms of dialogue. He may be a great novelist, a great essayist, a great poet, but he will be a very bad dramatist if he cannot tell his story in talk.

The talk, however, may be as various as the form of the novel. It may be full of long speeches, such as George Bernard Shaw's, or of short speeches, such as Noel Coward's. The single necessity is that it shall be talk.

The Inquisitor's speech in Shaw's *Saint Joan* fills about a couple of pages and takes ten minutes to deliver. There are few speeches in the whole of Noel Coward's plays that are longer than three or four lines, and a vast number of them are less than a line long. Which is right? The answer is that both are. Some people are long-tongued and others are short-tongued.

The Inquisitor's speech in *Saint Joan* is right in that particular place for a special reason. It is not part of a conversation: it is an address on a ceremonial occasion. The Inquisitor is not talking to his listeners: he is addressing them, expounding doctrine to them, delivering a speech. If he were taking part in a general chat round a table, he would speak less formally, in shorter sentences, and would be subject to interruption; but no one interrupts him, any more than a preacher is interrupted during a sermon or a lecturer during a lecture.

Every student should read *Saint Joan* and observe this characteristic of the Inquisitor's long talk on religious heresy. It is a set piece, a grave discourse on a serious subject, and it is, therefore, free from the features of ordinary conversation. Yet it is talk. Note that. The Inquisitor is *not* reading a paper to his listeners; he is talking to them; and although his sentences are well arranged, they are arranged in such a way that the conversational quality is present in them, although what he says is not part of a general conversation.

Stage Dialogue and Everyday Speech

Dialogue is not easily defined. Talk that seems all right in a novel is all wrong in a play. From the point of view of a dramatist few novelists write dialogue. What they write is literary, and seldom everyday speech. Their dialogue is what people mean when they say that a person talks like a book. But characters in plays never talk like people in a book unless, of course, the dramatist wishes to portray the kind of person given to affected talk. Dramatic dialogue should have the look of literature and the sound of the street. It must sound as if it had been overheard: it must not sound as if it had been read. Yet it must not be literally like conversation in a drawing-room or at a street-corner; for that is frequently incoherent, disconnected, interrupted, full of repetitions, and seldom finished. A single word in a conversation between two friends may be sufficient to communicate all that the listener needs to know. It instantly conveys to him what his friend wishes to tell him. The sentence, therefore, is left unfinished. But this will not often do for a play, and for this reason. The dialogue between two friends in a play is not dialogue for their ears only; it is intended for the ears of an audience; and that audience must be told everything, not in hints, but at some length.

Importance of Clarity

That brings us to a third point. A play is intended to be performed before an audience. It is not intended to be read in solitude. It is doubtful, for instance, that Shakespeare's plays are better in the study than on the stage. Shakespeare shared this belief so little that he did not trouble himself to prepare printed editions of his plays. Had he been as careful about publication as Ben Jonson was, a great deal of literary speculation would have proved unnecessary. The fact that a play is intended to be performed before an audience means that it must be instantly clear to a great variety of minds. Points must be made immediately and unmistakably. A confused audience loses the thread of the play, and becomes a disturbed and restless audience, with disastrous results on the performance.

A man by the fireside reading a book can, if he feels uncertain about a passage, turn back a page or two and re-read the passage. If it still baffles him, he can ask a friend to explain it to him. But the same man, sitting in the pit of a theatre, cannot ask the actors to repeat a scene because he has missed its meaning, and if he asks his neighbour to explain it to him, he will be hissed by those whom he prevents from hearing the rest of the play. The dramatist, therefore, must make his point quickly and plainly. Obscurity will destroy him.

It is when we realize this fact that we discover how brief a thing a play is.

AFTER AGINCOURT

Shakespeare's "King Henry V" was first performed in 1599. Its theme is the invasion of France, during which Harfleur was besieged and captured, and English bowmen won the battle of Agincourt. The play concludes with the wooing by the King of the French princess Katharine. The photograph reproduced above shows Richard Burton as Henry V, in a stage production at the Old Vic, London.

Shakespeare's *Hamlet* is very long, taking about four hours to perform in its entirety; yet it contains only between thirty and thirty-five thousand words. That would be very short measure, indeed, in a novel. Some of Noel Coward's plays last for less than ninety minutes. The time is eked out by long intervals between the acts. A novel with less than seventy thousand words in it would bring frowns to the face of a publisher, who would declare it to be little more than a long short story. It is doubtful if there are as many words in all J. B. Priestley's plays as there are in his novel, *The Good Companions.* A couple of novels by Dickens probably contain more words than are in all Shakespeare's plays.

The writer of drama is compelled to be more concise than the novelist. He has to do as much work with much less material. He cannot afford to waste a second. Every word must have a point. The shape of his play is dictated to a large extent by the social habits of his age. Plays in Shakespeare's times were longer than plays in ours because people in Elizabethan times ate their meals at different hours from those at which we eat ours, and they were willing to walk home after the performance. They were not harassed by the necessity to catch the last train. The length of the modern play is conditioned by late dinner and late trains, trams and buses. A novelist need not pay the slightest attention to any of these social institutions.

This discovery of the brevity of the play and its dependence on certain social habits, obliges the dramatist to lay out his play with the greatest care. He must make his points quickly, but he must not make them too quickly. It is fatal to his story to tell an important part of it in the first two minutes, during which the din of late-comers is preventing anybody in the theatre from hearing much that is said on the stage. Even if the entire audience is assembled when the curtain rises for the first time, the dramatist must not make any important point at once. He must remember that about a thousand persons are present in

NINETEENTH-CENTURY PLAYHOUSE
Above may be seen the audience at a play at the Sans Pareil Theatre in the Strand.

large theatres, to whom everything connected with his play is unknown. All has to be revealed, rather than explained, to this audience, which must, moreover, be given time to adjust itself to the world on the stage and to withdraw itself from the world in the auditorium. Before the ascent of the curtain, the people in the theatre are of all sorts, men and women, old and young, rich and poor, well-educated and ill-educated. They must, in a few moments, be persuaded to concentrate upon the play on the stage. The feat is performable. It is, in fact, performed every night on which a play is acted. But it is manifestly a feat requiring great skill in those who perform it.

Introducing the Characters

As a general rule, it is inadvisable to bring the chief character in the play on the stage immediately the curtain rises. But this has been done both by Shakespeare and by J. M. Barrie; by the first in *Richard III* and by the second in *The Admirable Crichton*. Here we have proof of the fact that men of genius make their own technique. But, in general, matters and people of importance must not be flung pell-mell on to the stage the moment the curtain rises or without some preparation for their entrance or announcement. At this point, it is necessary to draw the student's attention to a small, but important, point which is seldom observed by playgoers. In Shakespeare's day, there were no programmes. There are none today in cinemas. The most that an Elizabethan had in the way of a programme was a card brought on to the stage by an attendant, on which was inscribed a statement that the scene about to be performed was "another part of the wood" or "a graveyard." There is, it is true, a long and almost unreadable list of names thrown on to the moving-picture screen before the film is unreeled, but few people remember what it contains or have time to read the whole of it.

Now, this absence of programme involves a point in technique. Shakespeare had to tell his audience the name of each of his characters immediately before that character made his or her first entrance. A modern dramatist is largely relieved of this

necessity by the programme, which even tells the audience in what order the people will present themselves. How does *Hamlet* open? It starts on a dark platform outside the Castle at Elsinore. A sentry is pacing up and down. As he paces, he hears the sound of approaching footsteps. Here is the dialogue:

BERNARDO: Who's there?

FRANCISCO: Nay, answer me; stand, and unfold yourself.

BERNARDO: Long live the King!

FRANCISCO: Bernardo!

BERNARDO: He.

FRANCISCO: You come most carefully upon your hour.

BERNARDO: 'Tis now struck twelve; get thee to bed, Francisco.

FRANCISCO: For this relief, much thanks: 'tis bitter cold and I am sick at heart.

BERNARDO: Have you had quiet guard?

FRANCISCO: Not a mouse stirring.

BERNARDO: Well, good-night.
  If you do meet Horatio and Marcellus, the rivals of my watch, bid them make haste.

FRANCISCO: I think I hear them.— Stand, ho! Who is there?

HORATIO: Friends to this ground.

MARCELLUS: And liegemen to the Dane.

FRANCISCO: Give you good-night.

MARCELLUS: O! farewell, honest soldier:
  Who hath relieved you?

FRANCISCO: Bernardo has my place. Give you good-night.

MARCELLUS: Holla! Bernardo!

BERNARDO: Say, what, is Horatio there?

HORATIO: A piece of him.

BERNARDO: Welcome, Horatio: welcome, good Marcellus.

MARCELLUS: What, has this thing appear'd again to-night?

BERNARDO: I have seen nothing.

MARCELLUS: Horatio says 'tis but our fantasy.

This short opening scene, lasting, perhaps, for a minute, is technically superb. Here is a dramatist with so sure a sense of the theatre that he sets a scene almost instinctively. No one with any knowledge of dramatic craftsmanship can escape the knowledge that those lines were written by a man who was a dramatist in the marrow of his bones. Observe how he names all the characters. Before Horatio and Marcellus enter the scene, Bernardo mentions their names. Immediately after their names are mentioned, the two men appear. Bernardo, as he greets them, names them both. The least important person in the scene, the sentry, Francisco, is mentioned only once. Bernardo's name is spoken three times. Marcellus is named twice, Horatio four times. The most careless listener cannot fail to catch the names of these four men or to identify Horatio as the most important.

But that is not all. The scene opens in darkness which has a silencing effect on an audience and makes it attentive to the stage more immediately than a blaze of light. The sentry's statement that the weather is bitter cold and that he is sick at heart establishes an atmosphere beyond that of wintry weather. The unimportance of Francisco is manifested by Marcellus's dismissal of him. "O! farewell, honest soldier!" He does not trouble to repeat Francisco's name. It is unimportant to remember who he is. He will not be seen again. If his name is forgotten, it is no matter. But Horatio, Marcellus and Bernardo must be remembered, for they will reappear.

Then, when identities have been established, the business of the play is started. "What, has this thing appear'd again tonight?" "I have seen nothing." "Horatio says 'tis but our fantasy." In three lines, as short as any Noel Coward has written, the mystery is announced. Something queer is happening in and around this dark castle.

Learning the Craft

No one can teach a man how to set a scene in that fashion. He knows it in his own nature. Those of us who are not naturally dramatists can only copy the born dramatist's invention. It may, of course, be said that Shakespeare, like the great French playwright Molière (1622-73),

Richard Brinsley Sheridan (1751-1816), author of *The Rivals* and other great English comedies, the Norwegian dramatist, Henrik Ibsen (1828-1906), Anton Chekhov (1860-1904), whose interpretation of Russian life is so remarkable, together with Sir Arthur Pinero (1855-1934), Lennox Robinson (1886-1958) and Noel Coward, learnt his craft in the theatre, and that is undeniable, although it should preferably be said that each of them developed in the theatre what was already in his own heart and mind. G. B. Shaw, Somerset Maugham and John Galsworthy did not learn their craft there, but nobody will deny their skill in the technique of the theatre. G. B. Shaw, indeed, was a superb example of a man who was born a dramatist and not a novelist. The student has only to read his novels to perceive that he was not, and could never have become, a typical novelist; that he was first and last, and all the time, a dramatist, even when his plays were first criticized. A man can learn a lot about dramatic technique in the theatre, but he does not need to be behind the scenes to learn it. It is learnable from the auditorium of the theatre.

Sense of the Theatre

That raises another point. The best way in which to develop a sense of the theatre is to read plays and to see them performed. The student of the drama should habituate himself to the drama by frequent attendance at the theatre. If he does not *like* the theatre as a place of entertainment, then he is unlikely to understand drama. It is inconceivable that a man can understand music if he never attends a concert or enters an opera house. An art connoisseur would not boast that he had never been in the Louvre or the National Gallery.

All the great dramatists, however much they differ from each other, have in common a high sense of theatrical effect. They know how to play upon the feelings of an audience, and they do not disdain any trick that will increase the intensity of the audience's mood. It is the fashion among some critics to "write down" Shakespeare's *The Merchant of Venice*, and, indeed, this play is full of improbabilities; but observe with what superlative skill Shakespeare makes all these improbabilities seem plausible. The technique of the trial scene in this play is extraordinarily fine, and it never fails to stir the pulse of the audience.

Here are all those effects for which professors have invented a jargon, and they are displayed as simply and as easily as light and shadow are thrown upon a hillside by the setting sun. Has the student heard of *suspense* in drama? It is here. Observe with what skill Shakespeare keeps the audience on tenter-hooks about Antonio's fate. Is the usurer, Shylock, after all, to take that pound of flesh from his debtor? The suspense is maintained until the penultimate moment. Shylock has his knife almost in Antonio's breast before the advocate, Portia, utters the decisive sentence. The situation is preposterous. It is inconceivable that Antonio should ever have reached that plight, that not a single lawyer at the court of Venice knew that it was against the law of Venice for an alien to conspire against the life of a citizen. It is absurd to think that Portia should ever have appeared in the court at all. But Shakespeare makes these unplausible things appear perfectly plausible, and with extraordinary skill and dexterity he keeps the audience wondering how the scene will end. The student need only compare *The Merchant of Venice* with the Elizabethan dramatist Christopher Marlowe's *The Jew of Malta* to detect the difference between a poet who could write plays and a poet who could not.

Dramatic Effects

Sheridan's screen scene in his immortal comedy of manners, *The School for Scandal*, is another example of superb craftsmanship, of high skill in the manipulation of suspense.

On the other hand, Bernard Shaw professed to ignore the tricks of his trade, but he, too, works most effectively upon the feelings of his audience in the trial of the Maid in *Saint Joan*. Shaw relieves what might become tedium in his long disquisitory passages by utilizing every effect that will distract the audience from bore-

FREDERICK LONSDALE

Lonsdale's casual and witty plays include "The Last of Mrs. Cheyney," "The High Road" and "On Approval."

dom. He places his characters in unusual scenes, and is addicted to the habit of dressing them in eccentric clothes or brilliant garments that are rarely worn. The twins in *You Never Can Tell* appear as Columbine and Harlequin. A character in *Heartbreak House* wears Arab costume instead of evening dress. There is no device of scene or costume that Shaw does not employ to lighten the dialectics of his drama. Pinero, who was a very great craftsman, could turn the most commonplace implement into a highly dramatic effect. These effects are often obtained by successions of dramatists, from generation to generation, but an author will fail to make good use of these effects, however faithfully he copies them, if he has not in himself a high sense of the theatre and cannot adapt the old device to modern conditions.

Let me illustrate what I mean by four plays in which a summons, such as a knock on a door or the sound of a bell, is employed to obtain a dramatic effect. They are: Shakespeare's *Macbeth* and *Othello,*

Pinero's *The Gay Lord Quex* and Frederick Lonsdale's *The Last of Mrs. Cheyney*. How terribly intense is that scene in *Macbeth* in which the Porter comes sleepily in answer to the knocking on the gate of Macbeth's Castle after Duncan has been murdered. The intense effect of the bell-ringing in the third scene of the second act of *Othello* is terrific. No less intense is the scene in *The Gay Lord Quex* when Sophy Fullgarney pulls the bell-rope in the bedroom and there is a loud clangour throughout the house, which rouses and alarms all its occupants. In these three plays, we have a small mechanical effect used with extraordinary skill and impressive effect. The effect employed by Pinero is used by Lonsdale in almost exactly the same sort of situation, but it is less effective because in Mr. Lonsdale's play the bell is a modern electric one and there is no *clang*—the very word is dramatic—in *The Last of Mrs. Cheyney*. There was a loud *clang* in *The Gay Lord Quex*. The audience at the Pinero play does not wonder why everybody in the house is awakened by the bell. The cause is obvious. But the audience at the Lonsdale play may wonder how everyone was awakened by the electric bell, which, presumably, rang in the servants' hall where it was unlikely to be heard by anybody. The Pinero bell was of an old-fashioned sort which sounded throughout the house: the Lonsdale bell was of a sort which could normally be heard only in the kitchen.

Advantage of Simplicity

The great dramatist is up to every trick, but he is economical in his use of tricks. He employs those that are simple rather than those that are elaborate. He presses into his service all the familiar household things, and gives them an appearance of importance. Lonsdale, in *The High Road*, achieves a most dramatic effect by causing a character to switch on the wireless at a certain moment. An item of news is broadcast which alters the lives of the characters. It is the very simplicity of these effects that makes them so dramatic. Few plays reveal a high sense of the theatre in their author so vividly as Sir James Barrie's one-act play, *The Will*, which is a perfect

example of craftsmanship. Here, in the space of thirty or forty minutes, Barrie shows the passage of several generations through life, and does it with the greatest simplicity. Merely to observe how he gives his actors and actresses opportunities to change their clothes and make-up is instructive. He has only a short time at his disposal, but he contrives without effort to turn a young couple into an old couple, a middle-aged solicitor into a doating, senile old man, a boy into a middle-aged man —all in the space of little more than half an hour. The passage of time is denoted by a means so simple that merely to name it makes it seem banal. Yet only a master craftsman could have thought of it. In the first of the three scenes into which this one-act play is divided, the eyes of the audience are drawn instantly to a portrait of Queen Victoria in the middle of the room. This portrait is replaced in the second scene by a portrait of Edward VII. In the last scene, the portrait is of George V. Without a word, the audience is made aware that thirty years or so have passed away.

In Noel Coward's *Cavalcade*, a small scene of no great value in itself is rendered most moving by the revelation of a ship's name. We see a young honeymoon couple standing near the stern of the ship, making love and discussing their ambitions. Then the ship moves away from the harbour. As it moves, its name comes into view It is the *Titanic*. This scene depends for its effect on the knowledge the audience brings into the theatre. A generation which has never heard of the *Titanic* and its tragic sinking in the Atlantic will not be moved in the slightest degree by the scene, but its effect on those who do know about that great ship is overwhelming.

Coward is skilful at this sort of scene, and can obtain a tremendous effect by silence, as in another scene in *Cavalcade*, when we see people promenading in Birdcage Walk on the day of Queen Victoria's death. That effect is increased when a heedless errand boy comes by, whistling, and the shocked promenaders all cry "Ssh!"

These points are, in the main, a matter

PLAYWRIGHTS OF TODAY
J. B. Priestley (top left), though primarily a novelist, has achieved much success in the theatre. Noel Coward (top right) stands supreme for his sophisticated comedies and musical plays. Sean O'Casey (bottom left), the Irish dramatist, has depth, passion and humour, while Christopher Fry (bottom right) has re-established verse drama as a popular form.

of mechanics. They do not tell anyone how to write a play or compose dialogue. The author cannot be taught these things. He must teach himself. It is only the mechanical parts that can be shown to him, and even these he cannot be taught to use effectively unless he has the instinct of the dramatist. Darkness, skilfully used, can be most effective on the stage, but it is destructive of drama when it is used unskilfully.

What the Novice Should Remember

Let us consider a play submitted to a manager by a novice. The whole tragedy, apart from the scene-shifting, can be performed in twenty minutes. The scene of one of the acts is in the heroine's bedroom which is in darkness. The heroine is in bed. She opens her eyes, she shuts her eyes, she opens them again and gazes at the ceiling. She pitches and tosses, and then, clenching her fists, exclaims, "O God, help me to be brave!" Curtain. Need I explain why that scene could have had no dramatic effect whatever if it was performed? Not only is the character unidentified, but in these conditions her actions cannot even be seen. A single exclamation tells the audience nothing whatever, except that the young lady begs the Almighty to give her courage—for what?

A speech takes about as long to deliver on the stage as it takes to deliver in ordinary life. Apprentice authors seldom realize this fact, and act on the assumption that what takes ninety seconds to say in the street can be said in ten seconds on the stage. An actor cannot change his clothes in the theatre in less time than he takes to change them at home. This is another fact that apprentice authors have to learn. They will send a character off the stage in hunting kit and bring him back, two minutes later, in full evening dress. The lapse of time is seldom convincingly arranged by apprentice authors. The Elizabethan, Christopher Marlowe, was an amazing bungler in this respect. Although a powerful writer he won little power of plausibility. He was capable of sending a character off the stage to order a massacre of the inhabitants of a city, and of bringing him back again in less than a minute and a half to say that the entire population, a very large one, had been drowned in a lake.

The student must remember in connexion with a play that it has two times: time inside the play and time outside it. By this I mean, that the time occupied by the performance of the play is different and usually much less than the time which passes in the play itself. The author is driven to the use of various devices to indicate the passage of time inside the play. The most obvious one is the dropping of the curtain and the statement on the programme that "six months elapse." But this device cannot always be used. During the course of an act, for example, the author cannot drop the curtain every time a character leaves the stage to fulfil some purpose which cannot possibly be done in less, say, than an hour. He must, therefore, divert the attention of the audience from that character so that when, at last, he does return to the scene, he will appear to have been absent for an hour when, in plain physical fact, he has been away only a few moments. This is usually done by causing several characters to come on and go off the stage between that character's exit and his reappearance.

But these intervening characters must not be casual or sporadic or insignificant. To have a diverting effect on the audience, they must be important or have something highly interesting to say. Their purpose, at this point, is to make the audience forget about the character who has been sent on an errand, and they can do this only by absorbing its attention by what they say or do. This sort of diversion is usually made by two or three intervening characters, each making a separate entrance as a rule. Their effect is to make a long time seem to have passed, a long enough time for the departure and return of the messenger.

Tricks of this kind may be better learnt from the auditorium than from the back of the stage. There is no illusion behind the scenes, nor can the effect of the play on the audience be observed there. It is not necessary, however, for a dramatist to have an intimate knowledge of stage technique, much of which may be described as producer's stuff, and he will do well not

SCENE FROM "HENRY IV": PART I
This shows a scene from Shakespeare's play—the fight between Hotspur and Prince Hal (on the right). It is from a stage production at the Old Vic, London.

to fill his script with directions, since they are likely to be disregarded or useless. It will be enough for him to write only directions that are essential. To describe the heroine's appearance, including in it the colour of her eyes and hair, is to waste time and paper.

It may be necessary in certain circumstances to stipulate that the heroine shall have red hair or be tall or short or lame or blind, but unless the point of the play turns on some such physical feature accounts of personal appearance are futile. It is improbable that the actress who will play the part will resemble the character as the dramatist describes her. Here is an account of a girl taken from an unacted play. She "is a buxom girl with a shock of

fair hair combed relentlessly from her forehead and kept in place by a semi-circular comb pressed tightly from ear to ear. This gives the effect of a halo to her face, which is round, fat, rosy and innocent looking. Her mouth—she has very full lips —is usually half open, and this, with the fuzzy hair and round, blue eyes, gives her an expression of perpetual surprise." Is the producer expected to run around the country looking for a fuzzy-haired actress with very full lips and an expression of surprise, before he can put this play on the stage? And what likelihood is there that he will find one?

Shaw and Barrie, for the purposes of publication, but *only* for the purposes of publication, print elaborate stage directions

BORDER

BATTERY

PILOT LIGHT

PERCH SPOT

SPOTS

ELECTRICIAN'S BRIDGE

WINGS

BACK CLOTH

STAGE MANAGER'S BOX

PROMPT CORNER

FOOT LIGHTS

DOWN STAGE

UP STAGE

FLAT

PIN SPOT

GROUND SPOT

A GLIMPSE BEHIND THE SCENES

Beyond the footlights and the audience's view of the stage is the world of the players and dancers, the scene-shifters and technicians. The drawing above is designed to show the system of lighting governed by the electrician (top left) and the parts of the stage, including the back-cloth and the flats. To afford simplicity, a ballet instead of a play is shown.

in their plays. These are intended to make the play more readable, to mingle the method of the novel and the method of the play, and are published because many people find a play difficult to read.

It is as well for the dramatist, however, to use his head in composing his play, and to remember the physical limitations of the theatre. The stage is not a film studio. It is a small, unstretchable platform, and it is governed by stringent rules, imposed by local authorities, in respect of such matters as fire. Its site is fixed and defined. A dramatist who divides an act into three scenes ought to have enough common-sense to realize, without instruction, that he must not have two consecutive scenes in the same act requiring a change of scenery and furnishings. He would be a very simple-minded person who would divide an act so that its first scene was set on the promenade deck of an Atlantic liner, its second scene in the midst of a mountain pass, and its third scene on the floor of the House of Commons.

Dangers of Dialect

The use of dialect is the most delusive of the dangers that a dramatist can encounter, and he must be very careful how he uses it. It is local speech, and, as a rule, is incomprehensible outside the district in which it is spoken. The more faithfully it is reproduced, the less intelligible will it be to those who are unfamiliar with it. Authors who are unskilled in their work, attempt to cope with this trouble by including translations of dialect words in their text, forgetting that these translations, though they may be printed in a published play, cannot be pronounced on the stage. Here is an easy passage of Scots dialect, in which the author has embodied an explanation of an unfamiliar term:

"I'm sure good puddins is just wastit on a dried-up schoolmaster that eats his pottit heid"—i.e. meat from a bullock's head, cut up, and boiled as soup, and poured into small basins where it jellies when cold—"frae a shoppie in the toun."

Manifestly, the ruminations of the character who speaks that passage of dialect, cannot be interrupted during a performance while the explanation of her words in parenthesis is given to the audience. Because of this difficulty in understanding dialect, dramatists must use an appearance of local speech rather than the local speech itself. Their object is to be understood, and they cannot be understood if they use obscure turns of local phrase. What may be crystal clear in a provincial town will be as mysterious as Choctaw in London. The theatre has invented a form of dialect, derisively called "Mummerset," which is, despite the derision, a sensible effort to solve a seemingly intractable problem. There is no need, however, to resort to "Mummerset": the dramatist need only be discreet in his use of dialect, avoiding the unintelligible

Evolution of the Theatre

At this point, it is well to remind the student that although the drama is conditioned by its physical limitations more than any other art, it is not bound and fettered by them. Shakespeare would not recognize Shaw, so vast is the difference between his conception of the drama and Shaw's; but neither would he recognize our theatre as a theatre. The Elizabethan building was entirely different in its shape and its appointments from the modern theatre; and it, in its turn, was entirely different from the theatre in, say, the time of Shakespeare's grandfather. In the Middle Ages, the stage was movable, but not in our sense of that word. Each scene of a Miracle Play, the religious ancestor of plays as we know them, might be performed on a cart which, when the scene had been acted in one part of the village, was then drawn to another part and acted again. Development occurred when the play was performed in one place; on a cart or a platform in, perhaps, the partially enclosed yard of an inn. Further development occurred when a building was set apart for the performance of plays: a theatre, used for no other purpose. In this theatre, which had no roof, the stage jutted into the auditorium, and the spectators stood around three of its sides. It had no curtain, very little scenery and scarcely any furniture. The audience was invited, as

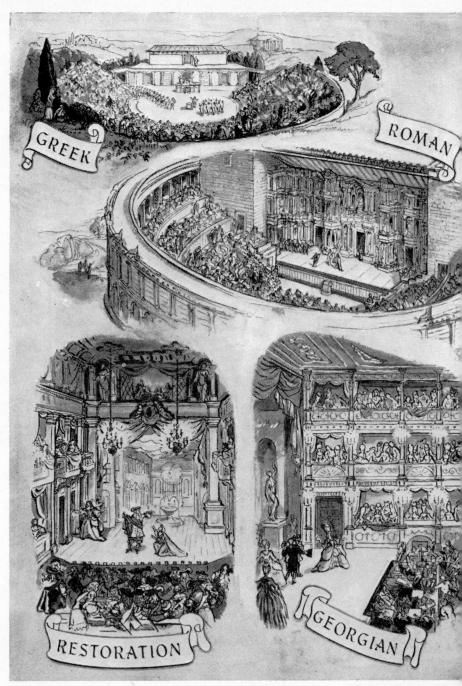

GREEK

ROMAN

RESTORATION

GEORGIAN

DEVELOPMENT OF

Influenced later by the re-discovery of classical plays, drama in England sprang from the

THE THEATRE
medieval Bible play, and passed by way of the morality to the Elizabethan theatre

Shakespeare invited it in the prologue to *Henry V*, to "work, work" its imagination, and to believe that the bare boards on which it gazed were indeed the veritable battlefield of Agincourt.

But even in the sixteenth century when Shakespeare was writing, alterations were being made in the theatre as a *building* which were to affect profoundly the nature and shape of the drama; and one of the most important of these changes was the decision to roof the theatre. This structural change opened up many new ways of presenting plays in public. Rain and wind no longer affected the performances as they had previously done. Performances could now be given at night instead of only in the day-time, and could be given as easily in winter as in summer. Light had to be used on the stage and in the auditorium, and light is easily manipulated. Seats began to appear in the auditorium where, formerly, the audience had had to stand as it does today at the Promenade Concerts. The stage started to recede from the auditorium, and was, eventually, pushed out of it. It no longer jutted into the auditorium: it jutted away from it. A proscenium arch was built, behind which the entire play was performed, and from this proscenium arch a curtain dropped at the end of every act.

Realism in Presentation

It thus became possible to change scenes without being overlooked by the audience. Actors who were supposed to fall dead on the stage, were not obliged to rise up at the end of a scene and walk off in full view of the audience. Illusion was increased, even if imagination was less violently stimulated. By the use of light and paint and strips of wood and canvas, the vast fields of Agincourt could be pictorially presented to the playgoers who were no longer asked to pretend that bare boards were battlefields. Some loss there was, no doubt, but there was greater gain. In this way, there came to be what is now known as the picture-frame stage.

It must be plain that these physical changes in the theatre, resulted eventually in changes, not only in the structure of the drama, but in changes in its nature. An open-air audience is radically different from an enclosed audience: the latter can listen better and more attentively than the former. Any politician today knows that he must use a broader and rougher method of oratory for a street crowd than he uses for a crowd inside a hall. So does a dramatist. It is broadly true to say that the man who first roofed a theatre made it possible for Bernard Shaw to write plays full of long intellectual arguments. Had that anonymous man never been born, *Getting Married* and *Heartbreak House* and *Back to Methuselah* would probably never have been written in their present form and certainly could never have been acted.

Here we have conclusive evidence of the interaction of the physical structure of the theatre and the spiritual substance of the play.

It was not, however, until about three centuries after the theatre had been roofed, that the full effects of the revolution the roofing had caused began to be seen. At first, indeed, the tendency to produce spectacular plays, with broad effects, was increased and accelerated, and we find Shakespeare's younger contemporary, Ben Jonson, bitterly complaining of the power and influence of mere painters and scene-builders to whom the dramatist was expected to defer. But that tendency could not long continue to prevail, and there began to be produced plays of an intimate and subtle character.

In the last quarter of Queen Victoria's reign, the revolution begun in the first quarter of Queen Elizabeth's was almost completed. The roof had *not* fallen in: it had become firmly fixed; and as a result of its fixture, the drama, which formerly had been scarcely varied in shape or style, became infinitely various, ranging not only from light entertainments, revues and musical comedies and even one-person entertainments, such as those given by the American actress, Ruth Draper, to personal problem plays, such as Ibsen's *The Doll's House*, and general sociological dramas, such as Eugène Brieux's *Damaged Goods*, John Galsworthy's *Justice* and *Strife* and Chekhov's *The Cherry Orchard*, but to

TEST OF AN ACTOR'S QUALITY

In all English drama there is no part more sought after than that of the posturing, vacillating, soul-searching Hamlet. To play Hamlet is the ambition of every male actor, whether he be a member of a travelling troupe like the nineteenth-century actor shown above, rehearsing the part in his lodging, or a modern actor seeking new effects by playing Hamlet in twentieth-century costume.   Two representative Hamlets in the history of English acting are John Kemble (below, left), brother of Mrs. Siddons, and, one hundred and sixty years later, John Gielgud (below, right), a member of the Terry family.

DESIGNS FOR STAGE SETTINGS

*Realistic drama demands that the stage setting should represent the scene faithfully and
naturalistically; poetical drama is best played against a simple setting symbolizing the
spirit of the play. Above is a realistic stage setting designed by Rex Whistler for a
production of Wilde's "An Ideal Husband." Below, as a contrast, we have a boldly simplified
setting designed by Michael Ayrton for the banquet scene in "Macbeth."*

more complicated psychological stuff, such as Chekhov's *The Three Sisters*, *The Seagull* and *Uncle Vanya*, Pirandello's *Six Characters in Search of an Author*, Eugene O'Neill's *Mourning Becomes Electra*, and the modern poetic plays, such as T. S. Eliot's *Murder in the Cathedral* and W. H. Auden and Christopher Isherwood's *The Dog Beneath the Skin*. It is doubtful if any of these plays could have been performed in a roofless theatre. There were no witty comedies in the open-air theatre, where all the laughter was dependent on slapstick and horseplay. Shakespeare's *Love's Labour's Lost* would have been as impossible in movable carts pulled around a village green as William Congreve's *The Way of the World*, Sheridan's *The School for Scandal*, Oscar Wilde's *The Importance of Being Earnest*, Shaw's *Man and Superman*, Somerset Maugham's *The Circle*, and almost the whole of Noel Coward's comedies.

Observe how dissimilar are all these plays from each other. What a flexible machine it is that can produce simultaneously such differing plays as Shaw's *Saint Joan* and Coward's *Cavalcade*, Pinero's *The Second Mrs. Tanqueray* and Wilde's *Lady Windermere's Fan*, Galsworthy's *The Silver Box* and Barrie's *Peter Pan*, the works of Auden and Isherwood and the revues of Charles B. Cochran. All this variety was made possible by the unknown genius who put a roof on the theatre. It was his unaided effort that enabled men of the most dissimilar sort to express themselves on the stage. It became possible in the roofed theatre, not only to produce comedies and tragedies, but to produce different varieties of each. The playgoer of the Middle Ages knew only one form of theatrical fun. To him, a comedy was a piece in which a man sat on a seat which was not there or put a horse-collar over his head and began to whinny or bray. When he aspired to intellectual laughter, he split his sides over a henpecked husband or the spectacle of a shrew being ducked in a pond. But after the theatre had been roofed, comedy took many forms. Slapstick remained, though it became more elaborate, but refinements of wit appeared.

SHAW CARICATURED

Of the scores of Shaw cartoons perhaps none has so felicitously caught the mixture of humour, arrogance, courage, originality and self-satisfaction as this forty years old drawing has done.

There was the play of verbal dexterity, with the pun prevailing, and the play of comic situations, in which the characters became involved in a ludicrous situation, as in Oliver Goldsmith's *She Stoops to Conquer* and the comedy of manners, in which social customs and fashions are portrayed, such as Congreve's *The Way of the World*, Sheridan's and Wilde's comedies, and the comedy of public institutions, such as

"AMATEUR THEATRES"

In this amusing sketch of the green room with "Macbeth" in progress, Cruikshank reminds us that there were amateur theatricals a hundred years ago no less than today. Every member of an amateur company will recognize the spirit, if not the substance, of the scene.

Arnold Bennett's *What the Public Wants.* Some authors were content to amuse: others insisted on giving instruction or reproof; and yet others were concerned only to put their point of view, leaving the audience to draw from it what conclusion they pleased. Sometimes, indeed, the distinction between comedy and tragedy was not always apparent. Is John Galsworthy's *Strife* a comedy or a tragedy? Can anyone safely label the contemporary Irish writer, Sean O'Casey's *Within the Gates*? Ought we to laugh or cry at John Millington Synge's play of Irish village life, *The Playboy of the Western World*? One audience, usually in England, may laugh at Sean O'Casey's *Juno and the Paycock*, while another audience, usually in Ireland, weeps over it. Which of them is right?

Enough has been written to show the diversity of the drama, particularly since it began to develop and expand after the theatre had been roofed. In the days of the Greeks, dramatists were closely restricted to certain themes, as they still are, or recently were, in China; though even in those days the personality of the author broke the restraint of convention.

Vicissitudes of Authorship

Authors nowadays range almost at will, subject to few restraints, and required only to fulfil one supreme demand, that what he writes shall interest his audience. The first duty of a dramatist is to be entertaining. He may write tragedies, satires, comedies, sociological works, musical pieces or revues, any or all of these; but if he is not entertaining, then he may abandon hope of ever winning an audience for his work. One fact stands out from all the facts of the theatre, and it is this, that no man who has anything to say worth hearing has ever, in the end, been barred from the stage. He may have to fight for his audience, and if he is a genius it is certain that he must fight for it, but he will win his audience at last. Ibsen was informed by the leading dramatic critic of Copenhagen that he had no conception of drama; Chekhov was advised by a leading actor to give up

all hope of ever writing a play worth performance; and Bernard Shaw was publicly begged by one of his best friends, the late William Archer, the dramatic critic, to cease his attempts on the theatre since he had no talent for writing plays. These are the vicissitudes of authorship and, indeed, of all arts. The great actress of the last century, Sarah Bernhardt, was assailed as incompetent; another, Eleanora Duse, was unable, at first, to obtain employment in Italy; the late Sir Henry Irving, the classic exemplar of Victorian acting, was booed off the stage in Dublin every night for weeks.

It is almost a law of life that original men and women shall be received with brickbats and abuse. We may believe that this is right and proper, for mankind dare not let itself be diverted from its purpose by every new thought that issues from the mind even of people of genius, but must feel sure that the genius is not only a genius but right. All life begins in a small way, but if the seed be sound, the fruit will follow. The genius, neglected today, will be applauded tomorrow. He will have been tried and found *not* wanting. If a man writes a play for which he cannot obtain production in his lifetime, assuming that he lives to the normal length of years, then we may safely suppose that his play is unfit for production. The world may reject or disregard a good or a great man for a season, but it does not reject or disregard him for ever.

Test Yourself

1. What is the chief difference between the craft of the novel and that of the play?
2. Give the names of three English playwright-novelists who have succeeded in producing examples of each type of work.
3. Give a brief account of the development of the theatre in this country.
4. Name a comedy by (*a*) Shakespeare; (*b*) Congreve; (*c*) Wilde; (*d*) Shaw; and (*e*) Barrie.

Answers will be found at the end of the book.

GRAND OLD MAN OF LETTERS

W. Somerset Maugham, novelist, dramatist and master of the short story, has been slow to win the acclaim he now receives; for we like our writers to express more warmheartedness than we normally do ourselves, whereas Mr. Maugham maintains the detachment of a Foreign Secretary towards the sharp dramas and melodramas which he so skilfully reveals.

CHAPTER XIX

THE NOVEL

As soon as we are old enough to understand them, stories are read to us. A little later, we read them for ourselves. Gradually we pass from tales about animals and toys and fairies to stories of treasure, adventure and mystery. Then we begin to read novels, which are stories about people like ourselves, who have to meet either difficulties which are known to all of us or an exceptional set of circumstances calling for the exercise of great courage and skill. We often identify ourselves with these people, and say that a book is good if we feel at home in it or if the characters do what we should like to have done. Some readers never get beyond this personal view. If the people in a novel are not "nice," and if they do not receive rewards for courage or sacrifice, that novel is not interesting to them. But if such readers go no further than this, they miss the extraordinary pleasure which one gains by understanding what authors are trying to do, and why and how they succeed.

Now the basis of all great novels, and most good ones, is character. The people in them are so vivid, so amusing or rich in vitality, that we can hardly believe we did not know them until we read about them. They are often more real to us than our friends, because we know them more completely.

There is a reason for this. Our friends are sometimes inconsistent. We see only the sides of them which are nearest. We do not always wish to know more, lest our happiness or our plans should be overset. Too often we are influenced by their looks, their attitude to ourselves, their manners, or their voices; looks, manners and voices being attributes of personality which, since they vary from moment to moment, a novelist cannot often make his readers see or hear. If, therefore, misled by the belief that we can draw from life, we use living models, as some authors have been accused of doing, we shall soon find that living models are not complete characters.

On this point Mr. Somerset Maugham has said, "Nothing is so unsafe as to put into a novel a person drawn line by line from life. His values are all wrong . . . he never convinces." Mr. Maugham, who means by values what a painter means when he indicates the lights and shadows of a picture in relation to one another and to the picture as a whole, is certainly right. A well-drawn character is always an imagined character. He, or she, is a person whom the novelist also knows better than he knows his friends, better than he knows himself; somebody who, however much he or she may owe to the observation of a lifetime, jumps from the writer's understanding like a vivid spark, and is then coaxed and petted into flame. The novelist's business, unlike the sociologist's business, is with individuals. If he makes this person, these persons, seem to be as much alive to us as they are to himself, he is a creative writer. He has created new life by his imagination.

Growth of Character in Fiction

One can make this clearer by saying that the persons in a book are made real or endearing by the author's insight, rather than by his conscious endeavour to draw them at more than life size. Don Quixote is a rare illumination of human nature because Cervantes saw and described him with such love and fun. My Uncle Toby, in Sterne's *Tristram Shandy*, is one of the best-loved characters in all fiction, for a similar reason. The two sisters, in Arnold Bennett's *The Old Wives' Tale*, move through the years, growing visibly older amid the progress of the Five Towns, because their creator knew and loved them, without sentimentality but with zest.

You can see how such characters gave rise to the stories which are told about them. They have only to put on a pair of shoes to suggest that something is going to happen. This is very important. Anybody can begin a tale by saying, "It was a fine day in December, and a girl was walking down from the top of Hampstead Heath"; but until that girl has been imagined she is meaningless. And by imagined is meant so warmly understood that whenever the author writes about her he is (for the time being) her very self. What she suffers, he suffers; what amuses her, amuses him; what she sees is immediately before his eyes with the thrilling convincingness of a tragic dream. The fact that he is simultaneously *not* her, but an extremely critical spectator of all she does, is a part of the novelist's art; but it is secondary to this extraordinary act of impersonation. The author who does not imagine may know mechanically where the girl is coming from, and where she is going; but unless he knows *her*, and why he is writing about her—it need not be with the laughter of Cervantes, or Sterne, or Arnold Bennett, but with as much assurance as these writers show—he is wasting his time.

Another consideration is that it is the novelist's job, not to describe life, in Somerset Maugham's phrase, "line by line," but, by the exercise of his fastidious selective power, to choose to describe only what is significant. He does not tell all —that would be impossible. He suggests. By the word he uses, by the gesture he indicates, by the speech he cuts short, he makes us understand what is passing in the minds of those whom he portrays. If he makes us want to know all that he knows, he has mastered the first secret of good novel writing.

Test of a Story

And the story? Well, a story is whatever invention carries the curiosity forward. It is not necessarily a *plot*. It is promise; suspense. The American author, Washington Irving, once wrote a most exciting and amusing story about the *Stout Gentleman in Room Thirteen*, of whom he learned nothing definite, and of whom all he ever saw was the plump seat of a pair of trousers as their owner climbed into a coach. A novelist who knew everything about the girl from Hampstead Heath could spin a whole book from her journey to Kensing-

ton. That would be a story, just as it would be a story if she were going to be married or divorced that day, or if she had escaped from a mad aunt and was to run risks of kidnapping, drugging, or murder before nightfall. The one test of a story is that we should follow it eagerly for as long as the author so determines; and that, having followed it, we should not, at the last page, feel that we have been cheated.

Types of Novel

This is why some novels ramble from the birth of hero or heroine, through a lifetime, and to death itself; others magnify the events of a few hours; and others again, such as *The Bridge of San Luis Rey*, by Thornton Wilder, or *Grand Hotel*, by Vicki Baum, assemble at one spot many persons whose lives, prior to the moment of crisis, are quickly sketched. What happens in the biographical novel like *David Copperfield* or H. G. Wells's *Tono-Bungay* is not carefully plotted beforehand; the author is rich enough in fancy, or improvisation, or knowledge of human nature, or all three, to keep his reader miscellaneously but progressively entertained. What happens in the novel of condensed time or chance assembly is that the unrelated short biographies or sketches of personality are given artificial unity by some crucial accident. In none of these books is there plot. There is a relation of events to some central character or to some central incident.

In another kind of novel, highly admired by those who prefer fancy to imagination, what matters most is not the body and character of the leading person of the tale but his or her temperament, moods, fantasies, associative memories and momentary observations. To this kind of novel has been given the description "the stream of consciousness." It is almost always an extension of the personality of the writer; and for its successful composition the novelist must be a poet, an introvert, a critical observer, and a literary virtuoso. Such a novelist, travelling from Hampstead to Kensington in the guise of a young girl, would fill the journey with fancy, with acute observation, with a

H. C. Wells.

LOW

H. G. WELLS, AS SEEN BY LOW

Many of Wells's novels, such as "The History of Mr. Polly," reflect the life and psychology of the "little man" in a piratical society developing into monopoly capitalism.

thousand delicacies of style; and would not once invoke the help of plot. Indeed, since it is an axiom with this kind of writer that all reality lies within the consciousness (which embraces both memory and present largely-evocative experience), form, in the sense in which that word was used by Henry James, whose novels are like dramatic pictures, is a thoroughly deplorable artificiality.

Dramatization of Character

Most novelists, however, find it wearisome to pursue for any long time, without resort to conflict or intrigue, the thoughts and feelings of a single character. They need milestones, good roads, journey's end, and quarrels, meals and drama *en route*. They represent, not the vagaries of mind, but active, physically adventurous man; and they write to please, as well as to edify, the majority of their fellow creatures. They accordingly, having imagined the girl from Hampstead, and having been really excited by the experience, begin busily to play with the possibilities of her day. This is the most fascinating part of their work, the part which links them again with childhood, when 'p'tend" was a magic word. It is like an applied day-dream, a day-dream with an object. You will recognize delight in what H. G. Wells once said in looking back over his own short stories:

> I found that, taking almost anything as a starting-point, and letting my thoughts play about it, there would presently come out of the darkness, in a manner quite inexplicable, some absurd or vivid little incident more or less relevant to that initial nucleus. Little men in canoes upon sunlit oceans would come floating out of nothingness, incubating the eggs of prehistoric monsters unaware; violent conflicts would break out amidst the flower-beds of suburban gardens; I would discover I was peering into remote and mysterious worlds ruled by an order logical indeed but other than our common sanity.

Of course, Mr. Wells's quickness and fertility in such matters are unrivalled, and because Mr. Wells is a genius what he says will not explain to a reader who has never written stories how and why such marvels should happen. But something of the sort does always happen with inventive writers. They cannot be content to let a girl walk and ride uneventfully from Hampstead to Kensington. If not dragons, then other threats to her peace and progress will arise, as they would have done a hundred and fifty years ago in the pages of a supposedly uneventful book by Jane Austen. The girl will remember something amusing or frightening; a shower of sleet will delay her, and so change the kaleidoscopic pattern of her day. She will impulsively go out of her path to visit a friend. Before an hour has passed, the entire prospect of her life may have changed. Such a view of her journey is not a plot; it is not something outside our own experience, and certainly is not at all outside the expectation of sanguine youth. But it is a colouring of probability, a dramatization; and it is such dramatization that helps characters in a novel to reveal themselves positively by means of actions or emotional response to inescapable events.

A novelist like Sterne, interested in his own sensations and so in the interior lives of his characters, is an introvert novelist; whereas Wells is an extrovert novelist, since he is interested in what happens outside himself and fills the lives of his characters with incident and action. Incident such as H. G. Wells describes comes freely. Having once reached his starting point in character, he is for ever glancing into possibility, taking this, rejecting that, being temporarily baffled, sometimes being forced to accept something less perfect than he could have wished, but always seeking situations and accessories to those situations which will make intelligible everything he has imagined.

A simple case taken from personal experience is illuminating. Once, having decided to write a short novel about an evening in the lives of five persons, the writer felt night descending upon him, and heard (not in fact, but just in Mr Wells's manner) Big Ben striking six o'clock. He saw, and made the heroine see, the River Thames as it would be visible from Westminster Bridge at that hour in winter, and, after long purposeful day-dreams in which was imagined the place where two lovers could meet and be together in London without interruption, there came, apparently, from nowhere, the word "yacht." Who could have told why that word leapt to a novelist's consciousness by association with Westminster Bridge? It was because, years earlier, the writer himself, in very different circumstances and in daylight, had gone on board a yacht at Westminster. The characters were independently imagined; the story was wholly invented; but the yacht, which gives the more emotional passages of that story a remote and romantic setting, was a positive reality, brought once again, this time at night, to Westminster

Bennett and "The Old Wives' Tale"

Here is another example of story-building, much more important, and (because it presents the first stages of a great novel) very illuminative of the novelist's art. Arnold Bennett was born, as everybody knows, in the heart of the Potteries. He lived there until he was twenty-one, when he came to London. And when he was about thirty he went to live in Paris. There he explored the back streets as well as the boulevards, and took his meals in all sorts of places, sometimes in those little restaurants outside which trees stand in green tubs, and sometimes in the economical *Restaurants Duval*. As he ate, he watched all who entered; for his curiosity was insatiable. And one day, when he was in a *Duval* in the rue de Clichy, an old woman came there to dine. "She was fat, shapeless, ugly, and grotesque. She had a ridiculous voice, and ridiculous gestures. It was easy to see that she lived alone, and that in the long lapse of years she had developed the kind of peculiarity which induces guffaws among the thoughtless." Everybody in the restaurant laughed at the old woman; but Bennett reflected: "This woman was once young, slim, perhaps beautiful; certainly free from these ridiculous mannerisms . . . her case is a tragedy. One ought to be

able to make a heart-rending novel out of the history of such a woman as she." This was the first inspiration for *The Old Wives' Tale*.

But Arnold Bennett's instinct told him that his genius was English; that although Paris could play its part in any book he might write he knew the city only with his eyes and his mind, whereas he knew the Potteries with all the certainty of a child's familiar experience. For five years, while he was doing other work, he thought about *The Old Wives' Tale*. The Five Towns were always there as a background to everything he now saw. Their early impression upon him was heightened and focused by distance. In particular, he remembered a certain shop near his childhood's home; and he resolved that his heroine should be born in a room above that very shop. But he also made another discovery, which was that if a novelist can use strong contrasts between two or more characters he is tremendously aided in the task of giving clear outlines to both, or all, characters. Quixote had his Sancho Panza, Cousin Pons his Schmucke, Elinor Dashwood her Marianne; Jane Austen, in particular, had set all later novelists an example in the use of *sisters*.

Constance and Sophia

Bennett pictured his Constance more and more vividly in the light of a contrast with one who should be all that she was not. Sophia, the sister who eloped, went to Paris, and returned to the spot which Constance never left, was likewise created. There was to be, not one old woman, but a pair of old women. Constance was still the heroine; but Sophia, her foil, had an essential part to play in the tale of one who, having been "once young, slim, perhaps beautiful; certainly free from ridiculous mannerisms" grew and matured and passed into middle life and old age in an English provincial city. Many incidental inventions were needed to suggest the passage of outward as well as inward time; one may read the book with an eye to the calculated details supporting the illusion of a changing age. But although it has thus, for those curious in such things, the interest of careful, if wayward, building by one who never had Mr. Wells's electrically-fast inventiveness, *The Old Wives' Tale* begins and ends with an entirely imaginative conception of individual character. Because it is in the main English tradition, it goes on to present imagined character objectively—that is, with all rough pencillings rubbed out, and in clear outline, without subjective analysis. It is one of the English novels of this century which has combined popularity with excellence. And it is one which all students of the art of novel writing can study with advantage.

Types of Opening

It begins abruptly:

> Those two girls, Constance and Sophia Baines, paid no heed to the manifold interest of their situation, of which, indeed, they had never been conscious.

And this leads one to note that novelists have always differed in their beliefs as to the best manner of opening a story; so that nowadays the set opening—the "once upon a time" of the fairy books, or Sir Walter Scott's easy "In the pleasant district of merry England which is watered by the River Don, there extended in ancient times a large forest"—has given place to something abrupt, resembling Browning's "My first thought was, he lied in every word." But the abrupt opening is an avoidance of convention. It is not an originality, however.

As the first page of a novel is intended to invite the reader's attention to what is to follow, and to foreshadow the whole manner and type of the book, writers will often at the outset sacrifice shock to consistency. Mention of the time, the day, the year, the place, and the appearance of the character who has been chosen to open the book may seem old-fashioned to the impatient; but if those things are important to what follows they will always be justified. Take this introduction to Honoré de Balzac's great book, *Cousin Pons*:

> Towards three o'clock in the afternoon of one October day in the year 1844, a man of sixty or thereabouts, whom anybody might have credited with more than his actual age, was walking along the Boulevard des Italiens with his head bent down, as if he were tracking someone. There was a smug expression about the mouth—he looked like a merchant who has just done a good stroke of business, or a bachelor emerging from a boudoir in the best of humours with himself; and in Paris this is the highest degree of self-satisfaction ever registered by a human countenance.
>
> As soon as the elderly person appeared in the distance, a smile broke out over the faces of the frequenters of the Boulevard, who daily, from their chairs, watch the passers-by, and indulge in the agreeable pastime of analysing them. That smile is peculiar to Parisians; it says so many things—ironical, quizzical, pitying; but nothing save the rarest of human curiosities can summon that look of interest to the faces of Parisians.

Cousin Pons has appeared. We are given, thereafter, several pages of detail about his clothes, bearing and former youth; and we pass, fully prepared, to his poignant history. Notice how, in these opening words, the milieu is indicated and our attention is bespoken for Pons. The author's sardonic amusement equals that of the Parisians; we ask at once why Pons should be so pleased. Since the fashion of 1844 is contrasted with that of his garments he becomes grotesque. Our attention being seized, we read on. Moreover, the first words of *Cousin Pons*, when afterwards re-read, bring the whole book back into our minds. They begin an immortal story. The modern colloquial novel may open less elaborately, with familiar clichés which slip cliché perceptions into the reader's quick mind; but it does not create the living portrait of a character. This is what Balzac does. Nobody has ever known better than he how to begin, and how to continue, a tale—often a terrible tale—about what he called "the human comedy." Once the novelist passes to page two, he

ARNOLD BENNETT—A BORN WRITER

Bennett was both man of the world and literary man. His zest for story telling was uninfluenced by any desire to make his novels vehicles for social reform, although the background of the Clayhanger series centres on the ugly reality of the pottery towns. His novels give a strong impression of truth by the amassing of vivid and accurate detail.

has another problem. If he keeps to the natural presentation of normal human beings, or what is sometimes called "the ordinary," he subjects himself to very close criticism from every one of his readers. We all have our own sense of probability, and we often refuse to believe something true, either because it is outside our experience, or because the author has expressed it in an incredible form. The novelist, knowing this, is tempted to run away from everything that may be familiar to his readers. He hastens to strange lands —even cloud cuckoo lands; he pretends not to admire the prosaic; he travels back or forward in time. But if, setting his teeth to the most courageous act of all, he determines to stick to real life, he will throw aside all temptation and risk the contempt of every dogmatic ignoramus.

It is essential, in this case, that his characters should be believed in. They may be superbly original; but besides being individuals they must be recognizable as real men of their time. He must make them behave with the most precise naturalness. They must only do things that we admit to be appropriate. They must earn their living, catch· the right omnibuses, know no more than what is within the range of their types. And when they speak they must speak in a way both proper to them as heroes and heroines and proper to their way of life. Conversation is thus one of the most difficult things to manage in the whole craft of novel writing.

Talk in the Novel

It is difficult because, if we could hear a recording of our own conversation, we should find it full of repetitions, stammerings, clumsy sentences and lost threads. The absolutely literal reproduction of ordinary talk in a novel would be entirely boring and would lead nowhere. But the novelist, while seeming to be literal, must make what his people say interesting and pointed. The characters speak, therefore, not just as real people speak, but with selected and heightened naturalness. They use the words and phrases we know, but use them suggestively, with fresh brevity, to tell us something, confirming always our

impressions of their personalities. Now nobody has ever written better dialogue than one of the earliest and most eccentric of the classic English novelists, the author of *Tristram Shandy*, Laurence Sterne.

You must remember that *Tristram Shandy* was written nearly two hundred years ago, and it is not easy to find a short passage which stands by itself. But although some of the author's amusing commentary has been left out, the quotation is a fair instance of Sterne's quick naturalness, and besides showing how the expectant, too-speculative Mr. Shandy and his sublimely sensible brother Toby react to the delay in Tristram's birth, it puts their personalities into charming opposition:

It is two hours and ten minutes —and no more—cried my father, looking at his watch, since Dr. Slop and Obadiah arrived—and I know not how it happens, brother Toby—but to my imagination it seems almost an age . . .

Though my father said, *he knew not how it happened*—yet he knew very well how it happened;—and at the instant he spoke it was pre-determined in his mind to give my uncle Toby a clear account of the matter by a metaphysical dissertation upon the subject of duration and its simple modes, in order to show my uncle Toby by what mechanism and mensurations in the brain it came to pass, that the rapid succession of their ideas, and the eternal scampering of the discourse from one thing to another . . . had lengthened out so short a period to so inconceivable an extent.—"I know not how it happens—cried my father—but it seems an age."

'Tis owing entirely, quoth my uncle Toby, to the succession of our ideas . . .

Do you understand the theory of that affair? replied my father.

Not I, quoth my uncle.

But you have some ideas, said my father, of what you talk about?

No more than my horse, replied my uncle Toby.

Gracious heaven! cried my father,

THE LIVELY EIGHTEENTH-CENTURY NOVEL

Rowlandson's illustrations catch the vigorous spirit of the eighteenth-century novel. Above we see the beginning of the adventures of Henry Fielding's "Tom Jones: a Foundling"; below, an exciting moment in Tobias Smollett's "Roderick Random" for which the author drew on memories of his own experiences as a surgeon in the British Navy.

HONORÉ DE BALZAC

Balzac's realistic studies of nineteenth-century French life and society have influenced the development of the novel in France and England.

looking upwards, and clasping his two hands together—there is a worth in thy honest ignorance, brother Toby —'twere almost a pity to exchange it for a knowledge.

Contrast this passage with one from Henry James, who depended much upon his power to suggest character and intrigue by dialogue. Here a young telegraphist in a small post office near the world of fashion has been tempted by a friend with the chance of arranging flowers in the homes of the élite. Mrs. Jordan, the flower arranger, has boasted of imaginary social contacts. The other girl is no less a snob. Their talk

had led to her saying, as if her friend's guarantee of a life of elegance were not quite definite: "Well, I see every one at *my* place!"
"Every one?"
"Lots of swells. They flock. They live, you know, all round, and the

place is filled with all the smart people, all the fast people, those whose names are in the papers . . . and who come up for the season!"
Mrs. Jordan took this in with complete intelligence. "Yes, and I daresay it's some of your people that *I* do!"
Her companion assented, but discriminated. "I doubt if you 'do' them as much as I! Their affairs, their appointments and arrangements, their little games and secrets and vices —these things all pass before me!"
This was a picture that could impose on a clergyman's widow a certain strain . . . "Their vices? Have they got vices?"
Our young critic even more remarkably stared; then with a touch of contempt in her amusement: "Haven't you found *that* out?" The homes of luxury, then, hadn't so much to give. "*I* find out everything!" she continued.
Mrs. Jordan, at bottom a very meek person, was visibly struck. "I see. You do 'have' them!"
"Oh, I don't care! Much good does it do me!"
Mrs. Jordan, after an instant, recovered her superiority. "No—it doesn't lead to much!" Her own initiations so clearly did. Still—after all; and she was not jealous: "There must be a charm!"
"In seeing them?" At this the girl suddenly let herself go. "I hate them: there's that charm!"

James, you will see, did not *enjoy* his characters as Sterne did. He was the artist, allowing them no more wit than was necessary. His dialogue misses precise veracity for the sake of literary polish (perhaps from a stranger's ignorance of idiom). But he was doing something which Sterne did not attempt. These two women, boasting, seeking information, disguising themselves to each other, thinking other thoughts as they speak, are also betraying every pretension so fast to the reader that he would be surprised to find, after a few pages, how much he had been helped to guess and how few facts he had been given.

This is the art of dialogue. It is the craft of the novel. The novelist is all the time slipping information into our minds about his characters and his story. The more subtle he is, the more does he communicate without apparently interrupting—let us say—two ladies in their talk. His ear and his dramatic sense help him. The reader's ear and dramatic sense help *him*. The truth is that with good novels the reader must do his best to understand not only what the novelist tells him, but also what the novelist leaves unsaid. Only the very simple novelist, the one who tells a plain story with a thrill at the end of every chapter and a kiss to end the book, can really be read without a constant sensitiveness of the reader's imagination to all that is undeclared. There are no limits to what can be shown, in a novel, of human nature.

The Novelist's Freedom

You have only to consider for a moment to realize that, although we have considered here what is sometimes called the traditional novel, and although men dogmatize about the qualities essential to any novel which is to please themselves, the novelist is freer from restrictive rules than any other kind of writer. His business is with human beings, high, low, normal and eccentric. He may deal with as small, as narrow a theme as he wishes (Jane Austen, for example, enchants us with miniatures about genteel country households whose sole excitements are walks, picnics and amateur theatricals; Joseph Conrad, though using tropical backgrounds, concentrates upon a single episode about which we learn through the illuminating knowledge and intelligence of half a dozen men sitting round a table). The novelist can crowd his pages, as Dickens did, with types and farcical or emotional incidents. Like Dostoevski, he can ride melodrama into the empyrean and show gamblers, saints and epileptics in a thrilling psychological *mélange*. He can picture his country in an historic age, as Tolstoy did in *War and Peace*, or make, as Balzac inventively did, or as Emile Zola systematically did, the whole of national life provide material for successive romances. And nobody will denounce him; for there is no theme or scene too small or too great to be attempted by the novelist. He is a free man.

With one reservation. It is a reservation sometimes forgotten. Unless he writes about individuals, he loses direct personal contact with the reader and becomes (within the wrong covers) an essayist or historian. He ceases to create.

And, since prigs abound who are impressed by grand design or solemnity, it should be said that a novel may be just as important as Tolstoy's *War and Peace* if it is a short dramatic book about life in a village, a city back street, a jungle clearing, or a ship afloat. What gives imaginative work importance is not earnestness or size, but the intense reality to the author of what he is describing. That makes it universal. The simplest needs of men and women—love, hunger, courage, steadfastness—are enough. No substitute has been found for them. All the cleverness in the world, the literary accomplishment and the stars of fashion, provide nothing unless imagination and belief lie at the heart of the novel. These qualities are essential. Most novels fail, not because ingenuity has been lacking, but because, while they were being written, they were not important enough to their authors. They were not *felt*.

Test Yourself

1. What is the most important element in all good novels?
2. The question of plot in a novel is a highly controversial one. Give examples of a novelist to whom a strong plot was a secondary matter, and one to whom a strong plot was essential for a good story.
3. What is the difference between an extrovert and an introvert novelist?
4. Should the dialogue of a novel be entirely realistic?

Answers will be found at the end of the book.

JAMES JOYCE, THE AUTHOR OF "ULYSSES"

His volume of short stories "Dubliners" is a landmark in the history of story writing.

CHAPTER XX

THE SHORT STORY

IN art, as in life, the most familiar things are often the hardest to define. The man in the street knows quite well what he means by a short story. He means a piece of prose fiction, long enough to hold his attention for a few minutes, and short enough to take its place among the contents of a single issue of a magazine or newspaper. This working definition is sufficient until doubts arise: doubts provoked by editors, who return manuscripts with the complaint that they are not short stories but sketches or conversation pieces, and by professional critics and reviewers, who object that they are anecdotes, novels in brief, mere pieces of reporting, anything except short stories.

Such strictures raise the need for a precise definition; and a precise definition is very hard to find. For one thing, the short story is a comparatively new form. Its vogue is a bare fifty years old, and during those years it has grown along at least two broad and diverging lines. If we wish to discuss an established art form, the sonnet for example, we meet little difficulty, since the basic form and the permissible variations are clearly laid down. Argument about sonnets is therefore directed to their quality, not to the question of whether they are sonnets. But, almost from the start of the century, argument has continued as to whether certain productions, which their authors roundly claim to be short stories, can properly be so described.

Most Flexible of Forms

When Henry James (the author of *The Art of the Novel*) wrote, "The only reason for the existence of a novel is that it does attempt to represent life," he was saying something which applied just as well to the short story. For, within its time limit, the short story can draw on the full range of life. It suffers local restrictions: the editors of popular magazines will not accept stories with themes which they imagine that their readers may dislike—but these are the restrictions of magazines, not of the short story. A short story, as one of its leading contemporary writers, H. E. Bates, has pointed out, is "the most flexible of all prose forms." It can be "anything from a prose-poem without plot or character to an analysis of the most complex human emotions." It can "deal with any subject under the sun, from the death of a horse to a young girl's first love affair."

The magazine editors, of course, would contest these claims, but we do better to take the word of the practitioner who studies and knows his art, rather than that of the middleman with a conservative estimate of his customers' taste and an apprehensive eye on his advertisement columns. The editors of popular magazines have been the English short story's worst enemies. In almost every instance it is the writers who, steadily broadening the form and scope of the short story, have caught the public imagination and forced editors to yield, slowly, point by point, reluctant, hostile, wailing that things are not what they were in the good old days: that the world has not obliged them by standing still.

No: definitions that limit development will not do. H. G. Wells, discussing the point in his brilliant and suggestive introduction to his own collected short stories, made the limit one of length only. Not more than ten thousand words, he suggested: something that can be read in half an hour. This is the sort of definition that a practising writer can accept.

Somerset Maugham, who brought to the short story an admirable economy and finish, asks rather more. He likes a story to have a beginning, a middle, and an end. A critic who did much for the art of the short story, here and in America, the late Edward J. O'Brien, gave on many occasions the principles which guided him in the choice for his annual anthologies of British and American short stories. He says (in excerpts from the *Introduction* to his

315

collection, *The Best Short Stories of 1932*):

> . I have set myself the task of
> disengaging the essential qualities in
> our contemporary fiction which, when
> chronicled conscientiously by our
> literary artists, may fairly be called a
> criticism of life.

Here, obviously, O'Brien agreed with
Henry James Then he continues:

> I am not at all interested in formulae,
> and organized criticism at its best would
> be nothing more than dead criticism, as
> all dogmatic interpretation of life is
> always dead. What has interested me . . .
> is the fresh living current which flows
> through the best . . . work, and the
> psychological and imaginative reality
> which writers have conferred upon it.
> No substance is of importance in
> fiction, unless it is organic substance,
> that is to say, substance in which the
> pulse of life is beating . . . I have
> sought to select . . . those stories
> . . which have rendered life imagi-
> natively in organic substance and
> artistic form. Substance is something
> achieved by the artist in every creation.
> rather than something already present,
> and accordingly a fact or a group of
> facts in a story only attains substantial
> embodiment when the artist's power
> of compelling imaginative persuasion
> transforms it into a living truth. The
> first test of a short story, therefore, in
> any qualitative analysis is the measure
> of how vitally compelling the writer
> makes his selected facts or incidents
> The test may be conveniently called
> the test of substance.
> But a second test is necessary if the
> story is to take rank above other
> stories. The true artist will seek to
> shape this living substance into the
> most beautiful and satisfying form, by
> skilful selection and arrangement of
> his materials, and by the most direct
> and appealing presentation of it in
> portrayal and characterization.

The first thing to be said about this is
that, while interesting and illuminating, it
outlines tests of quality for certain short
stories, rather than attempts a definition of
the short story itself. It is quoted because,
despite its vagueness, it does expose
the main problems of short story writing,
and suggest a road towards the only
definition of the short story which twenty-
five years of study and practice have
enabled the writer of this chapter, very
tentatively, to propose for his own guidance. As a practising writer of short
stories, he would not want to modify
Wells's emphasis on length: but as a
reader and reviewer he has met so many
pieces of prose fiction which, however
short, were not short stories, that he has
been forced to look for some difference
between them and the pieces of similar
length to which the title could be given
without hesitation. The difference seems
to be one of the degree of satisfaction: the
best short stories do more than satisfy
personal taste—they satisfy deeply by
giving a sense of their completeness.

Brevity with Completeness

A caricature, consisting of a few quick
lines only, may satisfy the mind because
it suggests the subject completely, appearance and character in one. We feel no need
to add more lines, or to join the gaps
between one scribbled stroke and the next.
On the contrary, we know that we could
only spoil the likeness, which is total,
exceeding many a detailed portrait, because
of the imaginative work which it demands
of us.

A one-act play by the Irish playwright,
J. M. Synge, for example, is satisfying
and complete, because every word and
every gesture of the characters are so
revealing, so typical, that, short though the
encounter is we know all about them. We
can foresee their future and guess their
past. Like the caricature, they give us a
complete experience. In the same way, a
short story has achieved what O'Brien
called "organic substance" when the
impression which it leaves with the reader
is complete: when the gestures of its
characters wholly reveal them: when each
line is typical, suggesting the total reality

from which it is drawn: when all adds up to something which satisfies the imagination. This is not at all the same thing as leaving the imagination nothing to do. The proof is the way in which people will often say, of a novel or a play or a story, "I felt as if the characters went on living after it was finished."

There is an epitaph in the Greek Anthology which has been freely translated thus:

Bill Jupp lies here, aged sixty year.
From Tavistock he came.
Single he bided, and he wished
His father done the same.

The Greek poet did not tell us why the man wished he had never been born. He left our imagination unhampered. At the same time, he satisfied it with a laconic but complete picture, a lightning sketch which revealed the whole man. We may accept then, very gratefully, H. G. Wells's definition of length: and suggest in addition that the short story should in some way give the reader a sense of completed experience.

Next, let us examine the short story and its history, so as to see in what way, if at all, this suggestion applies: since, unless it will cover any and every kind of short story, it will be just another useless and cumbersome lump of dogma.

Two Types of Modern Story

The student who undertakes to examine short stories in bulk will very quickly find that they fall into two broad divisions. One, containing the vast majority, is the type of short story published in popular periodicals, magazines and newspapers. The other, a small minority only, is the type appearing in a handful of reviews, intellectual weeklies, short story anthologies, and an occasional collected volume by a single author. The second type is generally called the serious, literary, or artistic short story, and is the subject of such critical study as the short story provokes. The first type is known as the popular or the commercial short story, and receives no critical attention, save, perhaps, an occasional contemptuous dismissal. There are small overlappings, as when a story by an author whom the critics admire appears in a popular magazine, and, very rarely indeed, when something by a "popular" author is printed in an eclectic review: but the main division holds good.

How the cleavage arose will appear from a very brief account of the short story's history. The author writes here of the short story in Britain. Leaving aside for the moment the question of influence from abroad, to which we shall return later, in the earlier stages of English literary history, short stories, though they were written from time to time, were almost always incorporated in longer works. Thus, though many of the leading writers tried their hand at the shorter form, there was no vogue for the short story as such until the late 'eighties or early 'nineties.

Pioneers in the 'Nineties

The pioneer writers, amongst whom one may name Robert Louis Stevenson (*New Arabian Nights*), Frederick Wedmore, Hubert Crackanthorpe and Arthur Morrison (*Tales of Mean Streets*) were at first rather more leisurely than suits the genius of the short story. Wedmore's once famous *Last Love at Pornic* and *Pastorals of France* read oddly today. But they were speedily reinforced by the tales of vigorous and prolific writers who gave the short story an energy and a compactness which have not since been surpassed. Rudyard Kipling, H. G. Wells, W. W. Jacobs (author of *Many Cargoes*), Conan Doyle (*The Green Flag and Other Stories*)—to name four only—poured out a flood of stories which, greatly as they differed in quality and flavour, had so much in common that they determined the form of the short story for close on twenty years. Kipling's glowing imagination, Wells's eager curiosity, Jacobs's comedies of riverside and country pub, Conan Doyle's costume pieces and detective stories, were all expressed in terms of plot and action. The other writers followed suit, and for years the only short stories which editors and public would recognize were stories of plot, action, or situation (i.e. stories in which the interest depended less on the characters than on the predicament in which they were placed).

KATHERINE MANSFIELD
Magazine editors saw nothing for their readers in Katherine Mansfield's stories. Discerning critics, however, recognized in Katherine Mansfield the most distinguished short-story writer of the 'twenties.

Thus, what was accidental came to be regarded as essential, and, to this day, most editors of popular magazines continue to insist on plot and action, and to refuse the name of short story to anything which is not worked out in these terms. The mistake was natural enough. If we grant that the short story should give a sense of completed experience, it is hardly surprising that an action-loving people like the British should derive satisfaction from a completed action, from the solution of a problem, from the decisive answer to every question raised in the course of the story, and from that neat tying together of the threads which editors call a plot.

Psychological Aim

Then, by the inevitable law of development in all art, came a reaction. A new generation of writers, no longer interested in plot and situation, began to explore character and atmosphere, not as incidentals, but as ends in themselves. In this they were much encouraged by translations from the Russian writer, Anton Chekhov, to which the editors of British magazines would assuredly have denied all title to be short stories. (Many of Chekhov's stories have been published in collections, of which *The Lady with the Dog* is typical.)

The aim of these writers was a psychological rather than a physical completeness. They were content if, like the Irish dramatist J. M. Synge, they allowed the reader simply to glance in through a window at their characters and watch them make a few gestures so revealing and so typical that the reader's imagination could be left to fill in the gaps and supply all that was left unsaid. Unfortunately, however, the great majority of the writers who rushed to imitate Chekhov, or to apply what they took to be his methods, did not realize what these methods were. Seizing on certain superficial characteristics, they failed to see the psychological completeness, the solid foundations of even the slightest of Chekhov's stories. They did not appreciate the preliminary work that makes his stories resemble the visible part of a rock at high tide, firmly based on all that lies under the water. All they realized was that they now had good authority for writing stories without a plot.

They were encouraged, too, by the work of Henry James to load their work with psychological detail, not seeing that with James detail grew leaf from twig and twig from branch out of the living trunk of his story, and was a vital part of it; whereas the detail in their derived stories was an addition only, a decoration externally applied, which could be transferred without loss from one story to another.

But these rebels, whatever their competence, had an exceedingly hard struggle to gain public recognition. Editors refused to recognize these new stories, good or bad, and persisted obdurately in their demand for plot and situation. They had been confirmed in this view by the influence of two American writers of genius, O. Henry and Jack London, whose qualities lent themselves to imitation. The editors repeated that the new productions were not stories at all, and lamented that the art had degenerated, and that authors were no longer writing as Kipling, Wells and Jacobs wrote. In order to please them, those writers who lived by their pen were obliged to serve up the old formula in a topical dress. Hence came the regrettable split between popular and literary stories.

The New versus the Hackneyed

As more and more writers of serious purpose were attracted to the newer type of story, the split widened, and the apostles of the new art were driven into an error which balanced the error of the editors. Plot stories came to be associated only with the magazines, and, as these declined in reputation owing to the formula work of commercial writers, and to the awakening interest in the serious short story created by newcomers of talent and by the championship of such critics as the late Edward O'Brien.

Many literary-minded readers thought that plot and situation stories must, *ipso facto*, be bad; and that any dissection of character or presentation of squalor, however shapeless and inconclusive, was better than the best-constructed yarn. This fallacy was helped by the grotesque badness of nineteen out of twenty magazine stories, a badness more readily apparent than the badness of so many of the newer stories, and by the all but total refusal to give the new writers a hearing. Hardly any of Katherine Mansfield's stories, for instance, were published in periodicals during her lifetime. A. E. Coppard had to fight hard for recognition, by way of anthologies and eclectic publishers. Ernest Hemingway was already famous before *Scribner's Magazine* took a chance with one of his best stories. James Joyce's *Dubliners*, a landmark in the growth of the short story, had to wait years for publication. H. E. Bates, in his book *The Modern Short Story*, gives a long list of short-story writers of the 'twenties who knew that appearance in any periodical was most unlikely. Now the five writers named above are recognized as important figures in the development of the short story.

Things grew so bad that the serious writer (by whom is meant the writer who writes to please himself with only an artistic end in view), if ever he were moved to write a plot story or to tell a yarn, had to face contemptuous rebuke from the literary weeklies for "descending to the level of the magazines." The criterion of a story's quality came to be the place where it appeared. If it was paid for by a popular magazine, it was damned. If it came out in an eclectic review, with so small a circulation that it could not afford to pay its contributors, it was acclaimed.

This mistake, the converse of the editors', is easier to detect now than it was in the 'twenties and early 'thirties. The whole controversy was one in which both sides were at fault. The bad plot and situation stories were bad, not because they made use of plot and situation, but because they were badly done. They were bad examples of a class which in itself is neither good nor bad, but depends, like any other art form, upon the way in which it is handled. The reason why so many plot

A. E. COPPARD

A. E. Coppard (1878-1957) was a great writer of lively and refreshing short stories. His writings possess poetic quality, humour, and sometimes a mischievous fantasy. Among his principal stories are "Adam and Eve and Pinch Me," "The Field of Mustard" and "Tapster's Tapestry."

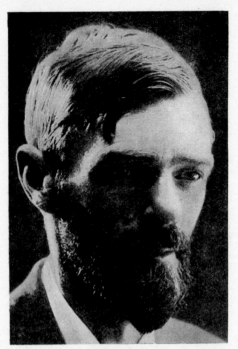

D. H. LAWRENCE, NOVELIST

Son of a coalminer, Lawrence propagated his faith in the importance for human welfare of sex and the life of the senses.

stories are bad is that the characters have been forced to fit the plot, or exist merely in order to embody it. Plot is neither a virtue nor a vice: but, when it arises naturally from character, it never did a story any harm.

In the same way, the shapeless and depressed studies written by the newer writers were bad, not because they lacked plot, but because they were shapeless and depressed. Those who extolled them above the plot stories forgot too much. Praising Chekhov, they forgot that he wrote *The Black Monk* as well as *The Head of the Family*, and quite often encouraged his reader to ask, "What happened then?" Hymning de Maupassant (the famous French author), they forgot that he loved situation. Waxing lyrical over Coppard, they had not the wit to see his supple, strongly knit framework and his unerring sense of movement and proportion. Rever-

ing D. H. Lawrence (author of *The Prussian Officer*), they missed his power of suspense, his gift for sheer narrative. Admiring Aldous Huxley's dissection of character (as for instance in *The Little American*), they did not realize how skilfully it was revealed in action. They did not perceive that Ernest Hemingway's laconic dialogue and economy of outline, corresponding indeed to the quick strokes of the caricaturist, like them were based on accurate anatomy and sound draughtsmanship. Enraptured by the atmosphere in a story of the Irish writer, Frank O'Connor—though perhaps offended by its gaiety, a quality much out of fashion —they missed the underlying discipline, and the structure so apt and shapely that, if it were to be symbolized in a drawing, the pencil would flow to a sweetly proportioned silver cup or vessel of shining glass.

This short account of the split between the two kinds of story is over-simplified, because it takes no account of exceptions: but the exceptions do not invalidate it. When a story by a serious writer appeared in a popular magazine, it was because it happened to deal, in straightforward, recognizable terms, with a subject of interest to nine ordinary people out of ten. The editors had no intrinsic prejudice against good writing, but they suffered from a number of local prejudices as to theme and treatment which they mistakenly elevated into rules for the short story. In view of those institutions which profess to teach short story writing, it cannot be repeated too often that these editorial prejudices have nothing whatever to do with the art or nature of the short story. They are merely a melancholy incident in its history.

The greatest development of the last fifty years has been that, whereas the short story used to be something which a novelist wrote on the side, for relaxation, and with much the same technique as he used in a novel, it has come to be an entirely separate form with a technique of its own: many techniques, rather, for with the serious short story there are as many techniques as there are writers . . . "The short story," writes the American critic, Mr. Ellery Sedgwick, "has become all sorts of things, situation, episode, characterization, or narrative—in effect a vehicle for every man's talent."

Hence it is clear that, although one can speedily analyse the magazine story, no analysis of the serious story is possible. One can expose the manufacturing secrets of "trade goods," since they are standardized, invented, written to formula and from set prescription, but one can say very little about the genuine article which is not manufactured but created. The writer of this chapter has read hundreds of first-class stories in the past twenty-five years, but beyond analysing them one by one, which would require several volumes, he could do no more than give a list of those that remain most distinctly in his memory. Of each one he could say that it gave that sense of a completed experience which was posited earlier in this chapter, that it measured up to all O'Brien's tests, and that, if it could not always be said to represent life as Henry James laid down, it satisfied the earlier, more imaginative definition of Herman Melville, the author of *Moby Dick*: "It is with fiction as with religion, it should present another world, yet one to which we feel the tie."

Influences from Abroad

Clearly, we must beware of definitions. The form is too fluid, the influences too many. The birthplace of the modern short story is Russia, but the Russian influence did not reach England until this century, when translations of Chekhov, Turgenev, and Tolstoy were made available. The English short story had drawn its early nourishment from France and from America. Flaubert with his *Trois Contes* had many disciples in this country, and Guy de Maupassant many more. The former inspired Wedmore, the latter Crackenthorpe, our pioneers. From America, Edgar Allan Poe gave hints to Wells in one direction and Conan Doyle in another. O. Henry, the short story's three-card-trick man, taught serious writers what to leave out, gave the magazines a formula, and showed everyone the power of a good opening. Jack London, at his best a master of the type of story in which things happen to people from outside—*The House of*

Mapuhi, in *South Sea Tales*, has lessons for all short story writers—was shallow and sentimental in his treatment of character, and so gave the magazines more than he gave the serious writers. Since then we have had Joyce, Katherine Mansfield, Coppard, Bates, Manhood, Hemingway, Saroyan, O'Connor, Elizabeth Bowen, O'Faolain, Pritchett, O'Hara, and many another, all giving their best and pouring their life blood into the short story, all serious artists honestly trying to set down true things about life and human beings in the best way they can.

We see, then, that arguments as to what is a short story are its strongest asset, since they prevent it from becoming standardized. What uniformity can be expected or desired in an art influenced by Poe, who stretched it taut as his own anguished nerves: by Turgenev, author of *A Sportsman's Sketches*, whose poetic sympathies made it eloquent both of natural beauty and social injustice: by Flaubert, who made a character the thread for a rich and intricate tapestry: by Maupassant, whose skill lay in the complete portrayal of a situation: by Chekhov, who made a mood or an episode the imaginative key to the whole lives of its actors: by writers as diverse as D. H. Lawrence, Sherwood Anderson and William Saroyan, each of whom made the short story a vehicle for the expression of personal feeling and conviction: an art fed from scores of individual streams, which is being revived daily by the newest writers, in almost every language, all over the world? Who but a pedant would dogmatize about it, or wish to circumscribe it?

Are there, then, no general rules of art that govern every type of short story? Is there nothing helpful that can be said to the reader or writer anxious to learn? He will learn more by reading twenty or even a dozen short stories of proved quality than from any attempted digest of principles. A story list is added at the end: but here, as evidence of good intention, are two or three elementary principles that apply to the vast majority of short stories.

The various parts of the story should bear such relation to one another as will make a symmetrical whole. There is no reason why a story should contain action, but, if it does, the action must be evenly spaced out so as to balance the "still," or purely descriptive, part of the story. The average beginner's story—let us suppose it introduce a second character, or describe a place, and the action of the story will not begin till more than half-way through. It is obvious on reflection that a story like this must be top-heavy and ill-balanced; yet, this mistake is commonly found

H. E. BATES, STORY-TELLER AND NOVELIST

Although primarily a novelist Mr. Bates has never lost his love for the short story—the medium in which he first practised his craft. His are delicately-woven sensitive tales which linger in the imagination long after more eventful stories are forgotten.

contains four thousand words—begins with several long, solid paragraphs, amounting to perhaps fifteen hundred words or more, introducing the main character and giving us chunks of his history. Often, as likely as not, it will then especially in efforts of the serious type.

A story should start only once. Having started, it should go straight ahead, and contain nothing that does not lead directly or indirectly to the climax. The reader's progress, from start to finish, should be ven and controlled. If the writer slows im up here, stops him abruptly there, then ushes him off his feet to make up for it; if e jolts him from traffic block to traffic lock, he will only irritate the reader and revent him from receiving the full effect f the story. To secure this smoothness, here must be no irrelevant detail. "No dmittance except on business" must be he short story teller's motto. The writer hould ask himself, when looking over his ory, whether each incident or each line f dialogue is pulling its weight by con- ributing to the story's total effect. Is it ssential? If not, it must go.

He might ask himself, too, whether any f the necessary facts could not be conveyed o the reader by means of dialogue between he characters, rather than in a chunky aragraph of information. A. E. Coppard uggests a further rule, that a story should e told from a single point of view, ither that of the author, or of a single haracter. This, though by no means niversal, is an exceedingly safe rule. To witch over from one character to another s dangerous, because it distracts the nterest and tends to split the story in two.

Summing Up

That is about all. "Any real examination f the story's development and shape," vrites H. E. Bates in his book, *The Modern hort Story*, "would involve the dissection f almost every short story written. No wo stories are alike; no two methods."

To sum up: A short story is a short piece of prose fiction. We need ask no closer definition. All we need require is that each short piece of prose fiction should have an aim worthy of an artist and should succeed in reaching it. Plot or no plot, situation or no situation, character study or no character study, action or no action, form what you like, manner as you please, setting what you fancy, length anything within reason: these are the needs for the short pieces of prose fiction of the future, plus the free extension of the term "short story" to cover them all. Without that freedom, the art of the short story can neither develop nor thrive.

Some Memorable Stories

For the student of the short story, here is a list that gives an excellent conception of the scope of the form:

The Overcoat, Gogol; *Un Cœur Simple*, Flaubert; *Boule de Suif* and *Miss Harriet*, Maupassant; *La Mule du Pape*, Daudet; *The Black Monk*, Chekhov; *The Knights of the Joyous Venture*, Kipling; *The Country of the Blind*, Wells; *A Change of Treatment*, Jacobs; *Gift of the Magi*, O. Henry; *The House of Mapuhi*, Jack London; *The Dead*, James Joyce; *Bliss*, Katherine Mansfield; *The Prussian Officer*, D. H. Lawrence; *The Traitor*, Somerset Maugham; *Death in Venice*, Thomas Mann; *Fifty Grand*, Hemingway; *The Higgler*, Coppard; *Green Thoughts*, John Collier; *Joining Charles*, Elizabeth Bowen; *I'm a Fool*, Sherwood Anderson; *Fishy*, V. S. Pritchett; and *Michael's Wife*, Frank O'Connor.

Test Yourself

1. What is the accepted limit for the number of words in a modern short story?
2. The development of the English short story has been influenced by those written in other countries. Name six foreign short story writers (including Americans) who have influenced short story writing in Britain.
3. Is a strong plot the first essential of a short story?
4. If you were a magazine editor, upon what main principles would you select short stories for publication?

Answers will be found at the end of the book.

PREPARING TO "SHOOT"

Perched in the crane above the players the director (left) and cameramen (right) mak
preparations for the shooting of a scene. Technically speaking, it will be a "long shot"—
that is, a general view without close-ups. Arc-lamps supplement natural lighting.

CHAPTER XXI

WRITING FOR THE FILMS

THERE are one or two outstanding geniuses in the film industry (Charles Chaplin is one) who can look back on a completed film and say with truth, "*I* made *that* film." They are very exceptional, for few have the necessary versatility and personality to superimpose themselves completely on the actors and technicians associated with them. No other art, no other craft, no other form of entertainment demands so much co-operation to ensure good quality—and that co-operation can only be achieved in a selfless manner. There are degrees of compromise, of course, but this selflessness must mean a certain withdrawal of one's personality for the common weal.

A film is made by a producer, a director, writers, designers, sound engineers, cameramen, cutters, actors . . . the work of each one of them being inextricably interlocked with that of each of the others. The combinations and permutations are enough to stagger one. Somebody with a love of statistics once worked out how many different professions, trades and arts are interlocked in the making of one film. The answer is, more than fifty. It is a co-operative society, then, that confronts the writer who wants to write films. A dozen people will wrestle with every line he writes (and among themselves over it) before it finally reaches the screen.

The prospect is one to discourage the newcomer, for writers are by heart and nature individualists and egoists.

New Field for Writers

But more writers are needed as films develop and improve, and the advantages awaiting screen-writers easily outweigh the sacrifice of that part of themselves which they will lose. The writer who turns to film work finds a new medium in which to practise a form of writing that is interrelated with sound and vision and which offers boundless possibilities for experiment. And not the least of the advantages —for even the creative artist has a stomach to fill and must have a roof to cover him— is a good income. It is there even for the novice who learns the craft. It is not essential to make a big reputation. Indeed, there are many writers steadily in demand of whom the public have never heard.

Script Treatments

Whether the subject is an original screen story or a translation to the screen of a novel or a play, the first step towards the finished script is what is known as a "treatment." The first treatment is, as a rule, a sketchy affair and is prepared by the writers after broad preliminary discussions with the producer and the scenario editor. It is quite possible that at this stage of the film no director has been assigned to it. His contribution to the writing will come.

A second (and, if necessary, a third and fourth) treatment will finally bring the story to the point when it can be "broken up" into the "shooting script." Treatments are written in narrative form. They serve to establish the construction of the story, the relative importance of situations and, of course, the characterization of the people in the story. Dialogue is rarely employed then, or if it is, it is of the sketchiest nature. No attempt is made to indicate the presence or the movement of the camera.

Up to this stage (and the finished treatment is a very important stage) the writer will have found little interference. The producer, having already agreed to the basic lines of the story, will have brief criticisms and suggestions to offer but rarely more than that. The writer will have had more to do with the scenario editor and (if one has been assigned) with the director. Each will have had his point of view, but it is an understood thing that the writer should be encouraged to develop the basic story line in his own way. Discussion rather than superimposition marks the treatment stage of a film script and it is generally in the treatment that the writer contributes his most important part to the co-operative effort.

The finished treatment having been finally approved by the producer, the first draft shooting script is the next stage. Here the writing begins to be entirely governed by the technicalities of film-making, and here the writer must needs subordinate himself a great deal to the desires expressed by, and the restrictions imposed on, the director, the cameraman, the art director, the sound engineer and —last but not least—either the associate producer or the production manager (not all films have associate producers) whose job it is, among other duties, to see that the cost of the finished film is approximately within the budget allowed for it. It is at this stage that the inexperienced writer may feel that his individuality is being taken away from him. He should remember, therefore, that the medium is not the written word, but the spoken word combined with the visual image, and that other creative people, of an importance equal to his, must work with him to bring that heard word and that seen image to life. The writer alone cannot do it in the same way as he can read an image in poem or novel.

Importance of Team Work

The moment he starts work on the shooting script, he is a member of a team. If this is grasped from the outset, he will not be troubled by the feeling that he is constantly being imposed upon. The old witticism of the screen-writer: "I write as they please" is a cynical interpretation of the system, and no writer who lives up to that attitude will ever write a film worth looking at. "*We* write as *we* please" sums up the situation more fairly, for no writer worth his salt will continue to co-operate with other technicians who do not allow him his fair contribution to the finished film. Generally speaking it will be found that teams develop naturally in a film studio; technicians who share the same interests and enthusiasms understand each other and work together whenever they

can. Occasional contact with other writers and technicians, however, is a mental stimulus to a team which might otherwise get stale from constantly working together.

The shooting script then is not a piece of literature. It is more akin to the architect's blue print; it is an elaborate briefing, not only for the actors who will play the parts and speak the lines, but for the director and the great team of technicians assembled under him. The shooting script embraces an elaborate and carefully prepared list of technical instructions. The producer's contact with the script virtually ends with his approval of it; it is at this point that the other technicians really begin to work on it for they now bring it physically to the screen. The producer keeps contact by seeing the "rushes" daily. Rushes are the daily screenings of what has been taken in the studio usually the day before.

Alternative "Takes"

As a rule there are alternative "takes" from which the producer and his soviet of technicians select the best; sometimes it will have been found that certain bits of dialogue once read better than they now sound and that a re-write and a re-take are necessary. The writer is at a disadvantage in that he does not always know the actor who will portray the characters he has created (more particularly those for the smaller parts) and dialogue may have to be modified to suit the people finally cast, but the principal parts will usually have been assigned to actors during the treatment stage of the script, and the writer when he gets on to the shooting script, can base or modify his characterization and dialogue on his own knowledge of the limitations of the actor concerned.

Here again let me stress the importance of the writer as a technician. The good film writer must at the same time be a film enthusiast, must make himself thoroughly conversant with the work of actors, directors, cameramen and cutters. And if in his early days he manages to put in a few months as an assistant to the cutter or to the cameraman, he will be the better writer for this experience.

So much for the broad processes through

A SCENE FROM "DUNKIRK"

British films, which in the early days of motion-picture production won world popularity, lost their lead during the first World War. In recent years they have revived in quality, and in realistic films, such as the Ealing Films production, "Dunkirk," are second to none.

which a story goes before it becomes a film script. We now come to a more detailed explanation of the functions of other technicians in so far as they affect the writer. Collaboration in an artistic medium is an art; it calls for the maximum of tact, sympathy and understanding on the part of each member of the team. Discouragement is easy, and the discouraged or frustrated contributor will never give his best work. There is every inducement in the film industry for the writer to lead a full and happy professional life and receive good rewards for his work; but the nature of the work is such that technicians working with him may influence him unduly.

To give the simplest illustration, it is proper for the cameraman to say that such and such a shot is a technical impossibility and he may (and should) suggest an alternative camera position. But it is not for him to suggest how the lines should be re-written in order to meet the new camera set-up, any more than it is for the writer to show *him* how to manipulate his camera. Unfortunately, most people believe that anyone can write and this is very irritating to the writer.

Who has not met the bore who says: "If only I could get down to it, *I* could write a book"? It is, of course, a confusion of thought; everyone has a book in him, since a book could certainly be written

MASTER SCENE SCRIPT

"DUNKIRK"

Sequence 48

The same Colonel who in the earlier sequence had told the doctors to get out, comes in at the door of the dressing station.

Through the open door the lines of men can be seen lying in the open. A Red Cross flag on an improvised pole floats over them. The same two doctors are still working at the tables, but the windows are open now and through the glassless openings some wounded can be seen.

The doctor who attended to Mike is working on a sergeant. He looks over him and says, his voice tired but still cheerful: "I thought you'd gone long ago, sir."

The Colonel says awkwardly: "We'll be going in half an hour. I—" he hesitates —"I had to tell you myself."

"That's all right," says the young doctor. "We're going to draw for it. Orders are for one doctor and ten men to every hundred patients. We've got two hundred and sixty we can't move. Jimmy!" he calls out loudly, "Jimmy! The Colonel will hold the hat for us—disinterested party. You don't mind me calling you a disinterested party, sir?"

The Colonel laughs wryly.

The doctors gather from outside. There are seventeen of them altogether. With them are seven chaplains. Somebody thrusts a tin hat filled with slips of paper into the Colonel's arms.

"First out, first to go. Last out, stay," says the young doctor flippantly.

Rapidly the Colonel draws the names and reads them. The papers diminish until there are only three left in the hat. The young doctor's name is the last to come from the hat.

The Colonel pauses as he reads it. He says: "Faulkner—that's you, isn't it?"

The young doctor nods. He says: "Ah, well, I'd have had to find my battledress top if I'd picked the lucky!"

He bends over the sergeant again and says: "You can thank God it's your elbow not your ankle, my lad! Anything I can do for you in Berlin, Colonel?"

The Colonel disregards the question. He says simply: "Thank you," and, turning, stumps out of the dressing station.

The doctors who are to leave are beginning to get their kit together.

A chaplain comes in and asks: "Can I help you with that?"

The young doctor says: "Are you going, Padre?"

The chaplain answers shortly: "No," and they begin to bandage the damaged arm.

FINAL SHOOTING SCRIPT

"DUNKIRK"

423 *INT. M.S. CASUALTY CLEARING STATION. DAY*
All three doctors straighten themselves from their work, look over to the
COLONEL for a moment and then go on with their work again.

LUCKHAM: I'll stay if you want me to, sir.

COLONEL: No, we'll draw lots.

RILEY (*to himself*): Two to one the field. Five to one I'm a loser.

COLONEL: Sergeant, write out the names on slips of paper (*he holds*
out his cap) and put them in my hat. How many doctors have we got
here?

SERGEANT: Sixteen, sir.

COLONEL: Seventeen. Put my name in with them.

The SERGEANT starts to write rapidly.

COLONEL: The first three out of the hat stay.

424 *INT. C.S. CASUALTY CLEARING STATION. DAY*
Through the open door comes BARLOW. An ORDERLY and BINNS are
supporting him. The CAMERA MOVES with them. They stop at a table
directly behind the COLONEL. BARLOW is told to sit on the table.
WESTERHAM crosses to attend him. The SERGEANT hands the cap to the
COLONEL, who holds it by the visor.

COLONEL: You'd better draw, Sergeant. You're more or less a disinterested party.

BARLOW is lying down now. The bandage on his face is being removed.
BINNS is dismissed. He makes his exit slowly.

425 *INT. LS. THE CASUALTY CLEARING STATION. DAY*
None of the three doctors looks up. The SERGEANT draws the first slip and
looks at it.

SERGEANT: Doctor Riley, sir.

RILEY: It was a snip at five to one. You couldn't lose.

SERGEANT: Doctor Dean, sir.

LUCKHAM: He was killed this morning.

SERGEANT: Doctor Kennedy, sir. He's outside.

COLONEL: Call him in, someone.

SERGEANT: Doctor Luckham, sir.

RILEY (*to Westerham*): Some people have all the luck, William.

WESTERHAM (*looking up for the first time*): I suppose you won't believe
it if I say I'm sorry. (*Bending down again*) Scissors!

RILEY (*laughing*): You wouldn't even ask me to.

about the life of each of us, however un-adventurous. But for every million people who have a story to tell, only a hundred know how to set it down on paper, only ten know how to set it down *well*, only one makes it a work of art—and that is probably putting the percentage too high.

Division of Labour

In film studios, as elsewhere, everyone thinks he can write. And not only technicians but actors, too, are quick to suggest an alternative line of dialogue. Here the writer must defend himself as best he can. Because his best ally is the director, let us review the director's relationship with the writer.

In our co-operative society the producer has the last word on all matters; if he is a good producer he will exercise his powers with the utmost care and preserve the balance by allowing himself to be over-ruled as often as he overrules. Next in power to the producer is the director, whose rule must needs be more firm and stringent; that is because the producer is co-ordinating the individual efforts of the team, whereas the other (as his title implies) is directing them. It is not easy to find an analogy but—roughly speaking—the relationship is that of the head of a steamship company and the captain of one of its liners; the first decides on the extent and course of the voyage, the number of passengers to be carried and so on; the second is responsible for the ship and its crew. So with the film; once this is "on the floor" (i.e. shooting in the studio has commenced) or once it is "on location" (i.e. shooting exteriors) the director takes over the main burden.

The movement of the camera, the use of sound, the interpretation of lines and the handling of performances—all these come under his direct control. Hence he is closely related to the writer, particularly where the shooting script is concerned. A shooting script is a waste of time unless the director has himself collaborated on it, for a shooting script indicates the movement of the camera, the use of long, medium and close shots—it indicates the final cutting and assembling of shots—all the

things which the writer can suggest but never control.

Some directors, of course, will accept the ready-made shooting script and after a minimum of work on it will interpret it in screen form as they go along. Many good films have been so made and the method can be made to work, particularly when the writers of the script (more often than not at least two writers work on the same script) are technically more accomplished and experienced than the director. But there is much to be said for the director who actively collaborates on the script. It is more satisfactory from everybody's point of view and not the least the writers', for they have the benefit of constructing the film shot by shot with the director and not seeing a totally different interpretation put on their work after it has been completed.

The film is primarily a visual medium; the eye more than the ear is the real receiving apparatus, and the story of the film is told in a series of changing, moving pictures. That, indeed, must sound obvious; but it is astonishing how difficult it is at first to make the newcomer appreciate it—and more difficult still to impress it on the established and successful writer of novels or tales; his familiarity with his own medium is in a sense a handicap. That series of moving pictures, then, is the director's responsibility; that is his language; that is the expression of his creativeness. He may not be a writer in the accepted literary sense, but his contribution to the script will not be the less vital on that account.

Film Dialogue

For the literature of film writing is a new literature; the dialogue is an integral part of the moving pictures. It is helped along and punctuated by a camera that can come so close to a face that the narrowing of the eyes, the twitch of a mouth, can be more eloquent than words. Because of the intimacy of the medium the dialogue can, when necessary, be economized down to those semi-intelligible sounds, the grunts, the tck's, the uh-huh's, the unfinished words, that are characteristic of everyday speech.

It is not the dialogue of the theatre which must be projected to the auditorium and which every spectator can listen to only from the level where he is sitting. Here the whisper has the same volume for the gallery as it has for the front stalls.

So much does the work of the writer and that of the director overlap that the ideal solution is, of course, for the writer and the director to be the same person without further collaboration. In rare cases it has been accomplished, mostly where the writer has graduated to direction. Preston Sturges is a famous example (I have already mentioned the unique Chaplin) and in Britain Noel Coward certainly had the qualifications to fulfil the dual role, although he had the good sense to have experts by his side in his initial venture as a director. But it is rare indeed to find these necessary qualifications in one man or woman; the next best is for the writer and the director to appreciate that they are dependent on each other and that neither is there to hinder or frustrate the other. It is often the case that the director's interference in the script is resented by the writer; this is the result either of the director imposing himself too uncompromisingly on the writer, or the writer not fully understanding the other's function.

It has already been explained why the mechanics of film production make it logical for the director to direct the writing of the script as much as the performance of the artistes and the movement of the camera; the scenario editor, though he be the executive in control of the writers, has no such powers nor does he seek them. He has two functions—to help the producer

DRAMATIC MOMENT

Films, like plays, may be symbolic, fantastic or realistic. The British film, "Sea of Sand," produced for Tempean Films Ltd., comes into the latter category. It is the story of a patrol of the Long Range Desert Group before the battle of El Alamein.

AN EXAMPLE OF REALISM

This scene from "The Shiralee," produced by Michael Balcon for Ealing Films, demonstrates the scope of the cinema in its handling of backgrounds. Extreme naturalness is achieved through the use of landscape.

and the director to find and shape broadly the stories they want to film, and to co-ordinate the work of the collaborating writers, the producer and the director. He is the umpire and the moving spirit of the script conference. He is—or certainly should be—an accomplished film writer himself and often he will work with the writers as a writer, but he helps and does not direct them.

Scenario Editor and Others

The scenario editor in many ways is like the producer; both are creative people in administrative positions. The script conference is a tricky affair; it is a parliament whose members include the writer or writers, the producer, the director, the associate producer, and (when the occasion demands) other technicians such as the cutter, the set designer and the cameraman. Unanimous decisions are not always easy to reach. The scenario editor, if you like, navigates the script conference through the troubled waters of Argument into the harbour of Resolution. At times a point has to be put to the majority vote; not, you may say, the ideal system for writing, but there are times when democracy has its drawbacks and we accept these as subservient to its blessings, and the film studio is by the nature of its work a microcosm of democracy.

Frank Capra and Alfred Hitchcock are two famous screen technicians who have frequently stated publicly that the film has been directed before shooting on it has commenced. They are right. The best film is that which has been most fully written and most fully planned (the two things should be synonymous) before actual studio work on it begins. For this reason it is important that the senior technicians should be kept in touch with the development of the script. Of these, perhaps the cutter and the designer are the most important. It is the designer's job to build sets which are not only good to look at, but which will accommodate the necessary movement of the camera, and reflect the mood of the scene: the cutter is responsible for the assembling of the film after the thousands of short takes have been delivered to him. The cutter's job is one of the greatest responsibility; he can improve an indifferent film almost out of all recognition by skilful manipulation, equally he can mar a perfectly good film by dragging out the scenes that should be played in quick tempo and so on. The presence of both these technicians at script conferences is an advantage.

True Roles of Film Collaborators

Producers have their own individual approaches to the preparation of a film and it is therefore more difficult to define their relationship to the writer than those of other technicians. Some producers work more closely with their writers than others, some indeed will go to the length of completing the script with the writers before assigning a director to the film. This is a topsy-turvy method and one to be discouraged. The producer should remain the one technician who retains an objective and critical attitude throughout the long period between the initial idea of the film and the first showing to the public.

For that reason, among others, the preparation of a script should be mainly a matter between the writer and the director, with an associate producer representing the producer throughout the preparation, and the producer called in from time to time as a senior arbitrator. The director, as already explained, directs the scriptwriters and other technicians and actors in the joint effort of translating the story into a series of moving pictures accompanied by sound. His relationship to them is close and intimate and expressed in every single shot. In a more remote way—or perhaps I should say with a more distant view of the film as a whole—the producer guides the director.

Final Responsibility

It is important that the writer should remember one thing when that general guidance affects his work. The relationship between writer and producer is not at all analogous to that between the author and his publisher. The film finally goes out under the producer's name. It is his film (into which, of course, others have put their work, too) and he stands or falls by the film as the man who has had the last word and made the final judgments. He is therefore creatively concerned with the film as well as being in an administrative capacity, and has his right to play an important part in the shaping and the detailed working out of the story.

Test Yourself

1. Name some of the participants in the making of a film.
2. The novelist's medium is the written word. What is the medium with which the film-maker is concerned?
3. Of the film-making team, who is the collaborator closest to the writer?
4. Why is a good novelist seldom a good script writer?

Answers will be found at the end of the book.

COMPLICATIONS OF TELEVISION

General view of a rehearsal under way in the studio for a television production of Shakespeare's "Romeo and Juliet." Microphones are held by long booms above the actors' heads, and each camera may need a team of three men.

CHAPTER XXII

BROADCASTING AND TELEVISION

ALL successful performance in public depends on the performer's ability to make a relationship with his audience.

The next obvious fact is that, in order to make this relationship, and keep it for as long as the performance lasts, the performer must be able to do two things. He must be able to calculate exactly his distance from his audience: and he must be able to bridge that distance. He must be able to make the precise effect he wants at the far side of the gap between him and those who listen and watch.

Without this power to bridge the gap, the most sincere performer is lost. It is no good being sincere on the stage or the platform if your sincerity does not reach the customers who are sitting fifty, a hundred, two hundred feet away. You need the power to project, as actors call it: in layman's terms, to make the relationship with your audience, at whatever distance. This calls for technique: and that is why people spend two or three years at stage schools, studying to acquire the rudiments of it.

Yes: but what has all this to do with television and broadcasting? Everything. In television the performer is close to his audience: in broadcasting very close indeed: closer even than in ordinary conversation. Both are intimate arts. Broadcasting is the most intimate of all public media of communication. This is to most people so strange a notion that we must look at it in detail. How can one speak of the broadcaster as close to his listeners, when some are hundreds of miles from the studio? How can one talk of intimacy, when perhaps his voice is bellowing at workers over the din of machines in a factory? How can one possibly generalise about a medium which varies from this bellowing to the whisper of a set by an invalid's bedside?

To answer this, we must consider what happens when a broadcaster comes into the studio to read a story or to give a talk. He sits down facing the microphone, which either stands on the table or hangs down from the ceiling. The engineer gives him a "level test," that is to say, asks him to read a few lines of his script, and listens on the loudspeaker in order to gauge the weight and quality of the speaker's voice, and to decide how near he should speak to the microphone. With most speakers, it will be between eighteen inches and two feet.

The red light flashes, the speaker reads, and the microphone receives his voice as it comes, from that short distance, with every nuance of tone and every small incidental sound—the catching of the breath, the moistening of the lips, the little huskiness that is cleared with a cough—exactly as the speaker utters it.

It follows, therefore, that the listener hears the broadcaster's voice as if it were coming to him from a distance of eighteen inches or a couple of feet. If it roars at him through a big loud speaker, all the little incidental sounds will be magnified, too. He will get, as it were, a gigantic close-up of the broadcaster's voice. If he tunes his set down to a whisper, the little sounds will be whispered to scale.

The moment we grasp this fact, we see why so many speakers, who are convincing on the platform of a large hall, fail at the microphone. Forgetting how close the microphone is bringing them to their listeners, they make a public speech into it. They orate, they use all the tricks and devices which a lifetime of experience has taught them. They do not stop to reflect that one does not address in this manner a person who is sitting at the other side of the fireplace, and that the vocal methods needed to throw one's voice across a big space become ridiculous when used in a small room.

A certain Minister of State, now a successful broadcaster, took some time to realize this. His first broadcast was of the public address type, three sizes larger than life; vocally, an intolerable intrusion into the quiet living-room where a man and his family listen after supper. Kind friends must have told him this, for, the next time he spoke on the air, he had scaled his voice down, but in the effort had lost all expression, and sounded dull and lifeless, like a worried schoolmaster. He stuck at this stage for two or three more broadcasts. Then the day came when he had a theme so compelling that he forgot all about being scared or self-conscious, and gave an intimate, man-to-man account of what he had to say. The result was first-class, and since that day he has never looked back.

If a beginner shows uneasiness at the microphone, announcers and producers will often tell him to imagine that he is talking to a friend seated at the other side of the table. They bid him banish all thought of the listening millions, and use an intimate manner. The hard, scientific fact at the bottom of this is that the microphone, the receiving instrument, must hand to the transmitter exactly what it receives, and just as it receives it. In other words, although the broadcaster, sitting eighteen inches or two feet from the microphone, is invited to address an imaginary friend sitting eighteen inches or two feet on the far side of it, his voice will actually be heard over the air as if it came from only eighteen inches or two feet away. The listener will hear it at even closer quarters than would the friend.

What the Microphone Heard

Once, in a poetry programme to schools, a broadcaster wished to include a girl who is an accomplished speaker of verse. She had several times broadcast in adult programmes, but the schools people wished to hear special tests. Accordingly it was arranged that three speakers, the girl, an actor, and the giver of the talk, should make records of the same poems, and that these records should be played to a selected audience of schoolchildren. If they liked the girl's records, she would appear in the programme.

The party travelled to Bristol, made the records, and felt that they had all done rather well. When they came to play them over, however, they found to their astonishment that the girl's record showed a distinct lisp. The giver of the talk protested that something must be wrong with the machine. Then he saw that the girl had gone very pink.

"What is it?" he asked her.

"Well," she said, "as a matter of fact, before I went to the drama school, I used to lisp. That was one reason why my parents sent me there."

Now, why had the microphone picked up a defect of which those in the studio, all trained and critical listeners, heard no trace? Some broadcasters will tell you that the microphone has an uncanny power of detecting the innermost qualities not only of voice but of personality: that it can at once reveal any sort of insincerity or fake. They have a superstitious awe of it, and credit it with magical powers. Up to a point, they are right. The microphone can detect insincerity. It does reveal qualities and characteristics that are not apparent in ordinary intercourse. Take the case of the girl and the lisp. The microphone heard what the people in the studio failed to hear, not because it had any magical powers, but for the simple reason that it was much nearer to the girl's mouth than they were. It gave her sibilants to the record exactly as it received them, and the record passed them back.

Why had she lisped? Because she knew she was on trial: she was nervous, she felt insecure and therefore young, as if she were up before the headmistress; and the ghost of the old defect that belonged to her schooldays, before her voice had been trained, came back, not so clearly that it could be heard in the studio, but clearly enough to be caught and recorded by the mechanical listener a few inches from her lips. As soon as she realized this, she made the record again, this time without a trace of lisp. The children approved, she got her booking, and duly went on the air.

The writer stresses the reason for the lisp, as well as the lisp itself, because it shows how the microphone reveals not only vocal characteristics but the psychological reasons beneath them. It is indeed a character detector. It pitilessly shows up insincerity, self-distrust, patronage, propagandist intention, shyness, pretentiousness, and many

REHEARSAL FOR BROADCAST

Whereas in television the players are seen as on the stage, in the radio play they are wholly dependent on voice and sound effects. The studio rehearsal is therefore like an informal reading circle, the artistes giving their whole attention to their scripts.

other qualities: not because it is magical but because it is so close to the lips of the speaker that it catches every intonation, every subtle sign that all is not well with the spirit behind the voice.

This preamble brings us to the first requisite of the broadcaster. If the instrument into which he speaks is so close to him that it is in fact a lie-detector, if it will catch him out in any form of affectation or insincerity and betray him to the listener, then he dare not be anything but sincere in his approach to it. The first requisite of the broadcaster, then, is sincerity.

This holds good whatever is being done. The straight talk, the duologue, the discussion, the short story, the radio play, all

subject the speaker to the same test of closeness to the listener. What is more, that listener will be hearing the performance in circumstances that favour him, not the performer. Instead of being one of an excited audience in a hall or theatre, looking at the figure of the performer on stage or well-lit platform, where he or she is able to exploit every advantage of stature, looks, or dress, and stands in a frame specially designed for just such a display —where everything is in the performer's favour—the listener sits at home, in his favourite chair, surrounded by all the familiar objects that give him confidence and make him feel the better entitled to his own opinion, and the performer, shorn of all advantages, is obliged to rely on voice alone.

An apparent exception is the broadcast of a public speech, where the speaker is addressing an audience in a hall or dining-room, and is therefore obliged to use a public technique. But this is not a broadcast in the ordinary sense, because the aim is to give listeners the illusion that they are present, and all the sounds from the audience are broadcast as well as the speaker's voice. It is not a studio broadcast, under broadcasting conditions, but eavesdropping at a public occasion.

Importance of Sincerity

Years of listening have made the listener critical. He has become accustomed to listen not only to what is said but to the voice that says it: and, in the stronghold of his own home, he is seldom deceived. The broadcasters who can put a thing over with their tongue in their cheek are few indeed (and even so, there are thousands whom they cannot fool). In almost every case, they are experienced professional actors; but their path is most perilous, and the listeners who are not deceived say things about them which they would not care to hear. The only safe maxim is sincerity.

The rest of our space could be filled with instances of this, and broadcasters of quality all agree that there is no substitute for sincerity. The human voice is an instrument of the greatest sensitivity. Its influence is incalculable: and radio, by concentrating upon it and making it all-important, offers to the speaker whose voice is the true expression of his personality possibilities such as have never been known in human history. Every year must produce new broadcasters: each of these voices, truly expressing the speaker's personality, makes thousands upon thousands of listeners feel that that speaker is a friend.

One often hears a great deal about microphone technique, and about the special gifts of good broadcasters, but both gifts and technique boil down to sincerity and a direct approach to other human beings. The good broadcaster must like his fellow creatures, and be capable of warmth towards them, but above all he must put on no airs, he must mean what he says, and do unto the listener as he would himself be done by: that is, approach him honestly, on the level, with no reservation and with no ulterior motive. Given this basic honesty of appeal, the rest will be added unto him. No one would deny that there is much to learn, and that good broadcasters are made by practice, and need a lot of practice before they become consistently good. They learn with every broadcast, and, as in every art, the job is never learned completely. But the heart of it is sincerity.

At this point the reader who knows something of broadcasting might very reasonably ask a question. Sincerity may not be so hard to achieve in the talk, and the discussion—though here the need to keep the ball moving, and the desire to cover this or that point, can offer temptations—but what about the radio play, where the players, standing around the microphone in their everyday clothes, without the help of an audience have to achieve their effects?

Tempo in Broadcasting

Before attempting to answer this, it is necessary to mention an essential circumstance which governs all story-telling over the air, whether it be a one-person narrative or a play with a cast of fifty.

To read a passage aloud at a pace within the limits that are practicable and pleasant in broadcasting takes considerably longer than to read the same passage silently to oneself. Naturally, people vary greatly in the speed at which they read silently, but whenever the experiment has been made in public, the audience has seen that, even with the slowest of silent readers, it takes twice as long to read the chosen passage aloud, and in certain cases, with quick silent readers, five or six times as long. The reader's eye is faster than speech.

This means that, in order not to seem slow, the timing of the broadcast story has to be considerably speeded up. If broadcasting has made a reputation for a few story-tellers only, it is because most of our writers have been slow to grasp this fact. When it is pointed out to them, they are apt to retort that you can read aloud in your family circle a story written for the printed page, and nobody will complain because your voice does not go as fast as one can read by himself. Why, then, should broadcasting be an exception?

It is because the members of an audience, when someone is reading to them, have every encouragement to adapt themselves to the reader's pace. They have plenty to look at: there are pauses for laughter, and for the exchange of glances of appreciation. Moreover, they are very often homogeneous, members of a family circle, and the reader can wait while someone whispers to little Teddy the meaning of a word he hasn't understood, or repeats to Granny a point she has missed. But the radio storyteller has a huge, unsorted audience, listening to him under all sorts of conditions, and, if their attention once wanders from their sole link with the story, the narrator's voice, then they lose the thread and cease to be interested. It is far safer to write in such a way that their attention will be held, from the first word to the last, and the pace of the story will seem to them natural, that is, their own pace.

Importance of Climax

The principles of the radio short story can only be stated from experience gained in practice, since the form is still very young, and there is no body of theory to which the student can be referred. We may go no further than a few broad generalizations, tips which a practising broadcaster has learned from experience and found useful. They have been checked by the experiences of other broadcasters, and of successive short story editors at Broadcasting House, but they remain generalizations to be accepted with caution.

The first essentials of the radio story are a clear direction, an interest which does not swerve and is easy to follow, and something going on all the time to hold the listener's attention. Any brief failure to listen, which corresponds to skipping details of the printed story, is fatal to the broadcast. Attention once lost is very hard

to recapture. The "something going on" need not, of course, be physical. It can be the thoughts in a character's mind, it can be anything at all, provided that it continues the movement of the story towards its climax. For the radio story, climax is far more valuable than plot. Plot is of doubtful value. No less an authority than Hilton Brown, whose experience as author, editor, and producer of broadcast stories gives him a triple right to judge, declares himself against it. The reason is that, for the listener, a single strand of straightforward narrative is easier to follow than a number of interwoven strands tied up neatly at the end. The eye can sort these out in its rapid journey across the printed page, but the ear, receiving more slowly, is liable to get confused.

All the requirements of the radio story are dictated by the convenience of the ear. Thus it is unwise to have more than a few characters; and the dialogue should never include more voices than the reader can clearly distinguish. The more versatile he is, the more he can handle: and the power to differentiate the characters vocally will save a great deal of time and space. The pointers necessary on the printed page can be left out, once the characters have been established firmly in the listener's mind: ". . . he said," ". . . she repeated slowly," ". . . the Cockney bitterly complained," ". . . stammered Harry": none of these will be necessary. The speaker will supply them with his voice.

An even more obvious way of giving the required speed of narrative is to cut all descriptions to a minimum. Descriptions of characters should consist of a few quick strokes, sufficient to compel the listener to form an immediate mental picture. Descriptions of scene and atmosphere likewise should be quick and suggestive. Atmosphere is best conveyed through dialogue, where tone of voice can suggest more than any detailed account.

Style in Radio Story-telling

Throughout the story, the writing should be spare and athletic, with a preference for short sentences, and for main verbs over participles. A series of completed movements is easier to follow with the mind's eye than the linked and dependent verbs of the printed page. Where, in print, such a sentence as "Glancing to left and right, and stooping swiftly, he picked up the wallet" might be adequate; over the air "He glanced left and right: he stooped swiftly, and picked up the wallet" comes with greater vividness and force. This does not mean that the writing should be jerky, but that its movement should exactly match what it relates. It cannot have too much variety. The reader, who is going to hold a listener for a quarter of an hour or twenty minutes by his voice alone, wants all the help he can get to avoid that chief bane of the broadcaster—monotony.

Since the writer of a talk or short story is usually invited to broadcast it, it will be relevant to consider briefly the art of reading for radio. Sincerity is the fundamental quality, but, like several other fundamental qualities, it is not enough by itself. The world is full of passionately honest bores. Sincerity must be reinforced by art, or it may not get the broadcaster beyond a single broadcast, even one based on personal experience. The shepherd or stevedore who makes one memorable appearance at the microphone is often ineffective the second or third time. He can sound one note only, and he sounds it in the same way each time. There are a few broadcasters of genius, who from the very start of their careers cannot go wrong, but regular broadcasters are made as well as born: and the maker is experience—one's own, and that of a good producer.

Talks and Talks Production

Most voices are apt to sound monotonous after one has listened to them for a few minutes. The story-teller's problem, and even more, the straight talker's, is to avoid monotony without apparent recourse to technical devices. Let no one imagine that the use of technical devices impugns sincerity. The devices are necessary to make the sincerity effective. Every actor, speaker, singer, and executant must use them. A great many he will use naturally. Listen to any girl in a teashop telling her friends of the interview she has just had with the

head of her department. She will use a number of inflexions, she will hurry over parts of her story, she will slow up to emphasize the climax, she will imitate the voice of her superior delivering the rebuke, or whatever it was. There will be a great deal of art in her telling of the story, none the less art for being unconscious. Set her down in front of the microphone, ask her to tell her story again, and ten to one she will fail miserably. She will be self-conscious, tongue-tied. Even if one handed her an exact typescript of her story, taken down in shorthand, at the teashop she would read it lifelessly. In the same way, her teashop performance, even if she could repeat it exactly, would fail on the stage of a theatre or in the Albert Hall, for the simple reason that what was effective at close quarters would not carry and sound natural across the larger space. Art is necessary, in order to sound natural to people sitting fifty or five hundred feet away, as every actor knows: and art is necessary in order to sound natural over the air when one is reading from a script.

Informality and Variety

Here a good producer is invaluable. In the case of a talk, he will see first of all that the script *is* a talk: that is to say, that it is easy, colloquial, informal, broken, "don't" and "can't" taking the place of "do not" and "cannot," with repetitions, loosely connected sentences, hesitations, etc., and that it sounds as if it were being spoken rather than read. The reader, if he has any talent at all, will vary his emphasis by nature. He will be a little louder here, a little softer there. What he may not do by nature, what the producer may have to teach him, is to vary his pace. Even greater variety can be obtained by changes of pace than by changes of tone or volume. Beginners are often reluctant to believe this, and it can be one of the hardest lessons to learn, but it is vital to the broadcaster. The actor has movement and gesture to help him, the platform speaker has facial expression, but the broadcaster has only his voice, and dare not neglect any means to make it a more effective expression of the honest purpose that is in him.

The teller of a story has scope for far greater variety than the giver of a first-person talk, since he has several voices at his command, the voices of his characters: but the same rules govern him. And he, no less than the first person talker, must never forget that he depends on the producer. The producer can hear him, as he cannot hear himself, and, coming to the script with a fresh and practised eye, can see more in it than the writer. A good producer will double the value of any broadcast.

Play Dialogue for Radio

The radio play demands an even greater speed than the radio story. The speed of its dialogue is often a surprise even to the professional actor, and the amateur is left gasping. The reason for this, like every other point of radio technique, is a matter of common sense. Take a short piece of stage dialogue. The scene is a study, the characters father and son.

FATHER *is waiting alone in the study, standing in front of the fire, his face set ominously. A timid knock sounds on the door.*
FATHER: Come in!
(*Enter* SON. FATHER *glares at him fixedly.*)
SON: You wanted to see me, father?
FATHER: I did. And you know why. (SON *attempts to look bewildered.*) Hand over that letter.
SON: Letter, father?
FATHER: Yes. Letter. I know she has written to you. Hand it over at once.
SON: (*attempting a dignified front*) It is a private letter.
FATHER: Hand it over.
SON: I'd very much rather not.
FATHER: I'm waiting.
SON: You have no right.———
FATHER: (*roaring*) Hand it over, I say.
(SON, *with a miserable gesture of resignation, fumbles in his pocket; produces the letter; hesitates; then weakly extends it.* FATHER *snatches it from him, unfolds it, takes out his glasses, puts them on, and begins to read. After a couple of lines, his face swells with rage.*)
FATHER: What! did she dare to write this?

Now imagine this as part of a radio play. What must go? Obviously, all the gesture and facial expression: about two-thirds of the playing time. If the scene were played on the air as it would be on the stage, there would be gaps of such intolerable length between some of the lines that the listener would suppose something had gone wrong with his set. In the stage version, we have the faces and movements of the actors to watch. Over the air, we have only the voices to listen to. Therefore the lines follow one another very quickly, with only the smallest of pauses where a pause is needed: for example, to mark the son's reluctance to hand the letter over, and to allow father time to open and read it.

The range of the radio play is enormous. Its only limits are those of the hearer's imagination. It has no scenery, it can go anywhere, and represent anything. Its scenes can be as short as you like, and as numerous. It is subject to none of the mechanical considerations of space which limit the stage play. It calls for a bigger effort from its audience, since it can appeal to them through one sense only: and it imposes a heavy strain upon its players. Not only can they generate no visual illusion—which, after all, should not hamper them much, trained as they are to use their imagination—but it deprives them of that mysterious electric contact with their audience which is life to the stage player; and it gives them little if any chance to work up any warmth of emotion among themselves. Standing at the microphone, in their everyday clothes, reading their script, they are thrown upon their own resources even more than is the film actor.

Small wonder, then, if many actors maintain that far greater care must be given to voice on the air than on the stage.

Television

Now—television. Everything we have been considering applies, with little modification, to television. True, the performers are not so close to their audience, and not quite so close to the microphone, as in broadcasting: but they are still close. They still need the special power to appear

natural at close quarters. The slightest
attempt to project, to "put across" as in
the theatre, is still fatal. They are far too
close for any of the tricks, any of the
technical devices which are not only
successful but necessary on platform or
stage.

The same basic sincerity, the same degree
of control over voice and inflection are
therefore essential in television as in
broadcasting. But television adds a fresh
hazard. The performer is not only being
heard at close quarters: he is being
watched. He must control not only his
voice but his whole body. He must make
no movement which does not point and
illustrate what he is saying.

A certain young actor was appearing in
one of Shakespeare's Roman plays at the
Old Vic. He gave his big speech splendidly
—but no one really listened to it. The
actor was wearing sandals, and in the
excitement of the big speech his two big
toes were jerking involuntarily and standing up on end. The attention of the whole
audience was focused on those hapless
toes, with disastrous effect to the speech.
An actor must make no involuntary movement. If in the big spaces of a theatre such
movement is distracting, in the close-up of
the television screen it would be quite fatal.
Even a panel member could embarrass and
annoy with a nervous trick, an uncontrolled
movement.

What we have said about sound radio,
therefore, applies to television: and television has peculiar needs of its own. What
extra burdens does it lay on those who
work for it?

Here let us once more get down to bed-
rock and consider the essentials of writing
for the television screen. We shall find that
writing for the screen has much in common
with writing for the air, but that television
has extra and very stringent needs.

The basic thing to remember about
television is its one enormous difference
from cinema, which at first sight it
resembles. Whereas the scenes in a film
may be shot in any order, and each played
many times until cast and director, sound
and camera men are satisfied, in television
the action is continuous and everything has

to be physically possible in time as well as
in space.

For example, let us imagine a play in
which one employee of a firm, Harry, has
told another, George, that the boss, Mr.
Smith, has made a certain statement about
him.

GEORGE: (*springing to his feet*) I don't
believe a word you say. I'm
going straight to Mr. Smith to
ask him if it is true.

Now, quite obviously, the audience will
expect to see George go into Mr. Smith's
office and put his question. They will be
all agog to hear Harry's lie shown up—if it
is a lie—and see how Mr. Smith reacts.
The writer's job is clear. We may expect
him to continue like this:

MEDIUM SHOT.   INTERIOR, MR. SMITH'S
OFFICE.   Mr. Smith is *seated at his desk,
reading a report. A knock at the door.*

MR. SMITH: (*frowning*) Come in.
(*Enter* GEORGE)

GEORGE: Excuse me, Sir, for disturbing
you like this. But. . . .

Fine—provided that the set representing
Mr. Smith's office is literally adjacent to the
set in which George was talking to Harry,
so that, in two or three seconds, the actor
playing George can leave Harry and go in
to see Mr. Smith. If, on the other hand,
Mr. Smith's office is set up in another
studio, the writer must somehow fill the
gap of time which will enable the actor
playing George to sprint from one point in
space to the other, and arrive not obviously
out of breath.

If a personal reminiscence may be
allowed—only because it illustrates a
technical hazard of television—the writer
was once appearing in a programme with
the distinguished actresses Thea Holme and
Sylvia Coleridge. The programme consisted of a series of short scenes on the
general theme of young women in love.
The climax of one scene left Sylvia
Coleridge at the far end of the studio. She
had, as quickly as possible, to change
costume, and rejoin me at the other end so
that I could ask her what the pair of them
were going to show us next. In the meantime I had to hold the screen, writing lines
for myself that would fill up the time

before she reached me, and walked into shot to receive my question.

We worked out a precision drill, pace by pace, whereby she was met at the far end of the studio by dresser A, who took hat and feather boa and handed her part of her new costume, which she put on while walking to dresser B, a third of the way down. Dresser B helped with a further exchange: Miss Coleridge walked to dresser C, who gave the finishing touches, after which she had only four paces more to make, and I could put my question.

Careful rehearsal of her moves and my lines made our timing accurate. But, when we came to the transmission, conditions were different. The distances were correct to the inch—but the floor space was no longer clear. Between dressers A and B stood a camera, between B and C cables and a clutch of buckets and miscellaneous gear. Thus the actress had to make a couple of detours, clambering round these obstacles, and, by the time I had reached the end of my carefully timed lines, she was little more than halfway down, and signalling eloquently. I could not gape open-mouthed into the camera: the producer could not have a blank screen. There was nothing for it but to gag and somehow go on talking until an inwardly agitated but outwardly serene Miss Coleridge appeared at my side. Seldom have I been so glad to see anyone!

I mention this experience only because it rams home the basic truth that in television

everything has to be physically possible.

As to the technical demands on actor or speaker, they are covered by the essential rule we stated at the start: the ability to judge exactly their distance from the audience and to perform in terms of it. The demands on sincerity are heavy. Any kind of affectation is at once shown up. There is a further limitation, imposed by the conditions in which most viewing is done. Flamboyant and exhibitionistic playing which would be all right in a theatre, in public, can be very much out of place in a private sitting room, and cause embarrassment to a family grouped round the set. Some stage favourites fail dismally on the television screen because they cannot get used to their reduced distance from their audience, cannot scale their performance down, cannot shed the technical devices which have brought them success in the theatre but destroy all illusion on the screen. I have heard an actor say that television combines the worst features of stage and film. Let us say that no medium hitherto has imposed greater difficulties on those who work for it.

At all events, try as they may, those who appear on the television screen cannot hide their real selves from their audience. They and the broadcaster can be welcome in millions of homes. They can make a legion of friends who trust them. It is their task and their privilege to be faithful to that trust, and to give their best to their unseen audience.

Test Yourself

1. What quality is most desirable in a speaker's voice while broadcasting?
2. What are the prime needs of a radio story?
3. "The range of the radio play is enormous: it is not a strictly limited type." Give reasons for this statement.

Answers will be found at the end of the book.

TWENTIETH-CENTURY POET

Edith Sitwell, together with her brothers, Osbert and Sacheverell, were perhaps the most talked-of poets of the 'twenties. Edith Sitwell's poems struck her contemporaries as owing little to tradition. They were forceful attempts to communicate sensations through the sheer originality of her metaphors and other imagery.

CHAPTER XXIII
LITERATURE AND MODERN LIFE

WHY do we want to read a novel or see a play? We may have many superficial and variable reasons, such as personal interest in the author or in a particular actor or actress, but the main reason is always the same: our deep-seated craving to live other lives than our own, to go through experiences which will never come our way or which (if we are young) we may try to seek out if they appeal to us.

Muddle-headed people condemn this as reprehensible, as liable to make us unfit to face the hard facts of our own condition; and the books and plays and films that indulge this craving most completely are labelled "escapist." Of course, emotionally false, silly, and sentimental stories deserve this condemnation, just as any other kind of book does which is bad or silly; but real literature, and that is what is being written about, though it may well be "escapist" in the sense that it takes us away from the narrow bounds of our own lives, is more likely to fit us to live than reduce us, as drugs do (and drugs are truly escapist), to total incapacity so that we merely become a burden for other more serious and hard-working people to shoulder. The craving to live other lives than our own through literature is a healthy craving; any writer who satisfies it is one of the most valuable members of society. The greater such a writer is, the less didactic will his aim be, and the more completely will he be inspired by the desire to portray the truth about life as he sees it; to tell us what happens when certain actions take place under certain circumstances, which we ourselves have not the experience and observation, or the power of imagination, to follow to their end without his help.

You may say it sounds rather dry and clinical, but no great play or story can ever be that, because it is not a report but a representation; and when it deals with human passions will represent those passions, so we have the illusion of actually taking part in the action and being left with certain conclusions of heart and mind which no mere description could give us. The factual truth about, say, a battle at sea can be contained in the driest of Admiralty *communiqués*, but for the other kind of truth we must go to a book like C. S. Forester's *The Ship*. A police report of the murders in the last scene of *Hamlet* would have sounded very different from Shakespeare's immortal drama, and would have had an incomparably smaller effect on us.

Shelley's View of Literature

For an effect a great story or play certainly does have on us, though very different from the effect of a book like *Mein Kampf*, or even something far nobler, such as Darwin's *Origin of Species*. This is fairly easy to understand in the case of a story or play, but it is rather more difficult when the work of literature in question is a poem. Shelley, who saw far more deeply into the springs of life and art than most of those who dismiss him as an "ineffectual angel," has some wonderfully illuminating words on the subject in his *Defence of Poetry*, words which can refer equally well to other forms of literature. "Poetry," said Shelley, "awakens and enlarges the mind by rendering it the receptacle of a thousand unapprehended combinations of thought. . . . The great secret of morals is love; or a going out of our own nature, and an identification of ourselves with the beautiful which exists in thought, action or person, not our own. A man, to be greatly good, must imagine intensely and comprehensively; he must put himself in the place of another and of many others; the pains and pleasures of his species must become his own. The great instrument of moral good is the imagination; and poetry administers to the effect by acting on the cause. . . . It exceeds all imagination to conceive what would have been the moral condition of the world if neither Dante, Petrarch, Boccaccio,

345

Chaucer, Shakespeare, Calderon, Lord Bacon, nor Milton had ever existed."

The plays of Shakespeare scarcely give us any practical information at all—the simplest handbook on electricity gives us more—nor do they directly instruct us how to behave in a way that any teacher of ethics would recognize; but they endow us with the vision from which we can draw our own conclusions about behaviour and about what is worth striving for in life, and in so doing give us something of far more ultimate value than the scientific handbooks.

The action of art—of literature—on our lives is almost impossible to trace or measure precisely because the effect lies in the most hidden parts of our nature and becomes the very climate of our mental life; but it is probable that the influence of English literature in general, and Shakespeare in particular (because he is the most richly endowed of all English writers), on the pattern of our actions and the background of our desires and judgments, and therefore on the course of English history, is more profound than that of any book of instruction or theory, however loudly its name resounds in the ears of contemporaries

Writer and Society

This is an important point to make when we are considering modern literature and its relation to our lives, because we live in a time in which clear thinking about art and propaganda is particularly necessary. Shakespeare is entirely without propaganda —he never breaks off, as Tolstoy does, to preach socialism, or anything else, at us— but we must not forget that some of the greatest English writers have had a direct effect on the social conditions of their day. Dickens is a case in point. There is no doubt at all that the revelations of social negligence, injustice and cruelty that Dickens made in his novels profoundly stirred the conscience of his contemporaries and helped to bring about the great reforms of the later Victorian Age. Some people would say that Dickens, like Tolstoy, too often forgot the artist in the preacher; and yet surely Dickens would not have had this extraordinarily powerful and immediate effect if he had not been a great artist before

anything else, whose characters live as human beings and not merely as wooden figures of his indignation. That he helped to abolish much squalor and misery that had grown up in the teeming cities of the industrial revolution was a secondary effect; today, he still exercises his sway over us as a great artist.

Where Life Leads Literature Follows

English literature is so rich, there have been authors of such giant stature in this country in the past six hundred years, that one might well be forgiven for wondering whether there was anything left to add to what they have said, or what the function of a poet or novelist today could be. But this would be to misunderstand the way the creative imagination works. Nothing is ever said completely, and even the cleverest description or definition leaves something out. Shakespeare's contemporaries felt that there was more to be told about life than he had managed to put into his plays, and they were right; John Ford is not so great a writer as Shakespeare, but he added something to literature, he did not just repeat as a clever imitator would have done. And if this happens even in a great writer's lifetime, how much more likely it is to happen as the decades pile up above his tomb. The outward circumstances of life change, at one period of history slower and at another faster, but they never remain fixed; and each new scene not only makes its predecessor appear rather old-fashioned but brings its own problems and interests with it.

But this does not mean that the writer of an earlier age is dead as soon as a new writer of sufficient talent emerges. Shakespeare has never died, except during the Civil Wars when the theatres were closed, and even then it is probable that he was diligently read in many a town and country house. But it does mean that without a contemporary literature even the appreciation of past literature may languish, because the stimulus of the "thousand unapprehended combinations of thought" of which Shelley spoke is absent. Again, language itself is constantly changing, old words lose their original meaning or drop out of use, and new words and metaphors are drafted into writing from common speech; and this also creates a demand for a new literature, for how can it gain its full effect unless it speaks with the voice of our own day? One should, however, beware of imagining that literature must slavishly follow the changes (perhaps corruptions) of language that arise elsewhere: great writers, to an extent that will never be exactly defined, control and create these changes of language themselves.

World After War

When the changes, both of the outward circumstances of life and of language, are very rapid and complex, literature is apt to become unstable, fragmentary, over-experimental, or to seek refuge in deliberately protracted archaism. The years between 1914 and today have been an example of such a period, perhaps the most extreme example in all history, and, as we might expect, our literature has produced a bewildering mixture of theories, experiments, styles, ideals and allegiances; a critic can do little more than point to the outstanding figures and the most firmly marked lines of development, and plead for the indulgence of his readers if, ten years hence, what now appears quite a small and insignificant plant should show the lustiest growth and the richest blossoms. It might, for instance, have been difficult for a critic at the end of the 1914-18 war to gauge how important certain writers, little known until then from an unassuming output, were rapidly to become, stealing the limelight first in advanced intellectual circles, and then, in wider masses of the reading public, from such writers as H. G. Wells, Bernard Shaw, John Galsworthy and Arnold Bennett, the established giants of the first two decades of the century.

At that period, could he foresee how explosive a book of essays called *Eminent Victorians* by Lytton Strachey, known only before the war for a small though excellent primer, *Landmarks in French Literature*, was to be in changing not only the attitude of the educated public towards the great figures of the previous century, but also the whole conception of how a biography

BIOGRAPHER OF ORIGINALITY
Lytton Strachey, whose treatment of famous "lives" revolutionized modern biography.

should be written? How a young Irishman, James Joyce, who had published during the war a book of short stories, *Dubliners*, and an autobiographical novel, *Portrait of the Artist as a Young Man*, both notable for a power of psychological penetration and artistic subtlety more in the French than the English tradition, was suddenly with his third book, *Ulysses*, to create an intellectual sensation (and a moral scandal) through the whole of the English-speaking world, among whom only very tiny circles had ever heard of him before? How a poet by the name of T. S. Eliot, born in New England but with a mind steeped in all the greatest poetry of the European tradition, who had published one small book called *Prufrock* in 1917, which contained poems blending an unusual realism and irony with a strong nostalgic romanticism, was a few years later to revolutionize the course of modern poetry and claim the allegiance of almost the whole of the younger intelligentsia with his long poem *The Waste Land*? Or how a tiny collection of sketches and stories called *Monday or Tuesday* by Virginia Woolf, who had previously written two novels, both distinguished and sensitive pieces of work, but not very different in total effect from the ordinary novels of the day, was to be the forerunner of a series of novels which broke almost every accepted rule of novel-making and opened up possibilities for the writer of prose fiction which no one before her would have believed to be the province of anyone but a poet?

The New Attacks the Old

Virginia Woolf herself attacked the methods and assumptions of Bennett, Wells and their school in her famous pamphlet, *Mr. Bennett and Mrs. Brown*, and continued the attack in an article entitled *Modern Fiction* (reprinted in *The Common Reader* in 1925) which also provided an important elucidation of her own work to come.

"Admitting," she wrote, "the vagueness which afflicts all criticism of novels, let us hazard the opinion that for us at this moment the form of fiction most in vogue now often misses rather than secures the thing we seek. Whether we call it life or spirit, truth or reality, this, the essential thing, has moved off, or on, and refuses to be contained any longer in such ill-fitting vestments as we provide. . . . So much of the enormous labour of proving the solidity, the likeness to life, of the story is not merely labour thrown away but labour misplaced to the extent of obscuring and blotting out the light of the conception. . . . Life is not a series of gig-lamps symmetrically arranged; life is a luminous halo, a semi-transparent envelope surrounding us from the beginning of consciousness to the end. Is it not the task of the novelist to convey this varying, this unknown and uncircumscribed spirit, whatever aberration or complexity it may display, with as little mixture of the alien and external as possible? We are not pleading merely for courage and sincerity; we are suggesting that the proper stuff of fiction is a little other than custom would have us believe it."

Here, then, was a great wave of dissatisfaction breaking over the literary shore in the years immediately following the first World War; and the interesting point to observe is that, though an element of *rebellion* unites all the new writers who

were making their name, there is a very distinct difference between the urbane mockery of human pretensions, the Voltairian note characteristic of Aldous Huxley's novels, of Lytton Strachey's historical and literary studies, and the spiritual inwardness of James Joyce and Virginia Woolf; between the gay romanticism and childlike freshness of Edith Sitwell's poems and the intellectual obscurities, the vast apparatus of erudition, underlying T. S. Eliot's *The Waste Land*; between any of these writers and D. H. Lawrence, with his increasing preoccupation with an anti-rational sex-mysticism which gradually dissolved the gift for poetic description and the subtle sense of character of his early novels into the interminable inchoate preachifyings of a book like *The Plumed Serpent*.

Such writers were united in little except their dissatisfaction, their feeling that the violently dislocated conditions of their time demanded a new attitude of mind and a remodelled framework of art in which to express itself; and so powerful was the expression of their dissatisfaction that they made the many other writers, poets and novelists and essayists who pursued the "even tenour of their way," seem insignificant and out of harmony with the temper of their age.

Writers of the 'Thirties

Scarcely, however, had this wave fallen crashing on the beaches, when it was followed by a second wave of dissatisfaction and iconoclasm. The change can be aptly gauged by a comparison of what Virginia Woolf was saying about her immediate predecessors in *Modern Fiction* and what, fifteen years or so later, she was saying about the new school of writers, her potential successors. "If you read current literary journalism," she writes in *The Leaning Tower*, published during the first year of the second World War, "you will be able to rattle off a string of names—Day, Lewis, Auden, Spender, Isherwood, Louis MacNeice and so on. They adhere much more closely than the names of their predecessors. But at first sight there seems little difference, in station, in education. Mr. Auden in a letter to Mr. Isherwood

AUDEN AND ISHERWOOD

Following rather the tradition of Jonson's satiric comedies than that of the romantic dramas of the eighteenth and nineteenth centuries, W. H. Auden (left) and Christopher Isherwood (right) criticize modern society in a play such as "The Dog Beneath the Skin."

says: 'Behind us we have stucco suburbs and expensive educations.' They are 'tower dwellers' like their predecessors, the sons of well-to-do parents who could afford to send them to public schools and universities. But what a difference in the tower itself, in what they saw from the tower! When they looked at human life, what did they see? Everywhere change, everywhere revolution. . . . Even in England towers that were built of gold and stucco were no longer steady towers. They were leaning towers. The books were written under the influence of change, under the threat of war. . . . They feel compelled to preach, if not by their living, at least by their writing, the creation of a society in which everyone is equal and everyone is free. It explains the pedagogic, the didactic, the loudspeaker strain that dominates their poetry. . . . The poet is a dweller in two worlds, one dying, the other struggling to be born. And so

we come to what is perhaps the most marked tendency of leaning-tower literature—the desire to be whole, to be human. 'All that I would like is to be human'— that cry rings through their books—the longing to be closer to their kind, to write the common speech of their kind, to share the emotions of their kind, no longer to be isolated and exalted in solitary state upon their tower, but to be down on the ground with the mass of human kind."

Virginia Woolf, one cannot help thinking, puts her finger on the central cause of the dissatisfactions that led to the emergence of these new authors, when she says that they were writing under the threat of war. In this precisely lay the difference between them and her own generation, the chief conditioning circumstance for whom was that they were writing after the experience of war. The cataclysm of 1914-18 seemed to most intellectuals to come out

DYLAN THOMAS

Son of a Swansea schoolmaster, Dylan Thomas was a reporter before he won fame with "Eighteen Poems" (1934), "Thirty-one Poems" (1936) and "Deaths and Entrances" (1946). It was, however, the posthumous broadcast of his dramatic poem "Under Milk Wood" in 1954 that brought his work to the notice of the wider world.

of a clear sky, and the misery and horror that it engendered in four years was something that they could never have imagined. In one way or another they were trying to create some counterbalancing world in art to the political and economic world of their time which produced such nightmares in reality: Virginia Woolf by a concentration on the inner life of the individual; Lytton Strachey and D. H. Lawrence by knocking away the intellectual and spiritual foundations of the nineteenth-century outlook (a task, one should not forget, made easier by the destructive dramatic wit of Bernard Shaw, which had begun its work many years before), the one by discreet ridicule and an appeal to the eighteenth-century virtues of tolerance, reason, and what might be called enlightened sensuality, the other by trying to substitute a worship of sex, a cult of the obscure primal instincts for what seemed a moribund Christianity;

and T. S. Eliot, on an opposite course, by a return to the ordered central tradition of a Christian and classical Europe.

The significant fact, however, about the new group of writers was that they began to emerge just when the post-war balance of civil and international peace was showing itself to be extremely precarious. The key date is 1929, when the boom collapsed in the United States, a collapse which reproduced itself gradually through the whole of the rest of the world (except the U.S.S.R.), bringing, especially in Central Europe, ruin to a large section of the middle classes, mass unemployment to the working classes, and the rise of extremist political parties, exploiting frustration and misery.

Social Consciousness and Criticism

The early poems of Auden and Spender, and Day Lewis's *From Feathers to Iron* (which showed such a decided break with his earlier work), were all published between 1929 and 1933; and in 1932 the anthology *New Signatures* appeared, in which a number of other young writers were grouped with these three and presented as a new school with certain aims in common the chief of which, the editor's preface maintained, was a desire not to withdraw from the wider social scene, but to extend their consciousness of it as far as possible. Much was made of their awareness of the machine in modern life; this awareness was not, as a matter of fact, to be found in more than a few of them, but it is interesting to note that political consciousness was still well in the background, though the anti-war theme could already be heard. In the next few years, however, as the condition of civilization rapidly worsened, social criticism and revolutionary partisanship grew louder and more dominant in their work. Auden's masque, *The Dance of Death*, Spender's long poem, *Vienna*, Day Lewis's book, *The Magnetic Mountain*, reveal a confident and at times brutally impatient revolutionary fervour. At the same time Christopher Isherwood was writing his stories of the Central European scene, where the clash between the old world and the new seemed to appear at its most naked; and Rex Warner and Edward

Upward were applying fantasy and allegory to the criticism of capitalist society.

By the time the civil war broke out in Spain, this political impulse, which had its deepest roots in the idea that only revolutionary action could stave off the international war that loomed ever nearer, had become so strong and so widespread among intellectuals of every kind, that it was possible to hold international conferences of a large proportion of the world's most distinguished writers to consider concerted anti-fascist action in connexion with Spain. Several of the younger writers from Britain went off to take up arms on behalf of the Republicans, and two of the most gifted, John Cornford and Ralph Fox, were among the many British sympathizers killed in action.

Retreat from Politics

In the Spanish Civil War the movement reached its zenith. As it became more and more evident that the Republicans were facing defeat, disillusionment began to set in; not simply disappointment, but a deeper feeling that the issues were more complex than had appeared on the surface, and that the idealism of writers had been in many ways unscrupulously exploited in an old-fashioned game of power politics. The writers began to reflect that they had not done themselves any particular good by their partisanship of what now seemed not so much a liberal cause as rather a narrowly organized political creed and had perhaps neglected their true duty as artists —to produce works of permanent value— in favour of ephemeral effusions and pamphleteering. When war with Germany broke out in September, 1939, the ebb was complete, except among those who had always been politicians first and artists second. Whatever the individual political views of writers have been, their politics have scarcely intruded into their writings since 1939; and even the patriotic note, which might have rapidly become strident after 1940 in a less mature and balanced civilization than Britain's, has been remarkable for its reticence.

There has been given here only the sketchiest survey of the development of English literature between the two wars; but inadequate as it is, it should at least prove that literature is profoundly affected by political, social and economic conditions, and especially by the speed at which those conditions change. But this is not the same thing as saying that the relationship is always easy to trace or present at all in some writers of the period. In the work of the Welsh poet, Dylan Thomas, for instance, we find a strange, "apocalyptic vision" with many personal symbols and few traces of the new scientific theories and techniques, new political and religious creeds, that so greatly possessed his contemporaries.

Nothing wears out more quickly than any form of propaganda in works of art; and when moral or political indignation in a community reaches the point where writers are deeply affected by it, the danger always arises that the richer and more permanent qualities in their work will be lost sight of as soon as their advocacy of a particular party, or formula of reform or salvation, is out of date. Already today many of the so-called communist poems of Auden, Day Lewis, Spender and MacNeice seem dated and superficial, and sometimes even slightly hysterical; luckily all four of them are poets of an altogether deeper inspiration, and those poems in particular in which what Virginia Woolf called their "desire to be whole, to be human" is most poignantly expressed are likely to survive far beyond the angry and divided years in which they were written, when the warring political ideologies and the rival claims of priest and psycho-analyst are a matter only for the study of the curious historian.

Fashions Outgrown

Already some of the debunking of great figures in the nineteenth century, the ancestor-ridicule in which the followers of Lytton Strachey joined with such zest, seems childish and tiresome; the incoherent sex-mysticism which D. H. Lawrence preached with such dedicated zeal in his later novels is so tedious to modern taste that it may carry with it into oblivion all that is beautiful and powerfully imagined in a highly original author; already the insistence on the terminology of modern psychiatry in certain novelists and playwrights is making them seem as old-fashioned as women's hats of the 'twenties, and the discovery is being made that almost all Freud can be found in Shakespeare— except the jargon; already the more extreme experiments in language and typography that caused a sensation in their day and brought small writers to big head-lines have passed, and left only the most faintly perceptible impression on the poets and novelists of the 'forties.

One cannot deny that the canvassing of what may be either the fashions and stunts of the day or urgent topical issues may provide a stimulus for both writer and reader out of which more significant literature and a greater readiness to assimilate it may develop; but it is rather those changes which proceed in a slower and more fundamental way that leave the more permanent mark on literature. And it is doubtful that any one would hesitate to point to the shifts in class structure, the spread of popular education (with the rise of a powerful popular Press which has followed it so swiftly), and the growth of American civilization, as the most important of these for us, and our language.

New Importance of Dialogue

In the fiction written in recent years, one of the most notable changes has been the development in the use of dialogue; in the stories and novels of J. B. Priestley, Christopher Isherwood, Graham Greene, V. S. Pritchett, Henry Green, Evelyn Waugh, and Walter Allen, all gifted and established practitioners of their art today, and in the work of many others who have risen to some prominence more recently, dialogue plays an increasingly important part: not only does it occupy a far greater proportion of the whole than in the past, but it is used, where description would have been used twenty-five years ago, for subtleties of characterization and atmosphere, for setting the tone and pace of an action; and it has become much more athletic in the process, it moves faster and with more point, and though these new qualities too often degenerate into a highly

mannered convention of "colloquialism," as smooth and as dull as the surface of a skyscraper, it has nevertheless given the novel a new vitality. This development of dialogue has been unmistakably accelerated by transatlantic examples, in particular by the novels of Ernest Hemingway.

American Novels and Modern Journalism

The modern American novel must also be held responsible in some degree for a kind of "levelling" that has been going on in fiction over here. This levelling is by no means characteristic of all prominent novelists; such women novelists as Ivy Compton-Burnett, Elizabeth Bowen and Rosamond Lehmann can produce effects both of style and of psychology that demand, as the writing of Henry James and Virginia Woolf demanded, a highly trained literary sense and the finest sensibility for their appreciation. Their background is still that of the cultured middle class and what remains of the aristocracy; but the scene that Graham Greene, for instance, in *Brighton Rock* or V. S. Pritchett in *Sense of Humour* introduces is one where the working classes and lower middle classes merge; and their aim in style would seem to be simplicity rather than complexity, however much art that simplicity may conceal. American influence, of course, is only part of the story: the increasing range of state-aided education, which has made far greater masses than ever before capable of appreciating something more than blood-and-thunder and the crude ballad; the gradual dissolution of the more extreme class barriers, which has been speeded up by both wars in a sensational way; and the power of the popular Press, have all played their role.

The influence of the Press has worked in two ways: it has helped to produce that almost completely modern phenomenon of "reportage," a kind of writing somewhere between journalism and fiction, seeking to give the information of the one with some of the colour and freedom of the other; and it has given the man who has chosen the writing of stories and novels as his career the possibility of a vast audience for whom he can write if he is ready to make the stuff of his art out of their background, their experiences and their language. It could be plausibly maintained that the cinema also has helped in the levelling process, and has affected the novel in other important ways; but that is a subject still large and obscure. . . .

Guardian of Spiritual Values

What critic would dare, at this point, to attempt to assess the full impact of the great cataclysm of society, through which we have lived since 1939, on the arts? It has accelerated the social and economic changes which, as the writer has endeavoured to show, are bound to have their effect on both the matter and the manner of imaginative literature if not on the judgment of its ultimate worth. It has given the writer great opportunities at the same time as it has confronted him with great dangers. If novelists and poets seemed only too often (though for reasons beyond their control) to have failed to rise to the stature of their opportunities, they at least withstood the temptations of propaganda that were presented to them in a new form—that of national unity. They showed that a writer can be, as an ordinary citizen, a loyal and courageous patriot, while in his art he continued to claim the right to voice the minority protest, to depict the unpopular misfit, to reflect doubt and fear if they are part of the truth, and to turn his eyes away altogether from the contemporary scene. The free play of the imagination and of the speculative mind are the essentials of a vital culture; and without a vital culture no country can remain great.

It is indeed those writers whose work during the past decade shows only the indirect influence of the war, if any at all, who seem to dominate the scene at the moment, and in particular the two poets T. S. Eliot and Edith Sitwell. It is impossible to estimate the loss to our cultural life if, instead of producing *Four Quartets* and *Green Song*, Mr. Eliot and Miss Sitwell had felt it incumbent on them (as might well have happened in other countries) to indite appeals to patriotism and, in elevated verse, report acts of heroism in the field. Silence, again, is a negative quality, but if E. M. Forster had filled the silence he maintained (as far as fiction is concerned) throughout the war with some tale, let us say, of German brutality avenged by invading British troops, the admiration and respect in which the author of those two great novels, *Howard's End* and *A Passage to India*—novels which have profoundly and often imperceptibly influenced so many writers of the last quarter of a century—is so generally held would not have been increased and might well have been diminished.

The word is a power, perhaps the greatest power of all; the function of the creative writer is not to serve the narrow political end or the fleeting topical fashion, but to be the guardian of those spiritual values which are the basic fabric of our civilization. If the hideous Nazi dream has done nothing else of constructive value, it has at least taught us again with painful insistence that culture is not a luxury but a necessity; that when a European people loses faith in those ways of life and values in judgment which have been built up through centuries out of our Christian and classical heritage, not a saviour but seven devils may enter in to lead them—to perdition.

Test Yourself

1. What was the main effect of the First World War on writers? What was the effect of the period leading up to the Second World War?

2. What element in fiction has been most remarkably developed in recent years?

Answers will be found at the end of the book.

ELL—M

GUIDE TO FURTHER STUDY

THE voyage of discovery through English literature is a journey everybody must make for himself. First-hand experience is the only sort that has any value. A book is good when you find it so; until then it is only thought to be good by other people. What is suggested here for reading is what other people have enjoyed, but you must form your own opinions and be prepared to follow your own interests. Ask yourself what each author you read is trying to do, and, if you remain unsure, try to find out about the author and his aims from one of the books mentioned as assistants to study. Having grasped the author's intentions, estimate his success and try to see how he has set about doing what he aimed at doing.

The ground you cover will depend, of course, on the time you spend. Each reader desiring an outline of further study can plan his own timetable and read as much or as little as he chooses. You will see, however, that the "Guide to Further Study" has been divided for convenience into nine parts or sections, and you would do well to think of these as covering broadly three subjects which can easily be studied together because they furnish parallel courses:

English Language . . Part 1
English Literature . . Parts 2-8
English Prose and the Art
 of Writing . . . Part 9

Of these three subjects English Literature requires most time and reading. Hence for convenience it has been divided into Parts 2 to 8 of the outline, any one of which will lead you into a more intensive study of some particular period or aspect of English Literature. If you have used this book to give yourself the broad background, you can feel free to follow up whatever part or aspect of English Literature interests you most. Indeed, it is better to investigate one or two of the periods thoroughly than attempt to skim through the entire course.

Part 1—The Study of Language

Language is our link with one another; but it is more. We learn to think by trying to make our meaning absolutely clear to other people, and we extend our experience by listening to what others have to tell us. Our minds develop through practice in expressing our ideas and perceptions fully and accurately: that is the benefit of the discipline of writing. But we also need to enlarge our experience by sharing that of others, which is transmitted to us in words, either spoken or written.

The study of anything so fundamental to all the processes of civilization, from the lowest to the highest, could well fill a lifetime. But the study of language is seldom an end in itself. It is language at work that is interesting and important. Hence to attempt to study language to a timetable or schedule would be a hard and sterile task. Rather should one be conscious of it all the time. Opportunity is constant. The material is all around you —in everyday chatter, in the newspapers, in the books. . . . We are constantly using language ourselves and hearing other people use it. All that requires training is our power of observation. Once our curiosity has been aroused, the habit of noticing tricks of speech will grow: it is fascinating. Every time an unusual word or expression is uttered we shall find ourselves pricking up our ears.

As we grow more experienced at word-watching, we shall turn common expressions over in our minds and stop in the middle of formulating a phrase to wonder how it came into existence and whether it says just what we want it to say. Language is not static; it is always changing. One reason for this is because the people using it try to make it convey their own shades of meaning, born of new and unique experiences. The commonest words and

354

expressions have histories behind them; they have developed their meanings, they have changed their meanings; and they will go on developing and changing as does the life of the people using them.

The observation of language at work can be carried on to some extent all the time. Conversation is generally too rapid and too preoccupied with practical considerations to allow much time for analysis, but reading provides better opportunities. Every now and then you will come across a word or expression that seems a little unusual. Try to find out more about it. The indispensable companion to intelligent reading is a good dictionary. The best reference book is the New English or Oxford Dictionary. It records the different meanings of all recognized English words; tells us when they first acquired those meanings and where they came from in the first place. It gives copious examples to show the words in action. The student, who is unlikely to possess a set himself because of its size and expense, should, however, discover one in a convenient reference library and make regular expeditions to it with lists of words about which he wants further information. The words to be looked up should be related to their contexts, which should be compared with the examples quoted in the Oxford Dictionary. This will reveal the length of time the word has been used in such circumstances, how it has gradually changed its meaning in the course of history and where it came from in the first instance.

Like all other types of purposeful observation, this continuous interest in the ways of words, which should accompany all one's reading and writing, requires a little preliminary training. It is well to spend a month or so reading a few books on language in general and then to go on to a course of study of the development of English in particular. An interesting book to start with is Sir Richard Paget's *Human Speech. Some Observations as to the Nature, Origin, Purpose and Possible Improvements of Human Speech*, 1930. This probably contains more than the beginner can digest, but he can perceive the general drift and learn much of interest, even if he misses some of the finer points. A simpler book is the same author's *This English*, 1935. L. Bloomfield's *Language*, 1935, is another good introduction.

For those interested enough to pursue the subject further there is O. Jespersen's *Language, Its Nature, Development, and Origin*, 1922. Part I deals with the history of linguistic science and is, perhaps, too advanced for the beginner. The rest of the book, however, presents the central problems of language. Part II is on the speech of children, Part III on the individual and the world, and Part IV on the development of language.

The student is warned not to get himself bogged in this preliminary reading. Language is an active study; one must watch words at work. It is better to push on to the study of English and then go back to the more general books with a wider experience of the ways of a particular language.

Language is shaped by the people who speak it; it embodies their history. They have gradually invented or borrowed words and modified grammar and sentence structure to express ideas as they have grown from the lives of different generations. A general survey of the development of English that contains chapters on English language and its history is L. Pearsall Smith's *The English Language* (Home University Library, 1912). Another good book to begin with is Professor E. Weekley's book with the same title (Benn's Sixpenny Library, 1928). Borrowing from other languages, word-making and the evolution of grammar are other topics dealt with in H. Bradley's *The Making of English*, 1904, and O. Jespersen's *Growth and Structure of the English Language*, 1906. Grammar and syntax in modern English are fully explained in O. Jespersen's *Modern English Grammar*, 1922-1931, which should be used as a reference book while the development of the language is being studied, for the aim in studying the development of the language is to understand modern English better by seeing how it has come to be what it is. This point of view is kept well in mind in

S. R. Robertson's *The Development of English*, 1934.

While language is continually developing in response to the needs of the people who speak it, there is value in taking stock of it at selected moments of its history. Old English is a good early form of the language from which to follow through the changes sketched in the books just recommended. W. J. Sedgefield's *A Skeleton Outline of Old English Accidence*, 1917, is easily memorized, and it is then possible to get the feel of Old English by passing on to A. S. Cook's *A First Book of Old English*, 1903, and reading some of the extracts with the aid of notes and vocabulary.

A later period at which to sample the language would be the time of Chaucer, whom the student will want to read, anyhow. K. Sisam's *Fourteenth-Century Verse and Prose*, 1921, contains a good appendix on "The English Language in the Fourteenth Century," which will help you to read Chaucer with facility.

Whether Old (Anglo-Saxon) or Middle (Chaucer's) English are read or not will depend on the time available: to try a little of each will make the history of the language more intelligible. Middle English is very much easier to pick up than Anglo-Saxon unless you happen to be a student of German, with which Old English has much in common. Middle English is the forerunner of our own speech, and you can learn enough of it to understand Chaucer in an hour or two

Things to Do

1. Make a list of about twenty words of Anglo-Saxon origin, and opposite each write a synonym of Romance origin (e.g. fatherly—paternal; quietness—silence). Try to explain the difference in usage between the two words in each pair.

2. Collect as many prefixes and suffixes as you can, dividing them into those surviving from Old English, those borrowed from French, those borrowed from Latin and those borrowed from Greek. Write down a number of words containing each affix. Which affixes are still used for making new words derived from existing words? (L. Pearsall Smith, *The English Language*, Chap. IV.)

3. Make a list of words borrowed from French but pronounced in an English way, and another list of words still retaining their French pronunciation. Find out when each word was introduced into English. (*New English Dictionary*.)

4. List fifty words commonly used in the physical sciences and trace the origin of each. (*New English Dictionary*.)

5. Write down as many strong and as many weak verbs as you can. Try to think of some verbs recently coined and see how many are strong and how many weak. (O. Jespersen, *Growth and Structure of the English Language*.)

6. Make a list of fifty local place names, tracing their origins. What do they tell about the history of your district? (Ekwall, *Dictionary of Place Names*.)

Part 2—Early and Medieval Literature

The English literary tradition, like the English language, begins with a fusion of Germanic and Romance elements. The Germanic poetry brought to the island by the Saxons did not develop much here, although it was early Christianized, but its verse structure contributed to modern English versification. It was based on a regular succession of strong stresses marked by alliteration. To get the feeling of it read aloud—it was meant for recitation to the harp—some of the great epic *Beowulf*, noticing the alliteration. The vocabulary is rich and difficult: it was almost a ritual, celebrating the prowess of heroes admired by a race of warriors and seafarers. Its subjects and spirit can be judged from modern renderings, such as those of R. K. Gordon's *Anglo-Saxon Poetry* (Everyman Library), J. D. Spaeth's *Old English Poetry* (Princeton, 1922), which imitates the original metre, or G. Sampson's *Cambridge Book of Prose and Verse*, 1924. A. S. Brooke's *English Literature from the Beginning to the Norman Conquest*, 1898, gives an excellent account of it.

The alliterative metre survived until the fourteenth century and was the metre of the great medieval poem, *Piers Plowman*. Much of the difficulty of this poem is due to the difference of the medieval from the modern outlook, and it is, therefore, a good representative of the medieval mind. There are modern versions by H. W. Wells (New York, 1935) and A. W. Burrell (Everyman's Library), and a running commentary in R. W. Chambers's *Man's Unconquerable Mind*, 1939.

The poem presents a social philosophy by means of allegory, a very popular medieval device. The student should investigate Langland's social teaching as expressed in the poem and consider the advantages and disadvantages of allegory as a medium for it. The picture of the times given by the sombre Langland should be compared with that given by Chaucer. his cheerful contemporary.

Chaucer did not use the alliterative metre but naturalized French versification, which depends on a fixed number of syllables to the line, French having weak accentuation compared with a Germanic tongue like English. Ever since, English verse has compromised between the two principles. Long before Chaucer's time England had been drawn into the European culture dominated by French literature. Before reading Chaucer the chief types of medieval literature should be sampled in such a selection as G. Sampson's (mentioned above), G. H. Gerould's *Old and Medieval Literature* (New York, 1934) or J. L. Weston's *Chief Middle English Poets* (Boston, 1914). An excellent guidebook is W. P. Ker's *English Literature: Medieval* (Home University Library). It is less important to study the examples in detail than to realize the characteristics (subject, method of development, characterization, etc.) of the main types into which they fall—romance, allegory, debate. animal tale, etc.

One type that is specially important is the romance. By this name are known the cycles of story that were common property throughout medieval Europe. Of these the chief one in England was the story-cycle that related the adventures of King Arthur and his knights. This can best be read in the late prose compilation of Sir Thomas Malory, the *Morte D'Arthur*. It is long, but delightful, and can be dipped into at any point. In reading it, try to picture the interests and standards of the society for whom the romance was intended, as well as to notice its atmosphere and narrative technique. It will be obvious why poets of later periods have always been attracted to Malory.

Chaucer translated and imitated fashionable French poetry but transformed the accepted types into something new. Even the structure of *The Canterbury Tales*—a series of tales bound together by a master-fiction—is not original, but the Prologue and the links between the tales do more than bind the stories into a unity. It is well to relate the tales to medieval types and, at the same time, to decide what is of permanent interest in the way Chaucer handles them. The Knight's Tale shows what he respected in chivalry, but he was a Londoner and not in sympathy with romance, being too much of a realist. The Nun's Priest's Tale is the most delightful of all animal tales. *Troilus and Criseyde* should not be missed. Note how the narrative technique improves in the second half of the poem, and consider Chaucer's attitude to his characters (the function of Pandarus is worth thinking about). There are innumerable guides to Chaucer: Grace Hadow's *Chaucer and His Times* (Home University Library) and D. Martin's *A First Book About Chaucer*, 1927, may serve as introductions. Rather more advanced are R. K. Root's *The Poetry of Chaucer*, 1934, and G. L. Kittredge's *Chaucer and His Poetry*, 1925. Chaucer can be enjoyed in his own words: the only help needed is a glossary, such as that in the Oxford edition, and the knowledge that every final *e* was sounded in his time.

During this period and long afterwards popular poetry was sung from memory. The ballad is the chief form. F. J. Child's great collection has been abbreviated by G. L. Kittredge (*English and Scottish Popular Ballads*, 1904), and other selections are F. Sidgwick's *Popular Ballads of the Olden Time* and A T. Quiller-Couch's

TIME CHART

PERIOD	POETRY	PROSE	PLAYS
1300	Langland (1330-1400) Chaucer (1340-1400) Ballads		MIRACLES MYSTERIES AND MORALITIES
1400	Lydgate (1370-1451) Henryson (1425-1506) Skelton (1460-1529)	Mandeville (*fl.* 1370) Malory (*fl.* 1470) Caxton (1422-1491)	
1500	Wyatt (1503-1542) Surrey (1517-1547) Sackville (1536-1608) Spenser (1552-1599) Sidney (1554-1586) Drayton (1563-1631) Marlowe (1564-1593) Shakespeare (1564-1616)	More (1478-1535) Ascham (1515-1568) Holinshed (*d.* 1580) Lyly (1554-1606) Sidney (1554-1586) Bacon (1561-1626) Prayer Book (1549)	Greene (1537-1583) Deloney (1543-1600) Lyly (1554-1606) Kyd (1558-1594) Marlowe (1564-1593) Shakespeare (1564-1616) Nashe (1567-1601) Dekker (1570-1632) Heywood (1575-1650)
1600	Donne (1573-1631) Wither (1588-1687) Herrick (1591-1674) Herbert (1593-1633) T. Carew (1598-1639) Davenant (1606-1668) Milton (1608-1674) Suckling (1609-1642) Butler (1612-1680) Cowley (1618-1667) Lovelace (1618-1668) Dryden (1631-1700)	The Bible (1611) Burton (1577-1640) Hobbes (1588-1679) Walton (1593-1683) Browne (1605-1682) Milton (1608-1674) Evelyn (1620-1706) Bunyan (1628-1688) Dryden (1631-1700) Locke (1632-1704) Pepys (1632-1704)	Jonson (1572-1637) Webster (1575-1625) Fletcher (1579-1625) Beaumont (1584-1616) Massinger (1584-1639) Ford (1586-1639) Milton (1608-1674) Dryden (1631-1700) Congreve (1670-1729)
1700	Pope (1688-1744) Thomson (1700-1748) Johnson (1709-1784) Gray (1716-1771) Collins (1721-1759) Cowper (1731-1800) Crabbe (1754-1832) Blake (1757-1827) Burns (1759-1796) Wordsworth (1770-1850) Coleridge (1772-1834)	Defoe (1660-1731) Swift (1667-1745) Addison (1672-1719) Steele (1672-1729) Richardson (1689-1761) Fielding (1707-1754) Johnson (1709-1784) Hume (1711-1776) Sterne (1713-1768) Gray (1716-1771) Smollett (1721-1771) Burke (1729-1797) Goldsmith (1728-1774) Gibbon (1737-1794)	Addison (1672-1719) Steele (1672-1729) Johnson (1709-1784) Goldsmith (1728-1774) Sheridan (1751-1816)

TIME CHART—*continued*

PERIOD	POETRY	PROSE	PLAYS
1800			
	Scott (1771-1832)	Cobbett (1762-1835)	Lord Byron (1788-1824)
	T. Moore (1779-1852)	Edgeworth (1767-1849)	Shelley (1792-1822)
	Lord Byron (1788-1824)	Scott (1771-1832)	Tennyson (1809-1892)
	Shelley (1792-1822)	Coleridge (1772-1834)	Browning (1812-1889)
	Keats (1795-1821)	Southey (1774-1843)	Swinburne (1837-1909)
	Fitzgerald (1809-1883)	Austen (1775-1817)	Jones (1851-1929)
	Tennyson (1809-1892)	Lamb (1775-1834)	Pinero (1855-1934)
	Browning (1812-1889)	Hazlitt (1778-1830)	Shaw (1856-1950)
	Clough (1819-1861)	De Quincey (1785-1853)	Wilde (1856-1900)
	Arnold (1822-1888)	Carlyle (1795-1881)	Yeats (1865-1939)
	Patmore (1823-1896)	Macaulay (1800-1858)	
	Meredith (1828-1909)	Borrow (1803-1881)	
	D. G. Rossetti (1828-1882)	Gaskell (1810-1865)	
	Morris (1834-1896)	Thackeray (1811-1863)	
	Swinburne (1837-1909)	Dickens (1812-1870)	
	Hardy (1840-1928)	Trollope (1815-1888)	
	Hopkins (1844-1889)	C. Brontë (1816-1855)	
	Henley (1849-1903)	E. Brontë (1818-1848)	
	Wilde (1856-1900)	Froude (1818-1894)	
	Housman (1859-1936)	George Eliot (1819-1880)	
	Thompson (1859-1907)	Ruskin (1819-1900)	
	Yeats (1865-1939)	Meredith (1828-1909)	
		Morris (1834-1896)	
		Butler (1835-1902)	
		Pater (1839-1894)	
		Hardy (1840-1928)	
		Stevenson (1850-1894)	
		Shaw (1856-1950)	
		Gissing (1857-1903)	
1900			
	Bridges (1844-1930)	G. Moore (1852-1933)	Barrie (1860-1937)
	Kipling (1865-1936)	Conrad (1856-1924)	Galsworthy (1867-1933)
	W. de la Mare (1873-1956)	Doyle (1859-1930)	Synge (1871-1909)
	Masefield (1875-)	Kipling (1865-1936)	Maugham (1874-)
	Sassoon (1886-)	Wells (1866-1946)	Drinkwater (1882-1937)
	Brooke (1887-1915)	Bennett (1867-1931)	Ervine (1883-)
	E. Sitwell (1887-)	Galsworthy (1867-1933)	James Bridie (1888-1951)
	T. S. Eliot (1888-)	Belloc (1870-1953)	O'Casey (1890-)
	Graves (1895-)	Chesterton (1874-1936)	Priestley (1894-)
	Blunden (1896-)	Maugham (1874-)	Coward (1899-)
	C. Day Lewis (1904-)	Trevelyan (1876-)	Emlyn Williams
	W. H. Auden (1907-)	Forster (1879-)	(1905-)
	Stephen Spender	Strachey (1880-1932)	Christopher Fry
	(1909-)	Joyce (1882-1941)	(1907-)
	Dylan Thomas (1914-1953)	Woolf (1882-1941)	Terence Rattigan
		Walpole (1884-1941)	(1911-)
		Lawrence (1885-1930)	
		Mansfield (1888-1923)	
		Huxley (1894-)	
		Priestley (1894-)	

Oxford Book of Ballads, 1910. The student need not concern himself with the origins of the ballad, which are obscure, but should note the features of subject and style that recur over and over again and the technique of story-telling, as well as the form. These uniform characteristics are to some extent due to the transmission of the ballads from mouth to mouth through a number of generations before they were written down by collectors.

Questions to Think Over

1. What do you learn from *Beowulf* of the lives of the Germanic peoples during the Heroic Age?

2. What are the characteristics of Old English epic, as exemplified in *Beowulf*? (Arrange your impressions under such headings as types of character, atmosphere, beliefs, standard of conduct, method of telling the story, vocabulary, style, etc.)

3. What do you learn from Malory's *Morte d'Arthur* about: (*a*) the normal occupations and interests of medieval knights; (*b*) the chivalric ideal of knightly behaviour; (*c*) the conventions of medieval courtly love; (*d*) medieval religion? How far do you think romance is based on actual medieval life and to what extent is it pure fantasy?

4. What was Langland's purpose in writing *Piers Plowman*? How does he hold the reader's interest? Is the use of allegory more or less effective than direct presentation of his message? (Chambers, *Man's Unconquerable Mind*.)

5. Compare Chaucer's *Troilus and Criseyde* with Shakespeare's *Troilus and Cressida*, noting the differences between the narrative and dramatic methods of presenting the story, the differences in characterization, the differences in the setting, the different attitudes to their subject of the two authors, etc.

6. What have you noticed in Chaucer that is medieval, and what qualities in him have appealed to readers of all times?

7. What are the distinctive features of the English and Scottish popular ballad? (G. L. Kittredge, *English and Scottish Popular Ballads*.)

Part 3—Sixteenth- and Seventeenth-Century Poetry

After Chaucer's death (1400) it became increasingly apparent that really original work could not be produced in the medieval literary forms, which had lost touch with the changing interests of society. But the rapid development of the language and the distractions of political and religious upheaval delayed the creation of a new style and technique.

It was only at the end of the sixteenth century that a new poetry could be written in English. Spenser's *The Shepherd's Calendar* (1579) preserved what was still alive in the Chaucer tradition but united it with lessons from the modern poetry of Italy and France and from the Greek and Latin authors who seemed so much more relevant than the medieval ones to sixteenth-century interests. Spenser's aims are explained in the commentary and notes to *The Shepherd's Calendar* by his friend E.K., but he wrote in a convention unfamiliar to us, and some knowledge of how his time viewed poetry is necessary to the full appreciation of his work. A contemporary expression of this is the *Apology for Poetry* by his friend Sir Philip Sidney. Professor W. L. Renwick's *Edmund Spenser, an Essay in Renaissance Poetry*, 1925, gives a very full account of what Spenser was trying to do. A good general introduction to his work is E. de Selincourt's in the Oxford edition. H. S. Jones's *Spenser Handbook* (New York, 1930) is a useful guide to be read with the poems.

The sixteenth and seventeenth centuries believed that the noblest form of poetry was the epic or heroic poem, such as the *Iliad* and *Odyssey* of Homer and the *Æneid* of Virgil. At this point it will be advisable to get to know a little about this type of poem, and Lascelles Abercrombie's *The Epic*, 1912, can be recommended. Spenser did not want to imitate the classical epics but to adapt their style to a genuinely English poetry, and he chose his subject and atmosphere from medieval romance. He also had a message for his own times to be conveyed through allegory. The inevitable complication of the plan, with two entirely different models of structure and two kinds of teaching to be worked out in the incidents, is not lessened by his failure to finish *The Faerie Queene.* The student should read as much as he can, without bothering too much about the details of the allegory, but rather enjoying the pictorial and rhythmical beauties that have made Spenser "the poets' poet."

The great heroic poem Spenser failed to write was achieved by Milton, whose form is that of the classical epic, undisturbed by medieval influences. *Paradise Lost* is unique, and there is no difficulty in noting for oneself the qualities that give it its grandeur. If there is not time to read it all, the structure of the poem should be studied from the arguments prefixed to the twelve books, and a few books should be read in their entirety. C. S. Lewis's *Introduction to Paradise Lost,* 1944, is suggestive. Other poems of Milton that should, if possible, be read are *Paradise Regained,* a unique example°of the brief epic and quite different from *Paradise Lost, Samson Agonistes,* a tragedy in the Greek manner, and the early *Comus,* a masque. J. H. Hanford's *Milton Handbook* and E. M. Tillyard's *Milton,* 1930, will help to make Milton's intentions clearer.

The sixteenth and seventeenth centuries are so rich in poetry of all kinds that the student can largely follow his inclinations. A dip into *The Oxford Book of Sixteenth-Century Verse* (edited by E. K. Chambers) and *The Oxford Book of Seventeenth-Century Verse* (edited by H. J. C. Grierson and H. Bullough) will illustrate the variety available.

There was, for instance, a vogue for personal poems, as a reaction against the long medieval narratives and allegories. An Italian form that was very popular in the late sixteenth century was the sonnet. It was generally love-poetry following a set convention. It is necessary only to read a few specimens to get to know the convention (Sidney Lee's *Eliza-* *bethan Sonnets* is a collection of them). Shakespeare's sonnets are exceptional and repay close study. Milton's, too, have a character of their own. (Incidentally these two poets illustrate the two different rhyme patterns of the sonnet in English.)

From this conventional love-poetry it is a relief to turn to the most interesting school of seventeenth-century poetry, the "metaphysical." They are so anxious to avoid clichés and commonplace sentiments that they sometimes allow oddness and cleverness for its own sake to run away with them. H. J. C. Grierson's *Metaphysical Lyrics and Poems of the Seventeenth Century,* 1921, is a representative selection of their work and has a valuable introduction. The "metaphysical" poets were fond of images drawn from contemporary learning and occasionally sufficiently obscure to us to require the help of an annotated edition. But the rapid play of fancy running to extremes— at first a cause of difficulty in reading— may soon become a delight. It is a new world of poetic thought, requiring and meriting our closest attention in the reading. Poets of the school particularly worth studying are Donne, Marvell and Herbert. Compare one or two of Marvell's best poems with other poems on the same subject. A like comparison may be made between a few of Herbert's poems and poems by later religious poets. Study of this kind will indicate why modern poets have gone back to the seventeenth century for qualities seldom found in poetry of other periods.

Questions to Think Over

1. What arguments does Sidney put forward for the superiority of poetry over other kinds of learning? What has he to say about the state of poetry at the time the *Apology for Poetry* was written?

2. How does Spenser try to "teach and delight" at the same time? Does the allegory hinder a modern reader's enjoyment of *The Faerie Queene*?

3. Briefly arrange in chronological order all the events recounted or referred to in *Paradise Lost.* Alongside this place a brief summary of the events as they occur in the poem, noting which are related as in retrospect or foretold in prophecy. What advantage has Milton gained by presenting them in accordance with epic practice? (J. H. Hanford, *Milton Handbook*.)

4. By what devices of style and rhythm does Milton sustain grandeur of tone in *Paradise Lost*? (J. H. Hanford, *Milton Handbook*; C. S. Lewis, *Introduction to*

Paradise Lost; E. M. Tillyard, *Milton*.)

5. What is generally meant by a "metaphysical" poet? What reason is there for calling Donne, Marvell or Herbert "metaphysical," and what individual qualities have you noticed that differentiate each from the others?

6. In what respects are Shakespeare's sonnets superior to other Elizabethan sonnets?

Part 4—English Drama

The great period of English drama is the late sixteenth and early seventeenth centuries. The life of that period found its fullest literary expression in the drama, which had a very wide appeal to all classes. The roots of this wonderful growth run deeply into the Middle Ages: specimens of folk-plays, miracle and mystery plays, moralities and early professional entertainments can be read in J. Q. Adams's *Pre-Shakespearian Drama*. But the rapid development of a fine drama became possible only when companies of professional actors established themselves in permanent theatres and turned to profit the general interest in dramatic spectacle by employing the best writers they could find.

The drama was a business carried on by companies of actors and producers, who commissioned plays to suit them. A play was not written first and cast afterwards: it was written for a definite company, whose property it became and who might later commission another writer, or more than one, to bring it up to date.

It is important to visualize the plays of the period as they would be performed on the stage of the time. G. B. Harrison's *Introducing Shakespeare* (Pelican Books) gives a brief account of the theatre and will serve for other matters mentioned in this section, too. His *Elizabethan Plays and Players* traces the history of the drama in relation to that of the companies. But, having got some notion of what the Elizabethan stage looked like, the student, while reading the plays, can imagine their effect when produced on that stage.

The technique of the Elizabethan drama was largely settled by the group of young university men attracted to the theatre during the 1580s, when the companies were trying to interest a better-class public than the crude early plays had secured. Robert Greene established what is known as the "romantic" play: notice how he combines into one play quite different types of action and character (*James IV* and *Friar Bacon and Friar Bungay* are representative of him). Kyd's *Spanish Tragedy* is the first important "revenge" tragedy (compare it with *Hamlet* to see how much Shakespeare owes to his predecessor and how far he improved upon him). Marlowe began as a poet, but if his plays are read in roughly chronological order (*Tamburlaine, Faustus, The Jew of Malta* and *Edward II*) the extent to which he learned stagecraft can be judged. Another dramatist to be read with this group, although he wrote politely for Court production, is John Lyly: *Endymion* is a fair specimen of his work.

Shakespeare, of course, is a study in himself. It is usual to classify his plays according to their dates of composition, and this is a convenient way of studying the development of his art. P. Alexander's *Shakespeare* is a reliable companion. In the early plays what he learned from his predecessors and how he improved on them will appear from the reading suggested above. *Love's Labour's Lost*, for instance, should be compared with the work of Lyly, *Richard III* and *Richard II* with Marlowe's *Edward II*, Shylock with Marlowe's Barrabas in *The Jew of Malta*. The comedies of his maturity (*Twelfth Night, As You Like It, Much Ado*) can be studied as a group to discover Shakespeare's idea of comedy, and similarly the

ELIZABETHAN STAGE TYPES AS SHOWN IN AN OLD PRINT
Whenever possible study the theatre through the eyes of contemporary artists of each period.

historical plays, especially *Richard II* and *Richard III* and *Henry IV*. The great tragedies will require more careful thought. Of the later romantic plays *The Tempest* and *The Winter's Tale* are the most important. A vast literature has grown up around the plays. Among books that will be illuminating after one's own study are: *The Shakespeare Companion*, edited by H. Granville Barker and G. B. Harrison, W. Raleigh's *Shakespeare*, Hazlitt's *Characters of Shakespeare's Plays*, A. T. Quiller-Couch's *Shakespeare's Workmanship*, A. C. Bradley's *Shakespearian Tragedy*, H. Granville Barker's *Prefaces to Shakespeare*, E. M. W. Tillyard's *Shakespeare's History Plays* and E. E. Stoll's *Art and Artifice in Shakespeare*.

But you must read the plays themselves, imagine them acted and see them acted as often as possible, reading *about* them only in so far as interest in particular points urges you to dig more deeply and consult other opinion. It cannot be too strongly emphasized that effectiveness on the stage was Shakespeare's governing aim, and each play should be appreciated separately as a dramatic construction.

Among Shakespeare's contemporaries and successors Jonson is pre-eminent. If you find him a taste hard to acquire, there is variety of choice among the other dramatists of the period, who can be sampled in N. J. Nielson's *Chief Elizabethan Dramatists*, or in the two Everyman volumes of *Minor Elizabethan Drama*. Jonson's *Volpone, The Alchemist* and *Bartholomew Fair* should be attempted, however. There is ample help to reading him in the large edition of E. H. Herford and P. Simpson, and a handy small edition in Everyman's Library.

The Restoration drama lacks the variety of the Elizabethan, partly because the audience tended to be restricted to the Court circle. *Restoration Plays* (Everyman's Library), M. Summers's *Restoration Comedies* and F. and J. W. Tupper's *Representative English Dramas from Dryden to Sheridan* are useful selections. Congreve in comedy is a good starting-point. *The Way of the World* might be compared with one of Jonson's or Shakespeare's comedies

to show the limitations as well as the polish of Restoration comedy. The tail-end of this tradition is Goldsmith (*She Stoops to Conquer* and *The Good-Natur'd Man*) and Sheridan, whose *Rivals* and *The School for Scandal* could also be compared with *The Way of the World*. Besides comedy, there was a Restoration vogue for the "heroic" play, though this is less interesting. It will probably be enough at first to read Dryden's *All for Love* and compare it with *Antony and Cleopatra*, but comparison with Shakespeare is a severe test, and one must be careful to do justice to Dryden's real merits. Look at Bonamy Dobree's *Restoration Comedy* and *Restoration Tragedy*.

During the nineteenth century drama lost touch with national life, and it was only in this century that it regained literary importance. G. B. Shaw ridiculed the romantic convention of the Victorians and used the drama for social propaganda. As his technique developed he relied less on the traditional methods of holding the audience and more on the ideas themselves. *Three Plays for Puritans, Man and Superman, Back to Methuselah, St. Joan, The Apple Cart* and any of his later plays show the progression. It is interesting to discuss just what Shaw's ideas are, but the important question is how far his plays are successful merely as plays—i.e. what is Shaw's dramatic technique and how far does it alone account for his success.

The Abbey Theatre, Dublin, was a centre of activity during the early part of the century. W. B. Yeats was more a poet than dramatist (*Countess Cathleen, The Land of Heart's Desire* and *Deirdre* are typical). J. M. Synge's *Playboy of the Western World* uses Irish idiom with great effect. Neither has had any significant followers in recent years. The most important living Irish dramatist, Sean O'Casey, although poetic in spirit and in his use of the Irish idiom, inclines to the realistic in general treatment and setting. *Juno and the Paycock* and *The Plough and the Stars* are good starting points. In the Irish school there is material for considering whether poetic or realistic drama is the more suitable for modern conditions.

In spite of Shaw's example, the realistic

drama in England never fulfilled its promise, and in recent years a poetic drama has developed. T. S. Eliot's *Murder in the Cathedral* and *The Family Reunion*, and W. H. Auden's and Christopher Isherwood's *The Ascent of F.6*, represent different aspects of it. The possibilities of twentieth-century poetic drama and the right subjects and verse for it are worth some thought. For the earlier part of the century the student should consult Allardyce Nicoll's *British Drama*, and current drama he can follow for himself.

Questions to Think Over

1. In what respects did the conditions of the Elizabethan theatre influence the drama of the period? (G. B. Harrison, *Introducing Shakespeare*; J. Q. Adams, *Pre-Shakespearian Drama*.)

2. Is it fair to say that Marlowe was more of a poet than a dramatist?

3. Compare the comedy of Shakespeare with that of Jonson.

4. What is the central conception behind Shakespeare's historical plays?

5. What are the purpose and the essential elements of tragedy to Shakespeare? (A. C. Bradley, *Shakespearian Tragedy*; H. Granville Barker, *Prefaces to Shakespeare*.)

6. Compare and contrast the kinds of comedy to be found in the plays of Wycherley and Congreve. (B. Dobrée, *Restoration Comedy*.)

7. How does the comedy of Goldsmith or Sheridan differ from that of the Restoration dramatists?

8. What are the sources of comedy in Shaw's plays? Which of them, if any, "date," and, if so, is this due to their underlying ideas or to the contemporary idiom and references?

9. In what way do the subjects, atmosphere and technique of modern poetic drama necessarily differ from those of prose drama?

Part 5—Eighteenth-Century and Romantic Poetry

The development of the physical sciences produced a change in the intellectual climate during the seventeenth century that had great influence on the subjects and style of poetry. B. Willey's *Seventeenth Century Background* and H. J. C. Grierson's *Cross Currents in the English Literature of the Seventeenth Century* describe the movements of thought. The first successfully to satisfy the need for a more disciplined poetry dealing with contemporary interests was Dryden, who is important as a critic and dramatist as well. The history of the last forty years of the century and Dryden's own development lie behind the series of satires and argumentative poems, *Absalom and Achitophel*, *The Medal*, *MacFlecknoe*, *Religio Laici* and *The Hind and the Panther*. To see the range of his poetry, however, these should be supplemented by reading some of the occasional poems, such as the *Ode in Memory of Mrs. Anne Killigrew*, *Alexander's Feast* and *The Secular Masque*. Johnson's essay in *The Lives of the Poets* (Everyman's

Library) and M. Van Doren's *Dryden* (1931) will help the reader to appreciate his poetic qualities and his historical importance.

Dryden's great successor, Pope, has again more variety than appears at first. *Eloisa to Abelard* and *An Elegy to the Memory of an Unfortunate Lady* reveal aspects of his genius not so obvious in the greater works, *The Rape of the Lock* and *The Dunciad*. Of the latter the fourth book, which is almost a separate poem, should particularly be read. The contemporary allusions may impede progress, but the general target of Pope's satire and the positive attitude behind it are more important than the detail. With him, as with Dryden, it is the poetic ability, what he makes of his material by imaginative choice of words and suggestion, that should be noted. G. Tillotson's *The Poetry of Pope* is an enlightening criticism.

The student with limited time can get a general view of the kinds of eighteenth-century poetry and their characteristics from *The Oxford Book of Eighteenth Century Verse*. From this various traditions can be followed by those with more time to spare—the elegiac and meditative in Gray and Collins, descriptive in Thomson's *Seasons*, moral satire in Johnson, and the development of realism from Goldsmith to Crabbe. Burns stands somewhat apart against his own background of Scottish popular song. The moods and diction of eighteenth-century poetry became rather stereotyped until at the end of the century a freshness was brought into poetry by Wordsworth and Coleridge.

These two were complementary influences and should be studied together. An account of their association and of Wordsworth's creative process is found in Dorothy Wordsworth's *Journal*, which is well worth reading for its own sake. The study of her brother's poetry must centre upon his greatest poem, *The Prelude*: Professor E. de Selincourt's edition is invaluable. From his own experiences Wordsworth evolved a particular kind of poetry and a philosophy: it is, therefore, best to read *The Prelude* first as a picture of his development, supplementing it with E. Legouis's *Early Life of Wordsworth*; then to go on to the earliest exemplification of his individuality in *The Lyrical Ballads*, in which he collaborated with Coleridge. Study *The Lyrical Ballads* as a group, for they throw light on his intentions as a poet and constitute a great departure from the work and style of his precursors. The Preface to the second edition is an indispensable commentary on it. Wordsworth's later development is treated by E. Batho in *The Later Wordsworth*. The best criticism of Wordsworth is that of Coleridge in *Biographia Literaria*.

Coleridge was, perhaps, the most penetrating of English literary critics. His great poems are few in number. There is a selection from his verse and prose in the Nonesuch Edition that gives all the important poems and will serve as an introduction to the critical works, which are fragmentary and discursive but full of insight.

Byron's personality reinforced the great influence of his poetry, especially on the Continent. His own letters, André Maurois's *Byron* and P. Quennell's *Byron: The Years of Fame* and *Byron in Italy* help to form a picture of him. The first two cantos of *Childe Harold* established his fame, and after them some of the tales (*The Giaour, The Bride of Abydos, The Corsair*) should be read before going on to the last two cantos, written after he left England for ever. *The Vision of Judgment* and *Don Juan* are his most characteristic works: it is interesting to compare them with the satires of Dryden and Pope.

All the poets of this period were much affected by the political upheaval caused by the French Revolution, on which H. N. Brailsford's *Shelley, Godwin and Their Circle* (Home University Library) is a useful commentary. A. Maurois's *Ariel* and the recent *Shelley* of Edmund Blunden deal more particularly with Shelley's life and character. A representative selection of his works would include *Alastor, Prometheus Unbound, The Masque of Anarchy, The Triumph of Life* and some of the shorter poems—e.g. *Ode to the West Wind, To a Skylark, Lines Written Among the Euganean Hills. Mont Blanc* should be compared with Wordsworth's description of the Simplon Pass in Book VI of *The Prelude* to appreciate the differing attitudes of the two.

Keats, like Shelley, died very young, before he could develop a poetic style satisfactory to his rigorous self-criticism. It is, therefore, necessary to follow the progress of his mind in his letters (the best edition is that of R. Buxton Forman) and to read the poems with them in chronological order—*Poems* (1817), *Endymion* (1818), *Lamia, Isabella, The Eve of St. Agnes, Hyperion*, and finally the Odes and the fragment of the revised *Hyperion*. The promise of further development lies primarily in these last two, and it is important to ask oneself what qualities they have that distinguish them from his earlier work, with which he was dissatisfied.

Questions to Think Over

1. What poetical qualities can you discern in the satires and argumentative poems of Dryden? (M. Van Doren, *Dryden*.)

2. Is there much variety of style and treat-

SCOTLAND IN THE EIGHTEEN-TWENTIES

Small-town street scenes such as this reproduction of an old engraving were homely sights to Burns and Scott—part of the everyday atmosphere of their lives. Always seek to reconstruct in your imagination the social background of the writers you are studying.

ment in Pope? (G. R. Tillotson, *The Poetry of Pope*.)

3. To what extent are Wordsworth's limitations due to his own theories about poetry and to the circumstances of his own development? What is of lasting value in his poetry? (Preface to *Lyrical Ballads*, etc.)

4. Why was *Childe Harold*, Cantos I and II, so immediately popular on its publication? What interest has it to a modern reader? Which of Byron's poems continue to be of interest to modern readers? (P. Quennell, *Byron: The Years of Fame*; *Byron in Italy*.)

5. What is meant by the statement that Shelley's genius was "essentially lyrical"? Is it true, and is there more to be said of his poetry?

6. Does his development during his short career and the quality of his latest works justify the belief that, if he had lived, Keats would have become the greatest poet of the nineteenth century?

*Part 6—*Victorian Poetry

The typical Victorian poet is Tennyson. The medieval dream-world of Keats's *Eve of St. Agnes* was a favourite resort of nineteenth-century poets. Tennyson's *Lady of Shalott* is an early example, but *Idylls of the King* were intended to have a message for his own time. The classical poems, such as *Ulysses* and *The Lotus-Eaters* and the lyrics in *The Princess*, represent other aspects of his poetry, but *In Memoriam* and *Maud* are his most individual poems

and show his relation to his time most clearly. What made him popular in his own day is a question to ask in reading him.

Browning's early work, in which he was trying to clarify his own thoughts, is involved, and of that probably only *Paracelsus* can now be read with enjoyment. He reached his own style and produced his best work in the dramatic monologues of *Men and Women* and

Dramatis Personae. In between is a series of plays, the most interesting being *Pippa Passes. The Ring and the Book* is, perhaps, too long to be read through: it is related in technique to the monologues. There is *A Browning Handbook* (1935) by W. C. de Vane. The Victorians valued Browning's thought more than his poetic qualities, but the modern student will do well to concentrate on the means by which he presents his characters and situations, and on his control of speech rhythm in verse—on his art, in other words—in the dramatic monologues.

The volume of Matthew Arnold's poetry is small. *The Strayed Reveller, The Scholar Gipsy, Thyrsis, Sohrab and Rustum* and *Dover Beach* are obvious inclusions in any selection, but his poems can be read almost entire. He was greatly troubled by the intellectual problems of his time, and it is interesting to see how far these are dealt with in his poetry and how far they merely give a general sense of uneasiness, for it is a serious limitation of any style of poetry that it cannot adequately cope with the most intelligent interests of the day.

Whatever their success in handling them, these three greater Victorian poets felt an obligation to deal with contemporary interests. In reaction against the intellectualism induced by this, the Pre-Raphaelite Movement concentrated its attention on aesthetic effect and on the suggestive power of poetry. The movement was merely an association of certain poets and painters in general sympathy. The pictures of Rossetti, the central figure in the movement, and of Burne-Jones lead us most quickly to an understanding of what these poets and painters preferred in subjects and treatment. Rossetti's love-poetry is full of symbolism. He is a master of the sonnet form (*The House of Life*) and experimented with variations on ballad metre in handling medieval narrative. William Morris recreated a whole body of medieval and Scandinavian story. *The Defence of Guenevere, The Life and Death of Jason* and *The Earthly Paradise* are very readable, but poetry was only one of many crafts Morris practised, and his full significance can be grasped only by looking at examples of his other work. The twenty-fifth and

FRIVOLOUS VICTORIANS

The Victorians were not always as serious as their literature might suggest. Look out for contemporary prints and pictures which give you the social background of the period being studied and start to make a small collection of those which interest you.

twenty-sixth volumes of the collected edition of his works, edited by his daughter, give accounts of him as an artist and as a socialist, and the standard *Life* by J. W. Mackail traces the development of his ideas.

Swinburne was influenced by the movement that started with the Pre-Raphaelites, but he excelled rather in the sensuous employment of sound effects. *Poems and Ballads* and *Atalanta in Calydon* are fair specimens of his style. In reading them one should think over the relative claims of sound and sense in poetry.

Questions to Think Over

1. In what ways does *In Memoriam* reflect Victorian ideas and interests?

2. Compare Tennyson's treatment of Arthurian legend with that of Spenser.

3. From what do Browning's dramatic monologues derive most of their interest? Is their technique adaptable to a longer poem? (*The Ring and the Book*.)

4. To Morris, poetry was a craft, like printing or weaving. Does this show itself in the shortcomings of his own poetry?

5. Is it true that Victorian poetry was "escapist"? Which poets of the time tried to deal with contemporary problems and with what success?

6. Did Matthew Arnold come anywhere near satisfying the high standards for poetry he upheld in his own critical writings? (Preface to *Empedocles*, *Essays in Criticism, Culture and Anarchy*.)

Part 7—Modern Poetry

The history of twentieth-century poetry can be traced in the career of W. B. Yeats. His early volumes were inspired by the end of the tradition running from the Pre-Raphaelites, but the later ones, from *The Tower* onwards, have an alert speech rhythm and a complexity of intention associated with recent poetry. His Irish mythology and references to mystical philosophies often make him difficult. There is an edition of *Collected Poems* (1933) and a study by Louis MacNeice.

A Victorian who went on writing into this century was Thomas Hardy. His poems are often clumsy and only a few are really great, but it is worth noticing how the clumsiness sometimes adds to the effect. His outlook and method of presenting it may be compared with those of A. E. Housman (*A Shropshire Lad, Last Poems* and *More Poems*). Kipling and Masefield brought into poetry features of modern life.

At this point you might consider what it is that makes a poem modern—the idiom, the reference to contemporary events and appliances, the underlying ideas, the rhythms and verse forms, or a combination of all of these.

At the beginning of the century it became evident that the traditions inherited from the Victorians were no longer capable of expressing the modern mind. The Georgian group, of whom Rupert Brooke is typical, did not succeed in giving the tradition much vitality. There were poets of talent—for example, Robert Bridges, Walter de la Mare, the two nature poets Edmund Blunden and Edward Thomas, and Wilfred Owen, who was killed in the 1914-18 war—but perhaps their technique and range of interest were too individual to constitute a new departure.

An attempt at greater originality was made by the Imagists (*The Imagist Anthology* gives a sufficient view of their efforts), who tried to combine classical form with free verse. One of the group was Ezra Pound, whose *Hugh Selwyn Mauberley* has had considerable influence. His *Collected Poems* contains an introduction by T. S. Eliot.

The major figure in recent poetry has been that of T. S. Eliot. His poetry is full of allusions to previous literature, and *The Waste Land* is annotated to help the reader see the force of the most important echoes. But the poetic effect should operate before the meaning is fully understood. It is wise to begin by getting the general significance of a poem on a first reading and then to follow imaginatively the suggestions of the detail. The rhythm is often as evocative as the individual words, and reading aloud often helps to give the effect. Eliot's use of the past as a commentary on the present can be studied in the early short poems in *Collected Poems*. A very cursory reading of Miss J. L. Weston's *From Ritual to Romance*, makes clear the background of *The Waste Land*. For *Ash Wednesday*, which marks a stage in Eliot's development, only a knowledge of religious symbolism is necessary. There is a study by F. O. Matthiessen, *The Achievement of T. S. Eliot*, and F. L. Leavis's *New Bearings in English Poetry* is a useful guide.

Gerard Manly Hopkins, although he lived in the Victorian period, must be reckoned a modern poet, for his works were not published until 1918 and were then found to be so original that they have had considerable influence on recent writers. His letters (edited by C. C. Abbott) throw light on what he was trying to do with words and rhythms.

It is not easy to determine the importance of more recent poets, but *The Faber Book of Modern Verse* gives a selection of them, and the student can follow up for himself those that interest him. Herbert Read's *Form in Modern Poetry* (*Essays in Order*, No. 11) may be suggestive, and Edwin Muir's *The Present Age* (*Introductions to English Literature*, edited by Bonamy Dobrée, volume 5) provides a commentary and a guide for further reading. For the most recent poets read *Auden and After*, by Francis Scarfe.

Questions to Think Over

1. Trace the development of Yeats's poetic style and show how it follows the general progress of twentieth-century poetry.
2. What has Hardy's poetry in common with his novels?
3. Compare the nature poetry of Edmund Blunden with that of Edward Thomas.
4. Why have modern poets found seventeenth-century verse so interesting, and what effect has the interest had on modern poetry?
5. Does T. S. Eliot's poetry make an immediate appeal before it is fully understood? If so, what are the qualities that give it such an appeal?
6. Why are modern poets so often thought difficult and obscure? Choose one whose work attracts you and try to decide whether his apparent obscurity is due to the nature of what he is trying to say.

Part 8—The English Novel

The novel as a distinctive literary form is comparatively modern. Chaucer had all the qualities of a great novelist, but the tale in verse was his natural medium. With the development of prose, attempts were made from the sixteenth century to turn life into prose fiction. An account of the novel's precursors will be found in Sir W. Raleigh's *The English Novel*. It was not until the eighteenth century, however, that anything like what we mean by the novel emerged. Defoe began as a journalist and drifted into imagining stories that looked like slices of real life. Everybody knows *Robinson Crusoe*, but *Moll Flanders* and *Roxana* are probably better examples of his mature technique. His methods of convincing the reader that he is reporting fact are worth notice.

The novel is more than a presentation of events: the inner life of the characters is as essential to it as the outer action. Richardson allowed the characters to reveal themselves by telling the story in a series of letters, and there is no doubt his readers followed the fortunes of Pamela Andrews and Clarissa Harlowe as though they were real people. The advantages and disadvantages of the letter form the student can easily see from these works.

The problem of form, however, remained to be solved. One of the commonest ways of stringing the events together was to follow the adventures of a single character: Smollett's *Roderick Random* and *Peregrine Pickle* are of this type—picaresque novels as they are called. *Humphry Clinker* borrows Richardson's device of letters. The only eighteenth-century novelist to have any idea of plot was Fielding. *Joseph*

Andrews was begun as a satire on Richardson and is remarkable mainly for the great comic figure of Parson Adams, but *Tom Jones* has a well-managed plot; its structure and purpose deserve our attention. Sterne's *Tristram Shandy* conforms to none of the eighteenth-century types but has a delightful individuality in refusing to tell a story, being content with character and gossip.

Fielding and Smollett deal with contemporary society, but in the later eighteenth century romantic fiction had a vogue. Horace Walpole's *The Castle of Otranto* and Mrs. Radcliffe's *The Mysteries of Udolpho* are examples. The absurdities of this kind of novel are ridiculed in Jane Austen's *Northanger Abbey*. Jane Austen's other books draw their materials from country house society: note how she restricts herself to what she knows and try to form an idea of her standards and point of view.

The early Victorian novels were often published serially and were loose in construction, but as the social prestige of the novel rose a sense of form gradually awakened. Dickens began with the picaresque, strings-of-incidents formula in *Pickwick Papers* and never achieved much unity of effect. In later life, however, he began to plan his novels more architecturally, learning something of the management of plot from his friend, Wilkie Collins. His characters are his great strength; but in *Bleak House* and *Great Expectations* the atmosphere of places is powerfully conveyed. Thackeray's novels are more coherent. What is more, he is a critic of society in a subtler way than Dickens, although Thackeray's freedom of criticism —as, indeed, all Victorian social criticism— seems pallid by comparison with the eighteenth-century Fielding, who flogs hypocrisy and pretentiousness. Trollope's Barsetshire novels should be read and compared with those of Thackeray and Jane Austen.

All these novelists deal critically with people in society, but do not question the basic assumptions of society itself, although Dickens strongly attacked particular social evils (*Oliver Twist, Hard Times, Bleak House* and *Little Dorrit* provide examples).

Disraeli propagated his Tory Democracy in *Sybil, Coningsby* and *Tancred*, and in spite of his over-ornate style his novels are in advance in that his characters think, as well as act and feel. Kingsley's *Yeast* and *Alton Locke* and Mrs. Gaskell's *Mary Barton* and *North and South* are concerned with the conditions of the working classes. With similar seriousness, George Gissing, towards the end of the century, was concerning himself with the fate of the lower-middle class. The suitability of the novel for social criticism is a topic for your consideration after reading some of these books.

Charlotte Brontë's *Shirley* deals with social conditions, but *Jane Eyre* and *Villette*, her more characteristic novels, are more remarkable for their emotional force. If Charlotte is melodramatic, her sister Emily is more so. Indeed, in *Wuthering Heights*, the melodrama has the quality of genius, so great is its force and intensity. The student should ask himself to what qualities *Wuthering Heights* owes its impressiveness and unity of effect.

George Eliot moves on more mundane levels but is historically the most important of the earlier Victorian novelists because she was the first to construct a novel round an idea and to show characters developing under the pressure of circumstances. *The Mill on the Floss, Adam Bede*, and *Middlemarch* contain the essence of the novel's mature technique. Her methods were developed by her great successor, Hardy, whose novels are so well known that it is necessary to draw attention only to *Jude the Obscure*, a masterpiece not to be omitted from any reading list. In reading both writers, the working out of the central idea should be traced through the details of situation, plot and characterization.

Critical works on the novel of this period that can be recommended are Lord David Cecil's *Early Victorian Novelists* and A. T. Quiller-Couch's *Charles Dickens and Other Victorians*. On the general problems of the novel and more relevant to the later writers now to be mentioned are E. M. Forster's *Aspects of the Novel*, Percy Lubbock's *The Craft of Fiction*, H. W. Leggatt's *The Idea in Fiction*. Read, too,

Edwin Muir's *The Structure of the Novel*.

Up to this time the great novelists were also the popular novelists. The separation of novel readers into levels of taste begins to be apparent with Meredith, whose style was found obscure by most readers *Beauchamp's Career, The Egoist* and *Diana of the Crossways* are representative. Henry James will never have a large audience, but some of his early and middle works should be attempted (the later ones are best avoided by beginners). The short stories, such as *The Aspern Papers* and *A Turn of the Screw* (available in the Everyman Library) are an excellent introduction. Conrad admired James and is another careful craftsman but has more popular appeal: indeed, he and Kipling are still so well known as to require only a reminder of their importance.

Galsworthy, Bennett and Wells, the chief novelists of the early years of the present century, worked within the tradition established by the Victorians, and later novelists like D. H. Lawrence, Aldous Huxley and E. M. Forster did not change it fundamentally, although they expressed modern points of view. There has, however, in recent years been a sense that the traditional technique had reached the limit of its possibilities, and James Joyce and Virginia Woolf have shifted the centre of interest from the outer scene to the consciousness of the characters. The former experimented so much with the evocative power of words that he ended by writing almost a language of his own. *Portrait of the Artist as a Young Man*, however, is reasonably straightforward, even for those who cannot face *Ulysses*. *To the Lighthouse* and *Mrs. Dalloway* are, perhaps, the best examples of Virginia Woolf. Edmund Wilson's *Axel's Castle* contains a chapter on James Joyce that relates him to other modern tendencies. Consider how far the novel can dispense with the traditional structure of plot and still remain a novel.

Questions to Think Over

1. What are the advantages and disadvantages of telling the story in a series of letters, as Richardson does?

2. What qualities has Fielding that Jane Austen lacks, and to what extent does she compensate for her limitations by merits of her own?

3. What constitutes the comedy in *Tom Jones, Pickwick Papers* and *Vanity Fair* respectively? What differences are there in the authors' points of view, intentions and scope of interest?

4. Compare two Victorian novels that deal with social problems of the time and estimate their success (*a*) as propaganda, and (*b*) as presentations of life.

5. Is it true that Virginia Woolf's technique gives a more natural representation of experience than the traditional technique of the novel? What are the advantages and disadvantages of her method?

6. Compare a modern novel with a Victorian one of a similar type and consider what makes the former distinctively twentieth century. (Technique, the writer's point of view, the scope of interest, the characterization, the standards of conduct assumed, the style, etc.)

Part 9—English Prose and the Art of Writing

Prose develops much later than verse in all literatures. Narrative prose achieved a noble simplicity in Malory's *Morte d'Arthur*, many of the sources of which were in verse, and this dignified and direct style became a never-failing inspiration to English writers when it was applied to the translation of the Bible. Bunyan is a testimony to its virtues as a teacher of eloquence. It was only in the sixteenth century, when printing had multiplied the reading public and there was a ferment of religious and political discussion, that English prose became as capable as verse of conveying ideas. The early model was Latin, producing a rhetorical prose that reached its first perfection in the early seventeenth century. Milton's pamphlets (*Areopagitica* is the most readable now) and Sir Thomas Browne's *Religio Medici* illustrate different kinds, the one controversial and the other almost poetic.

Real command of language implies ability to handle any style and produce any effect. This early rhetorical prose is worth study, not only for pleasure but for a knowledge of the resources of English. It is not a model for ordinary purposes, however. While it is imaginative and sonorous it is not suitable for clear thought or practical exposition. General utility prose, like so much else in the modern world, is a product of the seventeenth-century movement towards discipline and good sense, the corollary of the growth of science and rationalism. The Royal Society in the Restoration period decided to encourage prose near to ordinary speech. The first great master of colloquial yet elegant prose is Dryden, whose critical essays (edited by W. P. Ker) deserve to be read for their content as well as for their style. Following his lead, Addison and Steele set the standard for the eighteenth century in their contributions to periodicals, particularly the *Tatler* and the *Spectator*. Later essays of the same type are those of Goldsmith.

For the combination of ease with vigour there is probably no better model than Swift. It is almost impossible to pick out of his works any purple patches; he uses very few figures of speech; and the clarity of the style springs from the lucidity of the thought. There is nothing unnecessary and nothing strained or odd about his writing. A careful study of him is one of the surest roads to general competence as a writer.

The conversational tone of early eighteenth-century prose is partly due to the writer's sense of addressing a small circle of readers in agreement with him and with one another on values and taste. As the public widened the audience became vaguer, and a more rhetorical prose developed, full of words of Latin origin and elaborate periods, though not half-poetical as the earlier seventeenth-century prose had been. Johnson and Gibbon do not talk naturally but assume the attitude of the orator. Their sentences are carefully shaped and balanced and their paragraphs have an impressive rhythm. Macaulay is the end of this classical tradition. He over-does antithesis and the balance of his sentences is too obvious, but for historical narrative and exposition his style is very effective. His tricks are apparent and easy to learn, and used with moderation give shape to the writing.

The early nineteenth century revolted against the formalism of this rhetorical style, and went to the other extreme in pursuing individuality too far. Lamb, for instance, is a bad model, for his quaintness becomes affectation when imitated. It is hardly necessary to warn students against the crabbed eccentricity of Carlyle. In spite of excessive exploitation of personality, however, Victorian prose often became rather pompous, as in some of Ruskin, or precious, as in Pater, for instance. This usually means that the writer is keeping his eye on the effect instead of on what he is trying to say. It is not found in Newman, whose interest in his subject never tires and whose intelligence is always alert. Modern readers are suspicious of artifice, and modern prose has aimed at being natural. G. B. Shaw has affinities with Swift, although, of course, the staple of his speech is twentieth and not eighteenth century.

All writing implies a tradition, which is the accumulated experience of writers and readers and their agreement on usage. Grammar and idiom constitute the more mechanical parts of that usage. It is not possible to communicate effectively to the reader unless these are correct according to current practice. For those who want to make sure they are sound on these elementary points there are three volumes published by the English Universities Press—*Teach Yourself to Spell, Teach Yourself to Write* and *Teach Yourself Good English.* J. W. Marriott's *The Art and Craft of Writing,* Guy Pocock's *Brush Up Your Own Language* and L. A. G. Strong's *English for Pleasure* can also be recommended.

The exact connotation of words is an important part of correct usage. It can be learned only by practice and by looking up any word or expression about which there is any doubt. For continual reference of this kind H. W. and F. G. Fowler's *The King's English* and H. W. Fowler's *Dictionary of Modern English Usage* (both published by Oxford University Press) are invaluable. The practice of regular writing should be accompanied by reading oneself into the central tradition outlined above. To see more in the course of reading some lessons in observation are an asset. F. H. Pritchard's *Training in Literary Appreciation* (Harrap and Co.), and G. Townsend Warner's *On the Writing of English* (Blackie and Co.) provide sound instruction, and Sir A. Quiller-Couch's *The Art of Writing* (Cambridge University Press) gives stimulating advice on the proper use of words. For more advanced study of the elements of prose style, Herbert Read's *English Prose Style* (G. Bell and Sons) is illuminating and full of examples.

Practice in writing increases facility and awareness of the sense of words. Strictly speaking, however, each piece of writing is a separate problem. It involves two partners, the writer and the reader. The writer tries to produce an effect on the reader. Before starting, be quite sure what effect is to be sought. That will determine the style and the order of treatment.

If the writer's aim is to describe or explain something accurately, then the writer must be quite impersonal and must strive to be absolutely clear and objective, so that there is no possibility of misunderstanding, and he must be sure attention is concentrated on the most important points, not lost among a mass of detail. On the other hand, if the reader's feelings have to be moved until he enters into an experience imaginatively, then exactness of detail is less important than impression; and the words, instead of being merely precise, should be suggestive and full of association, while figures of speech, to be avoided in scientific exposition, or description, may help to create the right atmosphere or picture. The tone is an important part of the effect. For one audience, a detached, logical approach will be suitable; for another, a more familiar approach. The first will express itself in fairly abstract language and in an ordering of the material according to a process of reasoning; the second in a colloquial vocabulary and in sentences easily grasped and apparently like those of ordinary speech.

The secret of successful writing is to begin with the total effect to be produced on the reader. Once that is clear, the material to be included, the arrangement and the tone settle themselves, although in working them out there must be constant vigilance to ensure that every word and phrase, every reference and figure of speech, is controlled by the total effect. Almost any subject can be made interesting, if the writer remembers that he has to create in the mind of the reader, gradually as word piles upon word, a particular impression which he has clarified in his own mind before he starts.

The art of writing is the art of making the reader share the experience of the writer. Even as an exercise writing is valuable in that it forces the writer to examine his own experience more carefully in the effort to convey it fully and precisely.

Questions to Think Over

1. What are the merits of the prose style of the authorized version of the Bible?

2. Select a portion of Milton's argument in *Areopagitica*, memorize the main development of the thought, and then re-write it in good modern prose, afterwards comparing your version with the original.

3. Choose fairly comparable passages from *Gulliver's Travels* and the English translation of More's *Utopia* or Bacon's *New Atlantis*. Compare the prose of the two passages, paying attention to such details as vocabulary, use of abstract and concrete words and expressions, sentence structure, figures of speech, use of adjectives, etc. What do you learn from this about the development of English prose during the seventeenth century?

4. Study half a dozen consecutive paragraphs in Gibbon or Macaulay. Decide what is the main idea of each paragraph, note how it is expanded into a complete paragraph, and trace the progressive development of these main ideas.

ANSWERS TO "TEST YOURSELF"

THE purpose of most of the questions is to enable you to discover for yourself how closely you are following the text of the book. Few persons can assimilate all the main facts at a single reading, and there is no cause for discouragement if your answers show you that you have forgotten many of them. What is worth remembering is worth a second and, if necessary, a third reading.

CHAPTER I

1. The West-Saxon dialect predominated owing to its being the language of Alfred, King of Wessex, who had his court at Winchester.

2. Among verbs derived from Anglo-Saxon are: bless, build, shake, drive, sing, break, get, climb, help, melt. Among nouns derived from Old Norse are: anger, egg, leg, fellow, husband, plough, skill, skin, sky, trust, window, wing.

3. From the invasion of another race, the Vikings, whose language, Old Norse, resembled Anglo-Saxon. The two languages lost most of their inflexions and merged.

4. Compare your essay with the material given on pages 12 to 17.

5. Here are some common words of Latin derivation mentioned in Chapter I: junior, senior, maximum, minimum, genius, index, omen, tribunal. Re-read the chapter for further examples.

6. Examples given in Chapter I include: aerial, bump, countless, dwindle, eventful, fitful, gnarled, hurried, lonely, monumental.

CHAPTER II

1. Beowulf.

2. The Venerable Bede.

3. The Schoolmen were the scholars of the Middle Ages. Roger Bacon, an early scientist, was one of the most famous.

4. William Caxton set up the first printing press in England in 1476.

CHAPTER III

1. 1362.

2. *The Canterbury Tales.* A mixed party of pilgrims on their way to Thomas à Becket's shrine in Canterbury Cathedral beguile the journey with a series of stories, comic, tragic and romantic, each in keeping with the character of the narrator.

3. Edmund Spenser.

4. Life was simple and mainly rural; houses simple and fittings strictly utilitarian; for lights they had candles, for carpets, a sprinkling of rushes; window glass was a luxury. In the main men's outlook and interests were agricultural. They drew their food from the soil, and it accorded with the seasons. The most important industry was the woollen. Means of travel: on foot or on horseback, the horses being much inferior to the modern breeds.

5. The answer should mention the emergence of English as a language used for literature; the spirit of adventure involving sea travel and the discovery of new routes and lands; a romantic sense of the wonders of far places which the stay-at-homes will never see; the re-discovery by scholars of the classics of ancient Greece and Rome; the circulation of new ideas about life and religion by the medieval scholars.

CHAPTER IV

1. The drama started in special church services, in the attempt of the clergy to make clear the highlights of the Bible story. The church service being normally conducted in Latin, a charade-like interpretation of the key incidents of the Bible had an educative effect. Later this rudimentary drama was presented at the church door, the audience watching from the churchyard. Later still medieval craftsmen and traders, organized in their various guilds, took over the presentation of these plays on feast-days and holidays, using wheeled platforms called pageants for their stage. Whole cycles of little plays called "mystery" and "miracle plays" retold in simple, rough language the stories of the Old and New Testaments. These playlets could be given and repeated at a series of pre-arranged spots so that the waiting crowds could see there the presentation of many

parts of the Bible story on the same day.

2. Christopher Marlowe, Thomas Nash, Robert Greene, Thomas Kyd and George Peele.

3. Check your account by re-reading Chapter IV, pages 54 to 63.

4. Shakespeare's life, from the time when he arrived in London until he retired, was bound up with acting, refurbishing old plays, and writing new ones. Jonson was a bricklayer and a soldier before he became an actor.

Shakespeare's plays had no political or religious import likely to cause offence and, while he was the chief playwright at the Globe Theatre, there was never any difficulty in obtaining a licence for the players. Jonson, however, annoyed the court and was threatened with the loss of his ears.

Shakespeare wrote steadily, Jonson spasmodically. Shakespeare has greater depth of characterization, and magnificent sensuousness in dramatic poetry which Jonson, writing in prose, lacks. Shakespeare views his characters "in the round," giving them an unusual depth and fullness; Jonson stresses the principal trait in each of his— makes each stand for a particular quality— and attacks by ridicule (being a satirist) those human qualities which he dislikes.

5. The tragic weakness in Hamlet was indecision—incapacity for drastic action; in Othello, excessive proneness to jealousy; in Macbeth, ambition becoming unrestrained; in King Lear, the querulousness and lack of judgment which sometimes accompanies old age in decline. None of these characters was an out-and-out criminal. Even Macbeth had "too much of the milk of human kindness" to be a first-rate murderer. They all had imagination, the power to feel greatly, and a sense of right and wrong. In each play, however, circumstances combine to foster their tragic weaknesses and encourage them, of their own choice, to take the path which step by step leads them, and others, to disaster.

CHAPTER V

1. Re-read the account of Milton's life and works given in the chapter. Your account should make some mention of the following: Milton's education at St. Paul's and Cambridge, his deep religious convictions, his championship of the cause of Parliament which led him into political writings and an office under Cromwell, his blindness and retirement after the Restoration. Of his works the most important are *Paradise Lost, Paradise Regained* and *Samson Agonistes.* Also worthy of mention in the space of your answer are *Comus, Lycidas,* and the two delightful but lighter masterpieces, *L'Allegro* and *Il Penseroso.* Of his prose works his *Areopagitica* is the most noteworthy.

2. Sir Isaac Newton, author of *Principia Mathematica.*

3. Your essay should mention Bunyan's imprisonment in Bedford Gaol for his religious opinions, and also his obsession with his own personal sinfulness. Of his works *Pilgrim's Progress* is, of course, the best known, but mention *Grace Abounding* and *Life and Death of Mr. Badman.*

4. Andrew Marvell.

CHAPTER VI

1. The age of Queen Anne was called Augustan because its writers contributed to the glory of the State as Virgil, Horace and other Latin authors had contributed to the glory of Rome under Augustus.

2. Your account of Daniel Defoe should include a reference to his early career in commerce as a hosier, tile-maker and wool merchant (enlarging his knowledge of men and affairs), his skill as a journalist and pamphleteer (which once caused his imprisonment in the pillory). His construction is diffuse, but his knowledge of character and use of detail produces an amazing sense of realism. He is best remembered for his novels, *Robinson Crusoe, Moll Flanders, Journal of the Plague Year,* and *Roxana.*

3. Swift's writings were notable for their savage satire directed, not against individuals, but at mankind in general. His scorn is hidden by an air of gravity which momentarily deceives the reader.

4. Steele and Addison are the two essayists whose writings made the *Tatler* and the *Spectator* memorable.

5. Restoration drama marked the division of tragedy and comedy. Tragedy,

modelled on the French classical drama, became stilted and unreal; it is for its bawdy, witty comedy that the period is remembered—especially for the works of Wycherley and Congreve.

CHAPTER VII

1. Dr. Johnson. He was pre-eminent for his conversational powers. His personality was formidable, and his reputation for scholarship high.

2. Burke had personal integrity in an age of political corruption; he had a liberal outlook towards the governed, and a high sense of the duties of government. Check your answer with Chapter VII.

3. Your answer should include the names of Richardson, who wrote sentimental moralistic novels of great length in the form of letter-sequences: *Pamela, Clarissa Harlow*, etc.; Fielding, who wrote robust novels flavoured with irony: *Tom Jones, Joseph Andrews, The History of Jonathan Wild*; Smollett, who wrote loosely constructed picturesque novels, often coarse but vigorously alive, and mainly about life in the navy: *Roderick Random, Peregrine Pickle, Humphrey Clinker*; Laurence Sterne, who wrote sly, subjective novels which loiter along, touching upon situations, characters, and snatches of humorous dialogue as though they were the work of a natural essayist: *The Sentimental Journey, Tristram Shandy*; Jane Austen, who wrote drily humorous and realistic novels of contemporary middle-class life in small country towns and villages: *Pride and Prejudice, Sense and Sensibility, Northanger Abbey, Emma* and *Persuasion*.

4. Three of the following should be mentioned: Gray, Collins, Burns, Cowper, Blake.

CHAPTER VIII

1. Check your answer with the facts given on pages 123 to 129.

2. John Clare.

3. Check your answer with the facts given on pages 131 to 134.

4. Walter Savage Landor.

CHAPTER IX

1. Your essay should mention Scott's novelty in breaking away from the artificial Gothic fiction of the later eighteenth century. Using as his main material Scotland and its history, and with an antiquarian's love of the past, he based his stories on historic *fact*, and his characters on real life types. In comparison with other romantic writers he brought the breath of reality to romantic material; and his descriptions of wild scenery and events found an immediate public.

2. Hazlitt was a shrewd critic, ebullient in his opinions, a man with an inquiring mind, and a good, familiar, taut prose style. Lamb was equally shrewd as a critic, but his mind was inclined to fantasy and he wrote with delicate zest. There is much humour in him; also a streak of melancholy, but it is not bitter. His style is unique among English essayists.

3. *Confessions of an English Opium Eater*.

4. George Borrow.

CHAPTER X

1. Tennyson is best described as an instinctive poet with an uncanny power of observation as far as nature is concerned. He has described the English scene more beautifully and accurately than any other English poet. But he had other sides; he could write a patriotic poem with sincerity, and there was reasonableness in his attitude to the problems of the day.

Browning, on the other hand, was an intellectual poet, with the power of divining character and dramatizing situations. His style is both vigorous and subtle; he has an enormous range of feeling, but he is an interpreter and does not attempt to sit in judgment on the people he presents.

2. Check your answer with the details given in the chapter. The account should include his education at Marlborough and Oxford; his attraction to the craftsmanship of the Middle Ages; his work for socialism; his talent for illustration and interior decoration; his business acumen; his liking for the saga as a form of literature, e.g. *Sigurd the Volsung*.

3. Elizabeth Barrett Browning; Emily Brontë; Christina Rossetti.

4. D. G. Rossetti and A. C. Swinburne.

CHAPTER XI

1. Carlyle in style is weighty, frequently obscure; but the activity of his thought often gives a brilliant flash to his writing. He had a fondness for German philosophy and thought which influenced his own writing to a great extent. He was a near-atheist and this, in turn, is clearly seen in his writings; he was always seeking for what he believed might be the truth.

Macaulay, on the other hand, had a remarkably lucid style because he found writing an easy matter. He believed sincerely in the greatness of the age in which he lived. The classicism of the eighteenth century, and not the cloudy philosophy of the German School, shaped his thought and writing.

2. *Lady Windermere's Fan; A Woman of No Importance; An Ideal Husband; The Importance of Being Earnest.*

3. Check your accounts with the details given in the chapter. Dickens: son of a clerk; worked in a blacking factory; sketchy schooling; lawyer's office; reporter; training as an actor; 1833, first sketch by Boz; 1836, *Pickwick Papers*. His name made. Expansive style, much given to caricature; an uncanny master of atmosphere; his defence of the oppressed; his love for the poor; a reformer; a creator of some of the most vivid characters in literature.

Thackeray: Charterhouse and Cambridge University; studies abroad; art; man of the world; greatly attracted by the eighteenth century. Novels include *Vanity Fair, Henry Esmond* and *Pendennis*. His style is compact, orderly and full of detail; he is sympathetic to his characters but never overwhelmed by them.

Trollope: mother a novelist; he became a post-office official. Novels: *The Warden, Framley Parsonage, Barchester Towers*, etc. Characters are completely natural and drawn unerringly. Style is straightforward and unpretentious, but there is an extraordinary amount of detail in the analysis of character and background.

4. Charlotte Brontë: *Jane Eyre, Shirley, Villette.* Emily Brontë: *Wuthering Heights.* Mrs. Gaskell: *Cranford, Mary Barton, Sylvia's Lovers.* George Eliot: *Adam Bede, Silas Marner, The Mill on the Floss.*

Charlotte Yonge: *The Heir of Redclyffe.* Names of authors should include three of those listed above.

CHAPTER XII

1. Check your answer with the novels enumerated in the chapter. Three possible lists would be: (*a*) *The Bostonians; Washington Square; Daisy Miller.* (*b*) *Chance; Lord Jim; The Arrow of Gold.* (*c*) *Esther Waters; A Mummer's Wife; The Brook Kerith.*

2. Check your answer with the details given in the chapter. It should be emphasized that Galsworthy and Wells chose different strata of society on which to base their novels. Galsworthy concentrated on the commercial upper middle-class with its taboos and snobbery and limited mode of life already being threatened by the new business men, whose wealth was sufficient to crash any artificial social barrier. Wells, on the other hand, wrote of the lower middle-class with its talent for being exploited, its respectability, poverty and lack of education. Common to both writers is their sympathy for the human race, but whereas Galsworthy believed in stoicism Wells advocated socialism.

3. Check your answer with the account of Chesterton's works in the chapter. A possible list is: (*a*) *The Napoleon of Notting Hill*; (*b*) *The Innocence of Father Brown*; (*c*) *Magic*; (*d*) *Dickens*.

4. Check your answer with the following list: (1) Tolstoy; Turgenev; Chekhov; Dostoevski. (2) Flaubert; Maupassant; Balzac; Zola.

CHAPTER XIII

1. The outgoing breath comes into contact with the vocal cords (two membranes stretched across the windpipe) and makes them vibrate, producing sound.

2. récord, recórd; présent, presént; áccent, accént.

3. Bough, cough, enough, dough, through, borough, hiccough, etc.

CHAPTER XIV

1. See page 236. You should practise this with other nouns, adjectives and verbs.

2. *Le mot juste* means the exact word

for what you mean to convey—the right word in the right place. When you are conscious of lacking the right word, search around for it in your mind. Use a dictionary and Roget's *Thesaurus*.

3. We laugh at Mr. Micawber's speech because he always prefers a long high-sounding word to a short one (i.e. a Latinate word to a native English one). His speech lacks punch and directness. There is incongruity between the weight of his words and the trivial matters about which he usually talks. His style is inappropriate. None the less, we may like Mr. Micawber as a person—that is a different matter.

The chief characteristic of Dr. Johnson's writing is his love of abstract words which, by the way, are usually ponderous Latinate words. Unlike Mr. Micawber's thoughts Johnson's thoughts are not trivial; but his frequent use of words that do not refer to concrete things, but stand for ideas, such as *conception, rotundity, generosity*, etc., puts an additional strain on the reader. In a word, he often uses terms correct in themselves, but not easy to define, and therefore less definite to our minds.

4. See page 239 for the five rules. A useful rule to add is that any of the five rules may be broken in the interests of using *le mot juste*—the precise word to convey your meaning in the context.

5. Slang may be judiciously used: (*a*) in dialogue to give verisimilitude; (*b*) in straight writing when the slang word is *le mot juste* and has no exact equivalent in the language. If the slang word has really no equivalent in formal English, it will soon become an established word and shortly enter the dictionaries.

CHAPTER XV

1. Empress, prosecutrix, she-goat, ewe, mare, countess, duchess, author (or, more rarely, authoress). Bridegroom, widower, drake, gander, stallion, bull.

2. Pianos, brothers (or brethren), bureaux (or bureaus), termini, axes, phenomena.

3. A baby's rattle; ladies' cycles; foxes' brushes; oxen's tails; children's nursery.

4. (*a*) *S, es, en*, vowel changes, e.g. mouse to mice, foreign plurals, e.g. libretto to libretti (a few words do not change in the plural: sheep); (*b*) *-ed*, vowel changes, use of auxiliary verbs; (*c*) *-er* or use of *more* with the positive.

5. "I shall," "we shall" indicate simple future (whereas "I will" and "we will" express determination). "You will" and "they will" indicate simple future (whereas "you shall" and "they shall" express compulsion, command, determination).

CHAPTER XVI

1. Obliterate; misanthrope; prodigy; superficial; geography; contiguous; illiterate; proposition; hysterics; intercepted; alligator; influence; excavate; paralysed; particulars; apprehend; oral; arrangement of epithets.

2. By right means or wrong; ruining a job by refusing a small expenditure; attempting to rectify a matter long after it is possible to do so.

3. Practice—noun, practise—verb; respectful—showing respect, respectable—of good repute; oral—spoken by word of mouth, aural—pertaining to the ear; literary—of or pertaining to literature, literally—according to the letter of the word, not figurative.

CHAPTER XVII

1. Religion; battle; and love.

2. William Langland; *Piers Plowman*.

3. The five-foot iambic, which is particularly suited to the English language.

4. Shakespeare; Milton; Wordsworth; Keats.

CHAPTER XVIII

1. The novelist depends on his powers of description and actual telling of the story; the playwright has to depend chiefly on dialogue.

2. Any three of the following: Shaw, Priestley, Galsworthy and Maugham.

3. See page 293, "Evolution of the Theatre."

4. (*a*) *Love's Labour's Lost;* (*b*) *The Way of the World;* (*c*) *The Importance of Being Earnest;* (*d*) *You Never Can Tell;* (*e*) *The Admirable Crichton.* Check with other plays mentioned in the chapter.

CHAPTER XIX

1. Character.

2. Jane Austen, Bennett, Maugham and writers of detective stories are novelists who construct their plots carefully and work towards a climax. Defoe, Smollett, and usually Dickens, are novelists whose plots are a series of incidents interesting in themselves but not cumulative in effect. Writers like Sterne and Virginia Woolf are content with the most tenuous thread of incident (i.e. their books contain little action), but the mental and emotional life of their characters are revealed.

3. The extrovert tends to be more interested in the world outside himself, and, when a writer, he tends to tell about the actions of characters and leaves us to infer their feelings. The introvert tends to be more interested in the world of his own thought and imagination, and, when a writer, is more given to exploring the internal life of mind and feeling than the external world of objects and actions.

4. The novelist, while giving his dialogue an air of naturalness and truth, will do well to make it more lively and interesting than normal talk. This is even more important in plays, where every statement should help to reveal character or forward the action as well as having verisimilitude.

CHAPTER XX

1. Ten thousand words—or something that can be read in half an hour.

2. Any six of the following: O. Henry. Edgar Allan Poe, Chekhov, Maupassant, Turgenev, Flaubert, Jack London, Gogol; more recently, Kafka, Ernest Hemingway.

3. There are several possible answers to this question. Check your conclusions with those reached in the foregoing chapter.

4. Your answer will be in accord with your individual opinion on what constitutes a good short story. Qualities likely to be found in such a story are as follows: power to grip the attention in the first few paragraphs; readability and natural flow; evidence of careful selectivity in the introduction only of such characters, incidents and details as help to carry the story to its climax; action and climax to develop naturally out of the characters and not

vice versa; plot in the sense of strong action leading to climax is desirable, but a "surprise ending" not necessarily an advantage.

CHAPTER XXI

1. Producer, director, writers, designers, sound engineers, cameramen, cutters, scenario editor, actors.

2. The spoken word combined with the visual image.

3. The film director.

4. Because he is accustomed to think in terms of word pictures to describe character, place and action, while the script writer must think in terms of visual images (camera shots) and sounds (including dialogue).

CHAPTER XXII

1. Absolute sincerity. A broadcast talk should sound as though it were coming from a friend across the hearth.

2. Your answer should be checked with the details given in the foregoing chapter. A radio story must move fast; must be actively interesting throughout. It is unwise to have more than a few characters since the reader of the story cannot be expected to imitate more than a few people's voices. All descriptions should be brief.

3. Check your answer with the reasons given in the chapter. The actors are not limited by stage and setting; the audience is not hampered by visual limitations; music and other sounds can be used to effect and to indicate swift changes of place.

CHAPTER XXIII

1. The First World War shocked many writers into a mood of cynicism and disillusionment. See also pp. 349-350.

The period of the depression in the early thirties and the events leading to the Second World War made many of the ablest writers go "left" in their general outlook, though only a few became propagandist, and of these, fewer remained propagandist, because their new view of life became so much a part of themselves that it ceased to obtrude as something forced in their writings.

2. Dialogue. See page 354.

INDEX

Numbers in italics indicate illustrations

ACKNOWLEDGMENTS

The publishers wish to acknowledge permission from the National Portrait Gallery to reproduce the portraits appearing on pp. 30, 65, 67, 68, 76, 78, 81, 83, 84, 86, 90, 92, 93, 94, 95, 100, 105, 107, 109, 117, 119, 122, 128, 130, 140, 159, 163, 164, 166, 170, 194, 201, 211, and 270; from the Victoria and Albert Museum for the Blake illustration on p. 72 (Crown copyright reserved); from Elliott & Fry for the portraits of W. H. Hudson on p. 206, of Walter Pater, George Saintsbury and Sir A. Quiller-Couch on p. 256; and of Sean O'Casey on p. 289; from E. O. Hoppé for the portrait of Thomas Hardy on p. 186; from Cecil Beaton for the portrait of John Gielgud on p. 297; from Sir Max Beerbohm and William Heinemann Ltd., for the caricatures from *Poets' Corner* on pp. 270 and 278; from Jacob Epstein for permission to reproduce the bust of Joseph Conrad on p. 197; from Walker's Galleries, Ltd., for the print on p. 368; from Michael Ayrton and the National Gallery for the stage setting from *Macbeth* on p. 298; from Houston Rogers for the photographs on pp. 226 and 227; from Angus McBean for the photograph on p. 283; and from Ealing Films for the film scripts on pages 328 and 329.
